Python Image Processing Cookbook

Over 60 recipes to help you perform complex image processing and computer vision tasks with ease

Sandipan Dey

Packt>

BIRMINGHAM - MUMBAI

Python Image Processing Cookbook

Copyright © 2020 Packt Publishing

All rights reserved. No part of this book may be reproduced, stored in a retrieval system, or transmitted in any form or by any means, without the prior written permission of the publisher, except in the case of brief quotations embedded in critical articles or reviews.

Every effort has been made in the preparation of this book to ensure the accuracy of the information presented. However, the information contained in this book is sold without warranty, either express or implied. Neither the author(s), nor Packt Publishing or its dealers and distributors, will be held liable for any damages caused or alleged to have been caused directly or indirectly by this book.

Packt Publishing has endeavored to provide trademark information about all of the companies and products mentioned in this book by the appropriate use of capitals. However, Packt Publishing cannot guarantee the accuracy of this information.

Commissioning Editor: Pravin Dhandre
Acquisition Editor: Devika Battike
Content Development Editor: Athikho Sapuni Rishana
Senior Editor: Sofi Rogers
Technical Editor: Manikandan Kurup
Copy Editor: Safis Editing
Project Coordinator: Aishwarya Mohan
Proofreader: Safis Editing
Indexer: Pratik Shirodkar
Production Designer: Joshua Misquitta

First published: April 2020

Production reference: 1170420

Published by Packt Publishing Ltd.
Livery Place
35 Livery Street
Birmingham
B3 2PB, UK.

ISBN 978-1-78953-714-7

www.packt.com

Packt.com

Subscribe to our online digital library for full access to over 7,000 books and videos, as well as industry leading tools to help you plan your personal development and advance your career. For more information, please visit our website.

Why subscribe?

- Spend less time learning and more time coding with practical eBooks and Videos from over 4,000 industry professionals

- Improve your learning with Skill Plans built especially for you

- Get a free eBook or video every month

- Fully searchable for easy access to vital information

- Copy and paste, print, and bookmark content

Did you know that Packt offers eBook versions of every book published, with PDF and ePub files available? You can upgrade to the eBook version at www.packt.com and as a print book customer, you are entitled to a discount on the eBook copy. Get in touch with us at customercare@packtpub.com for more details.

At www.packt.com, you can also read a collection of free technical articles, sign up for a range of free newsletters, and receive exclusive discounts and offers on Packt books and eBooks.

I dedicate this book to my beloved parents and all the teachers in my life from all the schools:

- Ballygunge Government High School, Kolkata, India
- Jadavpur University, Kolkata, India
- University of Maryland, Baltimore County, USA
- MOOC platforms like Coursera and edX

Contributors

About the author

Sandipan Dey is a data scientist with a wide range of interests, covering topics such as machine learning, deep learning, image processing, and computer vision. He has worked in numerous data science fields, working with recommender systems, predictive models for the events industry, sensor localization models, sentiment analysis, and device prognostics. He earned his master's degree in computer science from the University of Maryland, Baltimore County, and has published in a few IEEE data mining conferences and journals. He has earned certifications from 100+ MOOCs on data science, machine learning, deep learning, image processing, and related courses. He is a regular blogger (sandipanweb) and is a machine learning education enthusiast.

About the reviewers

Srinjoy Ganguly holds a master's in Artificial Intelligence from the University of Southampton, UK and has over 4 years of experience in AI. He completed his bachelor's in Electronics and Communications from GGSIPU, Delhi, and gained a thorough knowledge of signal processing algorithms and neural networks. He has actively pursued the theory and principles of machine learning, deep learning, computer vision, and reinforcement learning. His research interests include Bayesian machine learning, Bayesian deep learning, and quantum machine learning. He is also an active contributor to Julia language. He strongly believes that this book will be an extremely valuable asset into the hands of beginners in the field of AI and computer vision.

Shankar Jha is a software engineer who has helped a lot of beginners get to grips with Python through his articles and talks. He writes about Python, Django, tackling climate change, and poverty alleviation. He lives by the philosophy of Richard Feynman and Swami Vivekananda. His latest endeavor is to help facilitate the use of environment-friendly products. He believes this book will give you enough hands-on experience to jump start your career in computer vision.

Packt is searching for authors like you

If you're interested in becoming an author for Packt, please visit `authors.packtpub.com` and apply today. We have worked with thousands of developers and tech professionals, just like you, to help them share their insight with the global tech community. You can make a general application, apply for a specific hot topic that we are recruiting an author for, or submit your own idea.

Table of Contents

Preface   1

Chapter 1: Image Manipulation and Transformation   9
  Technical requirements   9
  Transforming color space (RGB → Lab)   10
    Getting ready   10
    How to do it...   10
        Converting RGB image into grayscale by setting the Lab space color channels to zero   11
        Changing the brightness of the image by varying the luminosity channel   12
    How it works...   12
    There's more...   13
  Applying affine transformation   13
    Getting ready   14
    How to do it...   14
    How it works...   16
    There's more...   17
  Applying perspective transformation and homography   17
    Getting ready   18
    How to do it...   18
    How it works...   21
    There's more...   21
    See also   21
  Creating pencil sketches from images   22
    Getting ready   22
    How to do it...   22
    How it works...   25
    There's more...   25
    See also   26
  Creating cartoonish images   26
    Getting ready   27
    How to do it...   27
    How it works...   28
    There's more...   29
    See also   29
  Simulating light art/long exposure   30
    Getting ready   30
    How to do it...   31
    How it works...   33
    There's more...   33

Table of Contents

Extended depth of field with mahotas	33
See also	35
Object detection using color in HSV	**35**
Getting ready	36
How to do it...	36
How it works...	37
See also	39
Chapter 2: Image Enhancement	**41**
Applying filters to denoise different types of noise in an image	**42**
Getting ready	42
How to do it...	42
How it works...	44
There's more...	46
Image denoising with a denoising autoencoder	**46**
Getting ready	46
How to do it...	47
How it works...	50
There's more...	53
See also	53
Image denoising with PCA/DFT/DWT	**53**
Getting ready	53
How to do it...	54
How it works...	55
There's more...	57
See also	57
Image denoising with anisotropic diffusion	**57**
Getting ready	57
How to do it...	58
How it works...	60
There's more...	61
See also	61
Improving image contrast with histogram equalization	**61**
Getting ready	62
How to do it...	62
How it works...	63
There's more...	65
Implementing histogram matching	**65**
Getting ready	66
How to do it...	66
How it works...	67
There's more...	69
See also	69
Performing gradient blending	**70**
Getting ready	71

[ii]

How to do it...	71
How it works...	72
Edge detection with Canny, LoG/zero-crossing, and wavelets	72
Getting ready	73
How to do it...	73
Canny/hysteresis thresholding	74
LoG/zero-crossing	75
Wavelets	77
How it works...	79
There's more...	81
See also	81
Chapter 3: Image Restoration	**83**
Restoring an image with the Wiener filter	84
Getting ready	84
How to do it...	84
How it works...	87
See also	88
Restoring an image with the constrained least squares filter	89
Getting ready	89
How to do it...	89
How it works...	93
There's more...	94
See also	94
Image restoration with a Markov random field	95
Getting ready	95
How to do it...	96
How it works...	98
See also	99
Image inpainting	99
Getting ready	100
How to do it...	100
How it works...	101
There's more...	102
Image inpainting with convex optimization	103
See also	104
Image completion with inpainting using deep learning	105
Getting ready	105
How to do it...	105
There's more...	108
See also	109
Image restoration with dictionary learning	109
Getting ready	110
How to do it ...	110
There's more...	113
Online dictionary learning	113

[iii]

See also	115
Compressing an image using wavelets	115
Getting ready	115
How to do it...	116
How it works...	117
See also	118
Using steganography and steganalysis	118
Getting ready	119
How to do it...	119
How it works...	122
There's more...	123
See also	123
Chapter 4: Binary Image Processing	**125**
Applying morphological operators to a binary image	126
Getting ready	127
How to do it...	127
How it works...	130
There's more...	132
See also	134
Applying Morphological filters	134
Getting ready	134
How to do it...	135
Computing the Euler number, eccentricity, and center of mass with mahotas/scikit-image	135
Morphological image filters with mahotas	136
Binary image filters with SimpleITK	138
Dilation by reconstruction with skimage	141
How it works...	143
There's more...	144
See also	147
Morphological pattern matching	147
Getting ready	147
How to do it...	148
How it works...	151
There's more...	151
See also	152
Segmenting images with morphology	152
Getting ready	152
How to do it...	153
Morphological watershed	153
Blob detection with morphological watershed	156
How it works...	158
There's more...	159
Blob detection with LOG scale-space	159
See also	160

Counting objects — 160
Getting ready — 161
How to do it... — 161
Blob separation and detection with erosion — 161
Object counting with closing and opening — 163
How it works... — 164
There's more... — 165
See also — 167

Chapter 5: Image Registration — 169
Medical image registration with SimpleITK — 170
Getting ready — 171
How to do it... — 171
How it works... — 174
There's more — 174
See also — 176
Image alignment with ECC algorithm and warping — 177
Getting ready — 177
How to do it... — 178
How it works... — 180
There is more — 182
See also — 182
Face alignment with dlib — 182
Getting ready — 183
How to do it... — 183
How it works... — 186
There is more — 187
See also — 188
Robust matching and homography with the RANSAC algorithm — 189
Getting ready — 190
How to do it... — 190
How it works... — 192
See also — 194
Image mosaicing (panorama) — 194
Getting ready — 195
How to do it... — 195
Panorama with OpenCV-Python — 201
How it works... — 202
There is more — 203
See also — 203
Face morphing — 204
Getting ready — 205
How to do it... — 206
How it works — 211
There is more — 212
See also — 213

Table of Contents

Implementing an image search engine — 213
- Getting ready — 214
- How to do it... — 214
  - Finding similarity between an image and a set of images with SIFT — 214
  - Steps to implement a simple image search engine — 218
- There is more — 223
- See also — 223

Chapter 6: Image Segmentation — 225
Thresholding with Otsu and Riddler–Calvard — 226
- Getting ready — 227
- How to do it... — 227
- How it works... — 228
- There's more... — 229
- See also — 231

Image segmentation with self-organizing maps — 231
- Getting ready — 232
- How to do it... — 233
- How it works... — 235
- There's more... — 235
  - Clustering handwritten digit images with SOM — 236
- See also — 238

RandomWalk segmentation with scikit-image — 239
- Getting ready — 240
- How to do it... — 240
- How it works... — 242
- There's more... — 243
- See also — 244

Human skin segmentation with the GMM-EM algorithm — 244
- Getting ready — 245
- How to do it... — 245
- How it works... — 249
- See also — 250

Medical image segmentation — 250
- Getting ready — 251
- How to do it... — 251
  - Segmentation with GMM-EM — 251
  - Brain tumor segmentation using deep learning — 253
  - Segmentation with watershed — 256
- How it works... — 258
- There's more... — 258
- See also — 259

Deep semantic segmentation — 259
- Getting ready — 260
- How to do it... — 260
  - Semantic segmentation with DeepLabV3 — 260

[vi]

Semantic segmentation with FCN	264
See also	267
Deep instance segmentation	**267**
Getting ready	268
How to do it...	269
How it works...	271
See also	272

Chapter 7: Image Classification — 273

Classifying images with scikit-learn (HOG and logistic regression)	**275**
Getting ready	275
How to do it...	276
How it works...	280
There's more...	281
See also	282
Classifying textures with Gabor filter banks	**282**
Getting ready	283
How to do it...	283
How it works...	287
There's more...	288
See also	288
Classifying images with VGG19/Inception V3/MobileNet/ResNet101 (with PyTorch)	**289**
Getting ready	290
How to do it...	290
How it works...	292
There's more...	294
See also	294
Fine-tuning (with transfer learning) for image classification	**295**
Getting ready	296
How to do it...	297
How it works...	302
There's more...	304
See also	304
Classifying traffic signs using a deep learning model (with PyTorch)	**305**
Getting ready	305
How to do it...	306
How it works...	314
There's more...	315
See also	315
Estimating a human pose using a deep learning model	**316**
Getting ready	317
How to do it...	318
How it works...	322
See also	322

Chapter 8: Object Detection in Images — 323
Object detection with HOG/SVM — 324
Getting started — 326
How to do it... — 326
How it works... — 329
There's more... — 330
See also — 330
Object detection with Yolo V3 — 331
Getting started — 332
How to do it... — 333
How it works... — 336
There's more... — 336
See also — 336
Object detection with Faster R-CNN — 337
Getting started — 338
How to do it... — 339
How it works... — 341
There's more... — 342
See also — 342
Object detection with Mask R-CNN — 343
Getting started — 344
How to do it... — 344
How it works... — 348
There's more... — 348
See also — 348
Multiple object tracking with Python-OpenCV — 349
Getting started — 349
How to do it... — 350
How it works... — 352
There's more... — 352
See also — 352
Text detection/recognition in images with EAST/Tesseract — 353
Getting started — 354
How to do it... — 355
How it works... — 358
See also — 358
Face detection with Viola-Jones/Haar-like features — 359
Getting ready — 359
How to do it... — 360
How it works... — 361
There's more... — 362
See also — 362

Chapter 9: Face Recognition, Image Captioning, and More — 363
Face recognition using FaceNet — 364

Getting ready	365
How to do it...	366
How it works...	370
See also	372
Age, gender, and emotion recognition using deep learning models	372
Getting ready	373
How to do it...	373
There's more...	375
See also	375
Image colorization with deep learning	376
Getting ready	376
How to do it...	377
See also	378
Automatic image captioning with a CNN and an LSTM	379
Getting ready	380
How to do it...	381
How it works...	384
See also	384
Image generation with a GAN	384
Getting ready	385
How to do it...	386
How it works...	392
There's more...	392
See also	392
Using a variational autoencoder to reconstruct and generate images	393
Getting ready	394
How to do it...	394
There's more...	400
See also	401
Using a restricted Boltzmann machine to reconstruct Bangla MNIST images	402
Getting ready	403
How to do it...	403
See also	409

Other Books You May Enjoy — 411

Index — 415

Preface

With advancements in wireless devices and mobile technology, there's an increasing demand for digital image processing skills to extract useful information from the ever-growing volume of images. This book provides comprehensive coverage of tools and algorithms, along with guiding you through analysis and visualization for image processing.

With the help of over 60 cutting-edge recipes, you'll address common challenges in image processing and learn how to perform complex tasks such as image detection, image segmentation, and image reconstruction using large hybrid datasets. Dedicated sections will also take you through implementing various image enhancement and image restoration techniques such as cartooning, gradient blending, and sparse dictionary learning. As you advance, you'll get to grips with face morphing and image segmentation techniques. With an emphasis on practical solutions, this book will help you apply deep learning-based techniques such as transfer learning and fine-tuning to solve real-world problems.

By the end of this Python book, you'll be proficient in applying image processing techniques effectively to leverage the capabilities of the Python ecosystem.

Who this book is for

This Python cookbook is for image processing engineers, computer vision engineers, software developers, machine learning engineers, or anyone who wants to become well-versed with image processing techniques and methods using a recipe-based approach. Although no image processing knowledge is expected, prior Python coding experience is necessary to understand key concepts covered in the book.

What this book covers

`Chapter 1`, *Image Manipulation and Transformation*, is where you will learn how to use different Python libraries (NumPy, SciPy, scikit-image, OpenCV, and Matplotlib) for image manipulation and transformation. You will learn how to write Python code to do point transforms (log/gamma transform, Gotham filter, colorspace transformation, and increasing brightness/contrast) and geometric transforms (swirl transform, perspective transform, and homography).

Preface

Chapter 2, *Image Enhancement*, is where you will learn how to use different Python libraries (NumPy, SciPy, scikit-image, OpenCV, PyWavelet, and MedPy) to denoise images (using linear/nonlinear filters, **Fast Fourier transform** (FFT), and autoencoders). You'll learn how to implement image enhancement techniques such as histogram equalization/matching, sketching/cartoonizing, pyramid blending/gradient blending, and edge detection with zero crossing.

Chapter 3, *Image Restoration*, is where you will learn how to implement image restoration (using NumPy, scikit-image, OpenCV, and scikit-learn) with deconvolution (inverse/weiner/LMS) filters. You'll learn how to implement image restoration with inpainting, variational methods, and sparse dictionary learning. You'll also learn how to implement steganography/steganalysis techniques with pysteg.

Chapter 4, *Binary Image Processing*, is where you will learn how to use different Python libraries (NumPy, SciPy, scikit-image, and OpenCV) for binary image processing (with mathematical morphology). You'll learn how to implement morphological operators, filters, and pattern matching and how to apply them in segmentation, fingerprint enhancement, counting objects, and blob separation.

Chapter 5, *Image Registration*, is where you will learn how to use different Python libraries (NumPy, scikit-image, OpenCV, and PyStasm) for image matching/registration/stitching. You'll learn how to implement image registration techniques with warping/feature (SIFT/SURF/ORB)-based methods and the RANSAC algorithm. You'll also learn how to implement panorama image creation, and face morphing, as well as how to implement a basic image search engine.

Chapter 6, *Image Segmentation*, is where you will learn how to use different Python libraries (NumPy, scikit-image, OpenCV, SimpleITK, and DeepLab) for image segmentation. You'll learn how to implement image segmentation techniques with graph-based methods/clustering methods, super-pixelation, and machine learning algorithms. You'll also learn how to implement semantic segmentation with DeepLab.

Chapter 7, *Image Classification*, is where you will learn how to use different Python libraries (scikit-learn, OpenCV, TensorFlow, Keras, and PyTorch) for image classification. You'll learn how to implement deep learning-based techniques such as transfer learning/fine-tuning. You'll learn how to implement panorama image creation and face morphing. You'll also learn how to implement deep learning-based classification techniques for hand gestures and traffic signals.

Chapter 8, *Object Detection in Images*, is where you will learn how to use different Python libraries (scikit-learn, OpenCV, TensorFlow, Keras, and PyTorch) for object detection in images. You'll learn how to implement classical machine learning (HOG/SVM) techniques as well as deep learning models to detect objects. You'll also learn how to implement barcode detection and text detection from images.

Chapter 9, *Face Detection and Recognition*, is where you will learn how to use different Python libraries (scikit-learn, OpenCV, dlib, TensorFlow, Keras, PyTorch, DeepFace, and FaceNet) for face detection in images. You'll also learn how to implement facial keypoint recognition and facial/emotion/gender recognition with deep learning.

To get the most out of this book

Basic knowledge of Python and image processing is required to understand and run the code, along with access to a few online image datasets and the book's GitHub link.

Python 3.5+ (Python 3.7.4 was used to test the code) is needed with Anaconda preferably installed for the Windows users, along with Jupyter (to view/run notebooks).

All the code was tested on Windows 10 (Pro) with 32 GB RAM and an Intel i7-series processor. However, the code should require little/no change to be run on Linux.

You will need to install all the required Python packages using pip3.

Access to a GPU is recommended to run the recipes involving training with deep learning (that is, training that involves libraries such as TensorFlow, Keras, and PyTorch) much faster. The code that is best run with a GPU was tested on an Ubuntu 16.04 machine with an Nvidia Tesla K80 GPU (with CUDA 10.1).

A basic math background is also needed to understand the concepts in the book.

Software/hardware covered in the book	OS requirements
Python 3.7.4.	Windows 10.
Anaconda version 2019.10 (py37_0).	Windows 10.
For the GPU, you will need an NVIDIA graphics card or access to an AWS GPU instance (https://docs.aws.amazon.com/dlami/latest/devguide/gpu.html) or Google Colab (https://colab.research.google.com/).	Windows 10/Linux (Ubuntu 16).

If you are using the digital version of this book, we advise you to type the code yourself or access the code via the GitHub repository (link available in the next section). Doing so will help you avoid any potential errors related to the copying and pasting of code.

Preface

To access the notebooks and images, clone the repository from this URL: `https://github.com/PacktPublishing/Python-Image-Processing-Cookbook`.

Install Python 3.7 and the necessary libraries as and when required. Install Anaconda/Jupyter and open the notebooks for each chapter. Run the code for each recipe. Follow the instructions for each recipe for any additional steps (for instance, you may need to download a pre-trained model or an image dataset).

Some additional exercises are provided for most of the recipes in a *There's more...* section to test your understanding. Perform them independently and have fun!

Download the example code files

You can download the example code files for this book from your account at `www.packt.com`. If you purchased this book elsewhere, you can visit `www.packtpub.com/support` and register to have the files emailed directly to you.

You can download the code files by following these steps:

1. Log in or register at `www.packt.com`.
2. Select the **Support** tab.
3. Click on **Code Downloads**.
4. Enter the name of the book in the **Search** box and follow the onscreen instructions.

Once the file is downloaded, please make sure that you unzip or extract the folder using the latest version of:

- WinRAR/7-Zip for Windows
- Zipeg/iZip/UnRarX for Mac
- 7-Zip/PeaZip for Linux

The code bundle for the book is also hosted on GitHub at `https://github.com/PacktPublishing/Python-Image-Processing-Cookbook`. In case there's an update to the code, it will be updated on the existing GitHub repository.

We also have other code bundles from our rich catalog of books and videos available at `https://github.com/PacktPublishing/`. Check them out!

Download the color images

We also provide a PDF file that has color images of the screenshots/diagrams used in this book. You can download it here: https://static.packt-cdn.com/downloads/9781789537147_ColorImages.pdf.

Conventions used

There are a number of text conventions used throughout this book.

`CodeInText`: Indicates code words in text, database table names, folder names, filenames, file extensions, pathnames, dummy URLs, user input, and Twitter handles. Here is an example: "Implement a `bilinear_interpolate()` function, which interpolates over every image channel."

A block of code is set as follows:

```
def get_grid_coordinates(points):
    xmin, xmax = np.min(points[:, 0]), np.max(points[:, 0]) + 1
    ymin, ymax = np.min(points[:, 1]), np.max(points[:, 1]) + 1
    return np.asarray([(x, y) for y in range(ymin, ymax)
            for x in range(xmin, xmax)], np.uint32)
```

Any command-line input or output is written as follows:

```
$ pip install mtcnn
```

Bold: Indicates a new term, an important word, or words that you see onscreen. For example, words in menus or dialog boxes appear in the text like this. Here is an example: "**Face alignment** is a data normalization process—an essential preprocessing step for many facial recognition algorithms."

> Warnings or important notes appear like this.

> Tips and tricks appear like this.

Sections

In this book, you will find several headings that appear frequently (*Getting ready*, *How to do it...*, *How it works...*, *There's more...*, and *See also*).

To give clear instructions on how to complete a recipe, use these sections as follows:

Getting ready

This section tells you what to expect in the recipe and describes how to set up any software or any preliminary settings required for the recipe.

How to do it...

This section contains the steps required to follow the recipe.

How it works...

This section usually consists of a detailed explanation of what happened in the previous section.

There's more...

This section consists of additional information about the recipe in order to make you more knowledgeable about the recipe.

See also

This section provides helpful links to other useful information for the recipe.

Get in touch

Feedback from our readers is always welcome.

General feedback: If you have questions about any aspect of this book, mention the book title in the subject of your message and email us at customercare@packtpub.com.

Errata: Although we have taken every care to ensure the accuracy of our content, mistakes do happen. If you have found a mistake in this book, we would be grateful if you would report this to us. Please visit www.packtpub.com/support/errata, selecting your book, clicking on the Errata Submission Form link, and entering the details.

Piracy: If you come across any illegal copies of our works in any form on the Internet, we would be grateful if you would provide us with the location address or website name. Please contact us at copyright@packt.com with a link to the material.

If you are interested in becoming an author: If there is a topic that you have expertise in and you are interested in either writing or contributing to a book, please visit authors.packtpub.com.

Reviews

Please leave a review. Once you have read and used this book, why not leave a review on the site that you purchased it from? Potential readers can then see and use your unbiased opinion to make purchase decisions, we at Packt can understand what you think about our products, and our authors can see your feedback on their book. Thank you!

For more information about Packt, please visit packt.com.

1
Image Manipulation and Transformation

Image transformation is the art of transforming an image. With image transformation and manipulation, we can enhance the appearance of an image. The transformation and manipulation operation can also be used as preprocessing steps for more complex image processing tasks, such as classification or segmentation, which you will get more acquainted with in later chapters. In this chapter, you are going to learn how to use different Python libraries (NumPy, SciPy, scikit-image, OpenCV-Python, Mahotas, and Matplotlib) for image manipulation and transformation. Different recipes will help you to learn how to write Python code to implement color space transformation, geometric transformations, perspective transforms/homography, and so on.

In this chapter, we will cover the following recipes:

- Transforming color space (RGB → Lab)
- Applying affine transformation
- Applying perspective transformation and homography
- Creating pencil sketches from images
- Creating cartoonish images
- Simulating light art/long exposure
- Object detection using color in HSV

Technical requirements

To run the codes without any errors, you need to first install Python 3 (for example, 3.6) and the required libraries, if they are not already installed. If you are working on Windows, you are recommended to install the Anaconda distribution. You also need to install the `jupyter` library to work with the notebooks.

All of the code files in this book are available in the GitHub repository at `https://github.com/PacktPublishing/Python-Image-Processing-Cookbook`. You should clone the repository (to your working directory). Corresponding to each chapter, there is a folder and each folder contains a notebook with the complete code (for all of the recipes for each chapter); a subfolder named `images`, which contains all the input images (and related files) required for that chapter; and (optionally) another sub-folder named `models`, which contains the models and related files to be used for the recipes in that chapter.

Transforming color space (RGB → Lab)

The **CIELAB** (abbreviated as **Lab**) color space consists of three color channels, expressing the color of a pixel as three tuples **(L, a, b)**, where the **L** channel stands for **luminosity/illumination/intensity** (lightness). The **a** and **b** channels represent the **green-red** and **blue-yellow** color components, respectively. This color model separates the *intensity* from the *colors* completely. It's device-independent and has a large *gamut*. In this recipe, you will see how to convert from RGB into the Lab color space and vice versa and the usefulness of this color model.

Getting ready

In this recipe, we will use a flower RGB image as the input image. Let's start by importing the required libraries with the following code block:

```
import numpy as np
from skimage.io import imread
from skimage.color import rgb2lab, lab2rgb
import matplotlib.pylab as plt
```

How to do it...

In this recipe, you will see a few remarkable uses of the Lab color space and how it makes some image manipulation operations easy and elegant.

Converting RGB image into grayscale by setting the Lab space color channels to zero

Perform the following steps to convert an RGB color image into a grayscale image using the Lab color space and `scikit-image` library functions:

1. Read the input image. Perform a color space transformation—from RGB to Lab color space:

   ```
   im = imread('images/flowers.png')
   im1 = rgb2lab(im)
   ```

2. Set the color channel values (the second and third channels) to zeros:

   ```
   im1[...,1] = im1[...,2] = 0
   ```

3. Obtain the grayscale image by converting the image back into the RGB color space from the Lab color space:

   ```
   im1 = lab2rgb(im1)
   ```

4. Plot the input and output images, as shown in the following code:

   ```
   plt.figure(figsize=(20,10))
   plt.subplot(121), plt.imshow(im), plt.axis('off'),
   plt.title('Original image', size=20)
   plt.subplot(122), plt.imshow(im1), plt.axis('off'), plt.title('Gray scale image', size=20)
   plt.show()
   ```

The following screenshot shows the output of the preceding code block:

Changing the brightness of the image by varying the luminosity channel

Perform the following steps to change the brightness of a colored image using the Lab color space and `scikit-image` library functions:

1. Convert the input image from RGB into the Lab color space and increase the first channel values (by 50):

   ```
   im1 = rgb2lab(im)
   im1[...,0] = im1[...,0] + 50
   ```

2. Convert it back into the RGB color space and obtain a brighter image:

   ```
   im1 = lab2rgb(im1)
   ```

3. Convert the RGB image into the Lab color space and decrease only the first channel values (by 50, as seen in the following code) and then convert back into the RGB color space to get a darker image instead:

   ```
   im1 = rgb2lab(im)
   im1[...,0] = im1[...,0] - 50
   im1 = lab2rgb(im1)
   ```

If you run the preceding code and plot the input and output images, you will get an output similar to the one shown in the following screenshot:

How it works...

The `rgb2lab()` function from the scikit-image `color` module was used to convert an image from RGB into the Lab color space.

The modified image in the Lab color space was converted back into RGB using the `lab2rgb()` function from the scikit-image `color` module.

Since the color channels are separated in the a and b channels and in terms of intensity in the L channel by setting the color channel values to zero, we can obtain the grayscale image from a colored image in the Lab space.

The brightness of the input color image was changed by changing only the L channel values in the Lab space (unlike in the RGB color space where all the channel values need to be changed); there is no need to touch the color channels.

There's more...

There are many other uses of the Lab color space. For example, you can obtain a more natural inverted image in the Lab space since only the luminosity channel needs to be inverted, as demonstrated in the following code block:

```
im1 = rgb2lab(im)
im1[...,0] = np.max(im1[...,0]) - im1[...,0]
im1 = lab2rgb(im1)
```

If you run the preceding code and display the input image and the inverted images obtained in the RGB and the Lab space, you will get the following screenshot:

| Original image | Inverted image (Lab) | Inverted image (RGB) |

As you can see, the **Inverted image** in the **Lab** color space appears much more natural than the **Inverted image** in the **RGB** color space.

Applying affine transformation

An **affine transformation** is a geometric transformation that preserves points, straight lines, and planes. Lines that are parallel before the transform remain parallel post-application of the transform. For every pixel x in an image, the affine transformation can be represented by the mapping, $x \mapsto Mx+b$, where M is a linear transform (matrix) and b is an offset vector.

Image Manipulation and Transformation

In this recipe, we will use the `scipy ndimage` library function, `affine_transform()`, to implement such a transformation on an image.

Getting ready

First, let's import the libraries and the functions required to implement an affine transformation on a grayscale image:

```
import numpy as np
from scipy import ndimage as ndi
from skimage.io import imread
from skimage.color import import rgb2gray
```

How to do it...

Perform the following steps to apply an affine transformation to an image using the `scipy.ndimage` module functions:

1. Read the color image, convert it into grayscale, and obtain the grayscale image shape:

   ```
   img = rgb2gray(imread('images/humming.png'))
   w, h = img.shape
   ```

2. Apply identity transform:

   ```
   mat_identity = np.array([[1,0,0],[0,1,0],[0,0,1]])
   img1 = ndi.affine_transform(img, mat_identity)
   ```

3. Apply reflection transform (along the *x* axis):

   ```
   mat_reflect = np.array([[1,0,0],[0,-1,0],[0,0,1]]) @
   np.array([[1,0,0],[0,1,-h],[0,0,1]])
   img1 = ndi.affine_transform(img, mat_reflect) # offset=(0,h)
   ```

4. Scale the image (`0.75` times along the *x* axis and `1.25` times along the *y* axis):

   ```
   s_x, s_y = 0.75, 1.25
   mat_scale = np.array([[s_x,0,0],[0,s_y,0],[0,0,1]])
   img1 = ndi.affine_transform(img, mat_scale)
   ```

Chapter 1

5. Rotate the image by 30° counter-clockwise. It's a composite operation—first, you will need to shift/center the image, apply rotation, and then apply inverse shift:

   ```
   theta = np.pi/6
   mat_rotate = np.array([[1,0,w/2],[0,1,h/2],[0,0,1]]) @
   np.array([[np.cos(theta),np.sin(theta),0],[np.sin(theta),-
   np.cos(theta),0],[0,0,1]]) @ np.array([[1,0,-w/2],[0,1,-
   h/2],[0,0,1]])
   img1 = ndi.affine_transform(img1, mat_rotate)
   ```

6. Apply shear transform to the image:

   ```
   lambda1 = 0.5
   mat_shear = np.array([[1,lambda1,0],[lambda1,1,0],[0,0,1]])
   img1 = ndi.affine_transform(img1, mat_shear)
   ```

7. Finally apply all of the transforms together, in sequence:

   ```
   mat_all = mat_identity @ mat_reflect @ mat_scale @ mat_rotate @
   mat_shear
   ndi.affine_transform(img, mat_all)
   ```

The following screenshot shows the matrices (*M*) for each of the affine transformation operations:

Identity	$\begin{bmatrix} x' \\ y' \\ 1 \end{bmatrix} = \begin{bmatrix} 1 & 0 & 0 \\ 0 & 1 & 0 \\ 0 & 0 & 1 \end{bmatrix} \begin{bmatrix} x \\ y \\ 1 \end{bmatrix}$
Reflection	$\begin{bmatrix} x' \\ y' \\ 1 \end{bmatrix} = \begin{bmatrix} 1 & 0 & 0 \\ 0 & -1 & 0 \\ 0 & 0 & 1 \end{bmatrix} \begin{bmatrix} x \\ y \\ 1 \end{bmatrix}$
Translation	$\begin{bmatrix} x' \\ y' \\ 1 \end{bmatrix} = \begin{bmatrix} 1 & 0 & dx \\ 0 & 1 & dy \\ 0 & 0 & 1 \end{bmatrix} \begin{bmatrix} x \\ y \\ 1 \end{bmatrix}$
Scale	$\begin{bmatrix} x' \\ y' \\ 1 \end{bmatrix} = \begin{bmatrix} S_x & 0 & 0 \\ 0 & S_y & 0 \\ 0 & 0 & 1 \end{bmatrix} \begin{bmatrix} x \\ y \\ 1 \end{bmatrix}$
Rotation	$\begin{bmatrix} x' \\ y' \\ 1 \end{bmatrix} = \begin{bmatrix} \cos(\theta) & -\sin(\theta) & 0 \\ \sin(\theta) & \cos(\theta) & 0 \\ 0 & 0 & 1 \end{bmatrix} \begin{bmatrix} x \\ y \\ 1 \end{bmatrix}$
Shear-X	$\begin{bmatrix} x' \\ y' \\ 1 \end{bmatrix} = \begin{bmatrix} 1 & \lambda_x & 0 \\ 0 & 1 & 0 \\ 0 & 0 & 1 \end{bmatrix} \begin{bmatrix} x \\ y \\ 1 \end{bmatrix}$
Shear-Y	$\begin{bmatrix} x' \\ y' \\ 1 \end{bmatrix} = \begin{bmatrix} 1 & 0 & 0 \\ \lambda_y & 1 & 0 \\ 0 & 0 & 1 \end{bmatrix} \begin{bmatrix} x \\ y \\ 1 \end{bmatrix}$

Image Manipulation and Transformation

How it works...

Note that, for an image, the *x* axis is the vertical (**+ve downward**) axis and the *y* axis is the horizontal (**+ve left-to-right**) axis.

With the `affine_transform()` function, the pixel value at location **o** in the output (transformed) image is determined from the pixel value in the input image at *position np.dot(matrix, o) + offset*. Hence, the matrix that needs to be provided as input to the function is actually the inverse transformation matrix.

In some of the cases, an additional matrix is used for translation, to bring the transformed image within the frame of visualization.

The preceding code snippets show how to implement different affine transformations such as **reflection**, **scaling**, **rotation**, and **shear** using the `affine_transform()` function. We need to provide the proper transformation matrix, *M* (shown in the preceding diagram) for each of these cases (homogeneous coordinates are used).

We can use the product of all of the matrices to perform a combination of all of the affine transformations at once (for instance, if you want transformation *T1* followed by *T2*, you need to multiply the input image by the matrix *T2.T1*).

If all of the transformations are applied in sequence and the transformed images are plotted one by one, you will obtain an output like the following screenshot:

Chapter 1

There's more...

Again, in the previous example, the `affine_transform()` function was applied to a grayscale image. The same effect can be obtained with a color image also, such as by applying the mapping function to each of the image channels simultaneously and independently. Also, the `scikit-image` library provides the `AffineTransform` and `PiecewiseAffineTransform` classes; you may want to try them to implement affine transformation as well.

Applying perspective transformation and homography

The goal of perspective (projective) transform is to estimate homography (a matrix, **H**) from point correspondences between two images. Since the matrix has a **Depth Of Field (DOF)** of eight, you need at least four pairs of points to compute the homography matrix from two images. The following diagram shows the basic concepts required to compute the homography matrix:

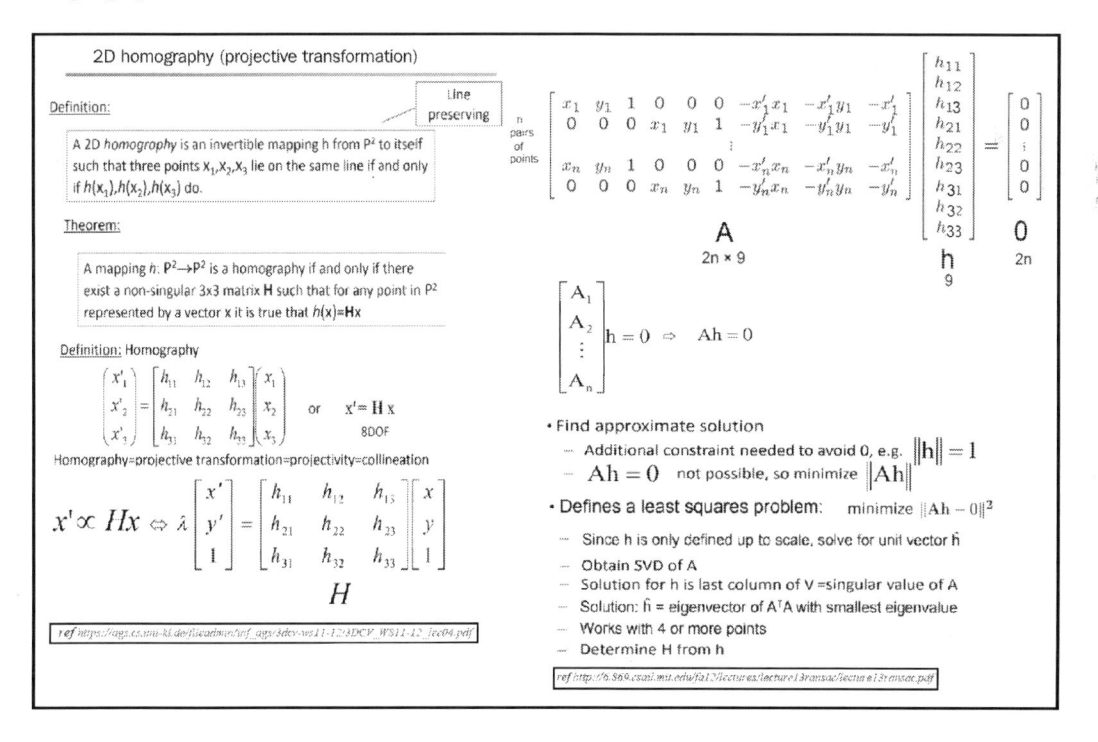

[17]

Image Manipulation and Transformation

Fortunately, we don't need to compute the SVD and the *H* matrix is computed automatically by the `ProjectiveTransform` function from the scikit-image `transform` module. In this recipe, we will use this function to implement homography.

Getting ready

We will use a humming bird's image and an image of an astronaut on the moon (taken from NASA's public domain images) as input images in this recipe. Again, let's start by importing the required libraries as usual:

```
from skimage.transform import ProjectiveTransform
from skimage.io import imread
import numpy as np
import matplotlib.pylab as plt
```

How to do it...

Perform the following steps to apply a projective transformation to an image using the `transform` module from scikit-image:

1. First, read the source image and create a destination image with the `np.zeros()` function:

    ```
    im_src = (imread('images/humming2.png'))
    height, width, dim = im_src.shape
    im_dst = np.zeros((height, width, dim))
    ```

2. Create an instance of the `ProjectiveTransform` class:

    ```
    pt = ProjectiveTransform()
    ```

3. You just need to provide four pairs of matching points between the source and destination images to estimate the homography matrix, *H*, automatically for you. Here, the four corners of the destination image and the four corners of the input hummingbird are provided as matching points, as shown in the following code block:

   ```
   src = np.array([[ 295., 174.],
    [ 540., 146. ],
    [ 400., 777.],
    [ 60., 422.]])
   dst = np.array([[ 0., 0.],
   [height-1, 0.],
   [height-1, width-1],
   [ 0., width-1]])
   ```

4. Obtain the source pixel index corresponding to each pixel index in the destination:

   ```
   x, y = np.mgrid[:height, :width]
   dst_indices = np.hstack((x.reshape(-1, 1), y.reshape(-1,1)))
   src_indices = np.round(pt.inverse(dst_indices), 0).astype(int)
   valid_idx = np.where((src_indices[:,0] < height) &
   (src_indices[:,1] < width) &
                       (src_indices[:,0] >= 0) & (src_indices[:,1] >= 0))
   dst_indicies_valid = dst_indices[valid_idx]
   src_indicies_valid = src_indices[valid_idx]
   ```

5. Copy pixels from the source to the destination images:

   ```
   im_dst[dst_indicies_valid[:,0],dst_indicies_valid[:,1]] = im_src[src_indicies_valid[:,0],src_indicies_valid[:,1]]
   ```

If you run the preceding code snippets, you will get an output like the following screenshot:

Image Manipulation and Transformation

The next screenshot shows the source image of an astronaut on the moon and the destination image of the canvas. Again, by providing four pairs of mapping points in between the source (corner points) and destination (corners of the canvas), the task is pretty straightforward:

The following screenshot shows the output image after the projective transform:

How it works...

In both of the preceding cases, the input image is projected onto the desired location of the output image.

A `ProjectiveTransform` object is needed to be created first to apply perspective transform to an image.

A set of 4-pixel positions from the source image and corresponding matching pixel positions in the destination image are needed to be passed to the `estimate()` function along with the object instance and this computes the homography matrix, *H* (and returns `True` if it can be computed).

The `inverse()` function is to be called on the object and this will give you the source pixel indices corresponding to all destination pixel indices.

There's more...

You can use the `warp()` function (instead of the `inverse()` function) to implement homography/projective transform.

See also

For more details, refer to the following links:

- `https://www.youtube.com/watch?v=YwIB9PbQkEM`
- `https://www.youtube.com/watch?v=2ggjHjRx2SQ`
- `https://www.youtube.com/watch?v=vviNh5y71ss`

Creating pencil sketches from images

Producing sketches from images is all about detecting edges in images. In this recipe, you will learn how to use different techniques, including the difference of **Gaussian** (and its extended version, **XDOG**), anisotropic diffusion, and dodging (applying Gaussian blur + invert + thresholding), to obtain sketches from images.

Getting ready

The following libraries need to be imported first:

```
import numpy as np
from skimage.io import imread
from skimage.color import rgb2gray
from skimage import util
from skimage import img_as_float
import matplotlib.pylab as plt
from medpy.filter.smoothing import anisotropic_diffusion
from skimage.filters import gaussian, threshold_otsu
```

How to do it...

The following steps need to be performed:

1. Define the `normalize()` function to implement min-max normalization in an image:

    ```
    def normalize(img):
        return (img-np.min(img))/(np.max(img)-np.min(img))
    ```

2. Implement the `sketch()` function that takes an image and the extracted edges as input:

    ```
    def sketch(img, edges):
        output = np.multiply(img, edges)
        output[output>1]=1
        output[edges==1]=1
        return output
    ```

Chapter 1

3. Implement a function to extract the edges from an image with anisotropic diffusion:

   ```
   def edges_with_anisotropic_diffusion(img, niter=100, kappa=10,
   gamma=0.1):
       output = img - anisotropic_diffusion(img, niter=niter, \
                kappa=kappa, gamma=gamma, voxelspacing=None, \
                option=1)
       output[output > 0] = 1
       output[output < 0] = 0
       return output
   ```

4. Implement a function to extract the edges from an image with the dodge operation (there are two implementations):

   ```
   def sketch_with_dodge(img):
    orig = img
    blur = gaussian(util.invert(img), sigma=20)
    result = blur / util.invert(orig)
    result[result>1] = 1
    result[orig==1] = 1
    return result

   def edges_with_dodge2(img):
    img_blurred = gaussian(util.invert(img), sigma=5)
    output = np.divide(img, util.invert(img_blurred) + 0.001)
    output = normalize(output)
    thresh = threshold_otsu(output)
    output = output > thresh
    return output
   ```

5. Implement a function to extract the edges from an image with a **Difference of Gaussian (DOG)** operation:

   ```
   def edges_with_DOG(img, k = 200, gamma = 1):
       sigma = 0.5
       output = gaussian(img, sigma=sigma) - gamma*gaussian(img, \
                 sigma=k*sigma)
       output[output > 0] = 1
       output[output < 0] = 0
       return output
   ```

[23]

Image Manipulation and Transformation

6. Implement a function to produce sketches from an image with an **Extended Difference of Gaussian (XDOG)** operation:

```
def sketch_with_XDOG(image, epsilon=0.01):
    phi = 10
    difference = edges_with_DOG(image, 200, 0.98).astype(np.uint8)
    for i in range(0, len(difference)):
        for j in range(0, len(difference[0])):
            if difference[i][j] >= epsilon:
                difference[i][j] = 1
            else:
                ht = np.tanh(phi*(difference[i][j] - epsilon))
                difference[i][j] = 1 + ht
    difference = normalize(difference)
    return difference
```

If you run the preceding code and plot all of the input/output images, you will obtain an output like the following screenshot:

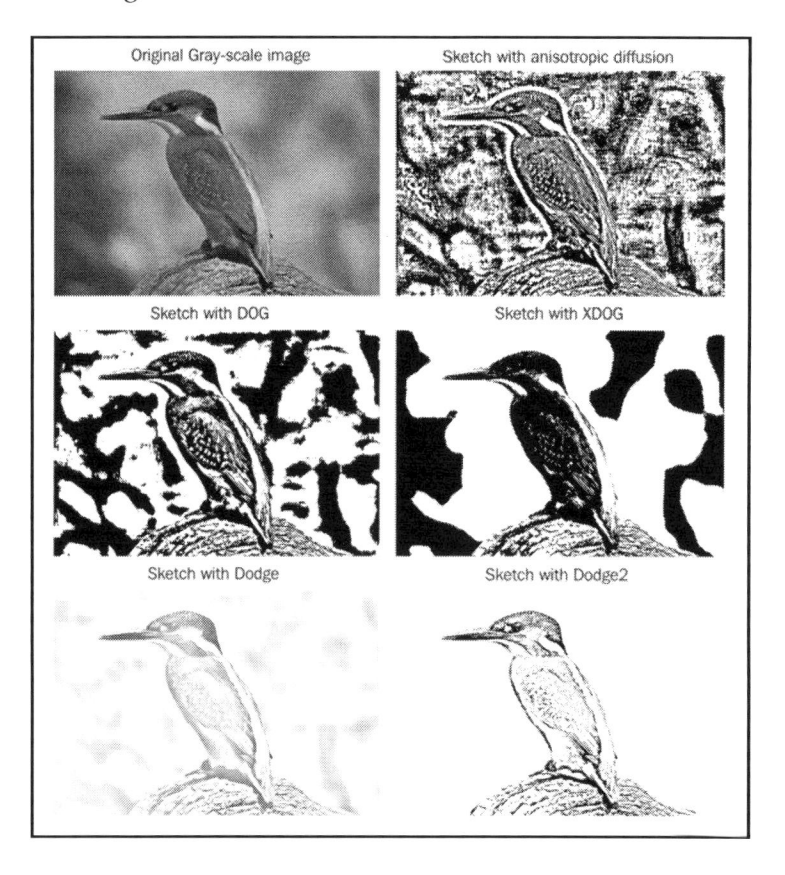

[24]

How it works...

As you can see from the previous section, many of the sketching techniques work by blurring the edges (for example, with Gaussian filter or diffusion) in the image and removing details to some extent and then subtracting the original image to get the sketch outlines.

The `gaussian()` function from the scikit-image filters module was used to blur the images.

The `anisotropic_diffusion()` function from the `filter.smoothing` module of the `medpy` library was used to find edges with anisotropic diffusion (a variational method).

The dodge operation divides (using `np.divide()`) the image by the inverted blurred image. This highlights the boldest edges in the image.

There's more...

There are a few more edge detection techniques, such as Canny (with hysteresis thresholds), that you can try to produce sketches from images. You can try them on your own and compare the sketches obtained using different algorithms. Also, by using OpenCV-Python's `pencilSketch()` and `sylization()` functions, you can produce black and white and color pencil sketches, as well as watercolor-like stylized images, with the following few lines of code:

```
import cv2
import matplotlib.pylab as plt
src = cv2.imread('images/bird.png')
#dst = cv2.detailEnhance(src, sigma_s=10, sigma_r=0.15)
dst_sketch, dst_color_sketch = cv2.pencilSketch(src, sigma_s=50, sigma_r=0.05, shade_factor=0.05)
dst_water_color = cv2.stylization(src, sigma_s=50, sigma_r=0.05)
```

Image Manipulation and Transformation

If you run this code and plot the images, you will get a diagram similar to the following screenshot:

See also

For more details, refer to the following link:

- https://www.youtube.com/watch?v=Zyl1gAIROxg

Creating cartoonish images

In this recipe, you will learn how to create cartoonish flat-textured images from an image. Again, there is more than one way to do the same; here, we will learn how to do it with edge-preserving bilateral filters.

Getting ready

The following libraries need to be imported first:

```
import cv2
import numpy as np
import matplotlib.pylab as plt
```

How to do it...

For this recipe, we will be using the `bilateralFilter()` function from OpenCV-Python. We need to start by downsampling the image to create an image pyramid (you will see more of this in the next chapter), followed by repeated application of small bilateral filters (to remove unimportant details) and upsampling the image to its original size. Next, you need to apply the median blur (to flatten the texture) followed by masking the original image with the binary image obtained by adaptive thresholding. The following code demonstrates the steps:

1. Read the input image and initialize the parameters to be used later:

    ```
    img = plt.imread("images/bean.png")

    num_down = 2 # number of downsampling steps
    num_bilateral = 7 # number of bilateral filtering steps

    w, h, _ = img.shape
    ```

2. Use the Gaussian pyramid's downsampling to reduce the image size (and make the subsequent operations faster):

    ```
    img_color = np.copy(img)
    for _ in range(num_down):
      img_color = cv2.pyrDown(img_color)
    ```

3. Apply bilateral filters (with a small *diameter* value) iteratively. The `d` parameter represents the diameter of the neighborhood for each pixel, where the `sigmaColor` and `sigmaSpace` parameters represent the filter sigma in the color and the coordinate spaces, respectively:

    ```
    for _ in range(num_bilateral):
      img_color = cv2.bilateralFilter(img_color, d=9, sigmaColor=0.1, sigmaSpace=0.01)
    ```

Image Manipulation and Transformation

4. Use upsampling to enlarge the image to the original size:

   ```
   for _ in range(num_down):
       img_color = cv2.pyrUp(img_color)
   ```

5. Convert to the output image obtained from the last step and blur the image with the `median` filter:

   ```
   img_gray = cv2.cvtColor(img, cv2.COLOR_RGB2GRAY)
   img_blur = cv2.medianBlur(img_gray, 7)
   ```

6. Detect and enhance the edges:

   ```
   img_edge = cv2.adaptiveThreshold((255*img_blur).astype(np.uint8), \
              255, cv2.ADAPTIVE_THRESH_MEAN_C, cv2.THRESH_BINARY, \
              blockSize=9, C=2)
   ```

7. Convert the grayscale edge image back into an RGB color image and compute bitwise AND with the RGB color image to get the final output cartoonish image:

   ```
   img_edge = cv2.cvtColor(img_edge, cv2.COLOR_GRAY2RGB)
   img_cartoon = cv2.bitwise_and(img_color, img_edge)
   ```

How it works...

As explained earlier, the `bilateralFilter()`, `medianBlur()`, `adaptiveThreshold()`, and `bitwise_and()` functions from OpenCV-Python were the key functions used to first remove weak edges, then convert into flat texture, and finally enhance the prominent edges in the image.

The `bilateralFilter()` function from OpenCV-Python was used to smooth the textures while keeping the edges fairly sharp:

- The higher the value of the `sigmaColor` parameter, the more the pixel colors in the neighborhood will be mixed together. This will produce larger areas of semi-equal color in the output image.
- The higher the value of the `sigmaSpace` parameter, the more the pixels with similar colors will influence each other.

The image was downsampled to create an image pyramid (you will see more of this in the next chapter).

Next, repeated application of small bilateral filters was used to remove unimportant details. A subsequent upsampling was used to resize the image to its original size.

Chapter 1

Finally, `medianBlur` was applied (to flatten the texture) followed by masking the original image with the binary image obtained by adaptive thresholding.

If you run the preceding code, you will get an output cartoonish image, as shown here:

There's more...

Play with the parameter values of the OpenCV functions to see the impact on the output image produced. Also, as mentioned earlier, there is more than one way to achieve the same effect. Try using anisotropic diffusion to obtain flat texture images. You should get an image like the following one (use the `anisotropic_diffusion()` function from the `medpy` library):

Image Manipulation and Transformation

See also

For more details, refer to the following links:

- `http://people.csail.mit.edu/sparis/bf_course/`
- `https://www.youtube.com/watch?v=DgRgPFkz6bg`

Simulating light art/long exposure

Long exposure (or **light art**) refers to the process of creating a photo that captures the effect of passing time. Some popular application examples of long exposure photographs are silky-smooth water and a single band of continuous-motion illumination of the highways with car headlights. In this recipe, we will simulate the long exposures by averaging the image frames from a video.

Getting ready

We will extract image frames from a video and then average the frames to simulate light art. Let's start by importing the required libraries:

```
from glob import glob
import cv2
import numpy as np
import matplotlib.pylab as plt
```

How to do it...

The following steps need to be performed:

1. Implement an `extract_frames()` function to extract the first 200 frames (at most) from a video passed as input to the function:

   ```
   def extract_frames(vid_file):
    vidcap = cv2.VideoCapture(vid_file)
    success,image = vidcap.read()
    i = 1
    success = True
    while success and i <= 200:
     cv2.imwrite('images/exposure/vid_{}.jpg'.format(i), image)
     success,image = vidcap.read()
     i += 1
   ```

2. Call the function to save all of the frames (as `.jpg`) extracted from the video of the waterfall in Godafost (Iceland) to the `exposure` folder:

   ```
   extract_frames('images/godafost.mp4') #cloud.mp4
   ```

3. Read all the `.jpg` files from the `exposure` folder; read them one by one (as float); split each image into B, G, and R channels; compute a running sum of the color channels; and finally, compute average values for the color channels:

   ```
   imfiles = glob('images/exposure/*.jpg')
   nfiles = len(imfiles)
   R1, G1, B1 = 0, 0, 0
   for i in range(nfiles):
    image = cv2.imread(imfiles[i]).astype(float)
    (B, G, R) = cv2.split(image)
    R1 += R
    B1 += B
    G1 += G
   R1, G1, B1 = R1 / nfiles, G1 / nfiles, B1 / nfiles
   ```

4. Merge the average values of the color channels obtained and save the final output image:

   ```
   final = cv2.merge([B1, G1, R1])
   cv2.imwrite('images/godafost.png', final)
   ```

Image Manipulation and Transformation

The following photo shows one of the extracted input frames:

An input image

If you run the preceding code block, you will obtain a long exposure-like image like the one shown here:

Output image

Notice the continuous effects in the clouds and the waterfall.

[32]

How it works...

The `VideoCapture()` function from OpenCV-Python was used to create a `VideoCapture` object with the video file as input. Then, the `read()` method of that object was used to capture frames from the video.

The `imread()` and `imwrite()` functions from OpenCV-Python were used to read/write images from/to disk.

The `cv2.split()` function was used to split an RGB image into individual color channels, while the `cv2.merge()` function was used to combine them back into an RGB image.

There's more...

Focus stacking (also known as extended depth of fields) is a technique (in image processing/computational photography) that takes multiple images (of the same subject but captured at different focus distances) as input and then creates an output image with a higher DOF than any of the individual source images by combining the input images. We can simulate focus stacking in Python. The following is an example of focus stacking grayscale image frames extracted from a video using the `mahotas` library.

Extended depth of field with mahotas

Perform the following steps to implement focus stacking with the `mahotas` library functions:

1. Create the image stack first by extracting grayscale image frames from a highway traffic video at night:

   ```
   import mahotas as mh
   def create_image_stack(vid_file, n = 200):
    vidcap = cv2.VideoCapture(vid_file)
    success,image = vidcap.read()
    i = 0
    success = True
    h, w = image.shape[:2]
    imstack = np.zeros((n, h, w))
    while success and i < n:
      imstack[i,...] = cv2.cvtColor(image, cv2.COLOR_BGR2GRAY)
      success,image = vidcap.read()
      i += 1
    return imstack
   ```

Image Manipulation and Transformation

```
image = create_image_stack('images/highway.mp4') #cloud.mp4
stack,h,w = image.shape
```

2. Use the `sobel()` function from `mahotas` as the pixel-level measure of infocusness:

   ```
   focus = np.array([mh.sobel(t, just_filter=True) for t in image])
   ```

3. At each pixel location, select the best slice (with maximum infocusness) and create the final image:

   ```
   best = np.argmax(focus, 0)
   image = image.reshape((stack,-1)) # image is now (stack, nr_pixels)
   image = image.transpose() # image is now (nr_pixels, stack)
   final = image[np.arange(len(image)), best.ravel()] # Select the right pixel at each location
   final = final.reshape((h,w)) # reshape to get final result
   ```

The following photo is an input image used in the image stack:

An input image

The following screenshot is the final output image produced by the algorithm implementation:

Output image

See also

For more details, refer to the following links:

- https://mahotas.readthedocs.io/en/latest/edf.html
- https://docs.opencv.org/3.0-beta/doc/py_tutorials/py_gui/py_video_display/py_video_display.html
- https://www.youtube.com/watch?v=5CTSc9GX3X8

Object detection using color in HSV

In this recipe, you will learn how to detect objects using colors in the **HSV color space** using OpenCV-Python. You need to specify a range of color values by means of which the object you are interested in will be identified and extracted. You can change the color of the object detected and even make the detected object transparent.

Image Manipulation and Transformation

Getting ready

In this recipe, the input image we will use will be an orange fish in an aquarium and the object of interest will be the fish. You will detect the fish, change its color, and make it transparent using the color range of the fish in HSV space. Let's start by importing the required libraries:

```
import cv2
import numpy as np
import matplotlib.pylab as plt
```

How to do it...

To do the recipe, the following steps need to be performed:

1. Read the input and background image. Convert the input image from BGR into the HSV color space:

   ```
   bck = cv2.imread("images/fish_bg.png")
   img = cv2.imread("images/fish.png")
   hsv = cv2.cvtColor(img, cv2.COLOR_BGR2HSV)
   ```

2. Create a mask for the fish by selecting a possible range of HSV colors that the fish can have:

   ```
   mask = cv2.inRange(hsv, (5, 75, 25), (25, 255, 255))
   ```

3. Slice the orange fish using the mask:

   ```
   imask = mask>0
   orange = np.zeros_like(img, np.uint8)
   orange[imask] = img[imask]
   ```

4. Change the color of the orange fish to yellow by changing the hue channel value only (add 20) and converting the image back into the BGR space:

   ```
   yellow = img.copy()
   hsv[...,0] = hsv[...,0] + 20
   yellow[imask] = cv2.cvtColor(hsv, cv2.COLOR_HSV2BGR)[imask]
   yellow = np.clip(yellow, 0, 255)
   ```

5. Finally, create the transparent fish image by first extracting the background without the input image with the fish, and then extracting the area corresponding to the foreground object (fish) from the background image and adding these two images:

```
bckfish = cv2.bitwise_and(bck, bck, mask=imask.astype(np.uint8))
nofish = img.copy()
nofish = cv2.bitwise_and(nofish, nofish,
mask=(np.bitwise_not(imask)).astype(np.uint8))
nofish = nofish + bckfish
```

How it works...

The following screenshot shows an HSV colormap for fast color lookup. The x axis denotes hue, with values in (0,180), the y axis (1) denotes saturation with values in (0,255), and the y axis (2) corresponds to the hue values corresponding to S = 255 and V = 255. To locate a particular color in the colormap, just look up the corresponding H and S range, and then set the range of V as (25, 255). For example, the orange color of the fish we are interested in can be searched in the HSV range from (5, 75, 25) to (25, 255, 255), as observed here:

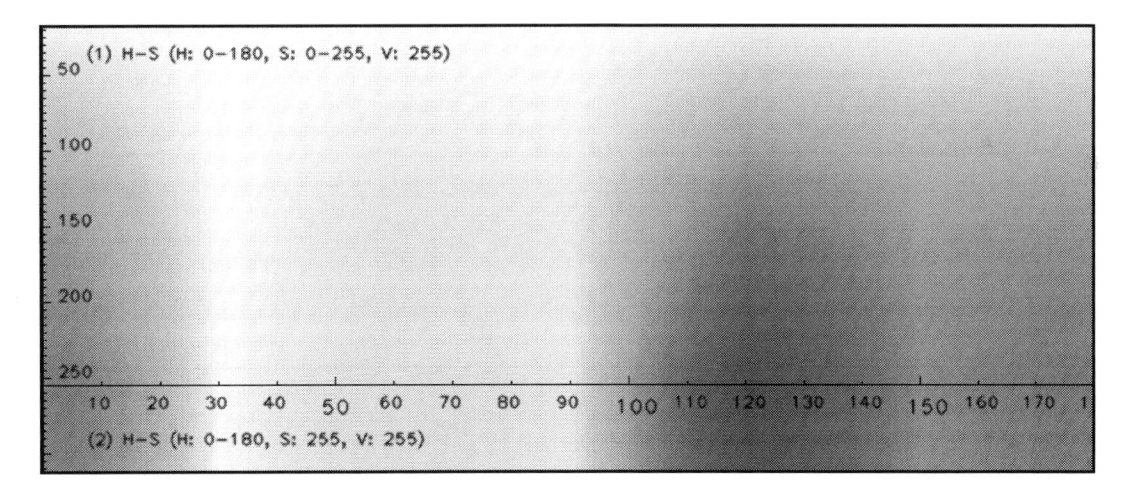

The inRange() function from OpenCV-Python was used for color detection. It accepts the HSV input image along with the color range (defined previously) as parameters.

Image Manipulation and Transformation

`cv2.inRange()` accepts three parameters—the input image, and the lower and upper limits of the color to be detected, respectively. It returns a binary mask, where white pixels represent the pixels within the range and black pixels represent the one outside the range specified.

To change the color of the fish detected, it is sufficient to change the hue (color) channel value only; we don't need to touch the saturation and value channels.

The bitwise arithmetic with OpenCV-Python was used to extract the foreground/background.

Notice that the background image has slightly different colors from the fish image's background; otherwise, transparent fish would have literally disappeared (invisible cloaking!).

If you run the preceding code snippets and plot all of the images, you will get the following output:

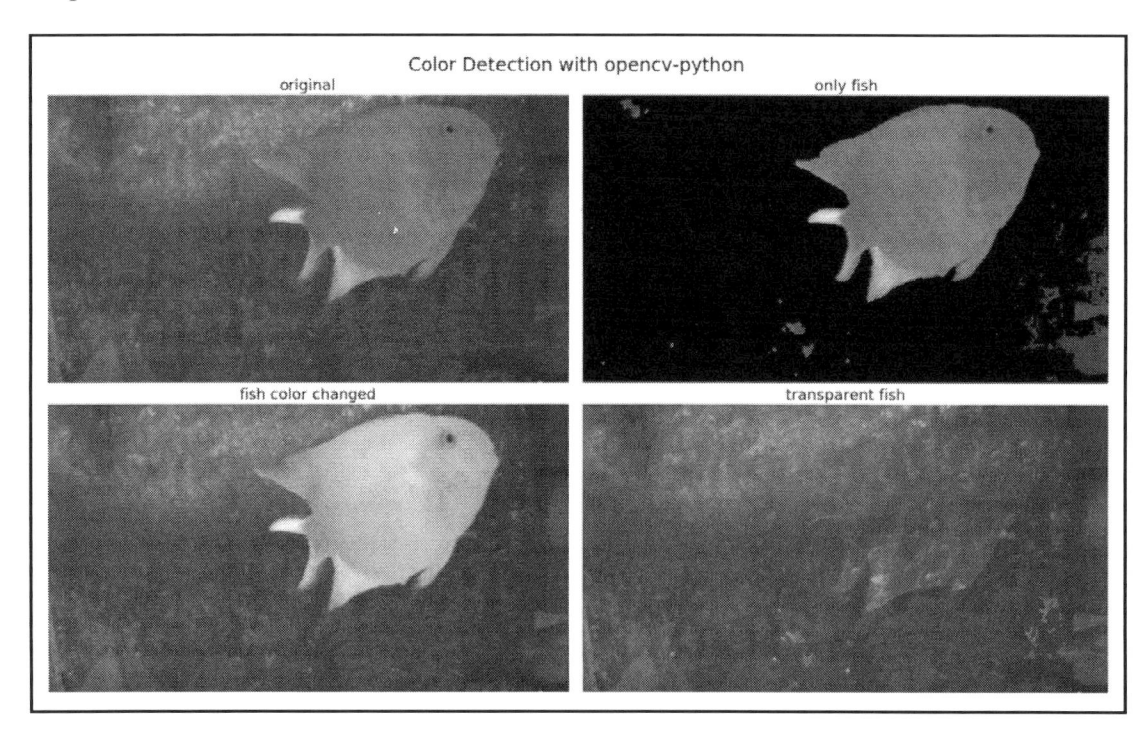

Note that, in OpenCV-Python, an image in the RGB color space is stored in BGR format. If we want to display the image in proper colors, before using `imshow()` from Matplotlib (which expects the image in RGB format instead), we must convert the image colors with `cv2.cvtColor(image, cv2.COLOR_BGR2RGB)`.

See also

For more details, refer to the following links:

- `https://opencv-python-tutroals.readthedocs.io/en/latest/py_tutorials/py_imgproc/py_colorspaces/py_colorspaces.html`
- `https://i.stack.imgur.com/gyuw4.png`
- `https://stackoverflow.com/questions/10948589/choosing-the-correct-upper-and-lower-hsv-boundaries-for-color-detection-withcv`
- `https://www.youtube.com/watch?v=1F0aOM3WJ74`

Image Enhancement

The objective of image enhancement is to improve the quality of an image or make particular features appear more prominent. The techniques used are often more general-purpose techniques and a strong model of the degradation process is not assumed (unlike image restoration, which we will see in the next chapter). Some examples of image enhancement techniques are denoising/smoothing (using different classical image processing, unsupervised machine learning, and deep learning techniques), contrast improvement, and sharpening.

In this chapter, we will cover the following recipes for image enhancement (and their implementations using Python libraries):

- Applying filters to denoise different types of noise in an image
- Image denoising with a denoising autoencoder
- Image denoising with PCA/DFT/DWT
- Image denoising with anisotropic diffusion
- Improving image contrast with histogram equalization
- Implementing histogram matching
- Performing gradient blending
- Edge detection with Canny, LoG/zero-crossing, and wavelets

Image Enhancement

Applying filters to denoise different types of noise in an image

Noise represents random variations of image intensity that cause image quality to deteriorate. Noise can be introduced when the image is captured or transmitted. Image denoising (noise removal) is a vital image processing task that must be done for most of the image processing applications. In this recipe, we will discuss different types of noise with different distributions, such as Gaussian, Salt and Pepper, Speckle, Poisson, and exponential, and image denoising performed for different noise types with a couple of popular filtering techniques (mean and median filters), using the `ndimage` module from SciPy. The results will be compared for all types of noise.

Getting ready

We will be using the Lena grayscale image and adding different types of random noise (by drawing random samples from different distributions) to the original image. We will apply a popular linear (mean) and a popular non-linear (median) filter to the noisy images obtained. We will also compare the performance of the filters by computing the **peak signal-to-noise ratio** (**PSNR**).

Let's start by loading the requisite libraries with the following code:

```
%matplotlib inline
from skimage.io import imread
from skimage.util import random_noise
from skimage.color import rgb2gray
from skimage.measure import compare_psnr
from scipy.ndimage import uniform_filter, median_filter
import numpy as np
import matplotlib.pylab as plt
```

How to do it...

Denoising different types of noises in an image is done with the following steps:

1. Define the `plt_hist()` function to plot the histogram of the noise added to the image:

    ```
    def plt_hist(noise, bins=None):
        plt.grid()
        plt.hist(np.ravel(noise), bins=bins, alpha=0.5, color='green')
    ```

```
            plt.tick_params(labelsize=15)
            plt.title('Noise Historgram', size=25)
```

2. Next, define the `plt_images()` function to plot all the images, that is, the original, noisy and denoised images, using the mean/median filters, and plot the noise histogram by calling the `plt_hist()` function defined previously. Also, compare the quality of the images denoised using the filters with the PSNR:

    ```
    def plt_images(im, im_noisy, noise, noise_type, i):
        im_denoised_mean = uniform_filter(im_noisy, 5)
        im_denoised_median = median_filter(im_noisy, 5)
        plt.subplot(7,4,i), plt.imshow(im_noisy), \
            plt.title('Noisy ({}), PSNR={}'.format(noise_type, \
            np.round(compare_psnr(im, im_noisy),3)), size=25), \
            plt.axis('off')
        plt.subplot(7,4,i+1), plt.imshow(im_denoised_mean), \
            plt.title('Denoised (mean), PSNR={}'.format(np.round\
            (compare_psnr(im, im_denoised_mean),3)), size=25), \
            plt.axis('off')
        plt.subplot(7,4,i+2), plt.imshow(im_denoised_median), \
            plt.title('Denoised (median), PSNR={}'.format(np.round\
            (compare_psnr(im, im_denoised_median),3)), size=25), \
            plt.axis('off')
        plt.subplot(7,4,i+3), plt_hist(noise)
    ```

3. Load the original Lena RGB color image and convert it to a grayscale image:

    ```
    im = rgb2gray(imread('images/lena.png'))
    ```

4. Now, add random noise to the original image by drawing samples from different distributions, along with appropriate parameters—one for each of the noise distributions. After this, call the `plt_images()` function defined earlier to plot the images and the noise distributions:

    ```
    im1 = random_noise(im, 'gaussian', var=0.15**2)
    plt_images(im, im1, im1-im, 'Gaussian', 1)

    im1 = random_noise(im, 's&p', amount=0.15)
    plt_images(im, im1, im1[((im1==0)|(im1==1))&((im!=0)&(im!=1))],
    'Impulse', 5)

    noise = np.random.poisson(lam=int(np.mean(255*im)),
    size=im.shape)/255 - np.mean(im)
    im1 = np.clip(im + noise, 0, 1)
    plt_images(im, im1, noise, 'Poisson', 9)

    im1 = random_noise(im, 'speckle', var=0.15**2)
    ```

Image Enhancement

```
            plt_images(im, im1, im1-im, 'Speckle', 13)

            noise = np.random.rayleigh(scale=0.15, size=im.shape) - 0.15
            im1 = np.clip(im + noise, 0, 1)
            plt_images(im, im1, noise, 'Rayleigh', 17)

            noise = np.random.exponential(scale=0.15, size=im.shape) - 0.15
            im1 = np.clip(im + noise, 0, 1)
            plt_images(im, im1, noise, 'Exponential', 21)

            noise = np.random.uniform(0, 0.5, size=im.shape) - 0.25
            im1 = np.clip(im + noise, 0, 1)
            plt_images(im, im1, noise, 'Uniform', 25)
```

How it works...

We started by applying the mean filter to the noisy images with the uniform_filter() function from the scipy.ndimage module. Then, we applied the median filter to the noisy images with median_filer() from the same module. For both the filters, the filter size used was 5, in order to apply a 5 x 5 convolution with the box kernel.

The compare_psnr() function from the skimage.measure module was used to compare the quality of the images denoised using the filters.

The imread() function from the scikit-image.io module was used to read the Lena RGB image and the rgb2gray() function from the scikit-image.color module was used to convert the image to grayscale.

We used either the random_noise() function from the scikit-image.util module, or used the corresponding distribution functions from the random module of NumPy (for example, np.random.possion()) to draw *random* noise samples from different distributions (for example, Gaussian, Poisson, and exponential), along with appropriate parameters (for example, mean, µ, and variance, σ2, for Gaussian noise, and mean, λ, for Poisson noise) for each of the noise distributions.

The plt_images() function accepts three arguments, the first one being the original image, the second being the noisy image, and the third being the noise added. Notice that for the impulse (s&p) noise, in order to compute the noise matrix, we had to find the locations where the pixel value switched from 0 to 1 (salt) or 1 to 0 (pepper) in the original image.

Chapter 2

The following screenshot is part of the output you should get after running the code in *step 4*:

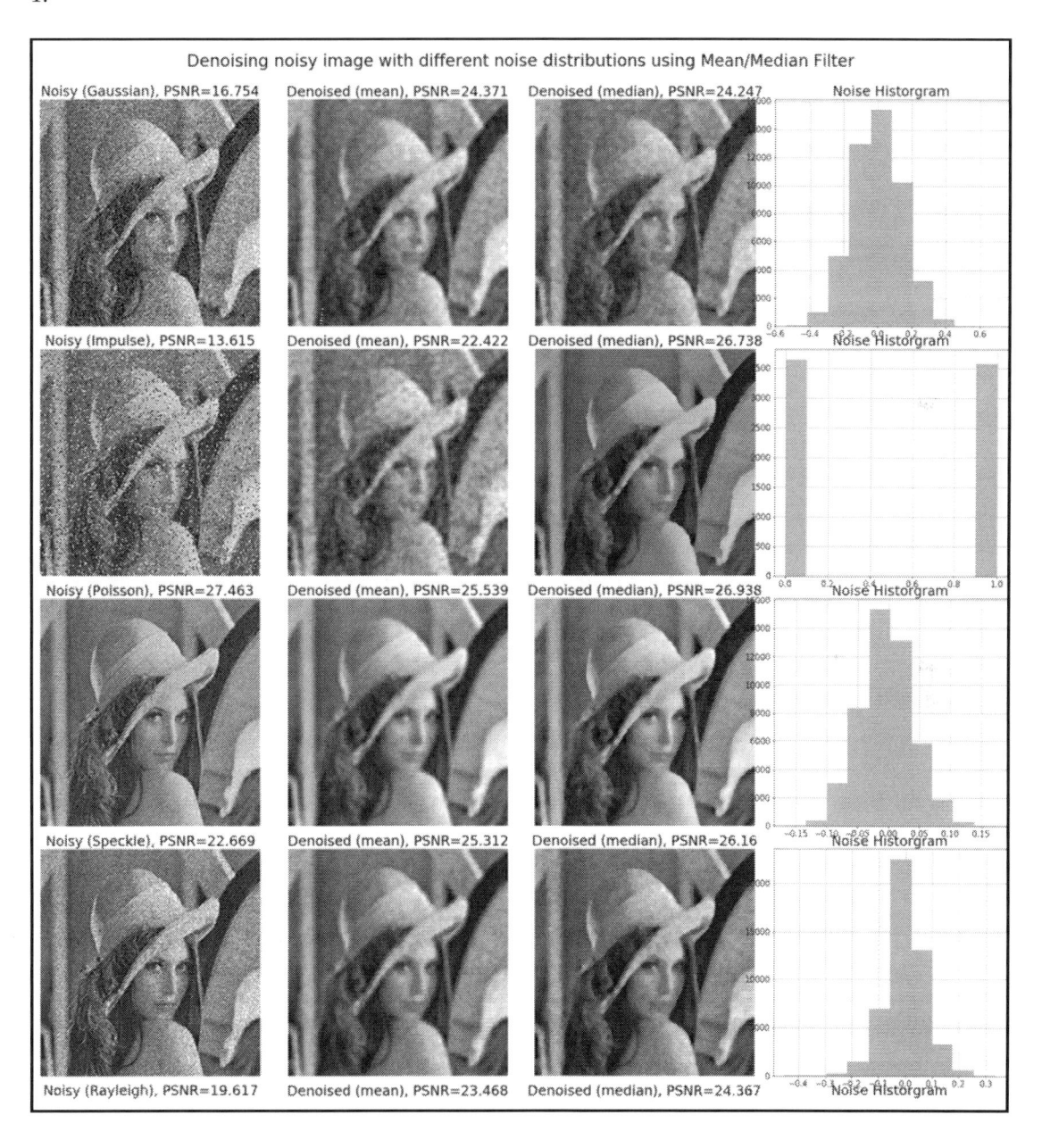

Image Enhancement

As seen from the last output, the median filter does particularly well for impulse (salt and pepper) noise and also does better jobs for Speckle, Poisson, and Rayleigh random noise, whereas for the other types of noise distributions, the mean filter performs well for this image. Also, notice how the shape of the random noise histograms change for each distribution (and they resemble the shape of the density functions).

There's more...

You could also use scikit-image implementations of the mean (for example, `rank.mean()`, `rank.mean_percentile()`, and `rank.mean_bilateral()`) and median filters (`filters.median()`). Try these functions on your own on the noisy images and compute the PSNR values of the denoised images.

Image denoising with a denoising autoencoder

An autoencoder is a neural network often used to learn an efficient representation of input data (typically in a reduced dimension) in an unsupervised way. A denoising autoencoder is a stochastic version of an autoencoder that takes (similar) inputs corrupted by noise and is trained to recover the original inputs (typically using some deep learning library functions) in order to obtain a good representation. We can use denoising autoencoders to learn robust representations from a set of similar input images (corrupted with noise) and then generate the denoised images.

Getting ready

We will be using the **labeled faces in the wild** (**lfw**) face dataset from scikit-learn (it contains face images of seven very famous politicians). We will add some random noise to these face images, use them as inputs to the autoencoder, and train it to learn to remove the noise. We will use PyTorch library functions for deep learning. As usual, let's start by importing the required libraries:

```
import os
import numpy as np
import matplotlib.pylab as plt
import torch
from torch import nn
from torch.autograd import Variable
```

```
from torch.utils.data import DataLoader
from torchvision import transforms
from torchvision.utils import save_image
from sklearn.datasets import fetch_lfw_people
```

How to do it...

We can now denoise using the denoising autoencoder in the following steps:

1. Define the `to_img()` and `plot_sample_img()` functions to convert a PyTorch tensor to an image from the `lfw` dataset (each grayscale image has a size of 50 x 37) and to save the image to disk, respectively:

   ```
   def to_img(x):
       x = x.view(x.size(0), 1, 50, 37)
       return x

   def plot_sample_img(img, name):
       img = img.view(1, 50, 37)
       save_image(img, './sample_{}.png'.format(name))
   ```

2. Define the `add_noise()` function to add random Gaussian noise to an image:

   ```
   def add_noise(img):
       noise = torch.randn(img.size()) * 0.2
       noisy_img = img + noise
       return noisy_img
   ```

3. Implement the `min_max_normalization()` and `tensor_round()` preprocessing functions to normalize and round a tensor, respectively. Also, create a transformation pipeline with the functions defined:

   ```
   def min_max_normalization(tensor, min_value, max_value):
       min_tensor = tensor.min()
       tensor = (tensor - min_tensor)
       max_tensor = tensor.max()
       tensor = tensor / max_tensor
       tensor = tensor * (max_value - min_value) + min_value
       return tensor

   def tensor_round(tensor):
       return torch.round(tensor)

   img_transform = transforms.Compose([
       transforms.ToTensor(),
       transforms.Lambda(lambda tensor:min_max_normalization(tensor, \
   ```

```
                        0, 1)),
        transforms.Lambda(lambda tensor:tensor_round(tensor))
    ])
```

4. Download the `lfw` dataset and create a `dataloader` with a batch size of 8:

```
batch_size = 8 # 16
dataset = fetch_lfw_people(min_faces_per_person=70, \
                            resize=0.4).images / 255
dataloader = DataLoader(dataset, batch_size=batch_size, \
                        shuffle=True)
```

5. Now, implement the `autoencoder` class, the encoder and decoder members, and the `forward()` method of the class:

```
class autoencoder(nn.Module):
    def __init__(self):
        super(autoencoder, self).__init__()
        self.encoder = nn.Sequential(
            nn.Linear(50 * 37, 512),
            nn.ReLU(True),
            nn.Linear(512, 128),
            nn.ReLU(True))
        self.decoder = nn.Sequential(
            nn.Linear(128, 512),
            nn.ReLU(True),
            nn.Linear(512, 50 * 37),
            nn.Sigmoid())

    def forward(self, x):
        x = self.encoder(x)
        x = self.decoder(x)
        return x
```

6. Instantiate the `autoencoder` class, and then define the loss function as binary cross-entropy (BCE) loss and the optimizer as the Adam optimizer using the following code snippet:

```
learning_rate = 1e-3
cuda = False #True
model = autoencoder()
if cuda:
 model = model.cuda()
criterion = nn.BCELoss()
optimizer = torch.optim.Adam(model.parameters(), \
            lr=learning_rate, weight_decay=1e-5)
```

7. Train the autoencoder for 100 epochs. In every epoch, use forward propagation for autoencoder prediction (and loss function computation) and backpropagation to update the weights in different layers:

```
num_epochs = 100
for epoch in range(1, num_epochs+1):
 for data in dataloader:
 img = data
 #...
 if cuda: noisy_img = noisy_img.cuda()
 img = Variable(img)
 if cuda: img = img.cuda()
 output = model(noisy_img) # forward-prop
 loss = criterion(output, img)
 MSE_loss = nn.MSELoss()(output, img)
 optimizer.zero_grad()
 loss.backward() # back-prop
 optimizer.step()
 print('epoch [{}/{}], loss:{:.4f}, MSE_loss:{:.4f}'
 .format(epoch, num_epochs, loss.data.item(),
MSE_loss.data.item()))
 if epoch % 10 == 0:
 x = to_img(img.cpu().data)
 x_hat = to_img(output.cpu().data)
 x_noisy = to_img(noisy_img.cpu().data)
 weights = to_img(model.encoder[0].weight.cpu().data)
```

8. Print the model to see the net architecture:

```
print(model)
# autoencoder(
#   (encoder): Sequential(
#     (0): Linear(in_features=1850, out_features=512, bias=True)
#     (1): ReLU(inplace)
#     (2): Linear(in_features=512, out_features=128, bias=True)
#     (3): ReLU(inplace)
#   )
#   (decoder): Sequential(
#     (0): Linear(in_features=128, out_features=512, bias=True)
#     (1): ReLU(inplace)
#     (2): Linear(in_features=512, out_features=1850, bias=True)
#     (3): Sigmoid()
#   )
# )
```

Image Enhancement

The following diagram shows the structure of the network and how the preceding denoising autoencoder works with the `lfw` faces dataset:

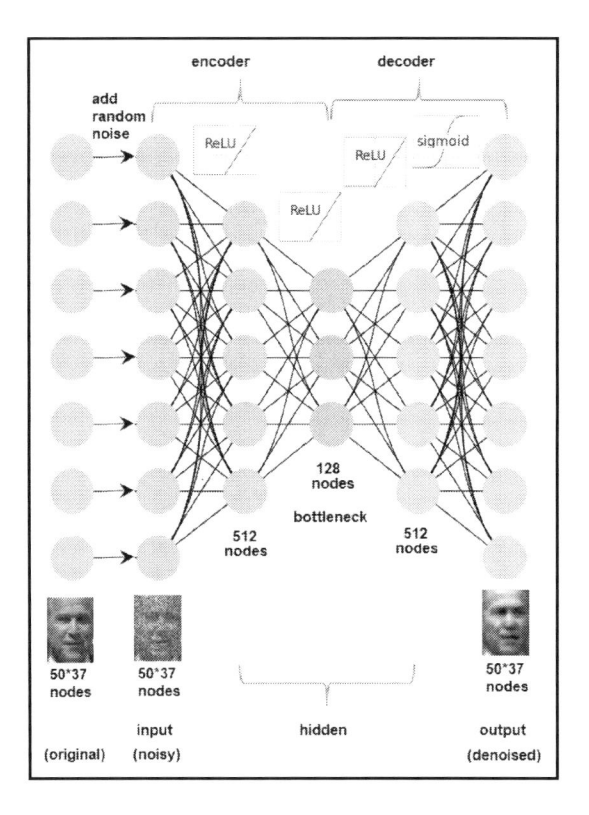

How it works...

We used `nn.Sequential()` from PyTorch to build the autoencoder by sequentially specifying the building blocks (`nn.Module`). Each pixel from a noisy image forms an input node, hence the input has 50*37 nodes. The output also has the same number of nodes.

A fully connected layer of size 1,850 x 512 was instantiated with `nn.Linear(50*37, 512)`. `nn.ReLU(True)` was used to apply in-place ReLU non-linearity in between the input/hidden layers and `nn.Sigmoid()` before the final layer to apply the sigmoid function at the output layer. Binary cross-entropy loss was used with `nn.BCEloss()`. The `backward()` function was used to backpropagate and recompute the weights in the neural net.

Chapter 2

We can run the code on a GPU by setting `cuda = True` to run it much faster.

The following screenshot shows the original image, the noisy image, the reconstructed output image with the autoencoder, and a few learned features in the first hidden layer of the encoder at the end of two different epochs:

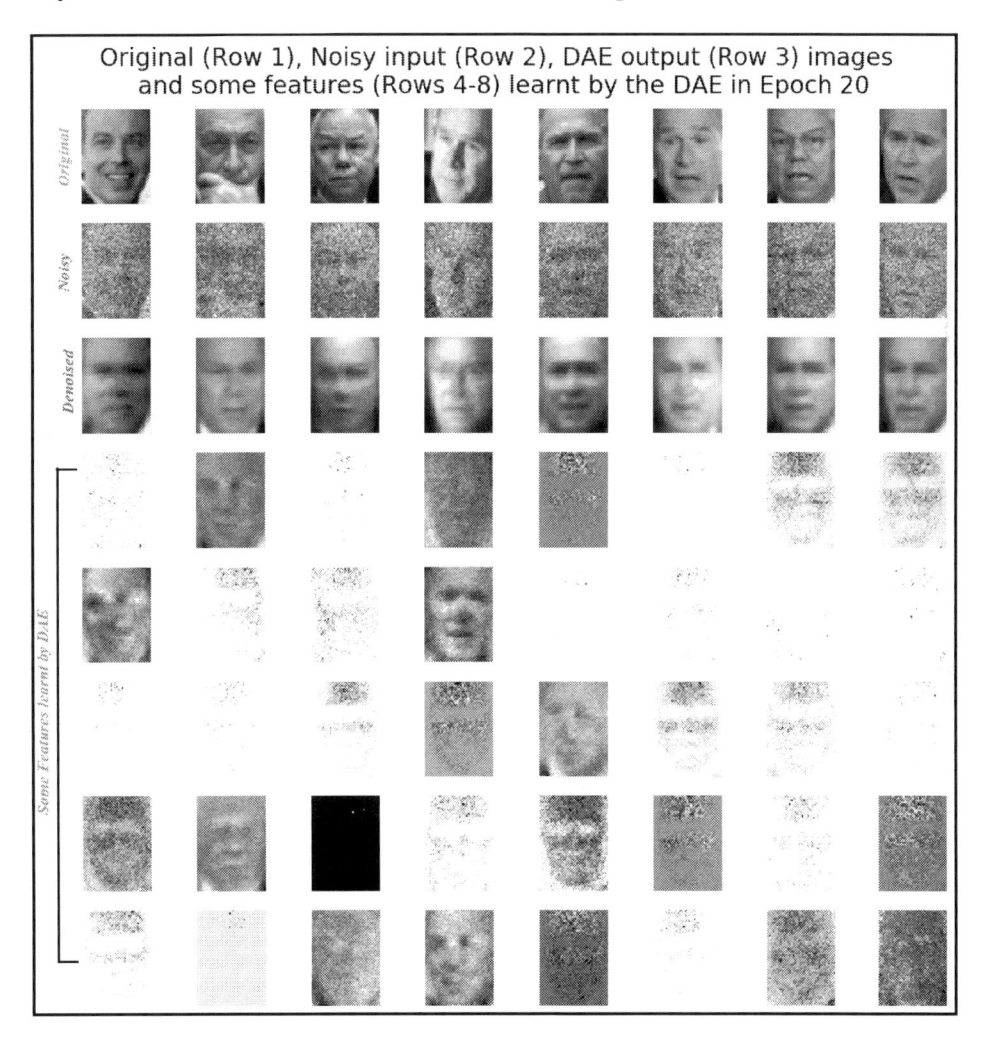

Original (Row 1), Noisy input (Row 2), DAE output (Row 3) images and some features (Rows 4-8) learnt by the DAE in Epoch 20

Image Enhancement

As you can see in the following screenshot, with more epochs, the denoised images generated as output by the autoencoder become more and more similar to the corresponding original image:

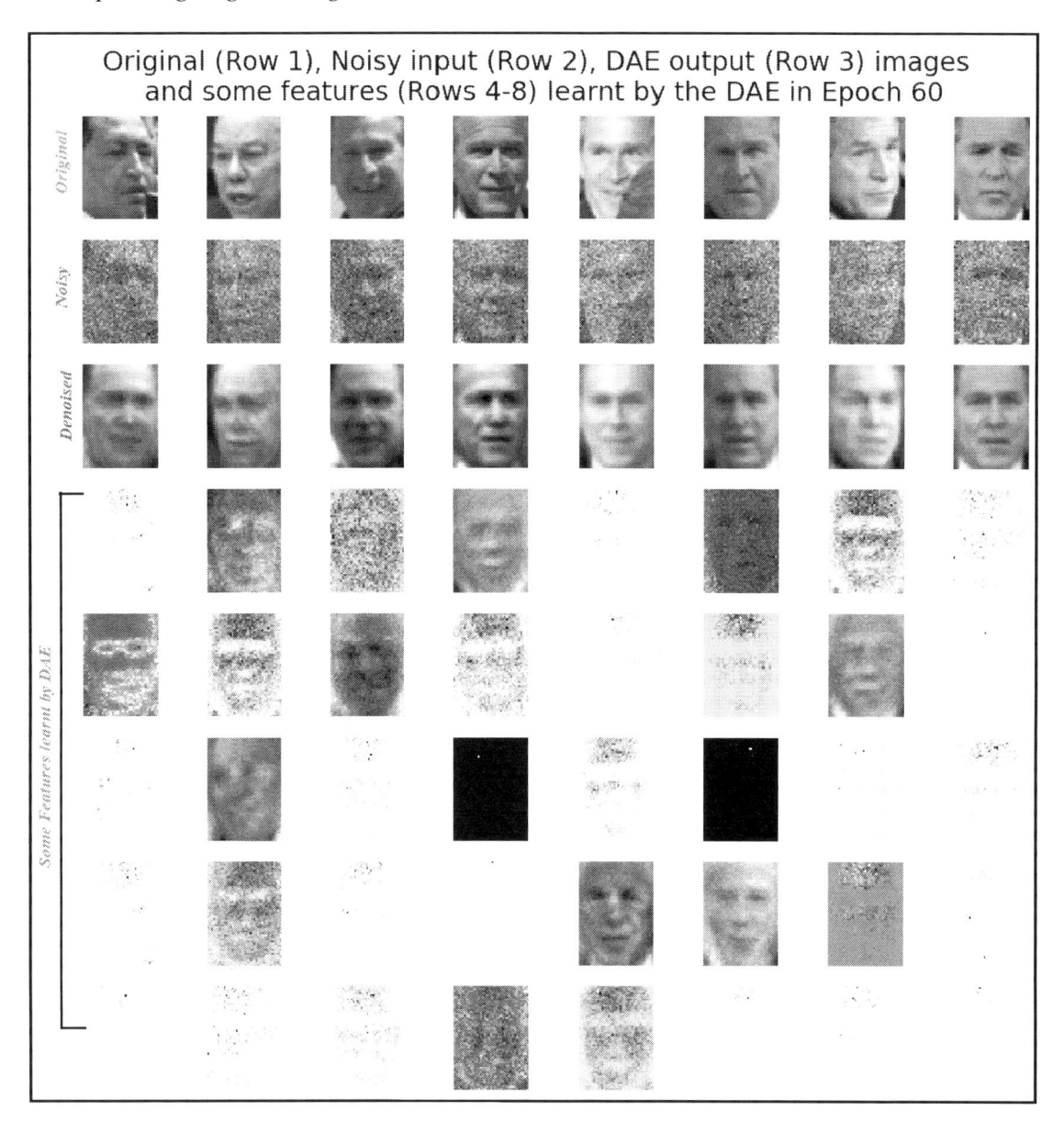

Original (Row 1), Noisy input (Row 2), DAE output (Row 3) images and some features (Rows 4-8) learnt by the DAE in Epoch 60

[52]

There's more...

Repeat the preceding denoising process with colored images (pass `color=True` to the `fetch_lfw_people()` function). Train an overcomplete autoencoder (where the number of hidden layer nodes is greater than the number of input nodes, with a single hidden layer) using the noisy images. What happens if you train this with the original images both at input and output? Now, train a sparse overcomplete autoencoder with original images both at input and output, but using an L1 regularizer at the hidden layer.

See also

For more information, refer to the following links:

- `http://vis-www.cs.umass.edu/lfw/`
- `https://scikit-learn.org/0.15/datasets/labeled_faces.html`
- `https://pytorch.org/docs/stable/_modules/torch/nn/modules/linear.html`
- `https://www.youtube.com/watch?v=B6YO5_RLALA`

Image denoising with PCA/DFT/DWT

Principal component analysis (PCA), **discrete Fourier transform (DFT)**, and **discrete wavelet transform (DWT)** are traditional machine learning techniques that can be used to denoise images as well. Each of these techniques will learn a representation (an approximation) of the image space and will retain mostly the information content in the images and remove the noise.

Getting ready

We will use the Olivetti faces dataset for this recipe. The dataset contains a total of 400 grayscale face images (each of size 64 x 64), 10 per each of the 40 objects. As usual, let's start by importing the required libraries:

```
import numpy as np
from numpy.random import RandomState
import matplotlib.pyplot as plt
from sklearn.datasets import fetch_olivetti_faces
from sklearn import decomposition
from skimage.util import random_noise
from skimage import img_as_float
```

Image Enhancement

```
from time import time
import scipy.fftpack as fp
import pywt
```

How to do it...

Perform the following steps to implement the filters:

1. Download the `faces` data first:

   ```
   dataset = fetch_olivetti_faces(shuffle=True, random_state=rng)
   original = img_as_float(dataset.data)
   faces = original.copy()
   print(faces.shape)
   # (400, 4096)
   ```

2. Add random Gaussian noise to the image with a variance of `0.005`:

   ```
   image_shape = (64, 64)
   rng = RandomState(0)
   n_samples, n_features = faces.shape
   faces = random_noise(faces, var=0.005)
   ```

3. Use `PCA` and reconstruct the images using only 50 dominant principal components:

   ```
   n_components = 50 # 256
   estimator = decomposition.PCA(n_components=n_components,
   svd_solver='randomized', whiten=True)
   print("Extracting the top %d PCs..." % (n_components))
   t0 = time()
   faces_recons =
   estimator.inverse_transform(estimator.fit_transform(faces)) #.T #+
   mean_face #.T
   train_time = (time() - t0)
   print("done in %0.3fs" % train_time)
   ```

4. Randomly select five image indices and display the original image, the noisy image, and the PCA reconstructions:

   ```
   indices = np.random.choice(n_samples, 5, replace=False)
   plt.figure(figsize=(20,4))
   for i in range(len(indices)):
       plt.subplot(1,5,i+1),
   plt.imshow(np.reshape(faces_recons[indices[i],:], image_shape)),
   plt.axis('off')
   ```

5. Use FFT **lowpass filter** (**LPF**) by discarding all but the thirty lowest-frequency components and reconstruct a noisy image with these basis vectors. Display the reconstructed images:

   ```
   n_components = 30
   plt.figure(figsize=(20,4))
   for i in range(len(indices)):
       freq = fp.fftshift(fp.fft2((np.reshape(faces[indices[i],:],
   image_shape)).astype(float)))
       freq[:freq.shape[0]//2 - n_components//2,:] =
   freq[freq.shape[0]//2 + n_components//2:,:] = 0
       freq[:,:freq.shape[1]//2 - n_components//2] = freq[:,
   freq.shape[1]//2 + n_components//2:] = 0
       plt.subplot(1,5,i+1),
   plt.imshow(fp.ifft2(fp.ifftshift(freq)).real), plt.axis('off')
   plt.suptitle('FFT LPF reconstruction with {} basis
   vectors'.format(n_components), size=25)
   plt.show()
   ```

6. Use DWT and discard the seventh band to reconstruct an image. Display the reconstructed images:

   ```
   plt.figure(figsize=(20,4))
   wavelet = pywt.Wavelet('haar')
   for i in range(len(indices)):
       wavelet_coeffs = pywt.wavedec2((np.reshape(faces[indices[i],:],
   image_shape)).astype(float), wavelet)
       plt.subplot(1,5,i+1),
   plt.imshow(pywt.waverec2(wavelet_coeffs[:-1], wavelet)),
   plt.axis('off')
   plt.suptitle('Wavelet reconstruction with {}
   subbands'.format(len(wavelet_coeffs)-1), size=25)
   plt.show()
   ```

How it works...

The `decomposition.PCA()` function from scikit-learn was used to instantiate a PCA object. The `fit_transform()` function was first used to project the images to a lower dimension (from 4096 to 50 dimensions), and then the `inverse_transform()` function was used to reconstruct the images from the lower-dimensional representations.

Image Enhancement

The `fft2()` function of `scipy.fftpack` was used to transform an image from the spatial to the frequency domain by forcing all the high-frequency basis vectors to be zero (except the lowest thirty basis vectors) and then the image was reconstructed with `ifft2()`.

Finally, the `pywt.Wavelet('haar')` function was used to instantiate a Haar wavelet object. The `pywt.wavedec2()` function was used to get all the wavelet coefficients, and then `pywt.waverec2()` was used to reconstruct the image from the coefficients by discarding the last band.

If you run the preceding code blocks, you will obtain an output along the lines of the following:

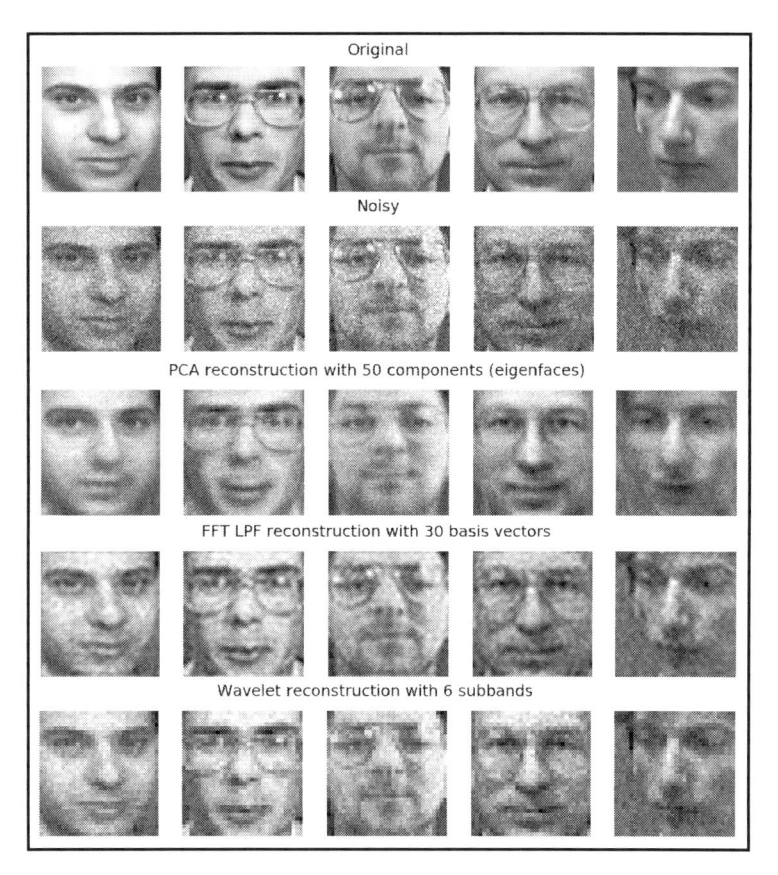

As can be seen from the preceding screenshot, PCA seems to do the best job in terms of reconstruction here.

There's more...

Try to implement PCA yourself using SVD and then project an image on the dominant singular vectors (you may use the `TruncatedSVD()` function from scikit-learn too). Use PSNR values to compare the output (denoised) image quality for different techniques.

See also

For more information, refer to the following links:

- https://scikit-learn.org/0.19/datasets/olivetti_faces.html
- https://scikit-learn.org/stable/modules/generated/sklearn.decomposition.TruncatedSVD.html
- https://www.youtube.com/watch?v=jDnIkyxwX4Y

Image denoising with anisotropic diffusion

In this recipe, you will learn how to use the anisotropic (heat) diffusion equation to denoise an image preserving the edges by using a `medpy` library function. Isotropic diffusion, on the other hand, is identical to applying a Gaussian filter, which does not preserve the edges in an image, as we have already seen.

Getting ready

In this recipe, we will use the cameraman grayscale image. As usual, let's start by importing the required libraries:

```
from medpy.filter.smoothing import anisotropic_diffusion
from skimage.util import random_noise
from skimage.io import imread
from skimage import img_as_float
import matplotlib.pylab as plt
import numpyp as np
```

Image Enhancement

How to do it...

Perform the following steps to denoise an image with the implementation of Perona-Malik anisotropic diffusion:

1. First, read the cameraman grayscale image from disk and add random Gaussian noise (with a variance of `0.025`) to it. Clip the noisy image to have values strictly between `0` and `1` (inclusive):

    ```
    img = img_as_float(imread('images/cameraman.png'))
    noisy = random_noise(img, var=0.005)
    noisy = np.clip(noisy, 0, 1)
    ```

2. Plot the original and noisy images:

    ```
    plt.figure(figsize=(15,18))
    plt.gray()
    plt.subplots_adjust(0,0,1,1,0.05,0.05)
    plt.subplot(221), plt.imshow(img), plt.axis('off'),
    plt.title('Original', size=20)
    plt.subplot(222), plt.imshow(noisy), plt.axis('off'),
    plt.title('Noisy', size=20)
    ```

3. Apply anisotropic diffusion (according to Perona-Malik equation 1) with parameters of `kappa=20` and `niter=20` to denoise the noisy image. Plot the smoothed image:

    ```
    diff_out = anisotropic_diffusion(noisy, niter=20, kappa=20,
    option=1)
    plt.subplot(223), plt.imshow(diff_out), plt.axis('off'), \
        plt.title(r'Anisotropic Diffusion (Perona Malik eq 1, \
        iter=20, $\kappa=20$)', size=20)
    ```

4. Again, apply anisotropic diffusion (according to Perona-Malik equation 2 this time), with parameters of `kappa=50` and `niter=50` to denoise the noisy image. Plot the smoothed image:

    ```
    diff_out = anisotropic_diffusion(noisy, niter=50, kappa=50,
    option=2)
    plt.subplot(224), plt.imshow(diff_out), plt.axis('off'), \
        plt.title(r'Anisotropic Diffusion (Perona Malik eq 2, \
        iter=50, $\kappa=50$)', size=20)
    plt.show()
    ```

If you run the preceding code snippets, you will get a diagram along the lines of the following:

You can see from the preceding output that, as the `kappa` value and the number of iterations are increased, the image becomes more blurry.

How it works...

Anisotropic diffusion was used to smooth (denoise) an image by keeping the edges mostly unchanged (even sharpened). In the anisotropic diffusion process (which is an iterative process), the Gaussian kernel is used as a conductivity function (c), according to Perona-Malik equation 1, as shown in the following screenshot:

Anisotropic Heat Diffusion Equation

$$I_t = \text{div}(c(x,y,t)\nabla I) = c(x,y,t) \cdot \Delta I + \nabla c \cdot \nabla I$$

Image at time t — divergence — Gradient — conductivity function — Laplacian

$$= \nabla \cdot (c \nabla I) = \frac{\partial}{\partial x}(c I_x) + \frac{\partial}{\partial y}(c I_y)$$

calculate the conductivity function c every iteration based on the current image I

$$c(x, y, t) = g(\|\nabla I(x, y, t)\|)$$

Perona-Malik edge-stopping function

$$g(\nabla I) = e^{(-(\|\nabla I\|/K)^2)} \quad \text{(equation 1)}$$

$$g(\nabla I) = \frac{1}{1 + \left(\frac{\|\nabla I\|}{K}\right)^2} \quad \text{(equation 2)}$$

Taken from http://image.diku.dk/imagecanon/material/PeronaMalik1990.pdf

The `anisotropic_diffusion()` function from the `filter.smoothing` module in the `medpy` library was used to implement the diffusion process. The `niter` parameter to this function represents the number of iterations on which the diffusion process is to be run. The `kappa` (K) parameter is an integer representing the conduction coefficient (for example, with values between 20 – 100). K controls the conduction, which is a function of the gradient. When K is small, the conduction and the diffusion across steep edges will be blocked. A higher K value decreases the impact of intensity gradients on conduction. The `gamma` parameter controls the speed of diffusion, and a `gamma` value of ≤ 0.25 should be used for stability.

There's more...

Compare the denoised image obtained using anisotropic diffusion with the one obtained by a convolution with a Gaussian kernel (also known as **isotropic diffusion**). Use PSNR to compare the quality. Try to implement the anisotropic diffusion on your own (refer to the second link given in the following *See also* section).

See also

For more information, refer to the following links:

- `http://image.diku.dk/imagecanon/material/PeronaMalik1990.pdf`
- `https://sandipanweb.wordpress.com/2017/10/08/some-more-variational-image-processing-diffusiontv-denoising-image-inpainting/`

Improving image contrast with histogram equalization

In `Chapter 1`, *Image Manipulation and Transformation*, we saw how the contrast stretching operation can be used to increase the contrast of an image. However, it is just a linear scaling function that is applied to image pixel values, and hence the image enhancement is less drastic than its more sophisticated counterpart, histogram equalization. This recipe will show how to implement contrast stretching using the histogram equalization. It is also a point transform that uses a non-linear mapping that reassigns the pixel intensity values in the input image in such a way that the output image has a uniform distribution of intensities (a flat histogram), and thereby enhances the contrast of the image.

Image Enhancement

Getting ready

In this recipe, we will implement histogram equalization with our own function, and also use scikit-image's global and local (adaptive) histogram equalization functions, starting with an RGB image. As usual, let's start by importing the required libraries:

```
import numpy as np
import matplotlib.pylab as plt
from skimage.io import imread
from skimage.exposure import import equalize_hist, equalize_adapthist
```

How to do it...

To execute this recipe, perform the following steps:

1. Define the `plot_image()` and `plot_hist()` functions to display an image and return its **cumulative distribution function** (cdf), respectively:

```
def plot_image(image, title):
 plt.imshow(image)
 plt.title(title, size=20)
 plt.axis('off')

def plot_hist(img):
 colors = ['r', 'g', 'b']
 cdf = np.zeros((256,3))
 for i in range(3):
  hist, bins = np.histogram(img[...,i].flatten(),256,[0,256], \
            normed=True)
  cdf[...,i] = hist.cumsum()
  cdf_normalized = cdf[...,i] * hist.max() / cdf.max()
  plt.plot(cdf_normalized, color = colors[i], \
        label='cdf ({})'.format(colors[i]))
  binWidth = bins[1] - bins[0]
  plt.bar(bins[:-1], hist*binWidth, binWidth,
        label='hist ({})'.format(colors[i]))
 plt.xlim([0,256])
 plt.legend(loc = 'upper left')
 return cdf
```

2. Implement the histogram equalization by reassigning the pixel values with the corresponding `cdf` value for that pixel using the following code:

```
img = imread('images/train.png')
cdf = plot_hist(img)
img2 = np.copy(img)
for i in range(3):
  cdf_m = np.ma.masked_equal(cdf[...,i],0)
  cdf_m = (cdf_m - cdf_m.min())*255/(cdf_m.max()-cdf_m.min())
          # min-max normalize
  cdf2 = np.ma.filled(cdf_m,0).astype('uint8')
  img2[...,i] = cdf2[img[...,i]]
```

3. Perform histogram equalization with the same input image using `scikit-image` library functions that implement global and adaptive histogram equalization:

```
equ1 = (255*equalize_hist(img)).astype(np.uint8)
equ2 = (255*equalize_adapthist(img)).astype(np.uint8)
```

How it works...

For each image channel, each pixel value needs to be reassigned to the corresponding `cdf` value for the pixel, as shown in the following diagram:

$$s_k = T(r_k) = \sum_{j=0}^{k} P_r(r_j) = \sum_{j=0}^{k} n_j / N$$

$$0 \leq r_k \leq 1, \quad k = 0,1,2,\ldots, 255$$

N: total number of pixels
n_j: frequency of pixel with gray-level j

The `equalize_hist()` and `equalize_adapthist()` functions from the `scikit-image.exposure` module were used to get the globally and locally contrast-enhanced images, respectively.

Image Enhancement

If you run the preceding code and plot the input and output images along with the corresponding histograms and cdfs, you will get the following output (the screenshot is just some part of the output):

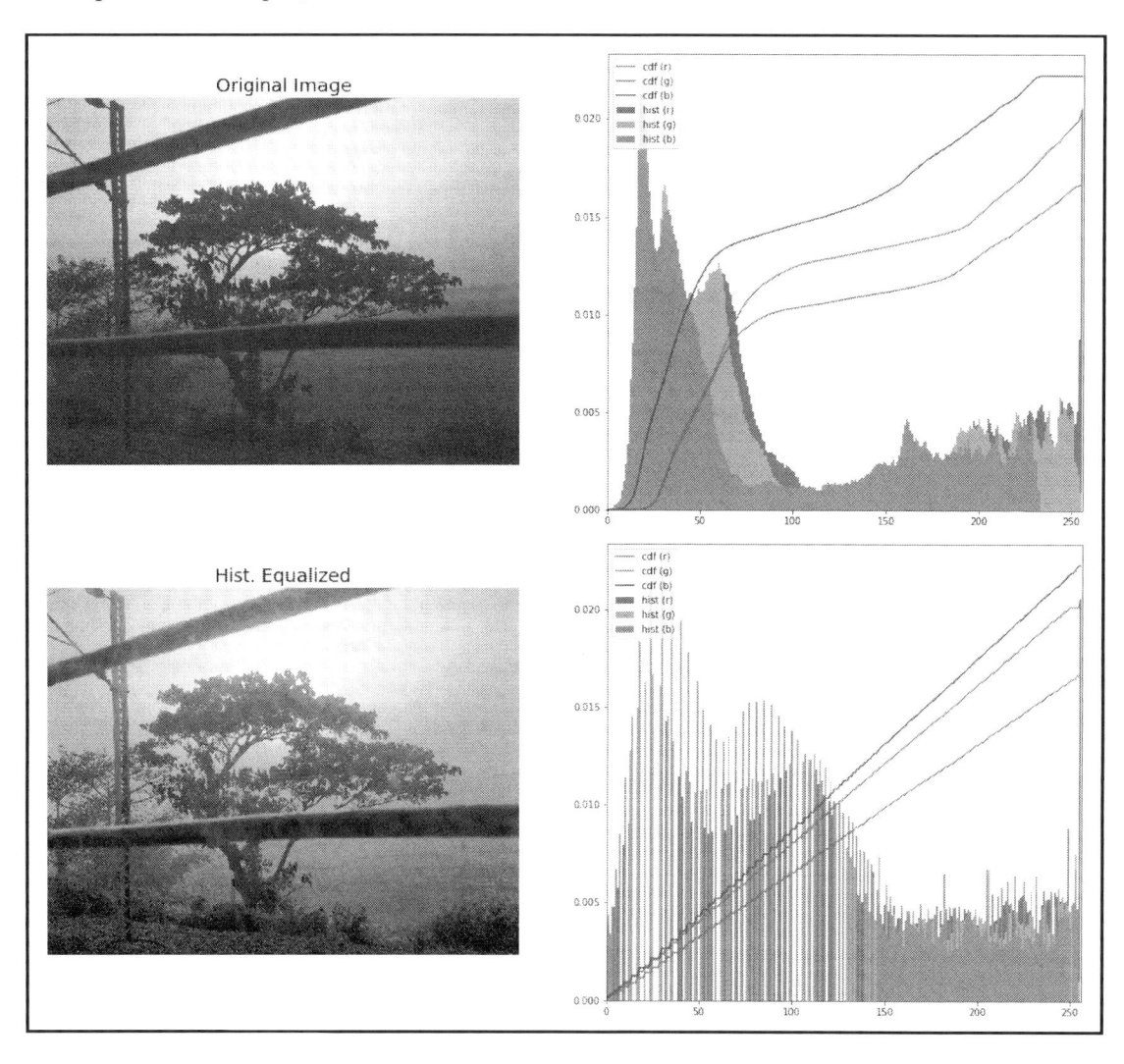

There's more...

Use the `createCLAHE()` function from OpenCV-Python to perform adaptive histogram equalization. Compare the quality of the output results obtained using different implementations. Also, run with a few different low-contrast images.

Implementing histogram matching

Histogram matching is an image processing task where an image is altered in such a way that its histogram matches the histogram of another reference (template) image's histogram. The algorithm is described as follows:

1. Compute the cumulative histogram for each image.
2. For any given pixel value, x_i, in the input image, find the corresponding pixel value, x_j, in the output image by matching the input image's histogram with the template image's histogram ($G(x_i)=H(x_j)$), as shown in the following diagram.
3. Replace pixel x_i in the input with x_j as shown in the following diagram:

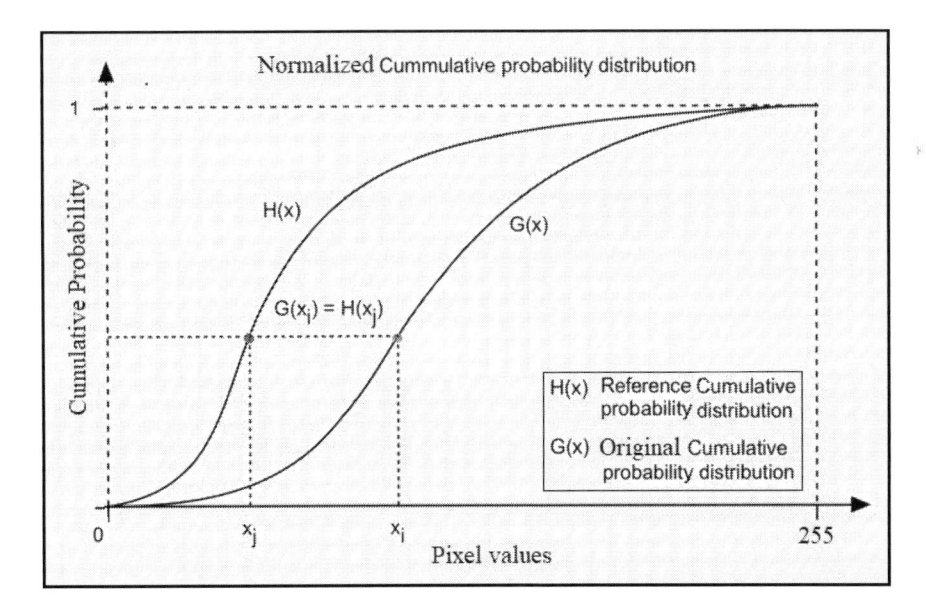

In this recipe, we will implement histogram matching for colored images on our own.

Image Enhancement

Getting ready

As usual, let's start by importing the required libraries:

```
from skimage.exposure import cumulative_distribution
from skimage.color import rgb2gray
import matplotlib.pylab as plt
import numpy as np
```

How to do it...

Perform the following steps to implement histogram matching:

1. Let's implement the histogram-matching algorithm with the `hist_matching()` function, which accepts the original and the template image's `cdf` along with the original image:

```
def hist_matching(c, c_t, im):
  b = np.interp(c, c_t, np.arange(256))
             # find closest matches to b_t
  pix_repl = {i:b[i] for i in range(256)}
             # dictionary to replace the pixels
  mp = np.arange(0,256)
  for (k, v) in pix_repl.items():
   mp[k] = v
  s = im.shape
  im = np.reshape(mp[im.ravel()], im.shape)
  im = np.reshape(im, s)
  return im
```

2. Compute `cdf` of an image with the following function:

```
def cdf(im):
  c, b = cumulative_distribution(im)
  for i in range(b[0]):
   c = np.insert(c, 0, 0)
  for i in range(b[-1]+1, 256):
   c = np.append(c, 1)
  return c
```

3. Finally, read the input and template images, compute their cdfs, and create the output image with the `hist_matching()` function. Plot the input, template, and output images by running the following code:

```
im = imread('images/goddess.png').astype(np.uint8)
im_t = imread('images/leaves.png')

im1 = np.zeros(im.shape).astype(np.uint8)
for i in range(3):
  c = cdf(im[...,i])
  c_t = cdf(im_t[...,i])
  im1[...,i] = hist_matching(c, c_t, im[...,i])

plt.figure(figsize=(20,17))
plt.subplots_adjust(left=0, top=0.95, right=1, bottom=0, \
                    wspace=0.05, hspace=0.05)
plt.subplot(221), plt.imshow(im), plt.axis('off'), \
                  plt.title('Input Image', size=25)
plt.subplot(222), plt.imshow(im_t), plt.axis('off'), \
                  plt.title('Template Image', size=25)
plt.subplot(223), plt.imshow(im1[...,:3]), plt.axis('off'), \
                  plt.title('Output Image', size=25)
plt.show()
```

How it works...

The `cumulative_distribution()` function from the `scikit-image.exposure` module was used to compute the `cdf` of an image.

> Note that the `cumulative_distribution()` function returns the bins in increasing order of consecutive pixel values, starting from the minimum pixel value present in the image up to the maximum pixel value present.

Since we needed all the pixel values starting from 0 to 255, we used `np.insert()` with an appropriate `cdf` value (0 for all the smaller pixel values and 1 for higher pixel values not present).

Image Enhancement

For each of the color channels, `cdf` was computed separately for the input and the template images using the `cdf()` function, and then the `hist_matching()` function was invoked with these values along with the input image to construct the corresponding color channel in the output image.

The following diagram shows the output image generated for these given input and template images:

There's more...

You can use histogram matching to change an image taken in daylight to a night-vision image using an appropriate template image. The next example shows a similar fun application of histogram matching:

See also

For more information, refer to the following links:

- `https://scikit-image.org/docs/dev/api/skimage.exposure.html#skimage.exposure.cumulative_distribution`
- `https://www.youtube.com/watch?v=4VLM1L90tLE`
- The *Histogram matching* section (Chapter 4) from the book *Hands-on Image Processing with Python*

Performing gradient blending

The goal of Poisson image editing is to perform seamless (gradient) blending (cloning) of an object or a texture from a source image (captured by a mask image) with a target image. We want to create a photomontage by pasting an image region onto a new background using Poisson image editing. The idea is from the SIGGRAPH 2003 paper, *Poisson Image Editing*, by *Perez et al.*, which shows that blending using the image gradients produces much more realistic results.

The gradient of the source and output images in the masked region will be the same after seamless cloning is done. Moreover, the intensity of the target image and the output image at the masked region boundary will be the same. The following diagram shows how a source image patch g is integrated seamlessly with a target image f^* (over the region Ω), with a new image patch f (over the region Ω) obtained as a solution with a Poisson solver:

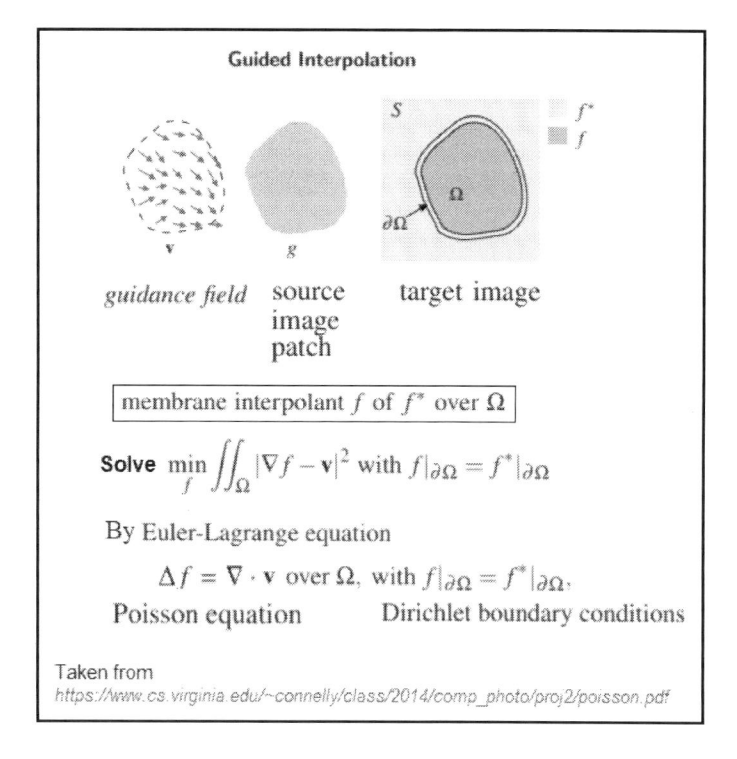

Guided Interpolation

guidance field   *source image patch*   *target image*

membrane interpolant f of f^* over Ω

Solve $\min_{f} \iint_{\Omega} |\nabla f - \mathbf{v}|^2$ with $f|_{\partial\Omega} = f^*|_{\partial\Omega}$

By Euler-Lagrange equation

$\Delta f = \nabla \cdot \mathbf{v}$ over Ω, with $f|_{\partial\Omega} = f^*|_{\partial\Omega}$.

Poisson equation   Dirichlet boundary conditions

Taken from
https://www.cs.virginia.edu/~connelly/class/2014/comp_photo/proj2/poisson.pdf

In this recipe, we will demonstrate seamless cloning with OpenCV-Python.

Getting ready

We will use an image of the Statue of Liberty as a source and an image of the Victoria Memorial Hall as the destination image. Let's start by importing the libraries. Make sure that the major version of OpenCV-Python is at least 3:

```
import cv2
import numpy as np
print(cv2.__version__)
# 3.4.2
```

How to do it...

The steps for this recipe are as follows:

1. Read the source, destination, and mask images:

    ```
    src = cv2.imread("images/liberty.png")
    dst = cv2.imread("images/victoria.png")
    src_mask = cv2.imread("images/cmask.png")
    print(src.shape, dst.shape, src_mask.shape)
    # (480, 698, 3) (576, 768, 3) (480, 698, 3)
    ```

2. Run seamless cloning to blend the masked source around a center in the destination image and save the output image:

    ```
    center = (275,250)
    output = cv2.seamlessClone(src, dst, src_mask, center, \
                               cv2.MIXED_CLONE)
    cv2.imwrite("images/liberty_victoria.png", output)
    ```

How it works...

The following screenshot shows the input and mask images used for gradient blending:

The `cv2.seamlessClone()` function was used with the `flags` parameter value as `cv2.MIXED_CLONE`, which is a `classic` method. This function implements Poisson image editing, using a Poisson solver to solve a system of (Poisson) equations, by keeping the gradients only at the edge locations (as Dirichlet boundary conditions).

You will get an output image along the lines of the following if you run the preceding code snippets:

Edge detection with Canny, LoG/zero-crossing, and wavelets

Edge detection is a preprocessing technique where the input is typically a two-dimensional (grayscale) image and the output is a set of curves (that are called the edges). The pixels that construct the edges in an image are the ones where there are sudden rapid changes (discontinuities) in the image intensity function, and the goal of edge detection is to identify these changes. Edges are typically detected by finding the local extrema of the first derivative (gradient) or by finding the zero-crossings of the second derivative (Laplacian) of the image. In this recipe, we will first implement two very popular edge detection techniques, namely, Canny and Marr-Hildreth (LoG with Zero crossings). Then, we will implement wavelet-based edge detection.

Getting ready

As usual, let's start by importing the required libraries:

```
import numpy as np
from scipy import ndimage, misc
import matplotlib.pyplot as plt
from skimage.color import rgb2gray
from skimage.filters import threshold_otsu
import pywt
import SimpleITK as sitk
```

How to do it...

Let's first start with the most popular edge detector, which is the Canny edge detector. We will use SimpleITK's implementation of the Canny edge detector for images that are scalar-valued (for example, grayscale images). This implementation uses second directional derivatives and zero crossings to find edges.

Image Enhancement

Canny/hysteresis thresholding

Perform the following steps to implement edge detection with Canny using `SimpleItk` library functions:

1. Read the input grayscale image and convert it to the `float64` datatype:

   ```
   image = sitk.ReadImage('images/cameraman.png')
           # 8-bit cameraman grayscale image
   image = sitk.Cast(image, sitk.sitkFloat64)
   ```

2. Compute the Canny filter for two values of σ of the Gaussian blur (1 and 3) with the same hysteresis thresholds:

   ```
   edges1 = sitk.CannyEdgeDetection(image, lowerThreshold=5, \
                   upperThreshold=10, variance=[1, 1])
   edges2 = sitk.CannyEdgeDetection(image, lowerThreshold=5, \
                   upperThreshold=10, variance=[3, 3])
   ```

3. Convert the output to the NumPy array for display:

   ```
   image = sitk.GetArrayFromImage(image)
   edges1 = sitk.GetArrayFromImage(edges1)
   edges2 = sitk.GetArrayFromImage(edges2)
   ```

4. Display the input and edge images:

   ```
   fig = plt.figure(figsize=(20, 6))
   plt.subplot(131), plt.imshow(image, cmap=plt.cm.gray), \
                   plt.axis('off')
   plt.title('Input image', fontsize=20)
   plt.subplot(132), plt.imshow(edges1, cmap=plt.cm.gray), \
                   plt.axis('off')
   plt.title('Canny filter, $\sigma=1$', fontsize=20)
   plt.subplot(133), plt.imshow(edges2, cmap=plt.cm.gray), \
                   plt.axis('off')
   plt.title('Canny filter, $\sigma=3$', fontsize=20)
   fig.tight_layout()
   plt.show()
   ```

If you run the preceding code snippet, you will get an output similar to the following:

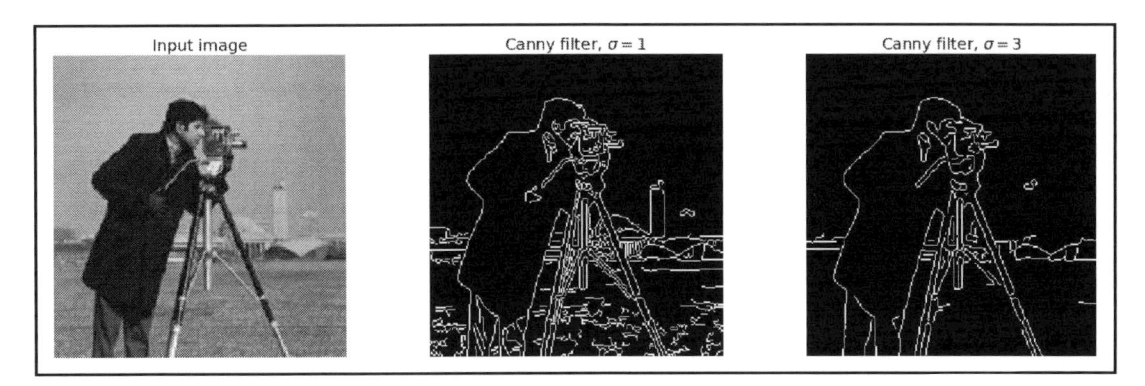

As you can see from the preceding image, a lower value of σ for the Gaussian blur outputs more detailed edges, whereas the higher value generates more prominent edges.

Next, let's implement edge detection with another popular algorithm known as the Marr-Hildret algorithm, for which we need to compute the zero-crossings in the **Laplacian of Gaussian** (**LoG**)-convolved image. The edge pixels can be identified by treating the LoG-smoothed image as a binary image and then determining the sign of the pixels.

LoG/zero-crossing

Perform the following steps to implement edge detection with LoG and zero-crossing:

1. First, let's define the `any_neighbor_zero()` function that takes a pixel in an image as input and returns `True` if any of the pixel's (8-connected) neighbors are zero:

    ```
    def any_neighbor_zero(img, i, j):
      for k in range(-1,2):
        for l in range(-1,2):
          if k == 0 and l == 0: continue # skip the input pixel
          if img[i+k, j+k] == 0:
            return True
      return False
    ```

Image Enhancement

2. Next, let's define the `zero_crossing()` function:

```
def zero_crossing(img):
  img[img > 0] = 1
  img[img < 0] = 0
  out_img = np.zeros(img.shape)
  for i in range(1,img.shape[0]-1):
    for j in range(1,img.shape[1]-1):
      if img[i,j] > 0 and any_neighbor_zero(img, i, j):
        out_img[i,j] = 255
  return out_img
```

3. Finally, invoke the `zero_crossing()` function on the LoG-convolved input image and plot the output:

```
img = rgb2gray(misc.imread('images/tiger.png'))
fig = plt.figure(figsize=(25,15))
plt.gray() # show the filtered result in grayscale
for sigma in range(2,10, 2):
 plt.subplot(2,2,sigma/2)
 result = ndimage.gaussian_laplace(img, sigma=sigma)
 result = zero_crossing(result)
 plt.imshow(result)
 plt.axis('off')
 plt.title('LoG with zero-crossing, sigma=' + str(sigma), size=30)
plt.tight_layout()
plt.show()
```

The following diagram shows the input image used for edge detection:

If you run the preceding code snippet, you will get an output similar to the following (using the preceding input image):

Chapter 2

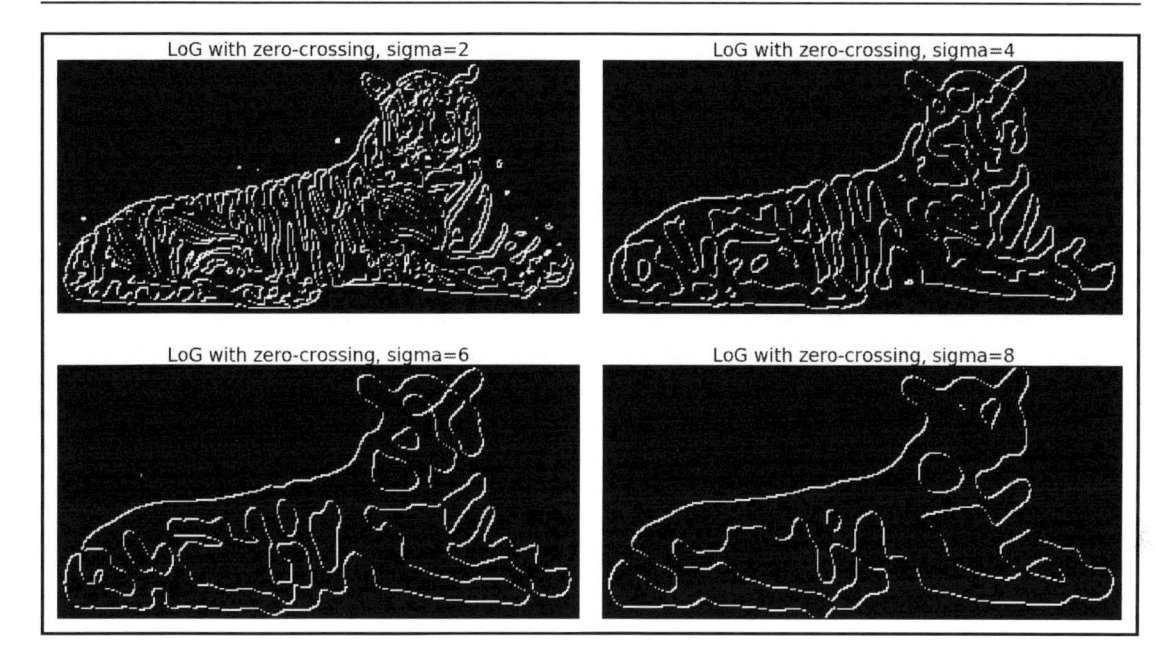

[Figure: LoG with zero-crossing at sigma=2, 4, 6, and 8]

Wavelets

Perform the following steps to implement edge detection with wavelets using `pywt` library functions:

1. Load the input image and convert it to grayscale:

   ```
   original = rgb2gray(imread('images/bird.png'))
   ```

2. Apply 2D-DWT to the image with a `haar` wavelet on the grayscale image. This will return the wavelet coefficients:

   ```
   coeffs2 = pywt.dwt2(original, 'haar')
   ```

3. Extract the approximation image along with the horizontal, vertical, and diagonal details (edges), respectively, using the following code:

   ```
   titles = ['Approximation', ' Horizontal detail', 'Vertical detail', \
             'Diagonal detail']
   LL, (LH, HL, HH) = coeffs2
   ```

[77]

Image Enhancement

4. Plot the approximation image and the horizontal, vertical, and diagonal edges (details) detected:

```
fig = plt.figure(figsize=(15, 20))
for i, a in enumerate([LL, LH, HL, HH]):
    ax = fig.add_subplot(2, 2, i + 1)
    a = abs(a)
    if i > 0:
        th = threshold_otsu(a)
        a[a > th] = 1
        a[a <= th] = 0
    ax.imshow(a, interpolation="nearest", cmap=plt.cm.gray)
    ax.set_title(titles[i], fontsize=20)
    ax.set_xticks([])
    ax.set_yticks([])
fig.tight_layout()
plt.show()
```

The following image shows the original input image:

The following image shows the output you will get if you run the preceding code:

Chapter 2

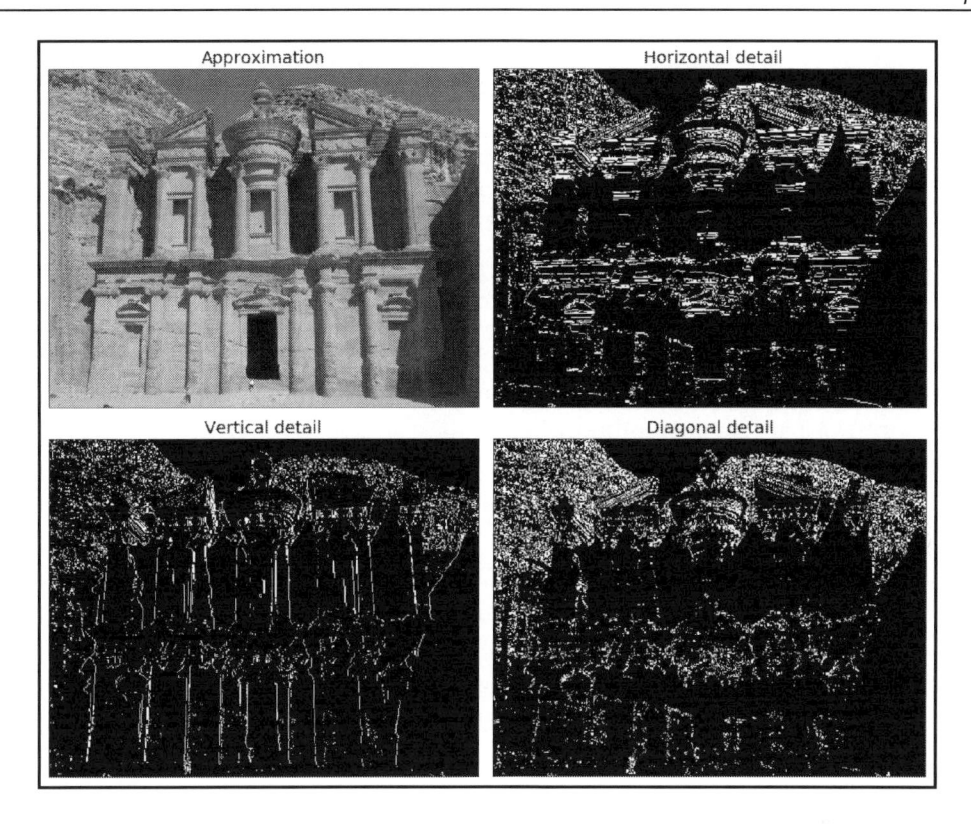

How it works...

The algorithm for edge detection using the `CannyEdgeDetection()` function from SimpleITK is listed as follows:

1. Smooth with a Gaussian filter (that is, remove the noise, since edge detection is sensitive to noise). The variance parameter for this function is used in the Gaussian smoothing.
2. Compute the second (directional) derivative of the image obtained from the preceding step.
3. Apply non-maximum suppression (to thin the edges and remove unwanted pixels), find the zero-crossings of the second derivatives, and find the correct extrema using the sign of the third derivative.

Image Enhancement

4. Apply the hysteresis thresholding to the gradient magnitude (multiplied by zero-crossings) to find and link the edges. The `lowerThreshold` and `upperThreshold` parameters to the function are the hysterisis thresholds. Sure edges are the ones that have an intensity gradient value higher than the `upperThreshold` parameter. Sure non-edges have an intensity gradient value below the `lowerThreshold` parameter. The edges for which the intensity gradient values fall in between the hysteresis thresholds are classified as edges or non-edges, depending on whether or not they are connected to the sure-edge pixels.

The `scipy ndimage` module's `gaussian_laplace()` function (which accepts σ as a parameter for the Gaussian smoothing) was used to apply LoG convolution to the input image.

The algorithm to compute zero-crossing (implemented with the `zero_crossing()` function) is as follows:

1. Create a binary image from the LoG-convolved image: replace the positive and negative pixel values with ones and zeros, respectively.
2. Consider the direct neighbors of the non-zero pixels in the binary image obtained to compute the zero-crossing pixels.
3. Mark the boundaries by finding any non-zero pixel having an immediate zero neighbor.
4. Summarizing, for each non-zero pixel in the binary image, check whether any of its (eight) neighboring pixels is zero and, if so, identify the (center) pixel as an edge pixel—this is implemented using the `any_neighbor_zero()` function.

The `pywt` library's `dwt2()` function was used to implement DWT. The wavelet object passed as a parameter is a HAAR family wavelet.

The `threshold_otsu()` function from the `scikit-image.filters` module was used to binarize the edge (details) images obtained using DWT.

There's more...

Try using different wavelet objects (db, sym, bior, and so on) from different wavelet families to extract edges (you can define your custom wavelets too). Implement a **Difference of Gaussian** (**DoG**) operation to approximate LoG for edge detection and compare the results (in terms of speed and quality). Use anisotropic diffusion to find edges in an image and compare the result with Canny (you will get a diagram along the lines of the following with anisotropic diffusion):

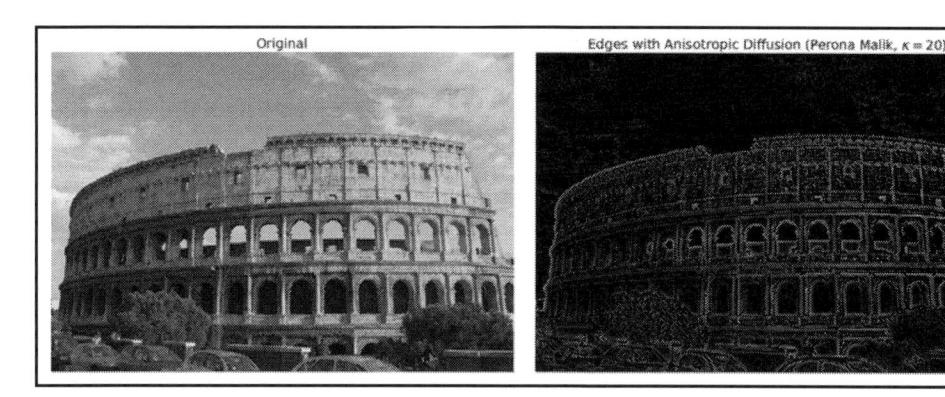

See also

For more information, refer to the following links:

- `http://citeseerx.ist.psu.edu/viewdoc/download?doi=10.1.1.420.3300rep=rep1type=pdf`
- `https://www.cs.virginia.edu/~connelly/class/2014/comp_photo/proj2/poisson.pdf`
- `https://pywavelets.readthedocs.io/en/latest/regression/wavelet.html`
- `http://image.diku.dk/imagecanon/material/PeronaMalik1990.pdf`
- `https://www.youtube.com/watch?v=Wpq0kMCPBU4`

3
Image Restoration

Image restoration is an image-processing technique that tries to recover a corrupted image by modeling the degradation process with prior knowledge (for example, the degradation filter is assumed to be known in most of the cases). Then, it improves the image by applying an inverse process to restore the original image. Unlike image enhancement techniques, in image restoration, the degradation is modeled. This enables the effects of the degradation to be (largely) removed. The challenge is the loss of information and noise. The following diagram shows a basic image degradation model, where the observed (degraded) image is assumed to be a sum of the original (noiseless) image convoluted with a degradation kernel and an additive noise component:

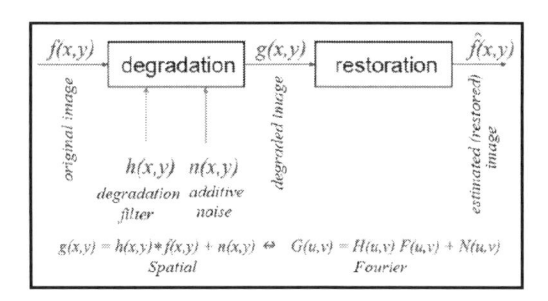

In this chapter, we will cover the following recipes for image restoration:

- Restoring an image with the Wiener filter
- Recovering an image with the CLS filter
- Image restoration with a Markov random field
- Image inpainting
- Image completion with inpainting using deep learning
- Image restoration with dictionary learning
- Image compression with wavelets
- Using steganography and steganalysis

Restoring an image with the Wiener filter

The Wiener filter is **Mean Squared Error** (**MSE**) filtering that incorporates both the degradation function and the statistical characteristics of noise. The underlying assumption is that the noise and image are uncorrelated. It optimizes the filter so that MSE is minimized. In this recipe, you will learn how to implement the Wiener filter using functions from scikit-image restoration module and how to apply the filter to restore a degraded image, both in a supervised and unsupervised manner.

Getting ready

In this recipe, we shall use a cactus image as input and corrupt it with noise/blur. As usual, let's first import all of the required libraries using the following lines of code:

```
from skimage.io import imread
import numpy as np
import matplotlib.pylab as plt
from matplotlib.ticker import LinearLocator, FormatStrFormatter
```

How to do it...

Follow the steps listed to implement the Wiener filter and apply it to restore images corrupted with blur/noise:

1. Read the image and convert it into grayscale:

    ```
    im = color.rgb2gray(imread('images/cactus.png'))
    ```

2. Define `convolve2d()` to implement the convolution in the frequency domain (by the convolution theorem, this implementation works much faster than the one in the spatial domain). Construct the 7x7 average (box-blur) point-spread function and use it as convolution-kernel to blur the image, with the following code:

    ```
    def convolve2d(im, psf, k):
        M, N = im.shape
        freq = fp.fft2(im)
        # assumption: min(M,N) > k > 0, k odd
        psf = np.pad(psf, (((M-k)//2,(M-k)//2+1), \
                          ((N-k)//2,(N-k)//2+1)), mode='constant')
        freq_kernel = fp.fft2(fp.ifftshift(psf))
        return np.abs(fp.ifft2(freq*freq_kernel))
    ```

```
k = 5
psf = np.ones((k, k)) / k**2 # box blur
im1 = convolution2d(im, psf, k)
```

3. Add noise to the blurred image to obtain the degraded image:

   ```
   im1 += 0.2 * im.std() * np.random.standard_normal(im.shape)
   ```

4. Apply the unsupervised Wiener filter on the degraded image along with the kernel as input to restore the image:

   ```
   im2, _ = restoration.unsupervised_wiener(im1, psf)
   ```

5. Apply the Wiener filter (this time with the `balance` parameter) on the degraded image along with the kernel as input to restore the image:

   ```
   im3 = restoration.wiener(im1, psf, balance=0.25)
   ```

If you plot the input and output images, you will get a screenshot like this:

Image Restoration

As you can see from the preceding screenshot, the Wiener restoration with the `balance` parameter performs better than the unsupervised Wiener restoration. We measured the restored image quality using the **Peak Signal-to-Noise Ratio (PSNR)** metric.

6. Plot the frequency spectra of the input/output images and kernel in 3D with the following code:

```
def plot_freq_spec_3d(freq):
    fig = plt.figure(figsize=(10,10))
    ax = fig.gca(projection='3d')
    Y = np.arange(-freq.shape[0]//2,freq.shape[0]-freq.shape[0]//2)
    X = np.arange(-freq.shape[1]//2,freq.shape[1]-freq.shape[1]//2)
    X, Y = np.meshgrid(X, Y)
    Z = (20*np.log10( 0.01 + fp.fftshift(freq))).real
    surf = ax.plot_surface(X, Y, Z, cmap=plt.cm.coolwarm, \
                           linewidth=0, antialiased=True)
    ax.zaxis.set_major_locator(LinearLocator(10))
    ax.zaxis.set_major_formatter(FormatStrFormatter('%.02f'))
    plt.show()

plot_freq_spec_3d(fp.fft2(im))
plot_freq_spec_3d(fp.fft2(im1))
plot_freq_spec_3d(fp.fft2(im2))
plot_freq_spec_3d(fp.fft2(im3))
```

The following screenshot is part of the output that you will get after running the preceding code:

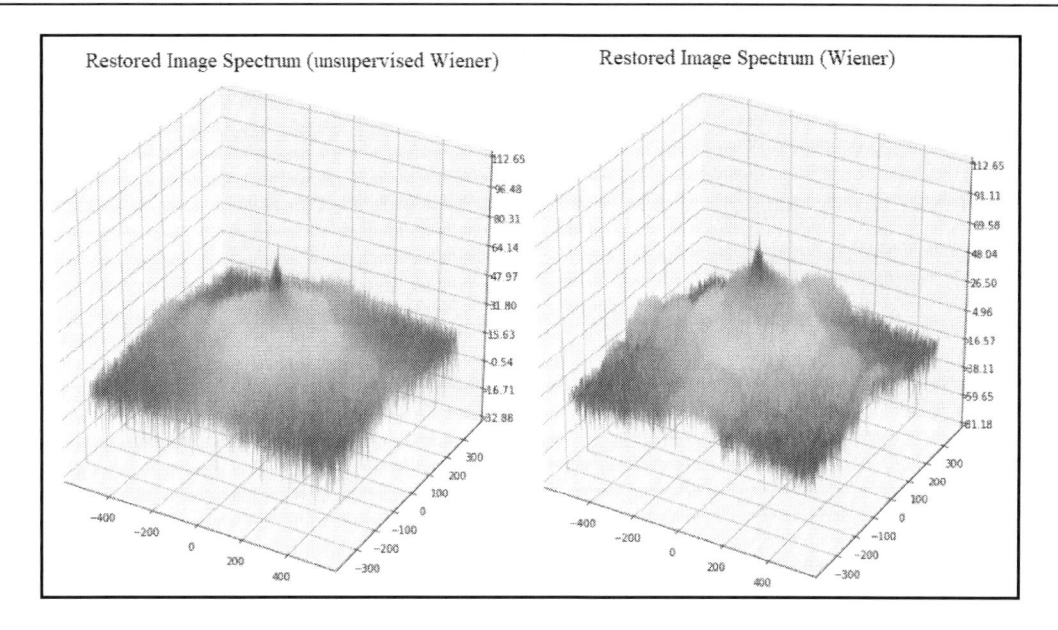

Restored Image Spectrum (unsupervised Wiener)   Restored Image Spectrum (Wiener)

How it works...

The following diagram shows how the Wiener filter can be computed. As can be seen, the Wiener filter is the filter that has the objective function of minimizing the MSE between the restored and the original image:

Wiener Filter

objective $\min_{W} E[(f - \hat{f})^2]$

$\quad\quad\quad = \min_{W} E[|F(u,v) - \hat{F}(u,v)|^2]$ by Parseval's Theorem

s.t. $\hat{F}(u,v) = G(u,v)W(u,v)$

solution:

$$W(u,v) = \frac{H^*(u,v)}{|H(u,v)|^2 + \frac{|N(u,v)|^2}{|F(u,v)|^2}} = \frac{H^*(u,v)}{|H(u,v)|^2 + K}$$

$$= \frac{1}{H(u,v)} \cdot \frac{|H(u,v)|^2}{|H(u,v)|^2 + \frac{|N(u,v)|^2}{|F(u,v)|^2}}$$

inverse filter   1/SNR

$$W(u,v) = \frac{H^*(u,v)}{|H(u,v)|^2 + \lambda|\Lambda_D|^2}$$ scikit-image restoration's wiener()

balance Freq. response of Laplacian

As you can see from the preceding diagram, the Wiener filter reduces to an inverse filter when no noise is added to the input image (N=0). Here, K is a constant (that is, it does not depend on u, v), to be chosen according to prior knowledge about the noise.

The `unsupervised_wiener()` function from the `scikit-image.restoration` module was used to denoise the degraded image using deconvolution with a Wiener-Hunt approach, where the hyperparameters are automatically estimated. For the unsupervised Wiener algorithm, the estimated image is defined as the posterior mean from a Bayesian analysis. The mean is defined as the total number of all possible images weighted according to their probability. The exact sum is not tractable, hence the **Markov Chain Monte Carlo (MCMC)** method (Gibbs sampler) is used to draw the image under the posterior law.

The Gibbs sampler draws highly probable images more (than the less probable images) since they have a higher contribution to the mean. The empirical mean of these samples is used as an estimation of the mean. The Laplacian is used as a regularization operator by default. The `wienner()` function from the `scikit-image.restoration` module was used, this time with an additional balance parameter to denoise the degraded image using the Wiener filter. Again, this filter returns the deconvolution with a Wiener-Hunt approach (that is, with Fourier diagonalization).

The `regularization` parameter (balance or λ) value changes the balance between the data and prior adequacy. The data adequacy helps to improve frequency restoration and prior adequacy helps to reduce frequency restoration to avoid noise artifacts. The Laplacian is used as a default regularization operator.

See also

Refer to the following articles to learn more about this recipe:

- `https://scikit-image.org/docs/dev/api/skimage.restoration.html#skimage.restoration.unsupervised_wiener`
- `http://sce2.umkc.edu/csee/lizhu/teaching/2018.fall.digital-image-processing/notes/lec11.pdf`

Restoring an image with the constrained least squares filter

In this recipe, we shall demonstrate yet another filter named the **Constrained Least Squares** (**CLS**) filter in the frequency-domain. As the name of the filter suggests, it's an inverse (least squares) filter with an additional smoothness constraint that does not allow arbitrary high-frequency fluctuation in the restored image by imposing a smoothness constraint. You shall now learn how to implement a CLS filter and how to restore a degraded image by applying the filter on the image. Also, you shall compare the qualities of the restored images using different frequency-domain filter implementations such as inverse, Wiener, and CLS.

Getting ready

Let's first import all of the libraries required, using the following code:

```
import numpy as np
import scipy.fftpack as fp
from skimage.io import imread
from skimage.color import rgb2gray
from skimage.restoration import wiener, unsupervised_wiener
from skimage.measure import compare_psnr
import matplotlib.pylab as plt
```

How to do it...

Execute the following steps to implement the CLS filter and to compare restored images with different frequency domain filters:

1. First, define the `cls_filter()` function to implement the constrained least squares filter:

   ```
   def cls_filter(y,h,c,lambd):
       Hf = fp.fft2(fp.ifftshift(h))
       Cf = fp.fft2(fp.ifftshift(c))
       Hf = np.conj(Hf) / (Hf*np.conj(Hf) + lambd*Cf*np.conj(Cf))
       Yf = fp.fft2(y)
       I = Yf*Hf
       im = np.abs(fp.ifft2(I))
       return (im, Hf)
   ```

Image Restoration

2. Read the input image and convert it into grayscale. Blur the input grayscale image using box-kernel (done in the frequency domain) and degrade the image using **White Gaussian Noise (WGN)** with a given standard deviation (σ):

    ```
    x = rgb2gray(imread('images/building.png'))
    M, N = x.shape
    h = np.ones((4,4))/16 # blur filter
    h = np.pad(h, [(M//2-2, M//2-2), (N//2-2, N//2-2)], \
                    mode='constant')
    sigma = 0.05
    Xf = fp.fft2(x)
    Hf = fp.fft2(fp.ifftshift(h))
    Y = Hf*Xf
    y = fp.ifft2(Y).real + sigma*np.random.normal(size=(M,N))
    ```

3. Apply the `pseudo_inverse` filter on the degraded image to get back the restored image along with the frequency response of the pseudo-inverse filter kernel:

    ```
    epsilon = 0.25
    pix, F_pseudo = pseudo_inverse_filter(y, h, epsilon)
    ```

4. Apply the `wiener` filter with the `balance` parameter as `0.25` to get back the restored image:

    ```
    wx = wiener(y, h, balance=0.25)
    ```

5. Next, apply the `unsupervised_wiener` filter to get back the restored image:

    ```
    uwx, _ = unsupervised_wiener(y, h)
    ```

6. Construct the high-pass filter (2D Laplacian) and convert it into the frequency domain, to use it as the constraint-kernel. Apply the CLS filter on the degraded image using the constraint kernel created, along with a regularization parameter (λ) value:

    ```
    c = np.array([[0,1/4,0],[1/4,-1,1/4],[0,1/4,0]])
    c = np.pad(c, [(M//2-1, M//2-2), (N//2-2, N//2-1)], \
                    mode='constant')
    Cf = fp.fft2(fp.ifftshift(c))
    lambd = 20
    clx, F_restored = cls_filter(y, h, c, lambd)
    print(r'Restored (CLS, $\lambda=${}) PSNR: {}'.format(lambd, \
                    np.round(compare_psnr(x, clx),3))
    # Restored (CLS, λ=20) PSNR: 28.924
    ```

[90]

Chapter 3

If you run the preceding code snippets and plot all input/output images and frequency response of the filters, you will get an output like the following screenshot (this is just some parts of the actual output):

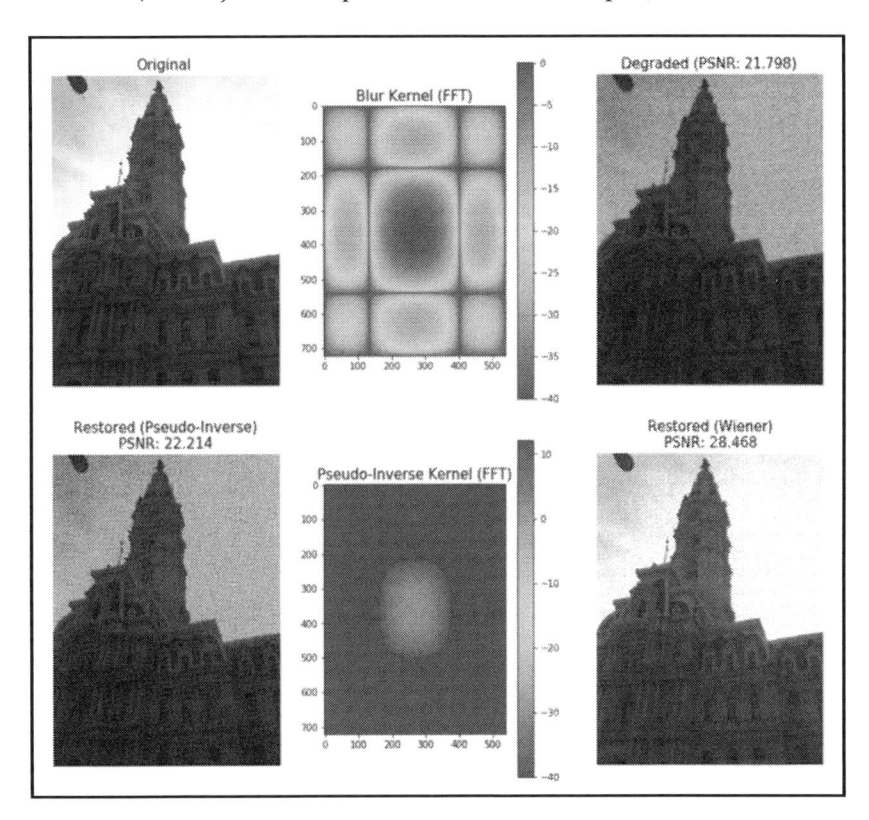

As you can see from the preceding output, the CLS filter (with higher values of λ) and the `wiener` filter perform quite well in terms of the quality of the image restored.

7. Plot the frequency responses of the kernels in 3D using the following code:

```
plot_freq_spec_3d(F_restored) # frequency response of CLS filter \
                                kernel
plot_freq_spec_3d(fp.fft2(x))
plot_freq_spec_3d(fp.fft2(y))
plot_freq_spec_3d(fp.fft2(clx))
plot_freq_spec_3d(fp.fft2(uwx))
```

Image Restoration

You will obtain the following screenshot as part of the output:

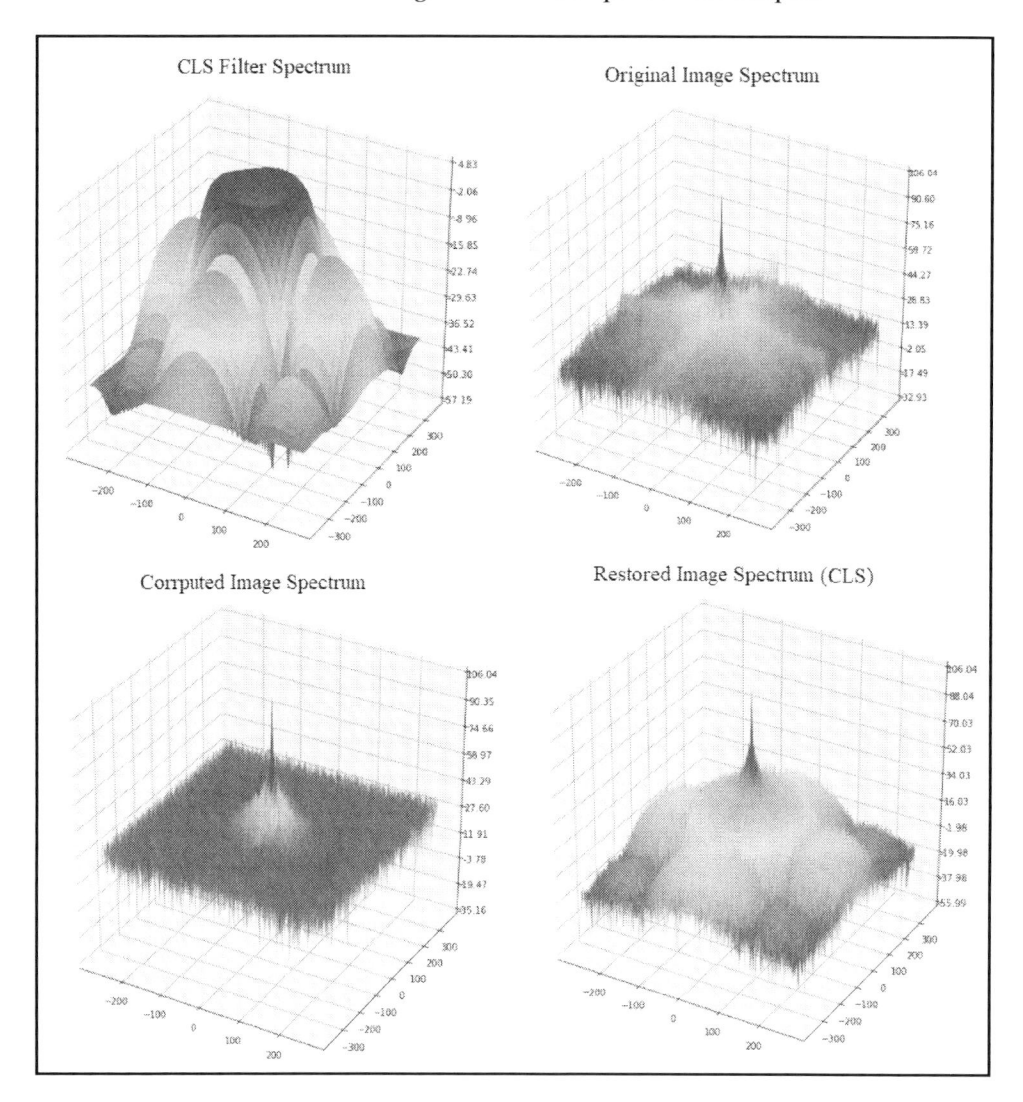

How it works...

The following diagram shows how to compute the CLS filter and restore a degraded image with it in the frequency domain:

Constrained Least-Squares Filter

$g = Hf + n$ (degradation equation)

objective: $\min_{f} \| g - Hf \|_2^2$

s.t. $\| Cf \|_2^2 < \varepsilon$ (smoothness constraint)

objective: $\min_{f} (\| g - Hf \|_2^2 + \lambda \| Cf \|_2^2)$

Data fidelity — Smoothness — Lagrange multiplier

solution: $\hat{f} = (H^T H + \lambda C^T C)^\dagger (H^T g)$
restored — Lagrange multiplier (regularization parameter) — high-pass filter

$$\hat{F}(u, v) = \frac{H^*(u, v) G(u, v)}{\| H(u, v) \|^2 + \lambda \| C(u, v) \|^2}$$

restored (in freq. domain)

As we can see, with λ=0, the CLS filter becomes an inverse filter. Parameter λ (the regularizer) controls the degree of smoothness—the higher the value of λ, the smoother the restored image will be.

The 2D Laplacian kernel `[[0,1/4,0], [1/4,-1,1/4], [0,1/4,0]]` is used as high-pass filter constraint kernel (C) for the CLS filter. The restored image qualities are compared using the `compare_psnr()` function from the `scikit-image.measurement` module, by comparing the restored (estimated) image (obtained using different filters) with the original image.

The `cls_filter()` function was used to actually implement the CLS filter. It accepts the degraded image, the blur kernel, the constraint high-pass filter (the Laplacian kernel), and the regularization parameter λ as input and returns the restored image along with the frequency response of the CLS filter.

Image Restoration

There's more...

Use different values of the regularization parameter (from a low value such as 0 to a high value such as 100) for the CLS filter and observe how the restored image quality changes. Compare the Wiener and CLS filters for restoring a degraded image with motion blur (for example, the following book image). You will get an output like the following screenshot (also use the MSE metric to test image quality):

See also

Refer to the following article to learn more about this recipe:

```
http://www.cs.uoi.gr/~cnikou/Courses/Digital_Image_Processing/Chapter_05b_
Image_Restoration_(Linear_Restoration).pdf
```

Chapter 3

Image restoration with a Markov random field

In this recipe, we shall discuss how a **Markov random field** (**MRF**) can be used to denoise an image. Let's say we have a noisy binary image, X, with pixel values $X_{ij} \in \{-1, +1\}$ and we want to recover the noiseless image, Y. If the amount of noise is assumed to be small, there will be a good correlation between a pixel in X and the corresponding pixel in Y and in a 4-connected neighborhood, pixels of X will be well-correlated. This can be modeled as an MRF as shown in the following diagram, with the total energy function that we shall like to minimize:

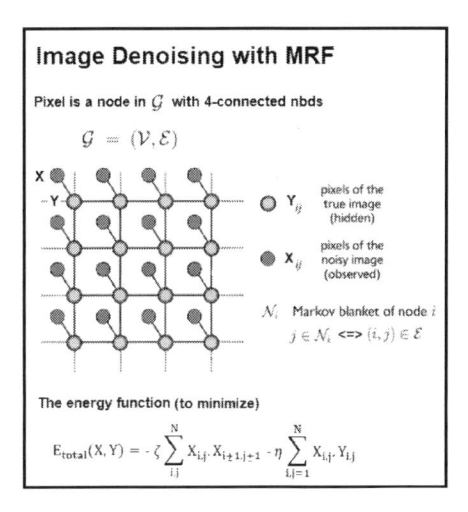

Image Denoising with MRF

Pixel is a node in $\mathcal{G}$ with 4-connected nbds

$$\mathcal{G} = (\mathcal{V}, \mathcal{E})$$

○ Y_{ij} pixels of the true image (hidden)

● X_{ij} pixels of the noisy image (observed)

$\mathcal{N}_i$ Markov blanket of node i
$j \in \mathcal{N}_i \iff (i,j) \in \mathcal{E}$

The energy function (to minimize)

$$E_{total}(X, Y) = -\zeta \sum_{i,j}^{N} X_{i,j} \cdot X_{i\pm 1, j\pm 1} - \eta \sum_{i,j=1}^{N} X_{i,j} \cdot Y_{i,j}$$

Getting ready

In this recipe, we will use the cameraman grayscale image and we will corrupt the image with noise. Next, we will use an MRF to denoise the image by minimizing the energy function. Let's start by importing the required libraries:

```
import numpy as np
from skimage.color import rgb2gray
import matplotlib.pylab as plt
```

Image Restoration

How to do it...

Execute the following steps to denoise image with an MRF:

1. Let's first implement the `read_image_and_binarized()` function to read the image and binarize (as pre-processing step). Note that the output binary image will have pixels with values from {-1, 1}:

   ```
   def read_image_and_binarize(image, threshold=128):
       im = (rgb2gray(plt.imread(image))).astype(int)
       im[im < threshold] = -1
       im[im >= threshold] = 1
       return im
   ```

2. Let's implement the `compute_energy_helper()` functions to compute the energy as a function of the noisy input image, X, and the output denoised image, Y, to be generated:

   ```
   def compute_energy_helper(Y, i, j):
       try:
           return Y[i][j]
       except IndexError:
           return 0

   def compute_energy(X, Y, i, j, zeta, eta, Y_i_j):
       energy = -eta * X[i][j] * Y_i_j
       for (k, l) in [(-1,0),(1,0),(0,-1),(0,1)]: # 4-connected nbd
           energy -= zeta * Y_i_j * compute_energy_helper(Y, i+k, j+l)
       return energy
   ```

3. Let's now implement a function to add noise to the image. The following function typically adds 10% noise to the image:

   ```
   def add_noise(im):
       im_noisy = im.copy()
       for i in range(im_noisy.shape[0]):
           for j in range(im_noisy.shape[1]):
               r = np.random.rand()
               if r < 0.1:
                   im_noisy[i][j] = -im_noisy[i][j]
       return im_noisy
   ```

Chapter 3

4. Next, let's implement the `denoise_image()` function, which actually denoises the image iteratively (typically, it runs for several iterations equal to 10 times the image size):

```
def denoise_image(O, X, zeta, eta):
    m, n = np.shape(X)
    Y = np.copy(X)
    max_iter = 10*m*n
    iters = []
    errors = []
    for iter in range(max_iter):
        # randomly pick a location
        i, j = np.random.randint(m), np.random.randint(n)
```

5. Compute energies for Y_{ij} = +1 and -1:

```
energy_neg = compute_energy(X, Y, i, j, zeta, eta, -1)
energy_pos = compute_energy(X, Y, i, j, zeta, eta, 1)
```

6. Assign Y_{ij} to the value with minimum energy:

```
if energy_neg < energy_pos:
    Y[i][j] = -1
else:
    Y[i][j] = 1
```

7. If the iteration is a multiple of 100,000, print the error in the reconstructed image. Plot how the error changes with iterations and return the output image recovered:

```
        if iter % 100000 == 0:
            print ('Completed', iter, 'iterations out of', max_iter)
            error = get_mismatched_percentage(O, Y)
            iters.append(iter)
            errors.append(error)
    plot_error(iters, errors)
    return Y
```

8. Finally, invoke the functions to read and binarize the input image, add 10% noise to it, and denoise using an MRF with energy minimization using the functions defined earlier, after initializing the parameters ς and η:

```
orig_image = read_image_and_binarize('images/cameraman.png')
zeta = 1.5
eta = 2

noisy_image = add_noise(orig_image)
```

[97]

```
            denoised_image = denoise_image(orig_image, noisy_image, w_e, w_s)

            print ('Percentage of mismatched pixels: ', \
                    get_mismatched_percentage(orig_image, denoised_image))
            plot_images(orig_image, noisy_image, denoised_image)
```

How it works...

The `compute_energy()` function takes the location of a particular pixel as input and computes the energy for different values of the output pixel. There are two types of energies typically:

- The first one remains low (negative) when the input and output pixel values match for that particular location, otherwise, it goes high. The η parameter is used to amplify this energy.
- The second one remains low (negative) if the pixel value in the noisy input image matches with those of its neighborhood values, otherwise, it goes high. The ς parameter is used to amplify this energy.

At every iteration of denoising, you choose a pixel location randomly and at that location in the output image, choose the pixel value that minimizes the energy of the pair of images. The following screenshot shows how the energy decreases through the iterations while denoising:

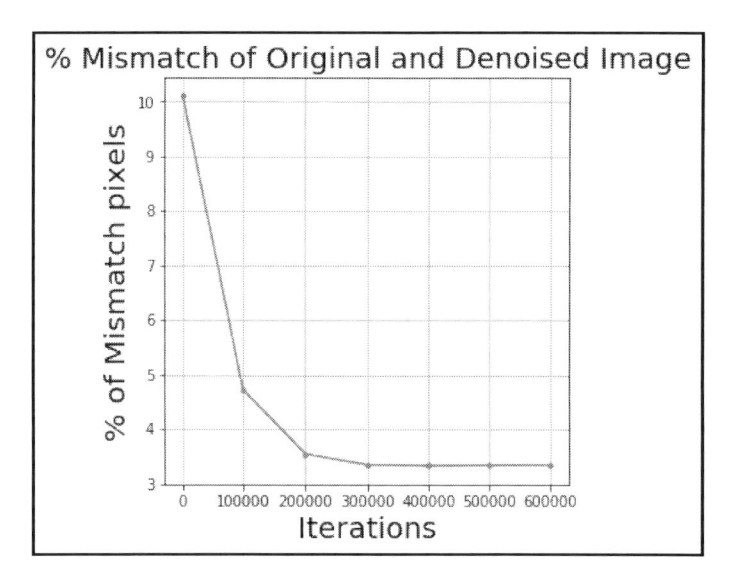

Finally, if you plot the original, noisy input and the denoised output images, you will get the following output:

See also

Refer to the following articles to learn more about this recipe:

- http://homepages.ecs.vuw.ac.nz/~marslast/MLbook.html
- https://www.youtube.com/watch?v=YAc0i36drEs

Image inpainting

Inpainting is the process of restoring the damaged or missing parts of an image. Suppose we have a binary input image, *D*, that specifies the location of the damaged pixels in the input image, *f*, as shown in the following equation:

$$D(x,y) = \begin{cases} 0 \text{ if pixel } (x,y) \text{ is damaged in image } f \\ 1 \text{ if pixel } (x,y) \text{ is not damaged in image } f \end{cases}$$

Once the damaged regions in the image are located with the mask, the lost/damaged pixels have to be reconstructed with some algorithm (for example, total variation inpainting). The reconstruction is supposed to be performed fully automatically by exploiting the information presented in non-damaged regions. In this recipe, you will learn how to use OpenCV-Python library functions to implement image inpainting, using two different algorithms.

Image Restoration

Getting ready

Import the following libraries before you start:

```
import cv2
import numpy as np
import matplotlib.pylab as plt
```

How to do it...

Follow the given steps to implement image-inpainting using two different algorithms from the OpenCV-Python library:

1. Read the RGB image and the grayscale mask image:

   ```
   im = cv2.imread('images/cat.png')
   mask = cv2.imread('images/cat_mask.png',0)
   ```

2. Binarize the mask image using `threshold`:

   ```
   _, mask = cv2.threshold(mask, 100, 255, cv2.THRESH_BINARY)
   ```

3. Remove the masked-out pixels from the input image using `bitwise_and` with the binary mask image:

   ```
   src = cv2.bitwise_and(im, im, mask=mask)
   mask = cv2.bitwise_not(mask)
   ```

4. Obtain the inpainted destination image returned by the `cv2.inpaint()` method using the `cv2.INPAINT_NS` algorithm:

   ```
   dst1 = cv2.inpaint(src, mask, 5, cv2.INPAINT_NS)
   ```

5. Obtain the inpainted destination image returned by the `cv2.inpaint()` method using the `cv2.INPAINT_TELEA` algorithm:

   ```
   dst2 = cv2.inpaint(src, mask, 5, cv2.INPAINT_TELEA)
   ```

   If you run the preceding code, you will get a figure like the following screenshot as the output image:

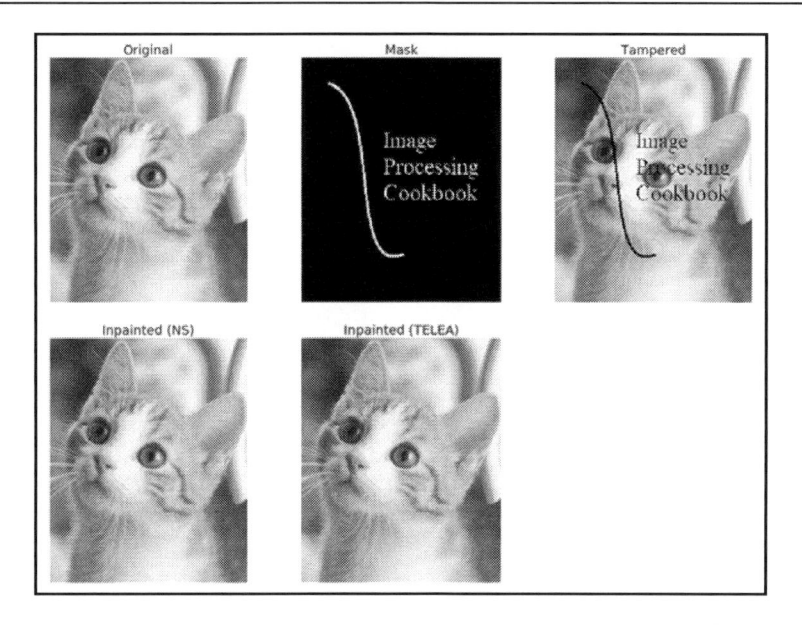

How it works...

The `cv2.inpaint()` function is used for inpainting the missing parts of the cat's image. The parameters this function accepts are the following:

- The source image
- The binary inpaint mask indicating pixels to be inpainted
- The neighborhood radius around a pixel to be inpainted (for thin inpainted regions, a smaller radius leads to less blurry results)
- The inpainting algorithm as flags—`cv2.INPAINT_NS` (a Navier-Stokes-based method) or `cv2.INPAINT_TELEA` (a method based on the fast marching algorithm)

`cv2.INPAINT_NS` uses a Navier-Stokes-based inpainting algorithm that imposes the following two constraints:

- Preserving gradients (that is, features such as edges)
- Propagating color to smooth regions

Image Restoration

The pixel intensities inside the target region (to be inpainted) with the aforementioned constraints are updated using a **Partial Differential Equation** (PDE). The Laplacian is used to estimate smoothness and the color is propagated along the contours of equal intensities (isophotes).

`cv2.INPAINT_TELEA` uses a fast marching method-based inpainting algorithm, which uses a weighted average over a known neighborhood's pixels and gradients to estimate the color of the pixel, for each pixel to be inpainted. The missing region of the image is treated as level sets and the fast marching method to update the boundary of pixel inpainted.

There's more...

Compare the speed (run time) and quality of the outputs produced by the two algorithms. You can do image inpainting with convex optimization too (for example, the image reconstruction problem solved by the forward-backward splitting algorithm). The convex optimization problem is the sum of a data fidelity term and a regularization term, which expresses a prior on the smoothness of the solution, given by the following:

Forward-Backward Splitting with Total Variation

$$\min_x \underbrace{\tau \underbrace{\|g(x) - y\|_2^2}_{\text{fidelity} \atop \text{L2-norm}}}_{\text{regularization}} + \underbrace{\|x\|_{\text{TV}}}_{\text{prior}}$$

where $f_2(x) = \tau\|g(x)-y\|_2^2$ and $f_1(x) = \|x\|_{\text{TV}}$.

Here, $\|\cdot\|_{\text{TV}}$ denotes the total variation, y are the measurements, g is a masking operator, and τ expresses the trade-off between the two terms (a regularization parameter).

Image inpainting with convex optimization

Follow these steps to pose the inpainting problem as a convex optimization problem and solve it using `pyunlocbox` library's `solvers`:

1. Import the required library functions, load the input cat image, and convert it into grayscale:

    ```
    #!pip install pyunlocbox
    from pyunlocbox import functions, solvers
    im_original = rgb2gray(imread('images/cat.png'))
    ```

2. Generate a random masking matrix that masks 80% of the pixels, apply it to the image, and obtain the corrupted image:

    ```
    np.random.seed(1) # Reproducible results.
    mask = np.random.uniform(size=im_original.shape)
    mask = mask > 0.8
    g = lambda x: mask * x
    im_corrupted = g(im_original)
    ```

3. The prior objective to minimize is defined by $f_1(x)=\|x\|_{TV}$. Express it using the toolbox `functions.norm_tv` object:

    ```
    f1 = functions.norm_tv(maxit=50, dim=2)
    ```

4. The fidelity objective to minimize is defined by $f_2(x)=\tau\|g(x)-y\|^2$. Express it using the toolbox `functions.norm_l2` object:

    ```
    f2 = functions.norm_l2(y=im_corrupted, A=g, lambda_=tau) #tau = 100
    ```

5. Set the τ parameter to a large value as we trust our measurements and want the solution to be close to them. For noisy measurements, a lower value should be considered:

    ```
    tau = 100
    ```

6. Finally, instantiate the forward-backward splitting algorithm and solve the optimization problem with the `solvers.solve()` method:

    ```
    solver = solvers.forward_backward(step=0.5/tau)
    x0 = np.array(im_corrupted) # Make a copy to preserve im_corrupted.
    ret = solvers.solve([f1, f2], x0, solver, maxit=100)
    im_restored = ret['sol']
    ```

Image Restoration

If you run the preceding code block and plot the original, noisy and inpainted images obtained using `solver`, you will get a screenshot as follows:

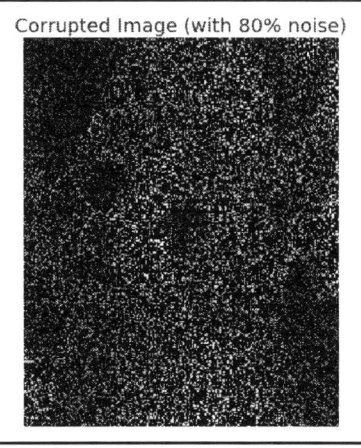

You could use the `cvxpy` library too for TV optimization-based inpainting; try it on your own (refer to the fifth link in the following *See also* section).
You can also use the scikit-image restoration module's `inpaint_biharmonic()` function to inpaint an image with yet another algorithm (refer to the sixth link in the following *See also* section).

See also

Refer to the following links to expand your skills more on this recipe:

- https://www.math.ucla.edu/~bertozzi/papers/cvpr01.pdf
- https://pdfs.semanticscholar.org/622d/5f432e515da69f8f220fb92b17c8426d0427.pdf
- https://www.learnopencv.com/image-inpainting-with-opencv-c-python/
- *https://pyunlocbox.readthedocs.io/en/stable/tutorials/reconstruction.html*
- https://web.stanford.edu/~boyd/papers/pdf/cvx_opt_intro.pdf
- Chapter 12, *Additional Problems in Image Processing*, in *Hands-on Image Processing in Python* by Sandipan Dey, Packt Publishing

Image completion with inpainting using deep learning

In this recipe, you will learn how a **Fully-Convolutional deep learning Network** (**FCN**, called a Completion Network model, from a recent paper, *Globally and Locally Consistent Image Completion* from *SIGGRAPH 2017*) can be used to complete the missing parts of a (previously unseen) image. We shall specifically use a *pre-trained* version of the neural network model to predict the missing parts in an image. The model will accept an input image and a mask (corresponding to the missing parts in the image) and try to predict the missing parts from the information provided by the remaining (incomplete) image.

Getting ready

Download the *pre-trained torch model* for *Globally and Locally Consistent Image Completion* from http://hi.cs.waseda.ac.jp/~iizuka/data/completionnet_places2.t7.

Then, import the required libraries:

```
import os
import torch
from torch import nn
from torch.nn.Sequential import Sequential
import cv2
import numpy as np
from torch.utils.serialization import load_lua
import torchvision.utils as vutils
```

How to do it...

Execute the following steps to complete the missing parts of an image:

1. Define the `tensor2image()` and `image2tensor()` functions to convert from a PyTorch tensor into an OpenCV-Python image and back, using the following code snippet:

    ```
    def tensor2image(src):
      out = src.copy() * 255
      out = out.transpose((1, 2, 0)).astype(np.uint8)
      out = cv2.cvtColor(out, cv2.COLOR_RGB2BGR)
      return out
    ```

Image Restoration

```
def image2tensor(src):
  out = src.copy()
  out = cv2.cvtColor(out, cv2.COLOR_BGR2RGB)
  out = out.transpose((2,0,1)).astype(np.float64) / 255
  return out
```

2. Define the input and mask image paths and the model path. Check whether the GPU is available:

```
image_path = 'images/zebra.png'
mask_path = 'images/inpaint_mask.png'
model_path = 'models/completionnet_places2.t7'
gpu = torch.cuda.is_available()
```

3. Load the pre-trained completion net model (in the evaluation mode):

```
data = load_lua(model_path, long_size=8)
model = data.model
model.evaluate()
```

4. Read the input and the mask images for inpainting. Create a binary mask image from the `mask` image by thresholding:

```
image = cv2.imread(image_path)
mask = cv2.imread(mask_path)
mask = cv2.cvtColor(mask, cv2.COLOR_BGR2GRAY) / 255
mask[mask <= 0.5] = 0.0
mask[mask > 0.5] = 1.0
```

5. Convert the input image and the binary `mask` image into a PyTorch tensor:

```
I = torch.from_numpy(image2tensor(image)).float()
M = torch.from_numpy(mask).float()
M = M.view(1, M.size(0), M.size(1))
assert I.size(1) == M.size(1) and I.size(2) == M.size(2)
```

6. Center the image by subtracting the mean from it:

```
for i in range(3):
  I[i, :, :] = I[i, :, :] - data.mean[i]
```

7. Set up the input tensors the way the model expects (for example, create a 3-channel input tensor). Then, run a forward pass on the pre-trained model to get the output result (as prediction). Use the GPU, if available, to predict faster:

    ```
    M3 = torch.cat((M, M, M), 0)
    im = I * (M3*(-1)+1)
    input = torch.cat((im, M), 0)
    input = input.view(1, input.size(0), input.size(1), \
                      input.size(2)).float()
    if gpu:
     model.cuda()
     input = input.cuda()
    res = model.forward(input)[0].cpu() # predict
    ```

8. Extract the output image from the result:

    ```
    for i in range(3):
      I[i, :, :] = I[i, :, :] + data.mean[i]
    out = res.float()*M3.float() + I.float()*(M3*(-1)+1).float()
    ```

9. Get the masked input image to plot:

    ```
    image[mask == 1] = 255
    ```

10. Finally, plot the input incomplete image with `mask` and the completed output image with inpainting using `CompletionNet`:

    ```
    plt.figure(figsize=(20,30))
    plt.subplot(211), plt.imshow(cv2.cvtColor(image, \
                cv2.COLOR_BGR2RGB)), plt.axis('off'), \
                plt.title('Incomplete Image', size=20)
    plt.subplot(212), plt.imshow(cv2.cvtColor \
                (tensor2cvimg(out.numpy()), cv2.COLOR_BGR2RGB)), \
                plt.axis('off'), plt.title('Completed Image \
                (with CompletionNet)', size=20)
    plt.show()
    ```

Image Restoration

If you run the preceding code and plot the input incomplete image and the output completed image, you will get the output shown in the following screenshot:

There's more...

Train a completion net using your own images (refer to the GitHub repository provided in the *See also* section for the code to train; you will need lots of images, a long time, and a GPU). Also, you can use the pre-trained Completion Network to complete (inpaint) faces too. Try it on your own—you should get an output as shown in the following screenshot:

Chapter 3

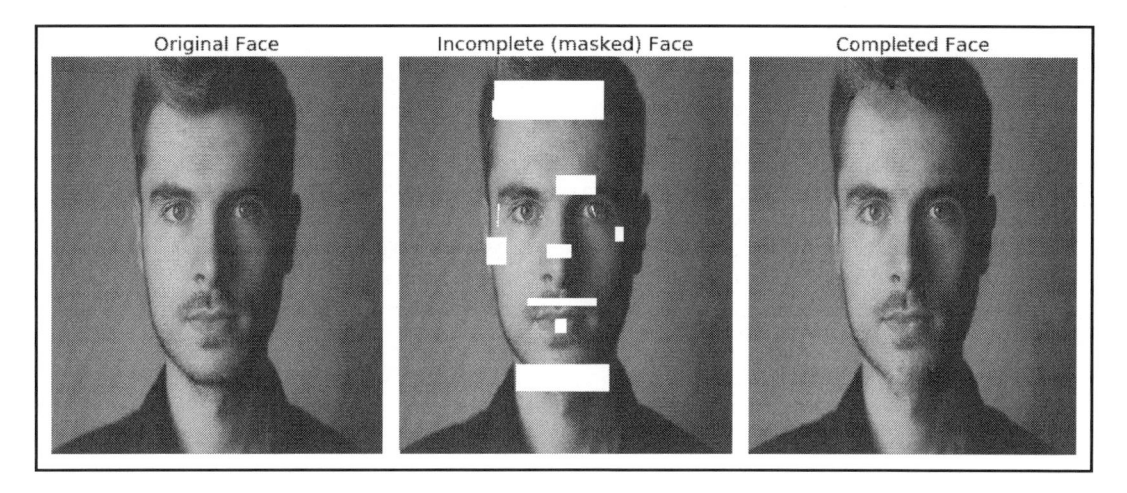

| Original Face | Incomplete (masked) Face | Completed Face |

See also

Refer to the following works to learn more about this recipe:

- http://iizuka.cs.tsukuba.ac.jp/projects/completion/data/completion_sig2017.pdf
- https://github.com/akmtn/pytorch-siggraph2017-inpainting
- http://iizuka.cs.tsukuba.ac.jp/projects/completion/en/
- https://www.youtube.com/watch?v=musgEEVatXs

Image restoration with dictionary learning

Dictionary learning (also known as **sparse coding**) is a representation learning technique that tries to find a sparse representation of the input data as a (sparse) linear combination of basis elements (known as **atoms**) that construct an over-complete spanning set (known as a **dictionary**). The mammalian primary visual cortex also works in the same way by exploiting the redundancy and flexibility of this type of representation. In image processing, dictionary learning has been applied on the image patches and it has shown promising results in different image processing problems such as image inpainting, image completion, and denoising. In this recipe, you will learn how to use dictionary learning for image denoising.

Image Restoration

Getting ready

In this recipe, we shall use the Lena grayscale image for reconstruction with dictionary learning. Let's start by importing the required libraries and the relevant modules:

```
from skimage.io import imread
from skimage.color import rgb2gray
from sklearn.decomposition import MiniBatchDictionaryLearning
from sklearn.feature_extraction.image import extract_patches_2d
from sklearn.feature_extraction.image import reconstruct_from_patches_2d
import numpy as np
import matplotlib.pylab as plt
from time import time
```

How to do it ...

You need to perform the following steps to implement image restoration with dictionary learning using the scikit-learn library functions:

1. Read the Lena image and degrade the lower half of the image with random Gaussian noise while keeping the upper half as it is:

   ```
   lena = rgb2gray(imread('images/lena.png'))
   height, width = lena.shape
   print('Distorting the lower half of the image...')
   distorted = lena.copy()
   distorted[height // 2:, :] += 0.085 * \
             np.random.randn(height // 2, width)
   ```

2. Extract all *7x7* reference patches from the upper half of the image. Compute the mean and standard deviation of the extracted patches and normalize the extracted patches:

   ```
   print('Extracting reference patches...')
   patch_size = (7, 7)
   data = extract_patches_2d(distorted[height // 2:, :], patch_size)
   data = data.reshape(data.shape[0], -1)
   data -= np.mean(data, axis=0)
   data /= np.std(data, axis=0)
   ```

3. Learn the dictionary (with 256 components) from the reference patches extracted:

   ```
   print('Learning the dictionary...')
   dico = MiniBatchDictionaryLearning(n_components=256, alpha=1, \
                                     n_iter=600)
   V = dico.fit(data).components_
   ```

Plot the components of the dictionary learned from the patches. You will obtain a figure like the following screenshot:

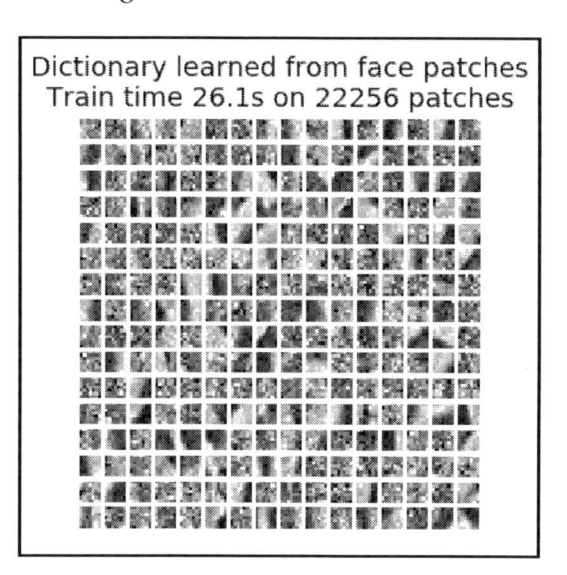

![Dictionary learned from face patches Train time 26.1s on 22256 patches]

4. Define the `show_with_diff()` function and invoke it to show the distorted image:

```
def show_with_diff(image, reference, title):
 plt.figure(figsize=(10, 5))
 plt.subplot(121), plt.title('Image')
 plt.imshow(image, vmin=0, vmax=1, cmap=plt.cm.gray, \
            interpolation='nearest'), plt.axis('off')
 plt.subplot(122)
 difference = image - reference
 plt.title('Difference (norm: %.2f)' % \
            np.sqrt(np.sum(difference ** 2)))
 plt.imshow(difference, vmin=-0.5, vmax=0.5, cmap=plt.cm.gray_r, \
            interpolation='nearest')
 plt.axis('off'), plt.suptitle(title, size=20)
 plt.subplots_adjust(0.02, 0.02, 0.98, 0.79, 0.02, 0.2)
 plt.show()

show_with_diff(distorted, lena, 'Distorted image')
```

Image Restoration

If you run the preceding code snippet, you will get an output as shown in the following screenshot:

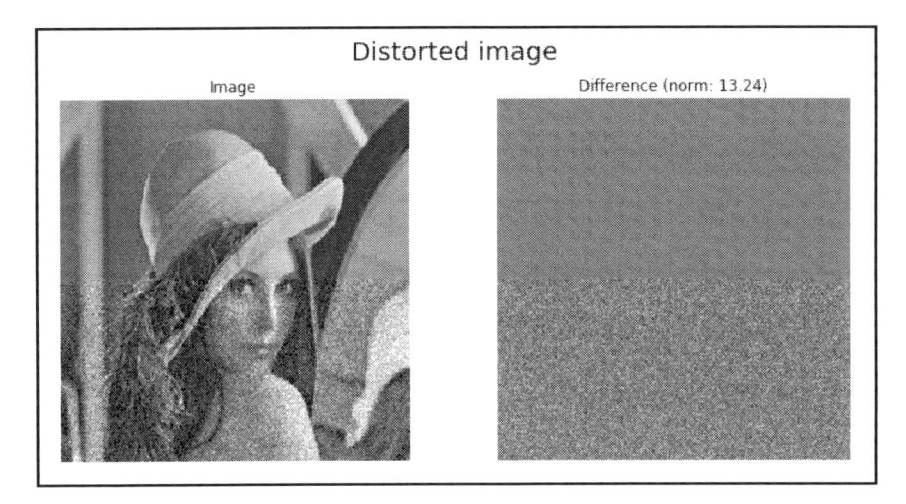

5. Extract patches from the noisy bottom half of the image and normalize the extracted noisy patches:

```
print('Extracting noisy patches... ')
data = extract_patches_2d(distorted[height // 2:, :], patch_size)
data = data.reshape(data.shape[0], -1)
intercept = np.mean(data, axis=0)
data -= intercept
```

6. Reconstruct the (noisy) bottom half of the image using the dictionary components (atoms):

```
print('Orthogonal Matching Pursuit\n2 atoms' + '...')
kwargs = {'transform_n_nonzero_coefs': 2}
reconstruction = lena.copy()
dico.set_params(transform_algorithm='omp', **kwargs)
code = dico.transform(data)
patches = np.dot(code, V)
patches += intercept
patches = patches.reshape(len(data), *patch_size)
reconstruction[height // 2:, :] = \
    reconstruct_from_patches_2d(patches, (height // 2, width))
show_with_diff(reconstruction, lena, 'Orthogonal Matching \
             Pursuit 2 atoms')
```

If you run the preceding code snippet, you will get the following output, which shows the reconstructed image:

[112]

Chapter 3

Orthogonal Matching Pursuit
2 atoms (time: 5.3s)

Image   Difference (norm: 6.97)

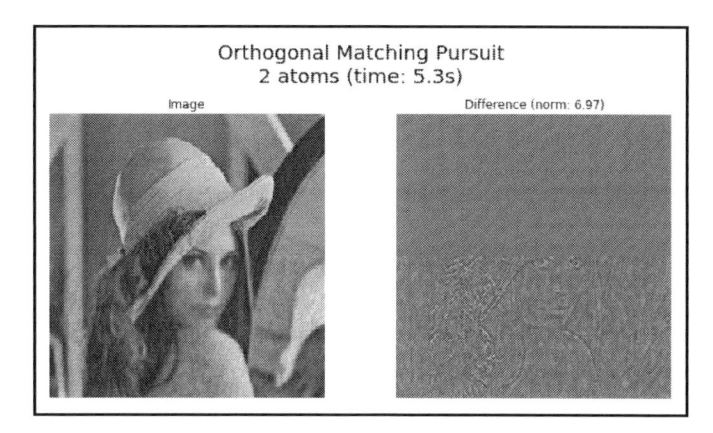

As you can see from the preceding screenshot, the difference norm has decreased a lot, which indicates that the reconstructed image is a much better approximation of the original image.

There's more...

You can learn the dictionary from the image patches in an online manner too; instead of providing all 22,256 image patches (from the upper half) at once to the `MiniBatchDictionaryLearning` object, for example, you can provide 128 patches at a time (as a batch) and learn the dictionary and reconstruct the noisy lower half of the image online, as demonstrated in the following section.

Online dictionary learning

Here are a few steps for online learning and reconstruction:

1. Define the constants:

```
batch_size = 128
n_epochs = 2
n_batches = len(data) // batch_size
```

2. Instantiate the `MiniBatchDictionaryLearning` object, this time with an additional argument, `batch_size`, to the constructor:

```
dico = MiniBatchDictionaryLearning(n_components=256, alpha=1, \
             n_iter=1, batch_size=batch_size)
# Now extract noisy patches as before
```

Image Restoration

3. Iteratively extract the current batch of patches and use `partial_fit()` to fit/update the dictionary from the current batch:

   ```
   for epoch in range(n_epochs):
    for i in range(n_batches):
    batch = data[i * batch_size: (i + 1) * batch_size]
    dico.partial_fit(batch)
    V = dico.components_
    n_updates += 1
    # Now reconstruct lower noisy half of the image using the current
   dictionary
   ```

4. If you run a few batches and plot the dictionary atoms, the reconstructed image, and the error in reconstruction, you will get the output shown in the following screenshot:

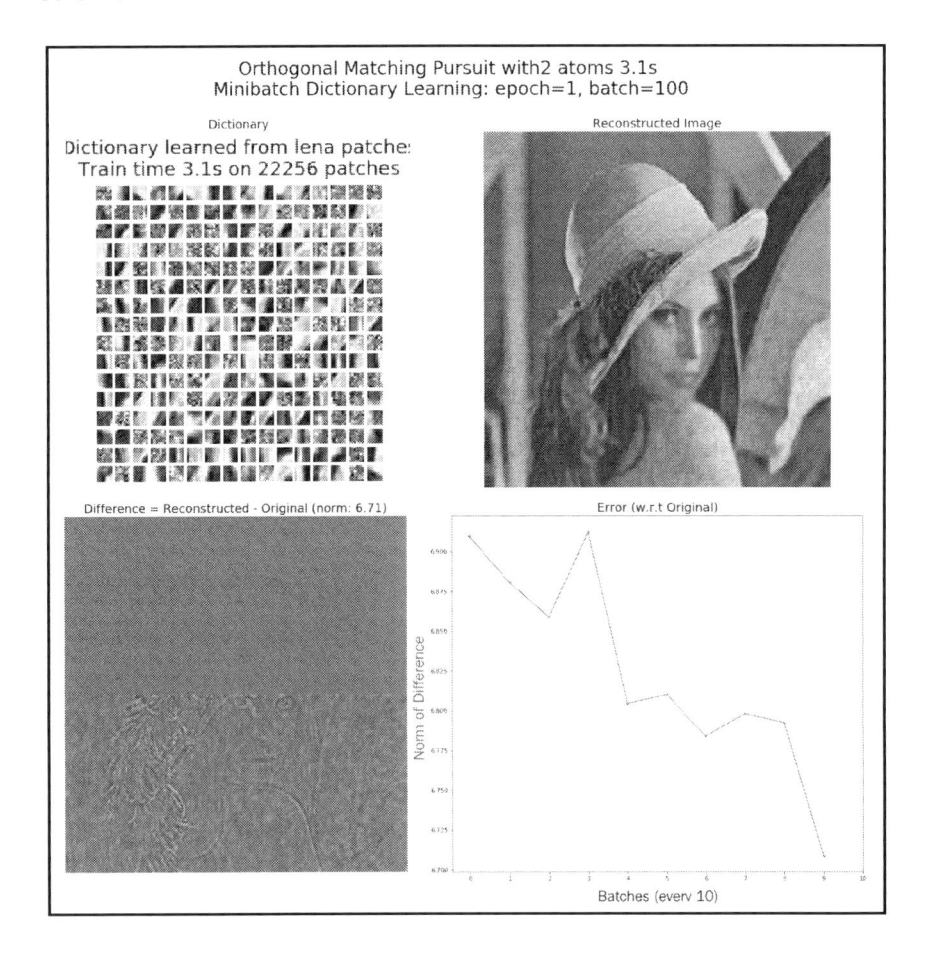

[114]

See also

Refer to the following links to learn more about this recipe:

- https://www.cs.technion.ac.il/~ronrubin/Publications/KSVD-OMP-v2.pdf
- https://github.com/scikit-learn/scikit-learn/blob/7813f7efb/sklearn/decomposition/dict_learning.py
- https://scikit-learn.org/stable/modules/linear_model.html#omp
- https://www.youtube.com/watch?v=Efbr3YP9wGw

Compressing an image using wavelets

In this recipe, you will learn how to use wavelets to transform an image and discard the lower-order bits from the output of the transform, so that most of its values are zero (or very small), but most of the signal (pixels) is preserved. We shall use the `mahotas` library functions for the demonstration.

Getting ready

In this recipe, we will use the cameraman grayscale image as input. Let's get started by importing the required libraries and modules:

```
import numpy as np
import mahotas
from mahotas.thresholding import soft_threshold
from matplotlib import pyplot as plt
import os
```

Image Restoration

How to do it...

Execute the following steps to implement image compression using *wavelets*:

1. First, read the input image and convert it into grayscale:

   ```
   im = mahotas.imread('images/cameraman.png', as_grey=True)
   im = im.astype(np.uint8)
   print(im.shape)
   # (256,256)
   f = np.mean(im==0)
   print("Fraction of zeros in original image: {}".format(f))
   # Fraction of zeros in original image: 0.0021514892578125
   ```

2. Try a baseline compression method using simple down-sampling (by saving every other pixel) and saving only the high-order bits:

   ```
   im1 = im[::2,::2].copy()
   im1 = im1 / 8
   im1 = im1.astype(np.uint8)
   f1 = np.mean(im1==0)
   print("Fraction of zeros in original image (after division \
           by 8): {}".format(f1))
   # Fraction of zeros in original image (after division by 8):
   0.01788330078125
   ```

3. Even though you have thrown away 75% of the values in the image in the previous step, still there are only a few zeros. Let's now transform the image using a Daubechies wavelet (D8) and then discard the low-order bits. Check whether you got a better image with the same number of values used:

   ```
   imw = mahotas.daubechies(mahotas.wavelet_center(im),'D8')
   imw /= 8 # discard lower order bits
   imw = imw.astype(np.int8)
   f2 = np.mean(imw==0)
   print("Fraction of zeros in wavelet transform (after division \
           by 8): {}".format(f2))
   # Fraction of zeros in wavelet transform (after division by 8):
   0.8892402648925781
   im2 = mahotas.wavelet_decenter(mahotas.idaubechies(imw, 'D8'), \
           im.shape)
   # min-max normalization to have pixel values in between 0-255
   im2 = (255 * (im2 - np.min(im2)) / (np.max(im2) - \
           np.min(im2))).astype(np.uint8)
   ```

[116]

4. Apply soft-thresholding to further increase the percentage of zeros in the transformed image:

```
imw = soft_threshold(imw, 12)
f3 = np.mean(imw==0)
print("Fraction of zeros in wavelet transform (after division \
       by 8 & soft thresholding): {}".format(f3))
# Fraction of zeros in wavelet transform (after division by 8 \
       & soft thresholding):   #0.9454727172851562
im3 = mahotas.wavelet_decenter(mahotas.idaubechies(imw, 'D8'), \
       im.shape)
im3 = (255 * (im3 - np.min(im3)) / (np.max(im3) - \
       np.min(im3))).astype(np.uint8)
```

A much higher compression ratio can be achieved with this image, enabling faster transmission over a communication channel and less bandwidth consumption, and after transmission, you will be able to reconstruct the image with a quality higher than the one reconstructed from the compressed image using baseline compression, created by just keeping every fourth pixel and low-order bits.

How it works...

If you execute the preceding code and plot the images, you will get a screenshot like the following one:

Image Restoration

The `im[::2,::2]` code selects every other pixel from the `im` image and `copy()` function from NumPy creates a clone of `ndarray`. The `wavelet_center()` and `wavelet_decenter()` functions from `mahotas` create a centered version of the image and undo the effect of the `wavelet_center()` function if applied on the transformed image, respectively. These functions correctly handle borders and removed artifacts at the border of the image that are created otherwise. The `mahotas.daubechies()` and `mahotas.idaubechies()` functions perform Daubechies wavelet transform and Daubechies inverse wavelet transform respectively and accept a code (`D8`) for the wavelet to obtain transformed/inverse-transformed image.

See also

Refer to the following links to find out more about this recipe:

- https://mahotas.readthedocs.io/en/latest/api.html?highlight=mahotas%20daubechies#mahotas.daubechies
- https://mahotas.readthedocs.io/en/latest/wavelets.html
- https://mahotas.readthedocs.io/en/latest/thresholding.html?highlight=soft_threshold

Using steganography and steganalysis

Steganography aims to hide a message (called **stego text**) imperceptibly in an input image (known as **cover image**) resulting in an output stego image (without visible distortion) so that the existence of the message isn't suspected. It provides security through obscurity and is used to convey messages secretly between a sender and a recipient. Steganography hides the message so that it is hard to be observed, unlike cryptography, which encrypts the message so that it is (computationally) hard to be decrypted or understood. On the contrary, steganalysis refers to the process of detecting secret messages that were hidden using steganography; cryptanalysis has a similar relationship with cryptography.

In this recipe, we shall demonstrate a very popular steganography technique known as **LSB data hiding** (secret messages can be hidden by storing information in the least significant bits of an image; this way, the change in pixel values is at most one and hence the stego image remains indistinguishable from the cover image by the human eye) in an RGB color image and steganalysis techniques to detect secret messages.

Getting ready

We shall use the Lena RGB color image to demonstrate the steganography/steganalysis techniques using the `stegano` library. Let's import the required packages, modules, and functions at the very outset, using the following code block:

```
#!pip install Stegano
import stegano
from PIL import Image, ImageChops
from stegano import lsb, lsbset
from stegano.steganalysis import statistics, parity
import matplotlib.pylab as plt
import pandas as pd
from stegano import lsbset
from stegano.lsbset import generators
from stegano import exifHeader
```

How to do it...

Execute the following steps to hide a secret message inside the Lena image using LSB data hiding and use (non-blind) steganalysis to detect the secret message:

1. Read the (cover) image and hide a long message (by concatenating a message 10 times) inside the image. Save the stego image:

   ```
   cover = Image.open('images/lena.png')
   stego = lsb.hide("images/lena.png", 10*"Python Image Processing \
                    Cookbook - LSB data hiding with Stegano")
   stego.save("images/lena-secret.png")
   ```

2. Print the message hidden inside the stego image:

   ```
   print(lsb.reveal("images/lena-secret.png"))
   ```

3. Do parity steganalysis and extract the parity encoded cover and stego images. Then, use statistical steganalysis to retrieve the common cover and stego images using the following code snippet:

   ```
   parity_encoded_cover = parity.steganalyse(cover)
   parity_encoded_stego = parity.steganalyse(stego)
   _, cover_common = statistics.steganalyse(cover)
   _, stego_common = statistics.steganalyse(stego)
   ```

Image Restoration

If you plot all of the images along with the difference between the stego and cover image and the difference between the parity encoded stego and cover images, you will get a figure like the following screenshot:

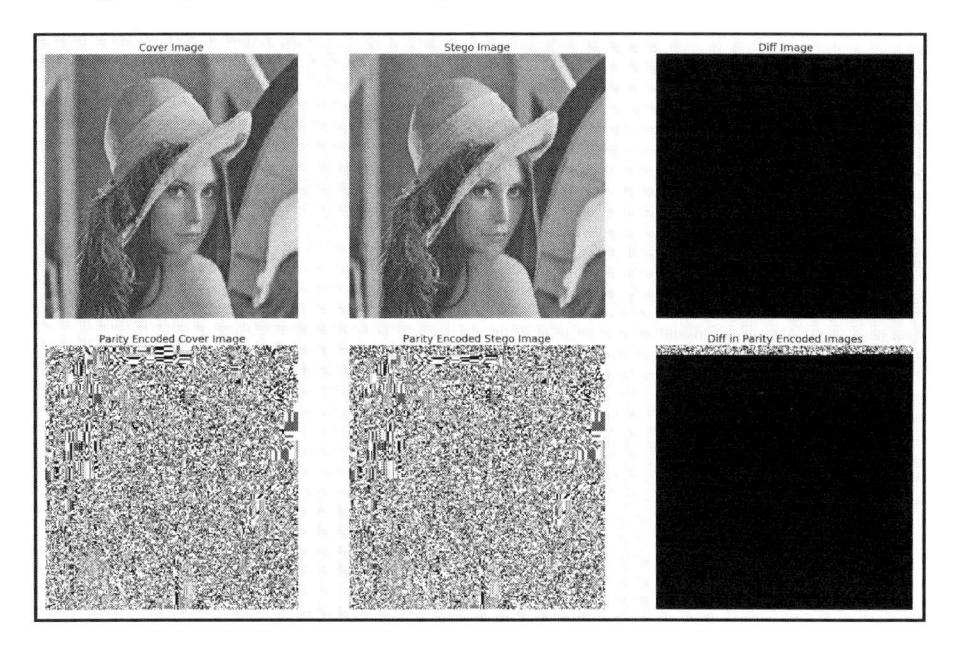

As you can see from the preceding screenshot, by seeing the difference in the image, between the stego and the cover image, the existence of the secret message can't be detected. The parity-encoded stego and cover image are not the same and the difference reveals that there is some secret message embedded inside the stego image.

4. Define a `plot_freq()` function to plot the histograms of the common pixel frequencies where the cover and stego images differ (obtained earlier with statistical steganalysis):

```
plot_freq(cover_common, stego_common)
```

You will get the output shown in the following screenshot, which clearly shows that the stego and the cover image were different:

Chapter 3

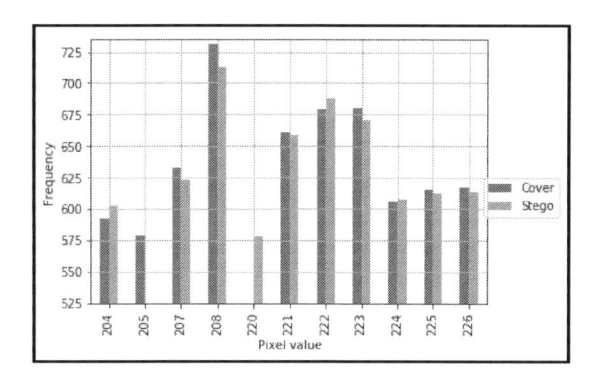

5. Next, use the LSB technique with sets based on generators (Sieve of Eratosthenes) to hide the secret message:

```
cover = Image.open("images/lena.png").convert('RGB')
 secret_message = "Python Image Processing Cookbook - LSB data \
                  hiding with Stegano lsbset!"
n = 1000
stego = lsbset.hide("images/lena.png",
secret_message,
generators.eratosthenes(),
shift = n).convert('RGB')
stego.save("images/stego.png")
```

If you plot the difference between the stego and cover image versus the difference between the parity-encoded stego and cover image, you will get the following screenshot:

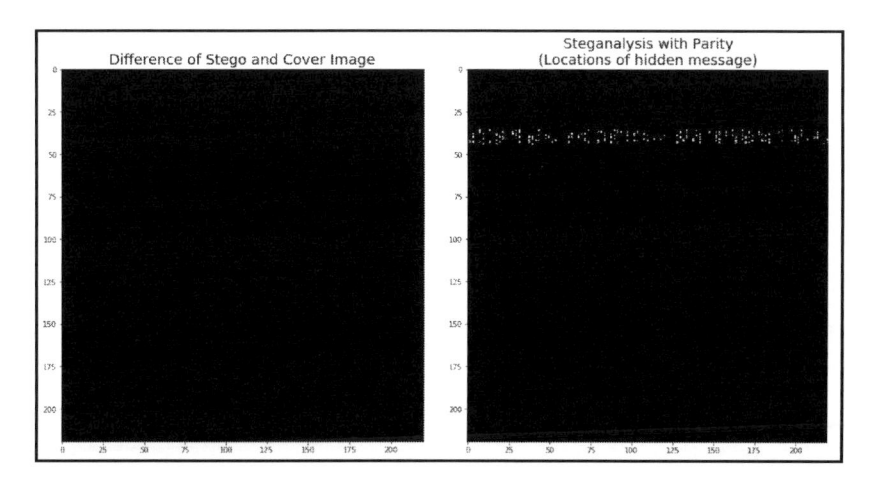

[121]

6. Now, try to retrieve the hidden message using the same generator (it will succeed) and a different one (it will fail):

```
try:
  message = lsbset.reveal("images/stego.png",
                          generators.fibonacci())
except:
print('Could not decode with the generator provided!')
# Could not decode with the generator provided!

message = lsbset.reveal("images/stego.png", \
                        generators.eratosthenes())
message
# 'Python Image Processing Cookbook - LSB data hiding with Stegano
lsbset!'
```

7. Finally, for JPEG and TIFF images, you can hide a message in the `exifHeader` (and reveal it) using the following code:

```
secret = exifHeader.hide("images/butterfly.jpg", \
                         "images/stego.png",
secret_message=5*"Python
  Image Processing Cookbook - LSB data hiding with Stegano")
print(exifHeader.reveal("images/stego.png"))
```

How it works...

The `open()` and `save()` methods from the PIL Image object were used to load and save and image, respectively. The `lsb.hide()` function was used for LSB data-hiding, which takes the cover image and the stego text as input parameters and returns the stego image. The `lsb.reveal()` function was used to get the stego text back from a stego image. `parity.steganalyse()` was used to obtain a parity-encoded image from an image (`stego` and `cover`).

The `difference()` function from PIL ImageChop was used to compute the difference image between two input images (for example, stego and cover). `statistics.steganalyse()` returns the pixel values with frequencies (histogram) where the cover and stego images differ in frequency.

There's more...

There are many different types of steganography techniques. You can find one based on number systems (refer to the first link in the following *See also* section) and implement it on your own.

See also

Refer to the following articles to further expand your skills in relation to this recipe:

- `https://arxiv.org/pdf/1003.3672.pdf`

- `https://buildmedia.readthedocs.org/media/pdf/stegano/latest/stegano.pdf`

Binary Image Processing

Morphological image processing refers to the application of a set of non-linear operation(s) that is related to the shape (that is, morphology) of image features. These operations are particularly suited to the processing of binary images (where pixels are represented as 0 or 1 and, by convention, the foreground of the object = 1 or white, and the background = 0 or black) since they don't depend on the exact numerical values of the pixels; rather, they depend only on how the pixel values are relatively ordered—although these operations can be extended to grayscale images.

Hence, in this chapter, we will discuss binary image processing with morphological operations, although a few grayscale morphological operations will also be discussed, for the sake of completeness. In morphological operations, a structuring element (a small template image) is used to probe the input image. The **Structuring Element (SE)** is placed at all possible locations in the input image and then an algorithm uses a set operator to compare it with the corresponding pixels' neighborhood. Morphological operations test whether the SE fits within, or hits or intersects, the corresponding neighborhood.

In this chapter, you will cover the following recipes:

- Applying morphological operators to a binary image
- Applying morphological filters
- Morphological pattern matching
- Segmenting images with morphology
- Counting objects

Applying morphological operators to a binary image

Dilation and erosion are two fundamental morphological operators. Erosion removes a pixel layer from the foreground (white) objects' boundaries and thereby shrinks the foreground in a binary image. The small-scale details get removed and the size of the regions of interest gets reduced by erosion in a binary image. On the other hand, dilation adds a pixel layer to the foreground objects' boundaries thereby expanding the foreground. The holes contained inside a single foreground object and gaps in between foreground objects (and boundaries) are reduced.

Many morphological operations can be obtained as combinations of erosion, dilation, and basic set operations (for example, complement). Morphological opening, closing, and hit-or-miss transform are the most popular ones. Opening is an idempotent operation (implemented with a dilation followed by erosion) that can disconnect the foreground objects connected by a thin layer of pixels, by keeping the surviving objects' size the same. Similarly, closing (dual operator of opening: implemented with an erosion followed by dilation) is another idempotent operation that can fill holes in the foreground regions while keeping the region sizes the same. The following screenshot shows how the fundamental and a few compound morphological operators are defined using the operators from set theory:

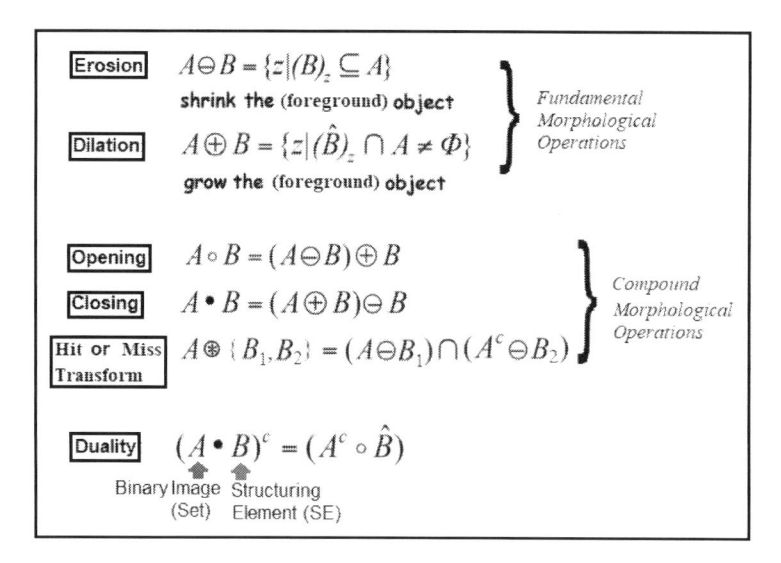

$$\text{Erosion} \quad A \ominus B = \{z | (B)_z \subseteq A\}$$
shrink the (foreground) object

$$\text{Dilation} \quad A \oplus B = \{z | (\hat{B})_z \cap A \neq \Phi\}$$
grow the (foreground) object

Fundamental Morphological Operations

$$\text{Opening} \quad A \circ B = (A \ominus B) \oplus B$$

$$\text{Closing} \quad A \bullet B = (A \oplus B) \ominus B$$

$$\text{Hit or Miss Transform} \quad A \circledast \{B_1, B_2\} = (A \ominus B_1) \cap (A^c \ominus B_2)$$

Compound Morphological Operations

$$\text{Duality} \quad (A \bullet B)^c = (A^c \circ \hat{B})$$

Binary Image (Set)   Structuring Element (SE)

In this recipe, you will learn how to apply a few morphological operators to a binary image.

Chapter 4

Getting ready

In this recipe, we will use a binary giraffe image to demonstrate how a few morphological operations can be applied to a binary image. Let's start by importing the required libraries:

```
%matplotlib inline
from skimage.io import imread
from skimage.color import rgb2gray
from skimage.filters import threshold_otsu
from scipy.ndimage.morphology import binary_erosion, binary_dilation, binary_fill_holes
from scipy.ndimage.morphology import morphological_gradient, distance_transform_edt
from skimage import morphology as morph
import numpy as np
import matplotlib.pylab as plt
```

How to do it...

You need to perform the following steps to be able to apply some of the morphological operators to a binary image using the functions from the `scipy.ndimage.morphology` module:

1. Read the input giraffe image and convert it into a binary image using thresholding. Obtain the optimal threshold with *Otsu's* algorithm and then change the pixels with values above the threshold to white and black:

   ```
   im = rgb2gray(imread('images/giraffe.jpg'))
   thres = threshold_otsu(im)
   im = (im > thres).astype(np.uint8)
   ```

2. Erode the image with a 2 x 2 square structuring element (SE/kernel) and invert the image:

   ```
   eroded = binary_erosion(im, structure=np.ones((2,2)),
   iterations=20)[20:,20:]
   eroded = 1 - eroded
   ```

3. Now, dilate the eroded image with an 11 x 11 square SE and compute the boundary of the image by taking the difference between the dilated and the eroded image. Next, use the (Euclidean) distance transform on the inverted boundary image:

   ```
   dilated = binary_dilation(eroded, structure=np.ones((11,11)))
   boundary = np.clip(dilated.astype(np.int) - eroded.astype(np.int),
   ```

```
    0, 1)
    dt = distance_transform_edt(np.logical_not(boundary))
```

4. Compute the `morphological_gradient` of the binary image. Invert the output to get the edges:

    ```
    edges = 1 - morphological_gradient(im, size=3)
    ```

If you plot the preceding images, you will get an output like the following diagram:

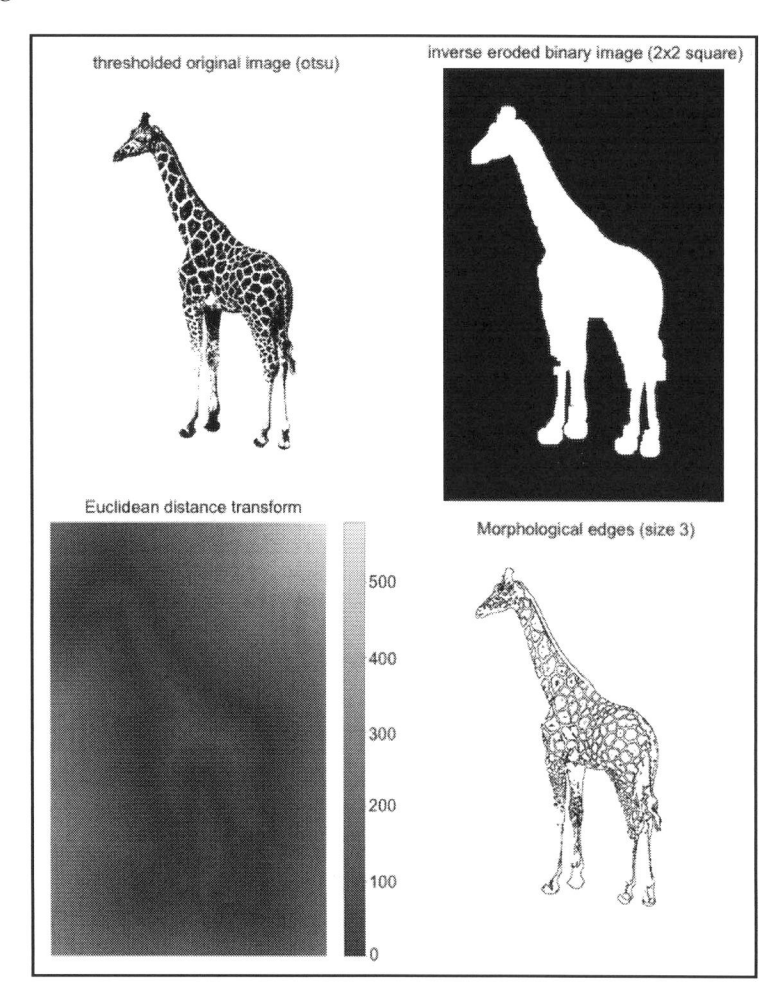

Chapter 4

Again, perform the following steps to be able to apply some more morphological operators to a binary image but, this time, using the functions from the `scikit-image.morphology` module:

1. Read the images of input circles and convert it into a binary image (choose a threshold of 0 this time):

    ```
    im = rgb2gray(imread('images/circles.png'))
    im = (im > 0).astype(np.uint8)
    ```

2. Erode the binary images with disk SEs of different sizes. Then, label the connected components of the eroded images with a connectivity of 1:

    ```
    disk2 = morph.disk(radius=2)
    disk8 = morph.disk(radius=8)
    eroded2 = morph.binary_erosion(im, selem=disk2)
    eroded8 = morph.binary_erosion(im, selem=disk8)
    labeled = morph.label(eroded8, connectivity=1)
    ```

3. Dilate the image and compute the edges in the image, this time computing `morphological_gradient` by taking the difference between the dilated and the eroded images:

    ```
    dilated2 = morph.binary_dilation(im, selem=disk2)
    edges = dilated2.astype(np.int) - eroded2.astype(np.int)
    ```

4. Skeletonize the binary image:

    ```
    skeleton = morph.skeletonize(im)
    ```

5. Plot all of the images obtained:

    ```
    plt.figure(figsize=(15,15))
    plt.subplot(221), plt.imshow(im), plt.axis('off'),
    plt.title('original binary image', size=15)
    plt.subplot(222), plt.imshow(labeled, cmap='spectral'),
    plt.axis('off')
    plt.title('eroded with connected components (radius 8)', size=15)
    plt.subplot(223), plt.imshow(edges), plt.axis('off'),
    plt.title('edges (radius 2)', size=15)
    plt.subplot(224), plt.imshow(skeleton), plt.axis('off')
    plt.title('skeleton binary image', size=15)
    plt.show()
    ```

If you run the preceding code, you will get something similar to the following:

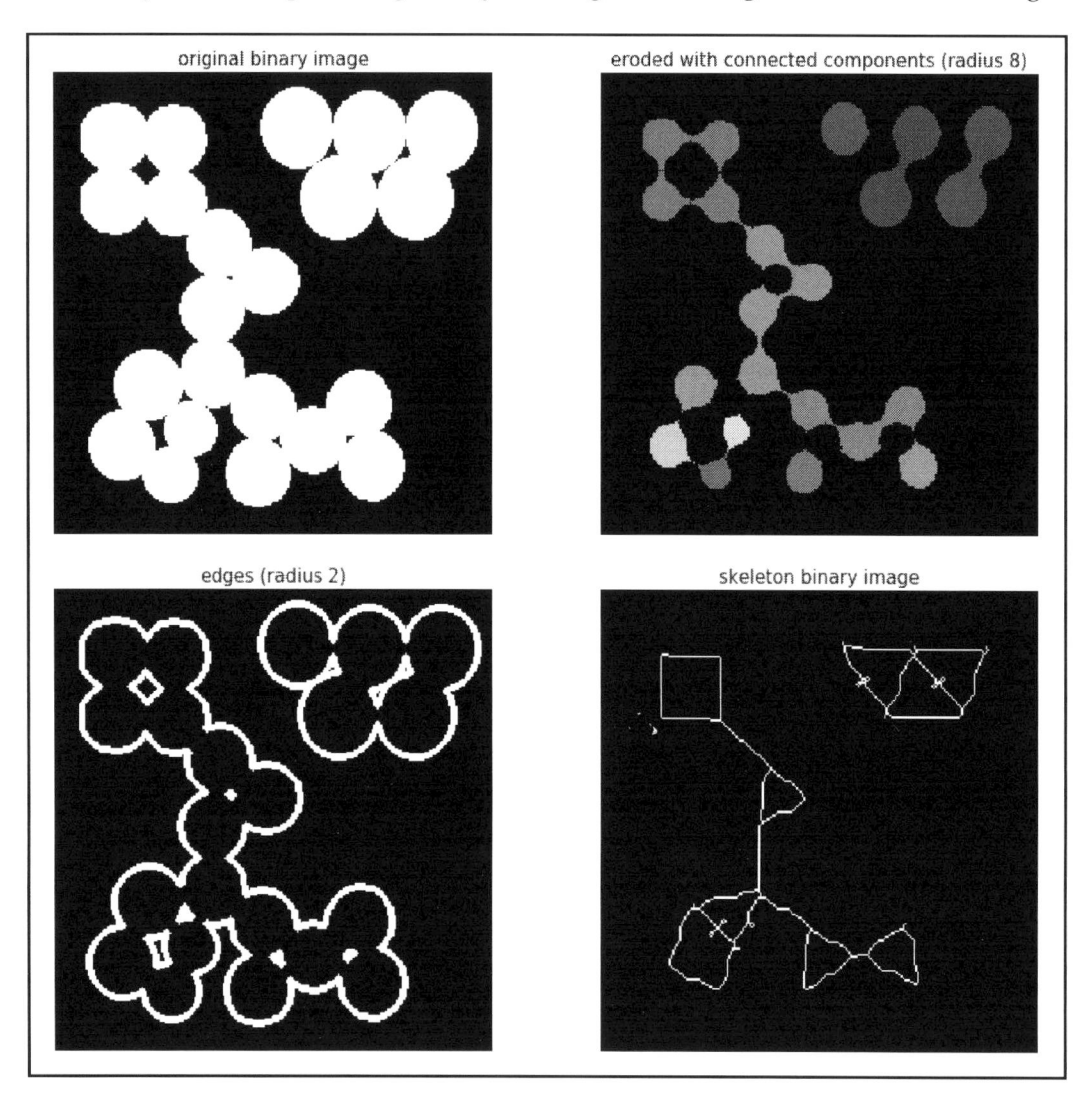

How it works...

In *step 1*, the `threshold_otsu()` function from the `scikit-image.filters` module was used to find the optimal threshold for creating the binary image (by thresholding the grayscale image).

In *step 2*, the `binary_erosion()` and `binary_dilation()` functions from `scipy.ndimage` were used to apply erosion and dilation operations to a binary image, respectively. These functions accept the binary image to be eroded/dilated, the structuring element to be used (the default SE is a square with connectivity 1), and the number of times the operation is to be repeated (default 1). Non-zero elements are considered `True`.

As you can observe, `np.ones((2,2)` was used to create a square SE of size 2, whereas `morph.disk(radius=2)` was used to generate a disk-shaped structuring element. This function is from the scikit-image morphology module. Here, a pixel is considered a neighbor of another pixel if the Euclidean distance between the pixels is at most the value of the radius. The compound operator morphological gradient was used to compute the edges in the input binary image and was computed by taking the difference between the dilated and eroded image with the same SE (a disk of radius 2), as shown here:

$$g_B(A) = A \oplus B - A \ominus B$$

The `skeletonize()` function from the `scikit-image.morphology` module was used to compute the skeleton of the binary image. It uses a *morphological thinning* operation to contract each connected component to a single pixel-wide skeleton. Mathematically, the morphological operator skeleton is defined as follows:

$$nB = \underbrace{B \oplus \cdots \oplus B}_{n \text{ times}},$$
$$0B = \{o\}, \quad \text{origin } o$$
$$S - n(A) = (A \ominus nB) - (A \ominus B) \circ B,$$
$$n = 0, 1, \ldots, N, \text{ size of the structuring element } B$$
$$S(X) = \bigcup_n S_n(X)$$
skeleton

The `label()` function from the `scikit-image.morphology` module was used to assign a unique value to each of the connected regions in the binary image (as an integer array). The connectivity parameter to this function denotes the maximum number of orthogonal hops that can be taken to consider a pixel as a neighbor of another pixel—which defaults to 2 for a binary image.

Binary Image Processing

There's more...

Detect holes in a chain-link fence and find the positions of the holes (there are two of them) in the following chain-link image, using morphological operators (hint: convert it to a binary image first):

Similarly, use morphological operations on the Tetris image provided to detect patterns and produce output, as in the following screenshot:

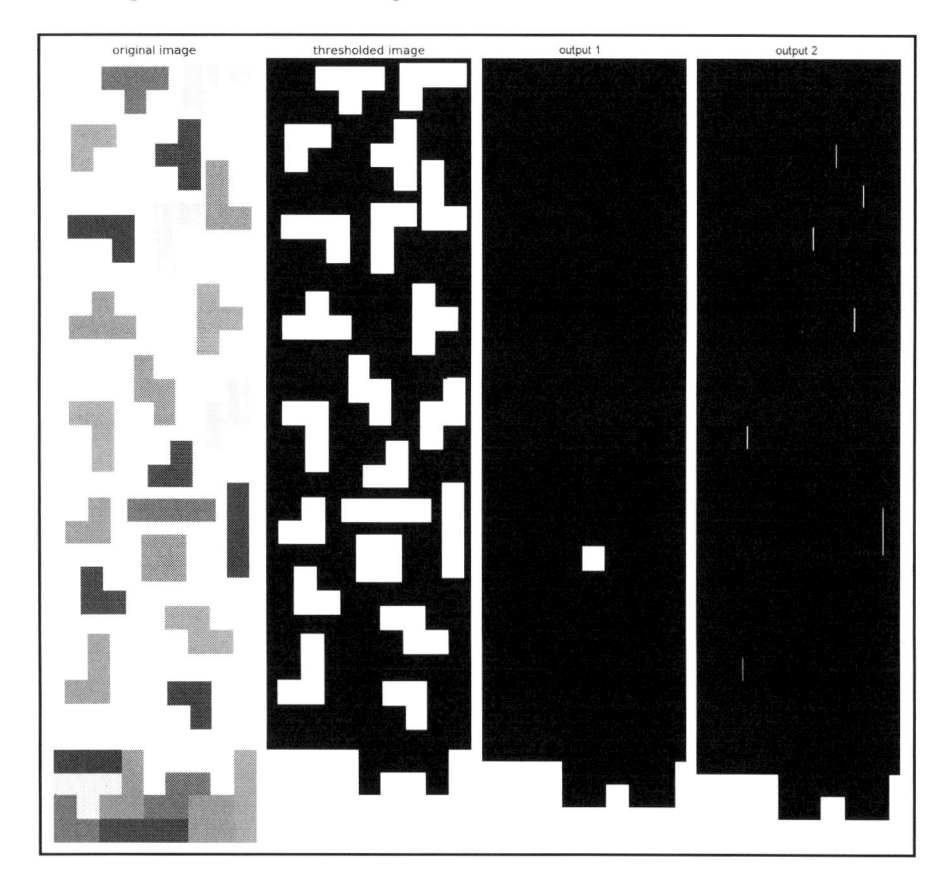

Chapter 4

Find the diamonds in the following image of a card using morphological operations, as shown here:

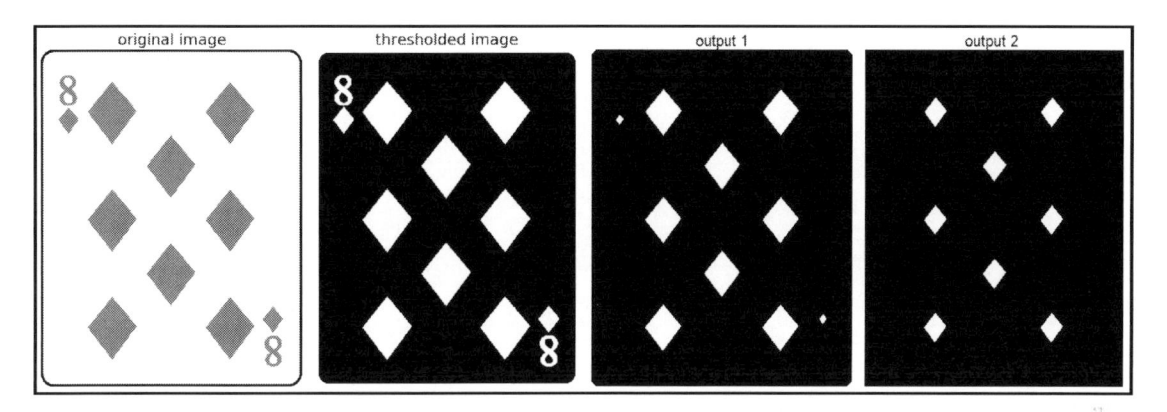

Use the following colored dice image and find the dots in it with morphological operations:

Compare *dilation* and *erosion* implementations from different libraries (for example, the morphology module from scikit-image's/scipy.ndimage's implementations with Mahotas, OpenCV-Python, and SimpleITK implementations), with respect to speed, features provided, output quality, and so on.

Morphological operators can be extended to processing grayscale input images as well; refer to the second link in the following *See also* section for examples.

See also

Refer to the following links to learn more about this recipe:

- https://web.stanford.edu/class/ee368/Handouts/Lectures/2019_Winter/7-Morphological.pdf
- https://www.cs.auckland.ac.nz/courses/compsci773s1c/lectures/ImageProcessing-html/topic4.htm
- *Chapter 6* of the book, *Hands-on Image Processing with Python*

Applying Morphological filters

As you have seen from the last recipe, morphological operators (such as erosion, dilation, erode, opening, and closing) can be applied through binary image filtering to grow/shrink image regions, as well as to remove or fill in image region boundary pixels. In this recipe, you will learn how to apply a few more morphological filters to a binary image to enhance the image or get the desired results. Some more morphology filters include *top-hat transforms*, *morphological gradient*, and *morphological Laplace*.

Getting ready

Import the necessary libraries, modules, and functions required to start by using the following code block:

```
#!pip install itk
from skimage.morphology import flood_fill, diameter_closing, binary_erosion, rectangle, reconstruction
from skimage.filters import threshold_otsu
import mahotas as mh
import itk
import SimpleITK as sitk
import matplotlib.pylab as plt
import numpy as np
```

How to do it...

In this recipe, you will learn how to use functions from different libraries (for example, `mahotas`, `skimage`, and `SimpleITK`) to apply a few different morphological filters to an input binary image. Let's first execute the following steps to compute a few basic metrics (for example, the Euler number) for a binary image (using `mahotas`) and to use filters such as `flood_fill` and `diameter_closing` (using the `skimage.morphology` module).

Computing the Euler number, eccentricity, and center of mass with mahotas/scikit-image

Perform the following steps to compute different metrics using the `mahotas` and `skimage` library functions:

1. Read the NASA black hole image (https://www.nasa.gov/sites/default/files/thumbnails/image/blackhole.png) and convert it into a binary image using a manual threshold (t=60). Compute the Euler number for the binary image:

   ```
   blackhole = mh.imread('images/blackhole.png')
   blackhole_gray = mh.colors.rgb2grey(blackhole).astype(np.uint8)
   t = 60
   bin_blackhole = (blackhole_gray > t).astype(np.uint8)
   print(mh.euler(bin_blackhole))
   # 0.0
   ```

2. Compute `center_of_mass` and `eccentricity` of the binary image:

   ```
   cms = mh.center_of_mass(bin_blackhole)
   print('Eccentricity =', mh.features.eccentricity(bin_blackhole))
   # 0.5449847073316407
   ```

3. Fill the black hole using either of `flood_fill` (starting from a seed inside the black hole) or `diameter_closing` (removing all holes of an area less than or equal to 100):

   ```
   bin_blackhole2 = flood_fill(bin_blackhole, (200,400), 1)
   bin_blackhole3 = diameter_closing(bin_blackhole, 100, connectivity=2)
   ```

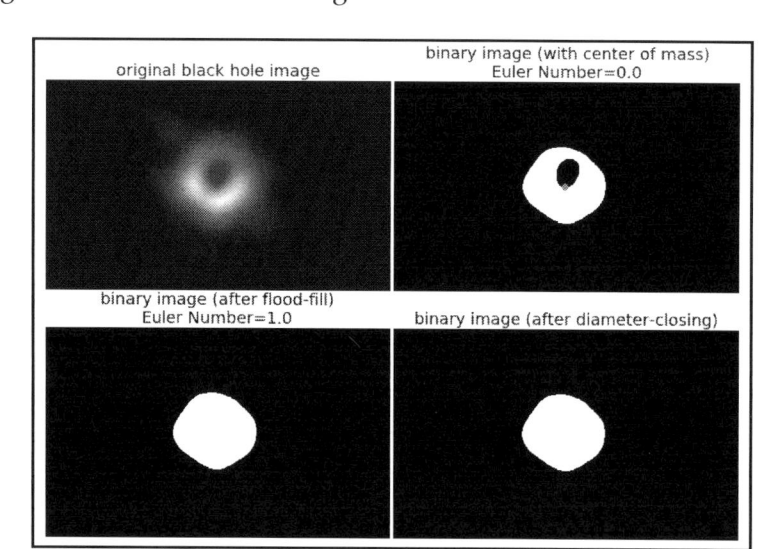

If you run the preceding code snippets and plot the images, you will get a diagram similar to the following:

The topology of a binary image is measured with the Euler number. It is defined as the difference in the total number of objects in the image and the number of holes present in those objects. For the first binary image, the Euler number is 0 = 1 - 1 (it has a single object that contains a single hole). On the other hand, for the second binary image, the Euler number is 1 - 0 = 1 (since the single object it contains does not have any hole in it).

Morphological image filters with mahotas

Perform the following steps to see the result of applying a few morphological image filters using mahotas library functions again:

1. Read the color mandelbrot (fractal) image, convert it into grayscale, and then use otsu thresholding to convert it into a binary image:

   ```
   fractal = mh.imread('images/mandelbrot.jpg')
   fractal_gray = mh.colors.rgb2grey(fractal).astype(np.uint8)
   t = mh.otsu(fractal_gray)
   bin_fractal = (fractal_gray > t).astype(np.uint8)
   ```

2. Compute the border between the white and black pixels using the following line of code:

   ```
   mh.border(bin_fractal, 0, 1)
   ```

3. Compute the regional minimum (with the region defined as a 3 x 3 cross SE around each pixel and taking the whole object into account) using the following line of code:

   ```
   mh.regmin(bin_fractal)
   ```

4. Close the holes in the image with the SE as a disk of radius 3, using the folllowing line of code:

   ```
   mh.close_holes(bin_fractal, mh.disk(3))
   ```

5. Apply `majority_filter` to the binary image using the next line of code:

   ```
   mh.majority_filter(bin_fractal)
   ```

   Finally, if you plot all of the images along with the center of mass of the original binary image, you will get a diagram similar to the following:

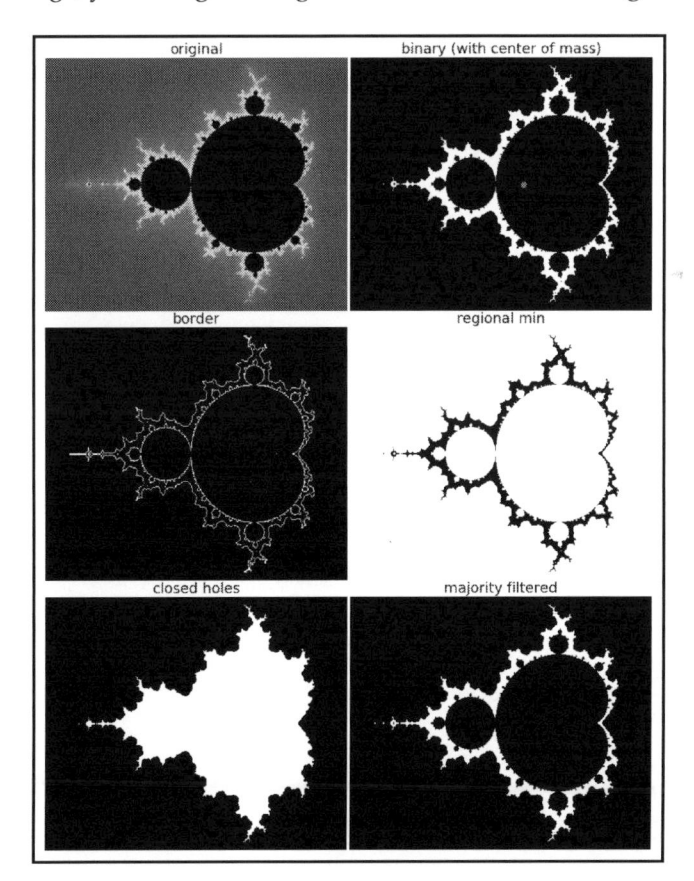

Binary Image Processing

Binary image filters with SimpleITK

Perform the following steps to demonstrate the application of a few more *binary filters* to a binary image, this time using `SimpleITK` library functions:

1. First, read the *NASA supernova* image (https://www.nasa.gov/image-feature/goddard/2019/hubble-sets-sights-on-an-explosive-galaxy) and convert the image into a binary one. Negate the binary image:

   ```
   supernova_gray = sitk.ReadImage('images/supernova.jpg',
   sitk.sitkFloat32)
   supernova_bin =
   sitk.BinaryNotImageFilter().Execute(sitk.OtsuThresholdImageFilter()
   .Execute(supernova_gray))
   ```

2. Instantiate the SimpleITK filter objects corresponding to the opening and closing morphological filters. Set the *SE* as a disk of radius 3. First, apply the opening filter followed by the closing filter to the binary supernova image:

   ```
   open_f = sitk.BinaryMorphologicalOpeningImageFilter()
   close_f = sitk.BinaryMorphologicalClosingImageFilter()
   open_f.SetKernelRadius(3)
   close_f.SetKernelRadius(3)
   supernova_bin1 = close_f.Execute(open_f.Execute(supernova_bin))
   ```

3. Apply the opening filter followed by the closing filter again to the input binary image, but this time with the SE as a circle with a radius of 7:

   ```
   open_f.SetKernelRadius(7)
   close_f.SetKernelRadius(7)
   supernova_bin2 = close_f.Execute(open_f.Execute(supernova_bin))
   ```

4. Next, apply the median filter with SEM as a disk with a radius of 3 to the input binary image:

   ```
   med_f = sitk.BinaryMedianImageFilter()
   med_f.SetRadius(3)
   supernova_bin3 = med_f.Execute(supernova_bin)
   ```

5. Apply `BinaryMinMaxCurvatureFlowImageFilter()` to the binary image using the following code snippet (with a stencil radius of 2 and a threshold parameter value of 60):

   ```
   curv_f = sitk.BinaryMinMaxCurvatureFlowImageFilter()
   curv_f.SetStencilRadius(2)
   curv_f.SetThreshold(60)
   supernova_bin4 = curv_f.Execute(sitk.Cast(supernova_bin,
   sitk.sitkFloat32))
   ```

6. Apply `BinaryContourImageFilter()` to the image after instantiating the corresponding object:

   ```
   cont_f = sitk.BinaryContourImageFilter()
   supernova_bin5 = cont_f.Execute(supernova_bin)
   ```

7. Finally, instantiate `VotingBinaryImageFilter()` on the binary image:

   ```
   vote_f = sitk.VotingBinaryImageFilter()
   vote_f.SetRadius(5)
   supernova_bin6 = vote_f.Execute(sitk.Cast(supernova_bin2,
   sitk.sitkInt32))
   ```

Binary Image Processing

If you run the preceding code snippets and plot all of the images, you will get a diagram similar to the following:

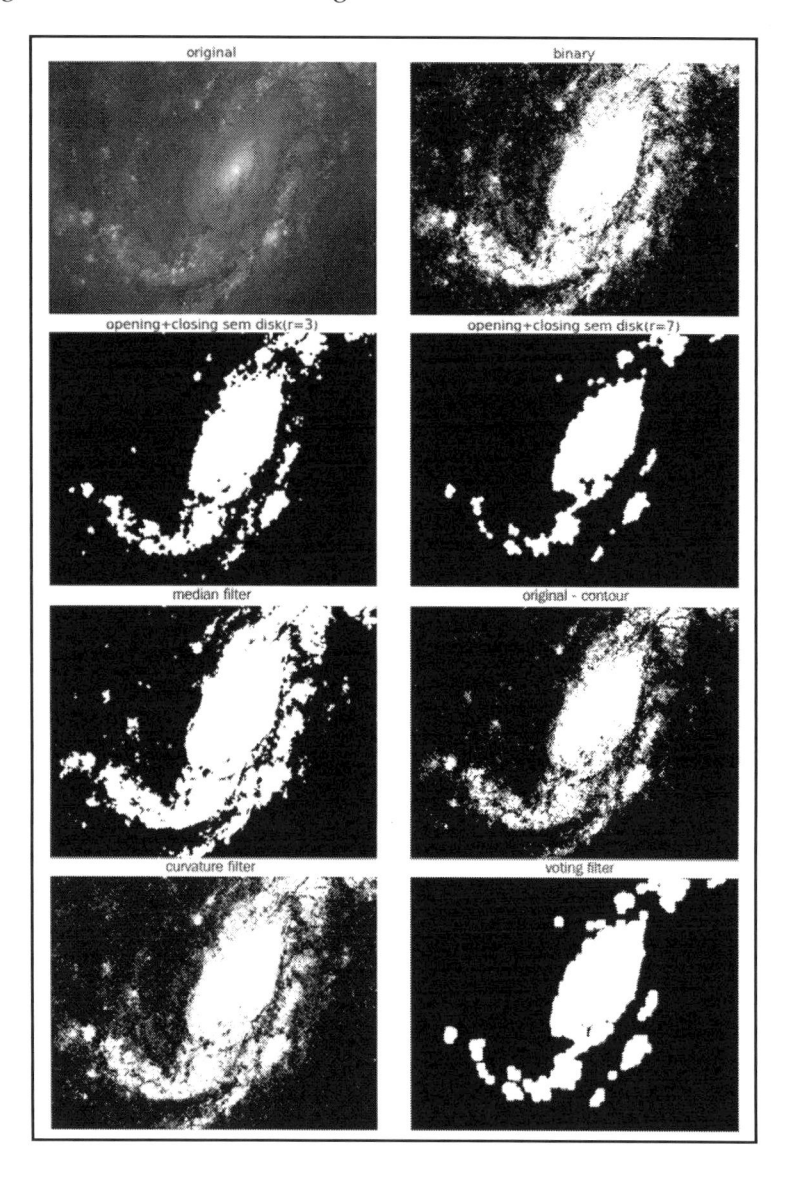

Dilation by reconstruction with skimage

Perform the following steps to separate drawing from text using dilation by reconstruction using the `skimage` library functions:

1. Read the input image (*Tagore's drawing-ridden Bengali manuscript* of one of his songs in his own handwriting) and convert it into a binary image with thresholding followed by binary inversion (you want to have the alphabets as foreground objects, that is, in white):

   ```
   img = rgb2gray(imread('images/tagore_manuscript.jpg'))
   th = 0.6 #threshold_otsu(img)
   img[img <= th] = 0
   img[img > th] = 1
   img = 1 - img
   ```

2. The mask image required for reconstruction by dilation is simply the binary image obtained previously. Create the `seed` image (*reconstruction by dilation*) using the `binary_erosion` operation with a *vertical line* filter. Finally, perform the reconstruction by dilation using the `mask` and `seed` images created:

   ```
   mask = img
   seed = binary_erosion(img, rectangle(1,50))
   words = reconstruction(seed, mask, 'dilation')
   ```

Binary Image Processing

If you run the preceding code snippets and plot all of the images, you will get the drawing separated from the writing (words), as shown in the following diagram:

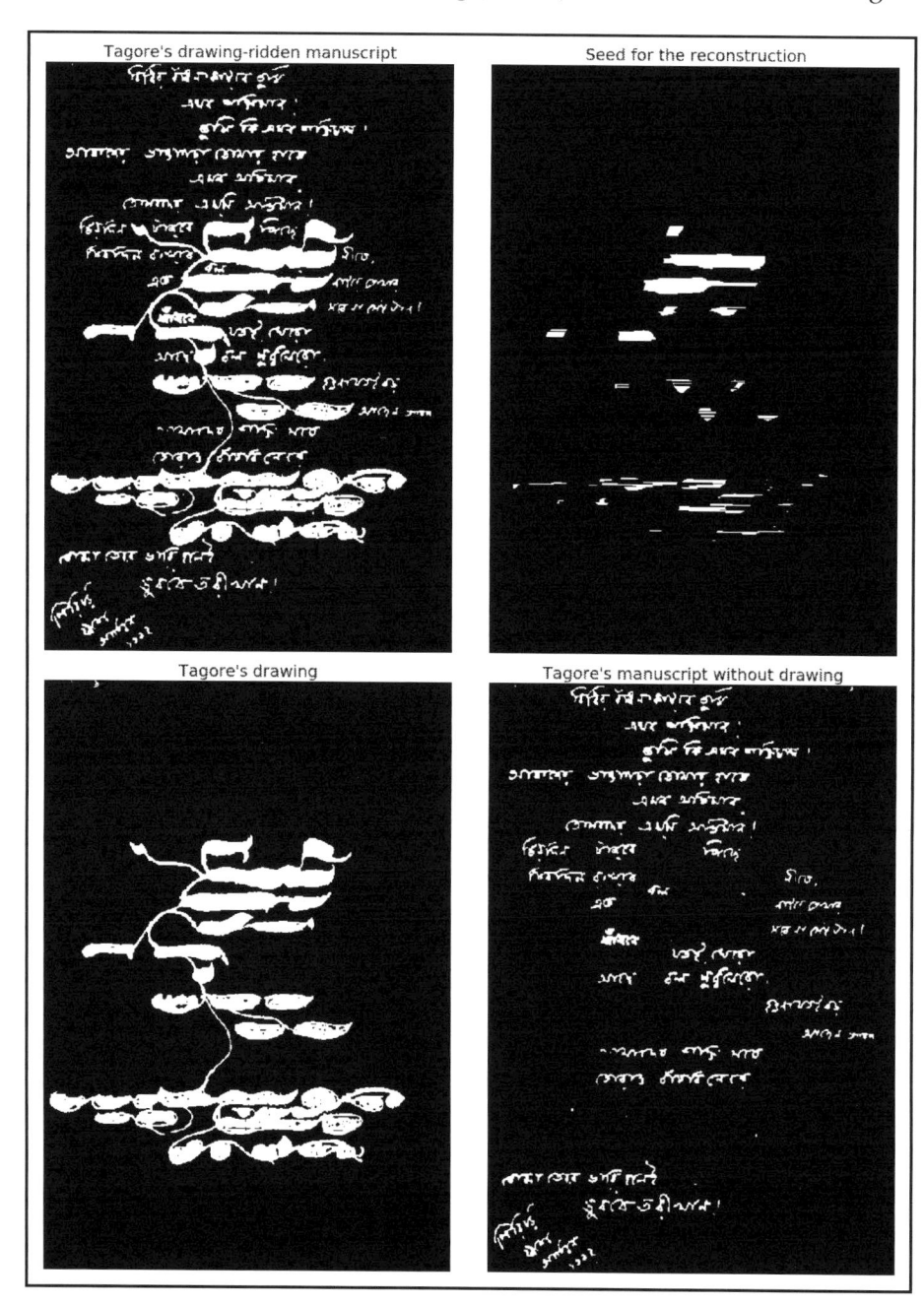

[142]

How it works...

The `euler()` function from the `mahotas` library was used to compute the Euler number (or characteristics) of the input binary image. By default, it uses *8-connectivity*.

The `flood_fill()` function from the `skimage.morphology` module was used to perform flood filling on the black hole binary image, starting at a specific seed point (200,400) on the dark region inside the black hole (passed as the second argument to the function); the connected points equal to the *seed pixel value* (here, 0 or black) are found and then set to `new_value` (here, 1 or white), which is the third input parameter of the function.

The `diameter_closing()` function from the `skimage.morphology` module was used to remove all *holes* of the black hole image with *maximum extension* (a side of the *bounding box* enclosing a *hole*) smaller than the `diameter_threshold` parameter (that is, 100). This operator is also known as **bounding box closing**.

The `reconstruction()` function from the `skimage.morphology` module was used to implement dilation by reconstruction.

The dilation by reconstruction operation uses a `seed` and a `mask` image. The seed image specifies the values to start with (that *spreads* iteratively using the *SE* for *dilation*), whereas the mask image (the original image was used as the mask image) specifies the maximum value allowed at each pixel. The mask image puts a constraint on the *spread* of the *foreground* values.

The `BinaryMedianImageFilter()` constructor was used to instantiate the binary median filter (for denoising the supernova image) and the radius of the disk SE for this morphological filter was set using the `SetRadius()` method. The filter is applied to the input binary image using the `Execute()` method, and likewise for other SimpleITK filters.

There's more...

Here are a few more useful morphological functions that you can try on your own (similar to the ones shown in this recipe). Use the `mahotas.bwperim()` function in the fractal binary image to compute the border and the `mahotas.thin()` function for morphological thinning/skeletonization.

Use morphological filters to get rid of the noise and the smaller planets (as shown in the following screenshot) from the binary image obtained by thresholding the image of the colored planet from *NASA* public domain images (https://www.flickr.com/photos/nasacommons/), as shown here:

Also, start with the following MRI grayscale image and apply white/black top hat morphological filters to obtain the output shown:

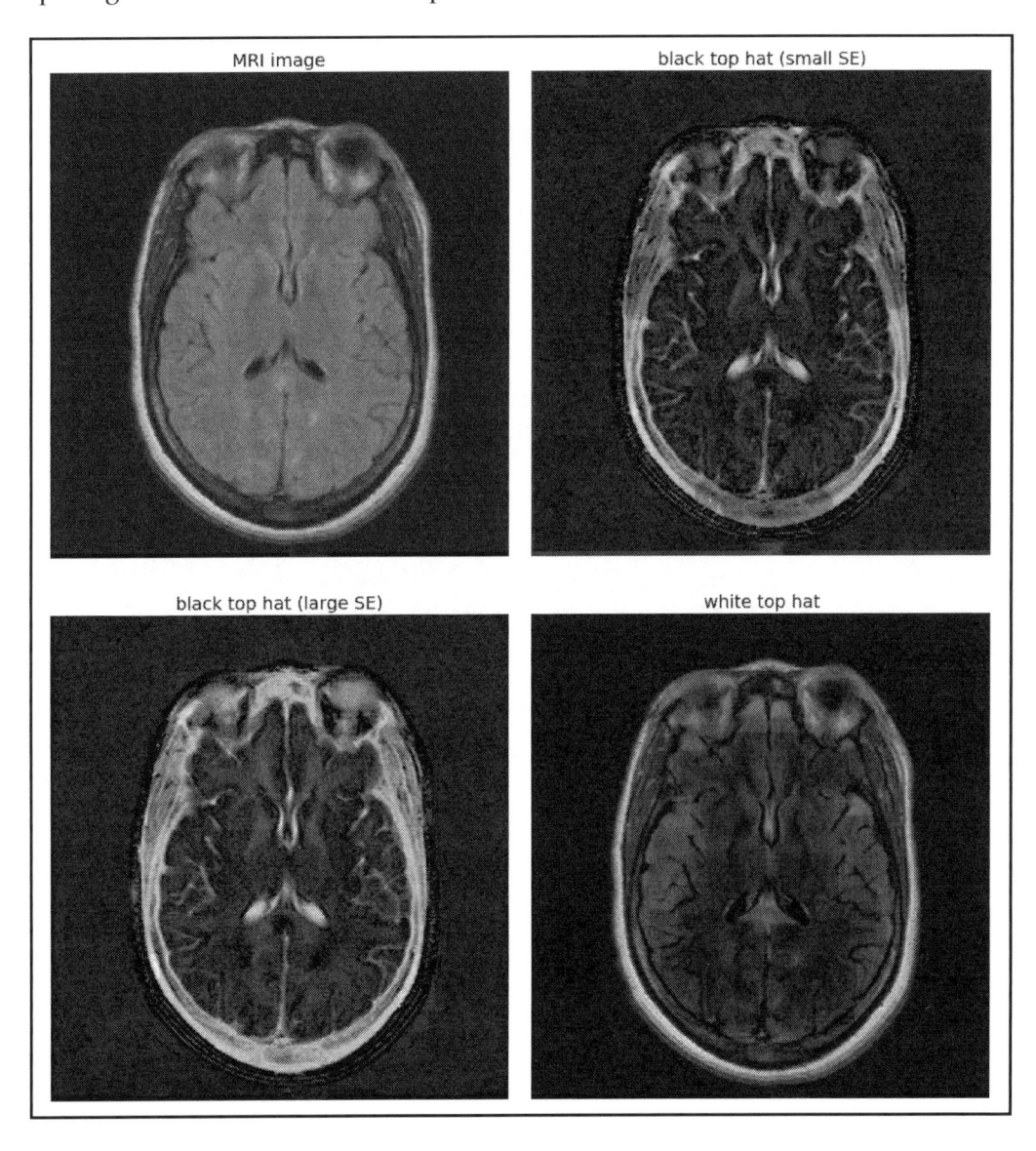

Binary Image Processing

Start with the keyboard binary image and get rid of all of the symbols to get the output image shown here (hint: use binary erosion by reconstruction with an appropriate structuring element):

Compare morphological diameter closing with closing by applying them to binary images where the results obtained are different when these two filters are applied.

Apply `mahotas` functions to apply the morphological local minima (and maxima) filters to a binary image. How are regional minima (and maxima) different from local minima (maxima)? Demonstrate with a binary image where these two are different. You can apply morphological filters to grayscale images as well (refer to the first link in the following *See also* and *Grayscale operations* sections for a demonstration of such an implementation).

See also

Refer to the following works to further enrich your knowledge of this recipe:

- *Chapter 6 of the book, Hands-on Image Processing with Python*
- https://mahotas.readthedocs.io/en/latest/api.html
- https://simpleitk.readthedocs.io/en/master/Documentation/docs/source/filters.html
- http://people.ciirc.cvut.cz/~hlavac/TeachPresEn/11ImageProc/71-3MatMorpholBinEn.pdf
- http://www.cs.uu.nl/docs/vakken/ibv/reader/chapter6.pdf

Morphological pattern matching

In this recipe, you will learn how to use the morphological compound operation, hit-or-miss-transform, to find patterns from a binary image. **Hit-or-miss transform** is a morphological operation that is used to detect a given pattern in a binary image. It uses a pair of disjointed structuring elements to define the pattern to be matched and the morphological erosion operator to implement the pattern matching. The hit-or-miss transform returns a binary image as output in which only those sets of positions are non-zero where the first SE matches and the second SE completely misses the foreground, respectively, in the input binary image.

Getting ready

In this recipe, we will use an image of a script of a Bengali poem by Tagore and search the image to find the occurrence of a Bengali character (ব) using morphological pattern matching. Let's start by importing the Python libraries, modules, and functions required:

```
import numpy as np
import matplotlib.pylab as plt
from skimage.io import imread
from skimage.color import import rgb2gray, gray2rgb
from scipy import import ndimage
```

Binary Image Processing

How to do it...

Perform the following steps to implement morphological pattern matching with hit-or-miss-transform:

1. Define the `hit_or_miss_transform()` function that accepts the filenames corresponding to the input image and two SEs (the first one for *hit* and the second one for *miss*) as input:

   ```
   def hit_or_miss_transform(im, s1, s2):
   ```

2. Inside the function, read the input image and structuring elements, consequently converting them into grayscale:

   ```
   im = rgb2gray(imread(im))
   m, n = im.shape
   s1 = rgb2gray(imread(s1))
   s2 = rgb2gray(imread(s2))
   ```

3. Apply the hit-or-miss transform using corresponding functions from the `scipy.ndimage` module, which returns a Boolean NumPy `ndarray` where the elements corresponding to the match position are set to `True`. Convert the output type into an unsigned 8-bit integer:

   ```
   hom_transformed = ndimage.binary_hit_or_miss(im, structure1=s1, \
                          structure2=s2).astype(np.uint8)
   ```

4. Now, highlight the matches (pixels with the value 1) with red squares and plot the highlighted output image using the following code snippet:

   ```
   xs, ys = np.where(hom_transformed == 1)
   hom_transformed = gray2rgb(hom_transformed)
   w, h = 10, 12
   for i in range(len(xs)):
       x, y = (xs[i], ys[i])
       for j in range(max(0, x-h), min(m-1, x+h)):
           for k in range(max(0, y-w), min(n, y+w)):
               hom_transformed[j, k, 0] = 1.
       for j in range(max(0, x-h), min(m, x+h)):
           for k in range(max(0, y-w), min(n-1, y+w)):
               hom_transformed[j, k, 0] = 1.
   # plot the highlighted output image hom_transformed here with
   matplotlib
   ```

Chapter 4

5. Finally, call the `hit_or_miss_transform()` function to match patterns such as the Bengali letter ব only, but not similar to letters such as র. The first SE matches both the patterns ব and র, but the second SE discards the pattern র by ensuring the corresponding mismatch:

    ```
    hit_or_miss_transform('images/poem.png', 'images/bo.png',
    'images/bo_inv_1.png')
    ```

The structuring elements you need to specify (corresponding to hit and miss, respectively) are shown in the following screenshot:

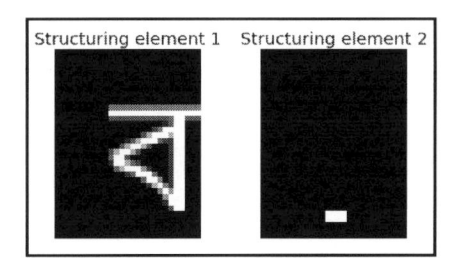

If you run the preceding code snippets with the given structuring elements and plot the input and output images, you will get a diagram along the lines of the following:

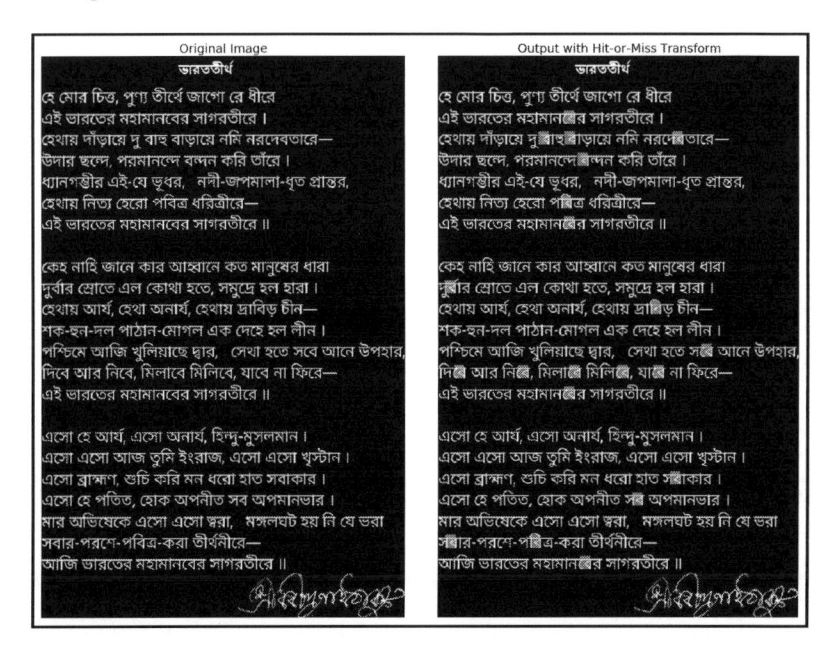

[149]

Binary Image Processing

As you can see from the preceding screenshot, all of the ব patterns are matched but not the র pattern.

6. Again, call the `hit_or_miss_transform()` function to match patterns such as the Bengali letter ব, except for the ones with vowel signs, such as বি and বে:

   ```
   hit_or_miss_transform('images/poem.png', 'images/bo.png',
   'images/bo_inv_2.png')
   ```

   The structuring elements you need to specify (corresponding to hit and miss, respectively) this time are shown in the following screenshot:

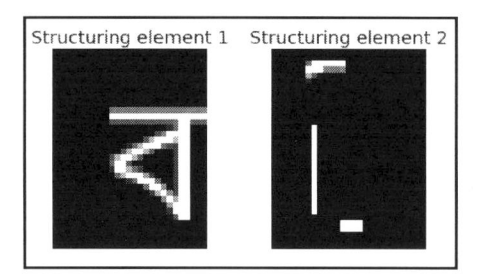

   If you run the code snippets with the new given structuring elements and plot the input and output images, you will get a diagram along the lines of the following:

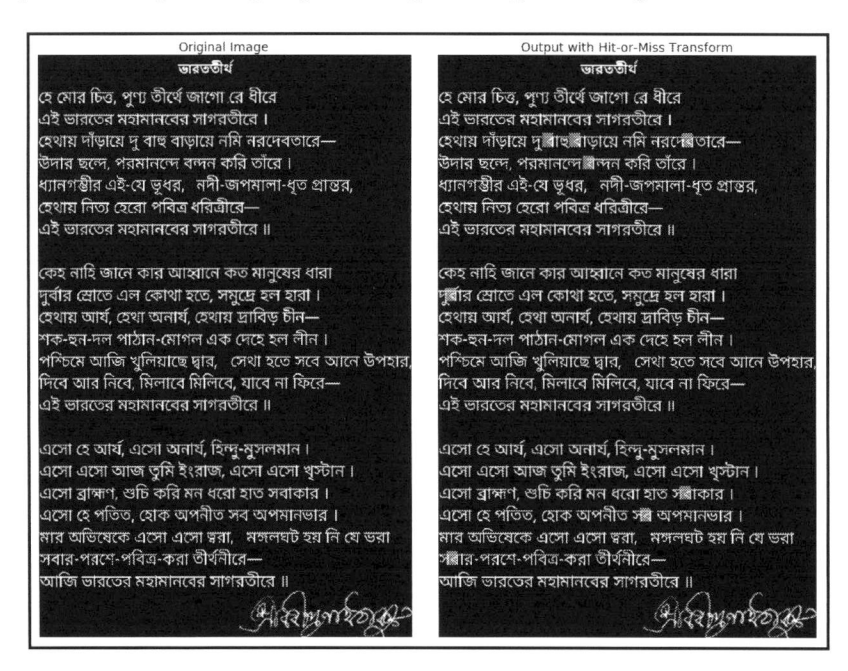

[150]

How it works...

As you can see in the preceding section, the `binary_hit_or_miss()` function from the `scipy.ndimage.morphology` module was used to apply the morphological hit-or-miss transform operation (shown in the following screenshot) to a binary image:

$$A \otimes B = (A \ominus B_1) \cap (A^c \ominus B_2)$$

binary image; composite SE

$$B = (B_1, B_2), B_1 \cap B_2 = \emptyset.$$

SE1 SE2

$$A \otimes B = \{x : B_1 \subset A \text{ and } B_2 \subset A^c\}$$

The input binary image, along with a couple of disjointed structuring elements, are passed to the function. The first SE argument represents part of the SE that must match (hit) the foreground. The second SE argument represents part of the SE that must miss the foreground completely.

This `binary_hit_or_miss()` function finds the locations inside the input image that match the given pattern (defined by the SEs).

The `np.where()` function was used to find the match coordinates and those matched pixels were then highlighted in red (using the `gray2rgb()` function from the `skimage.color` module to convert the 2D binary image into a 3D color image).

There's more...

Let's now apply the morphological pattern extraction to organic chemistry: find -O- and =O bonding from the following structure of the triglyceride molecule and highlight them, as shown in the next screenshot:

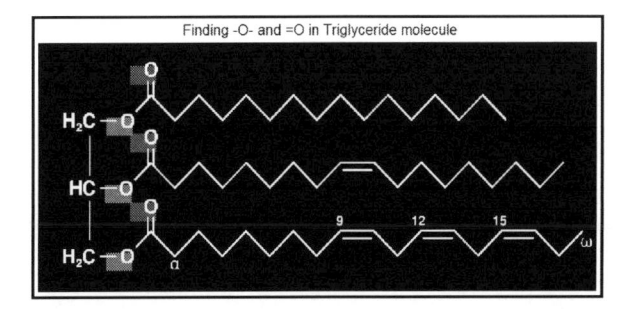

See also

Refer to the following link to learn more about this recipe:

- https://docs.scipy.org/doc/scipy-0.14.0/reference/generated/scipy.ndimage.morphology.binary_hit_or_miss.html

Segmenting images with morphology

Image segmentation is the partitioning of an image into distinct regions or categories that correspond to different objects or parts of objects. In this recipe, you will learn how to use a region-based segmentation method to a binary image using the morphological watershed algorithm. We can think of a grayscale image as a topographic surface. If we flood this surface from its minimum values and prevent the merging of waters from different sources, then the image gets partitioned into two different sets, namely, the *catchment basins* (*segments*) and the *watershed lines*. To prevent over-segmentation, a pre-defined set of markers is used and the flooding of the surface starts from these markers. The following are the steps involved in the segmentation of an image by the watershed transformation:

1. Find the markers and the segmentation criterion (the function that is to be used to split the regions; often, this is the contrast/gradient).
2. Run a marker-controlled watershed algorithm with these two elements.

Getting ready

Let's import all of the packages, modules, and functions required to demonstrate morphological segmentation with the watershed algorithm:

```
from scipy import ndimage as ndi
from skimage.morphology import watershed, binary_dilation, binary_erosion, remove_small_objects
from skimage.morphology import disk, square
from scipy.ndimage import distance_transform_edt
from skimage.measure import label, regionprops
from skimage.segmentation import clear_border
from skimage.filters import rank, threshold_otsu
from skimage.feature import peak_local_max, blob_log
from skimage.util import img_as_ubyte
from skimage.io import imread
from skimage.color import rgb2gray
import numpy as np
import matplotlib.pyplot as plt
```

How to do it...

In this recipe, we will segment a couple of images (the first one is a binary image and the second is a grayscale image) using scikit-image's morphological watershed implementation, by creating the markers in two different ways:

- By finding peaks in the Euclidean distance image
- By finding low-gradient regions in the gradient image

Morphological watershed

Perform the following steps to use `skimage.morphology` module's implementation of a morphological watershed for binary image segmentation:

1. First, read the image of input binary circles and convert it into grayscale with an unsigned integer type:

   ```
   image = img_as_ubyte(rgb2gray(imread('images/circles.png')))
   ```

2. Compute the exact Euclidean distance transform and find peaks in it, labeling them subsequently to use them as markers for the watershed algorithm:

   ```
   distance = ndi.distance_transform_edt(image)
   local_maximum = peak_local_max(distance, indices=False,
   footprint=np.ones((3, 3)), labels=image)
   markers = ndi.label(local_maximum)[0]
   ```

3. Now, run the `watershed` algorithm with the marker created to get the output segmentation labels. Remove small objects to get rid of noise, if necessary:

   ```
   labels = watershed(-distance, markers, mask=image)
   labels = remove_small_objects(labels, min_size=100)
   ```

4. Compute the number of segmented objects (`labels`) in the output and the number of unique classes (`labels`):

   ```
   props = regionprops(labels)
   print(len(np.unique(labels)), len(props))
   # 23 22
   ```

[153]

Binary Image Processing

If you run the preceding code snippets and plot the images, you will get a diagram along the lines of the following:

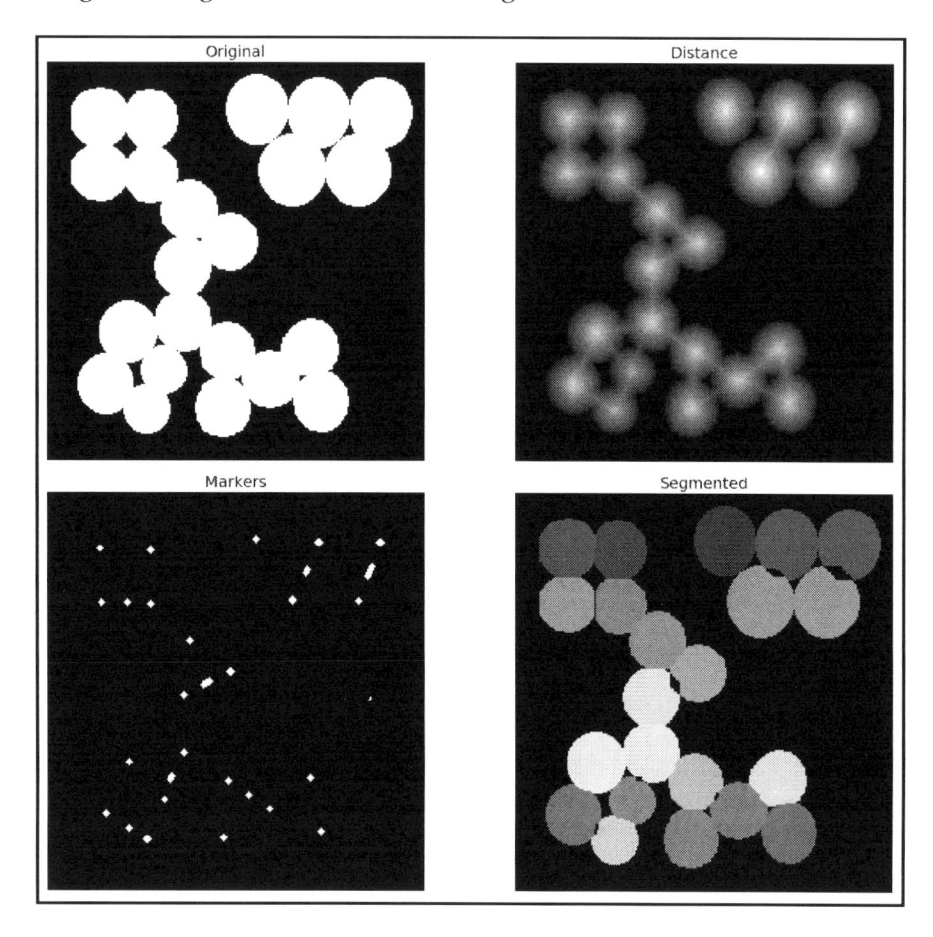

5. Now, run the morphological watershed algorithm on another image (of a lotus), but this time, create the markers by thresholding on the gradient (find continuous low gradient regions as markers and use a disk SE with a radius of 5 to get a smoother image). Denoise the image with the `median` filter to start with:

```
denoised = rank.median(image, disk(2))
markers = rank.gradient(denoised, disk(5)) < 20
markers = ndi.label(markers)[0]
```

6. Run the morphological watershed as you did last time, but this time, with `gradient` and `marker` as input (use the local gradient with SE as a disk of a small radius, 2, to keep the edges thin):

```
gradient = rank.gradient(denoised, disk(2))
labels = watershed(gradient, markers)
labels = remove_small_objects(labels, min_size=100)
props = regionprops(labels)
print(len(np.unique(labels)), len(props))
# 111 110
```

If you run the preceding code snippets and plot the images, you will get the following output:

If you plot the gradient image in 3D, you will get the following output:

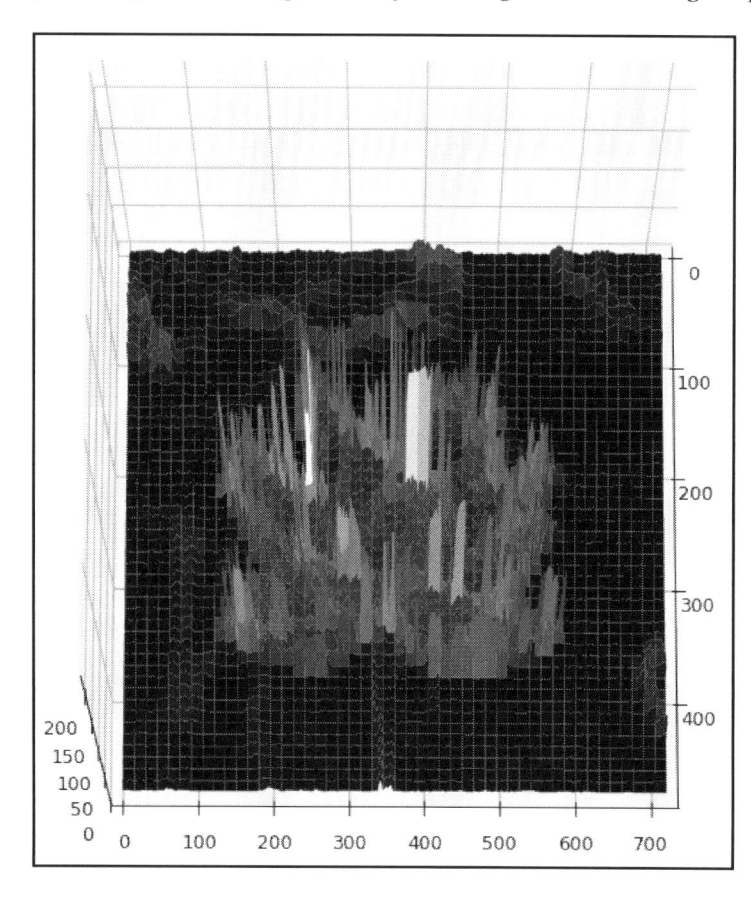

Blob detection with morphological watershed

Perform the following steps to use the `skimage.morphology` module's watershed again, this time for blob detection:

1. Implement the `segment_with_watershed()` function, which will detect the blobs in an image:

```
def segment_with_watershed(im, cell_thresh, bg_thresh):
  if np.max(im) != 1.0:
      im = (im - im.min()) / (im.max() - im.min())
  im_mask = im < cell_thresh
```

2. Generate the catchment, basins:

   ```
   basins = np.zeros_like(im)
   basins[im < cell_thresh] = 2
   basins[im > bg_thresh] = 1
   ```

3. Run the watershed segmentation by flooding basins:

   ```
   flood_seg = watershed(im , basins)
   flood_seg = flood_seg > 1.0
   ```

4. Now, erode the boundaries and compute the distance transform:

   ```
   selem = square(3)
   flood_erode = binary_erosion(flood_seg, selem=selem)
   flood_seg = clear_border(flood_seg, buffer_size=10)
   ```

5. Compute the distance matrix with the following line of code:

   ```
   distances = distance_transform_edt(flood_seg)
   ```

6. Find the local maxima in the distance matrix:

   ```
   local_max = peak_local_max(distances, indices=False,
   footprint=None, labels=flood_seg,
   min_distance=1)
   max_lab = label(local_max)
   ```

7. Perform the topological watershed. Remove any stray small objects:

   ```
   final_seg = watershed(-distances, max_lab, mask=flood_seg)
   final_seg = remove_small_objects(final_seg, min_size=100)
   ```

8. Extract the region properties and determine the number of cells. Return the results:

   ```
   props = regionprops(final_seg)
   num_cells = len(props)
   return final_seg, distances, basins, num_cells
   ```

9. Now, read the input image, convert it into grayscale, denoise it, and find the blobs in it by calling the img_as_ubyte() function. Print the number of segments returned:

   ```
   image = img_as_ubyte(rgb2gray(imread('images/sunflowers.jpg')))
   image = rank.median(image, disk(2))
   labels, distances, markers, nseg = segment_with_watershed(image,
   0.25, 0.28)
   ```

Binary Image Processing

```
print(nseg)
# 44
```

If you run the preceding code snippets, you will get the following output, with the blobs detected, as shown:

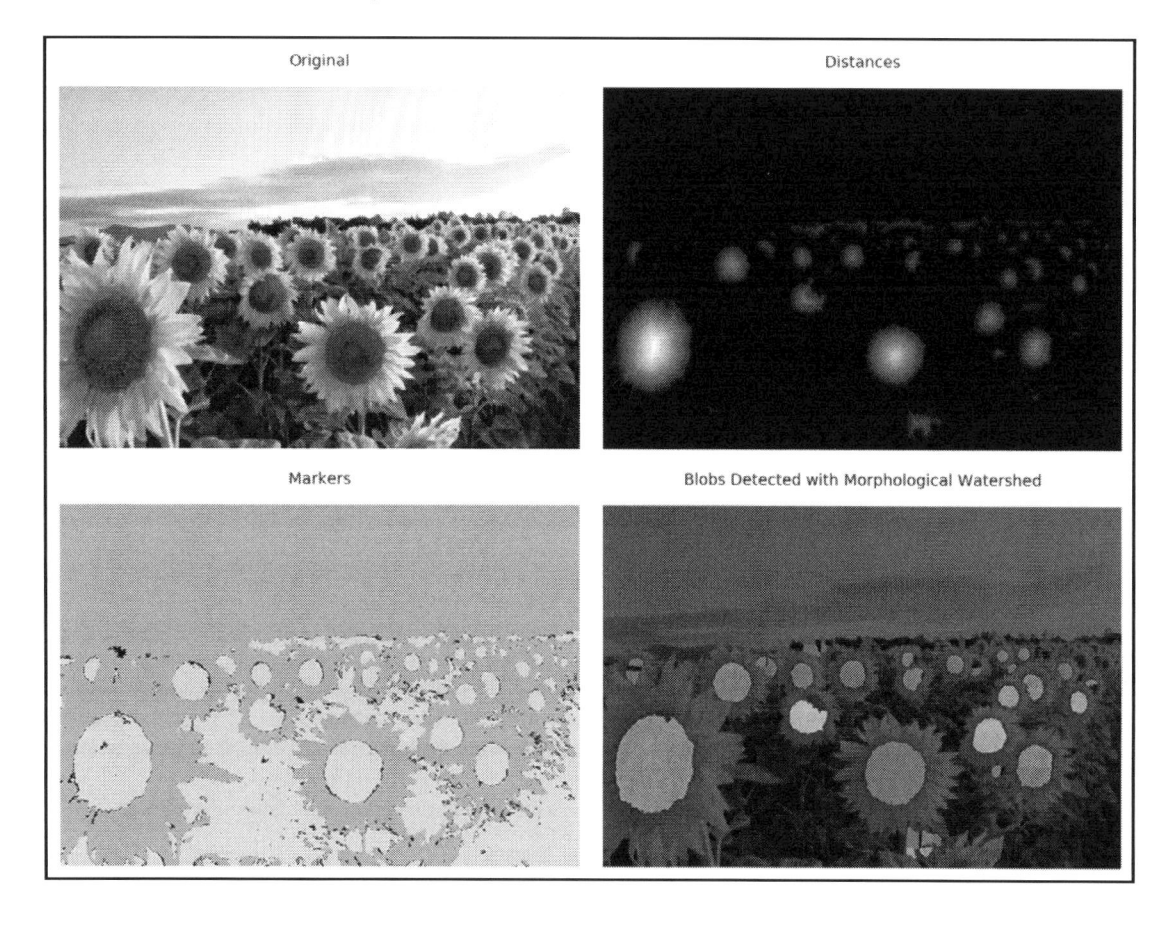

How it works...

The `watershed()` function from the `skimage.morphology` module was used to find the watershed basins in the input image, where the flooding started from the given markers. This function accepts the image and the markers (optional) as input arguments. The `watershed()` function accepts an ndarray marker with locations of the basins marked (the pixel values are used to assign the pixels in the label matrix) as the second argument (0 means not a marker).

The `distance_transform_edt()` function from `scipy.ndimage.morphology` was used to compute the exact Euclidean transform given by the following equation:

$$d_p = \sqrt{(p_x - b_x)^2 + (p_y - b_y)^2}$$

Here, *b* is the nearest background pixel to an input pixel, *p* (having the smallest Euclidean distance); the distance, d_p, between *p* and *b* is returned.

The `label()` function from the `ski.ndimage` module was used to label the features in the markers obtained by peaking the local maximum values from the Euclidean distance transform or by thresholding the gradient image. This function assigns a unique label to each of the unique features in the input image. The `regionprops()` function from the `skimage.measure` module was used to obtain a list of region properties, where each item describes one labeled region.

There's more...

You can detect blobs using LOG scale-space also. The following is a demonstration of blob detection using this method; compare it with the one obtained using morphological watershed.

Blob detection with LOG scale-space

Perform the following steps for blob detection in the LOG space:

1. Find the blobs in the image using the `blob_log()` function:

   ```
   blobs_log = blob_log(np.invert(image), max_sigma=40, num_sigma=10,
   threshold=.2)
   ```

2. Compute radii in the third column:

   ```
   blobs_log[:, 2] = blobs_log[:, 2] * np.sqrt(2)
   ```

3. Loop over the blobs found and draw them on the output image, ignoring blobs with a small radius:

   ```
   for blob in blobs_log:
     y, x, r = blob
     if np.pi*r**2 > 150:
       c = plt.Circle((x, y), r, color=[0.75] + \
           np.random.rand(2).tolist(), linewidth=2, \
   ```

```
        fill=True, alpha=.7)
# add the blobs to the plot
```

If you run the preceding code snippets and plot the images, you will get a diagram along the lines of in the following:

See also

Refer to the following links to learn more about this recipe:

- `https://www.doc.ic.ac.uk/~dfg/vision/v02.html`
- `https://scikit-image.org/docs/dev/api/skimage.morphology.html#skimage.morphology.watershed`
- `https://docs.scipy.org/doc/scipy/reference/generated/scipy.ndimage.label.html`

Counting objects

In this recipe, you will learn how to use morphological filters to count objects in a binary image. Often, the objects (blobs) in a binary image are overlapping and, before counting them, we need to do some necessary preprocessing, such as blob separation and detection. Morphological erosion can be quite useful in these cases. Then, contour-finding can be used to count the separated objects. You can use morphological watershed segmentation, too, to separate the blobs and then count them.

Getting ready

Let's import the packages and modules required to start with:

```
import cv2
import numpy as np
import matplotlib.pylab as plt
```

How to do it...

First, we will detect blobs and separate them, and then we will start with object counting.

Blob separation and detection with erosion

Perform the following steps to detect and separate blobs using morphological erosion, this time using OpenCV-Python functions:

1. Read the image of grayscale circles and convert it into a binary image using thresholding:

   ```
   image = cv2.imread('images/circles.png', 0)
   image = cv2.threshold(image, 100, 255, cv2.THRESH_BINARY)[1]
   ```

2. Create the SE (kernel) for binary erosion (with a different kernel size) and erode the image:

   ```
   kernel = np.ones((21,21),np.uint8)
   eroded = cv2.morphologyEx(image, cv2.MORPH_ERODE, kernel)
   kernel = np.ones((11,11),np.uint8)
   eroded1 = cv2.morphologyEx(image, cv2.MORPH_ERODE, kernel)
   ```

3. Now, find the contours of the eroded image with the following line of code:

   ```
   cnts, _ = cv2.findContours(eroded, cv2.RETR_EXTERNAL, cv2.CHAIN_APPROX_SIMPLE)
   ```

4. Finally, draw the contours on the input image, using different colors:

   ```
   output = cv2.cvtColor(image.copy(), cv2.COLOR_GRAY2RGB)
   count = 0
   for c in cnts:
     cv2.drawContours(output, [c], -1, (np.random.randint(0,255), \
           np.random.randint(0,255), np.random.randint(0,255)), 2)
     count += 1
   ```

Binary Image Processing

If you run the preceding code snippets and plot the images, you will get the following output:

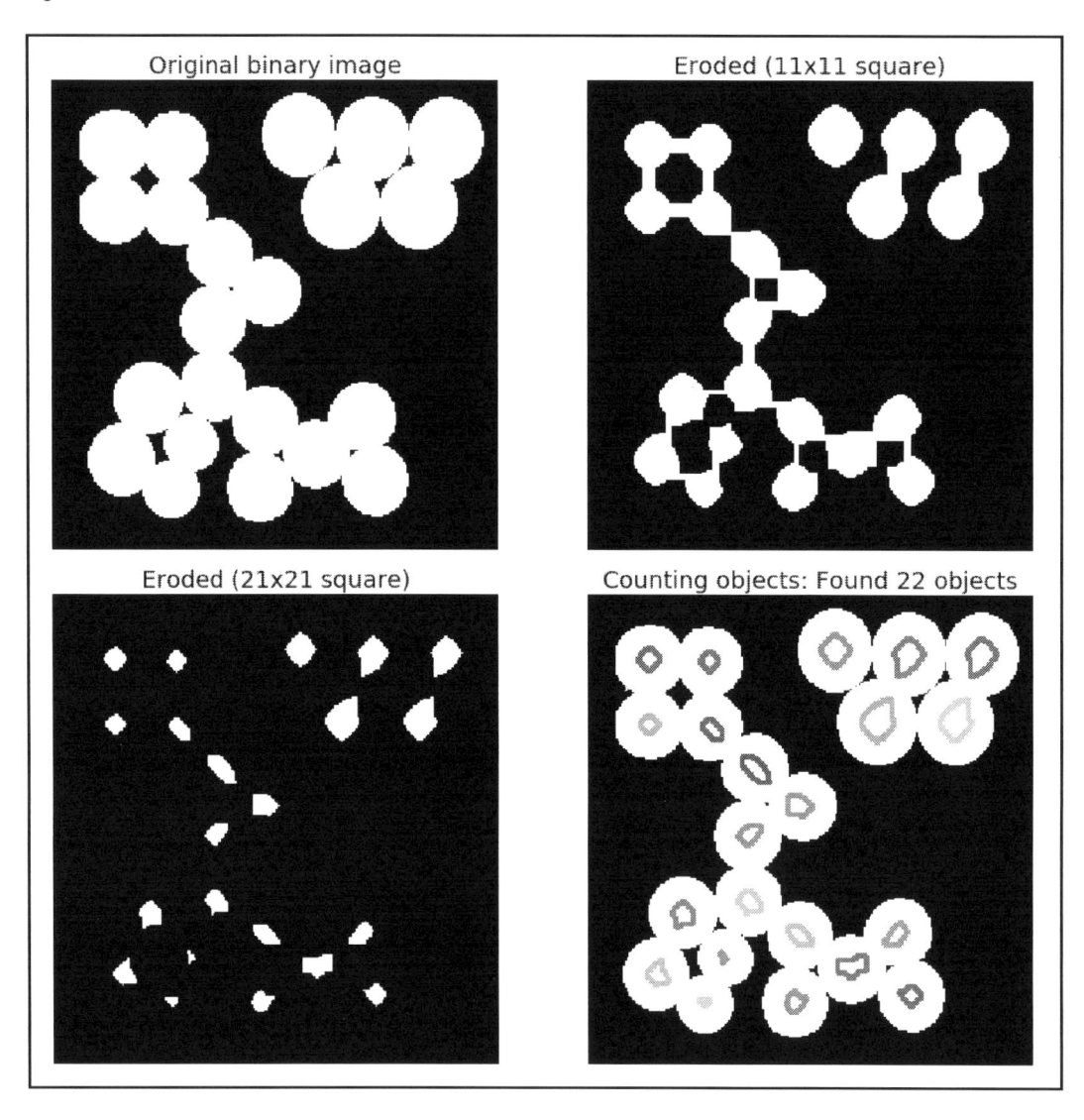

As you can see from the preceding output, the connected circles are separated and all of the 22 circles are detected.

Object counting with closing and opening

Perform the following steps to count objects using morphological closing and opening, again using OpenCV-Python functions:

1. Read the `rasagolla` input (a typical Bengali sweet dish) image, convert it into grayscale, and invert:

   ```
   image = cv2.imread('images/rasagolla.jpg')
   gray = cv2.cvtColor(image, cv2.COLOR_BGR2GRAY)
   gray = cv2.bitwise_not(gray) #255 - gray
   ```

2. Use the Canny edge detector to find the edges in the image, threshold the edge image, and then, using a 4 x 4 square SE, apply binary closing followed by binary opening to the thresholded edge image (to separate the objects):

   ```
   edged = cv2.Canny(gray, 50, 150)
   thresh = cv2.threshold(gray, 100, 255, cv2.THRESH_BINARY_INV)[1]
   kernel = np.ones((4,4),np.uint8)
   thresh = cv2.morphologyEx(thresh, cv2.MORPH_CLOSE, kernel) #Close
   thresh = cv2.morphologyEx(thresh, cv2.MORPH_OPEN, kernel)  #Open
   ```

3. Now, find the contours (that is, outlines) of the foreground objects in the image obtained from the preceding code:

   ```
   _, cnts, _ = cv2.findContours(thresh.copy(), cv2.RETR_EXTERNAL, cv2.CHAIN_APPROX_SIMPLE)
   ```

4. Finally, iterate over the contours found, to draw them on the output image (using different colors again), by ignoring the small objects:

   ```
   output = image.copy()
   count = 0
   for c in cnts:
       if cv2.contourArea(c) > 5: # ignore small objects
           cv2.drawContours(output, [c], -1, \
                    (np.random.randint(0,255), \
                     np.random.randint(0,255), \
                     np.random.randint(0,255)), 2)
           count += 1
   ```

If you run the preceding code snippets and plot the images, you will get the following output with all eight objects detected:

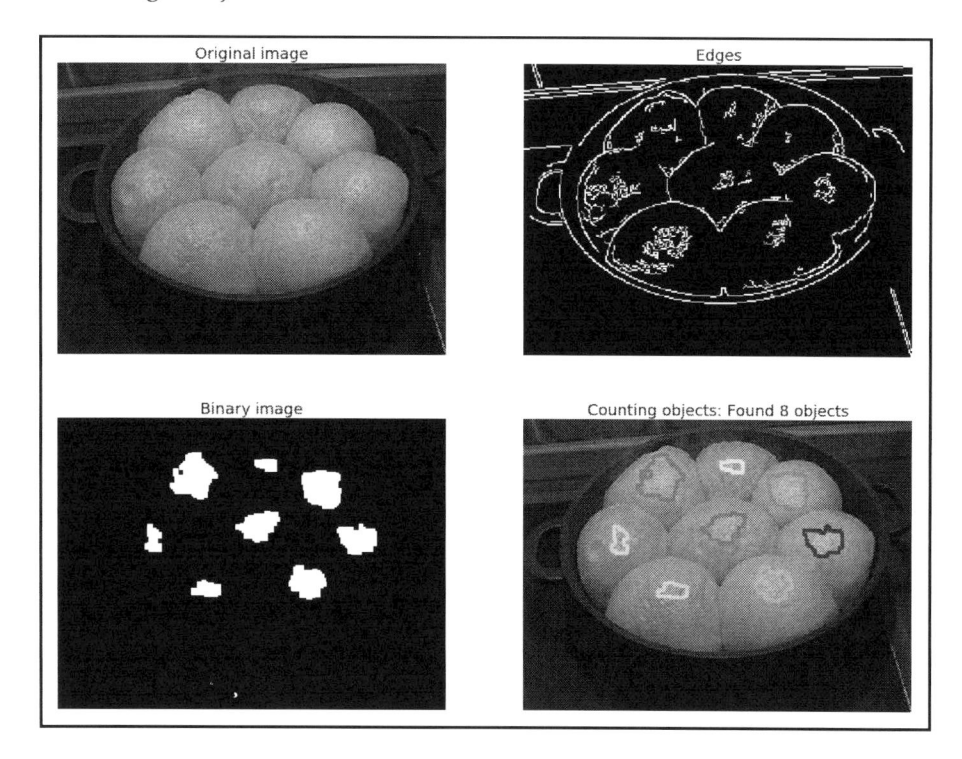

How it works...

The `morphologyEx()` function from `opencv-python` is used to apply morphological operations to an image. The function accepts the source image (that is, the binary image) and a morphological operation (such as `cv2.MORPH_CLOSE` and `cv2.MORPH_OPEN`) and the SE kernel (for example, `np.ones((4,4),np.uint8)` for a 4 x 4 square kernel) for the morphological operation.

The `cv2.findContours()` and `cv2.drawContours()` functions were used to find and draw the contours, respectively. Each contour on the output image was drawn with a random color outline and then displayed one at a time by looping over the contours found.

`(np.random.randint(0,255), np.random.randint(0,255), np.random.randint(0,255))` was used to generate a random *BGR* tuple. The `cv2.contourArea()` function was used to discard small objects with an area less than or equal to 5.

Chapter 4

There's more...

Detect and separate the objects from the following binary image using morphological operations:

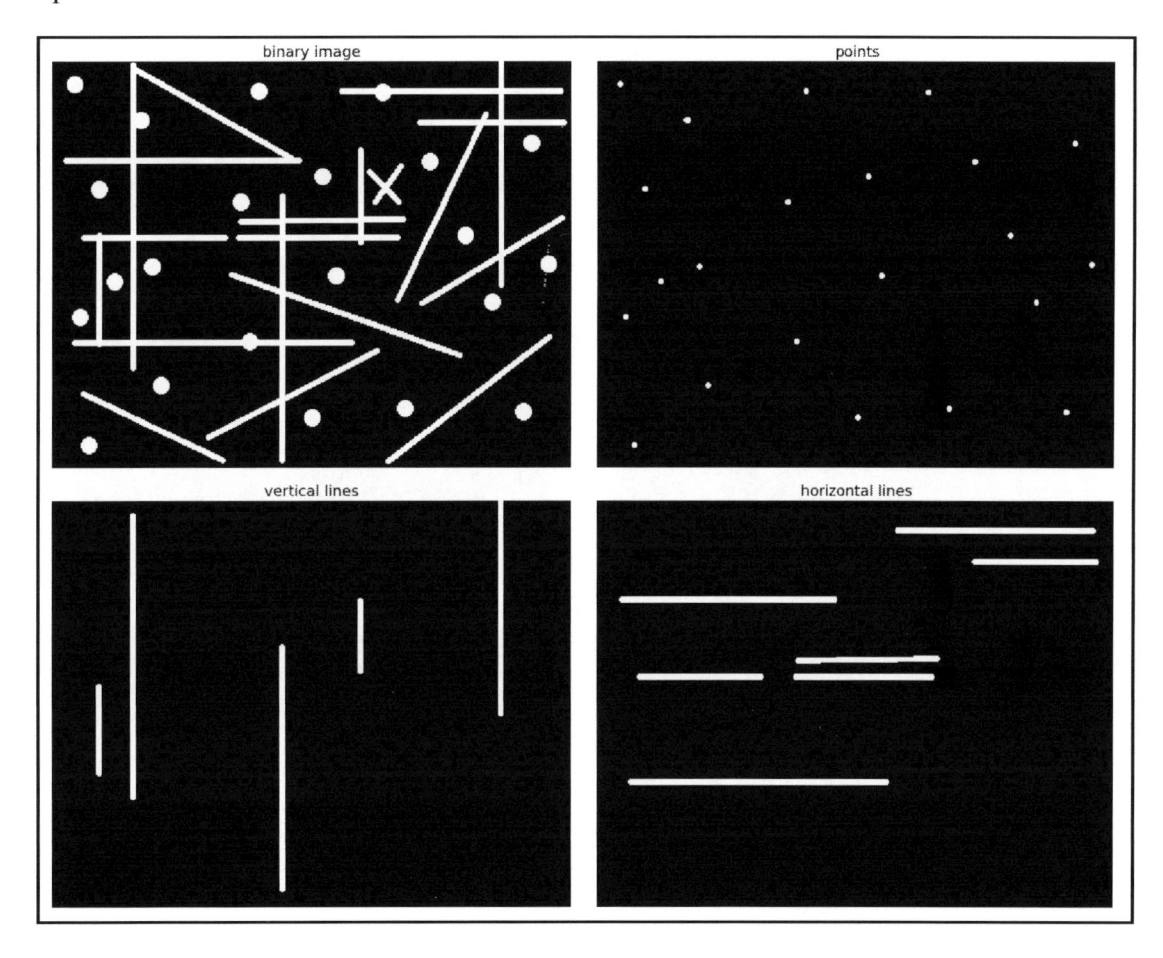

Can you also detect the lines that are neither vertical nor horizontal from the binary input image?

Binary Image Processing

Now, do some geospatial image processing: count the number of islands from the following map image (of a mangrove forest in India named *Sundarban*), and you will get diagram along the lines of the following:

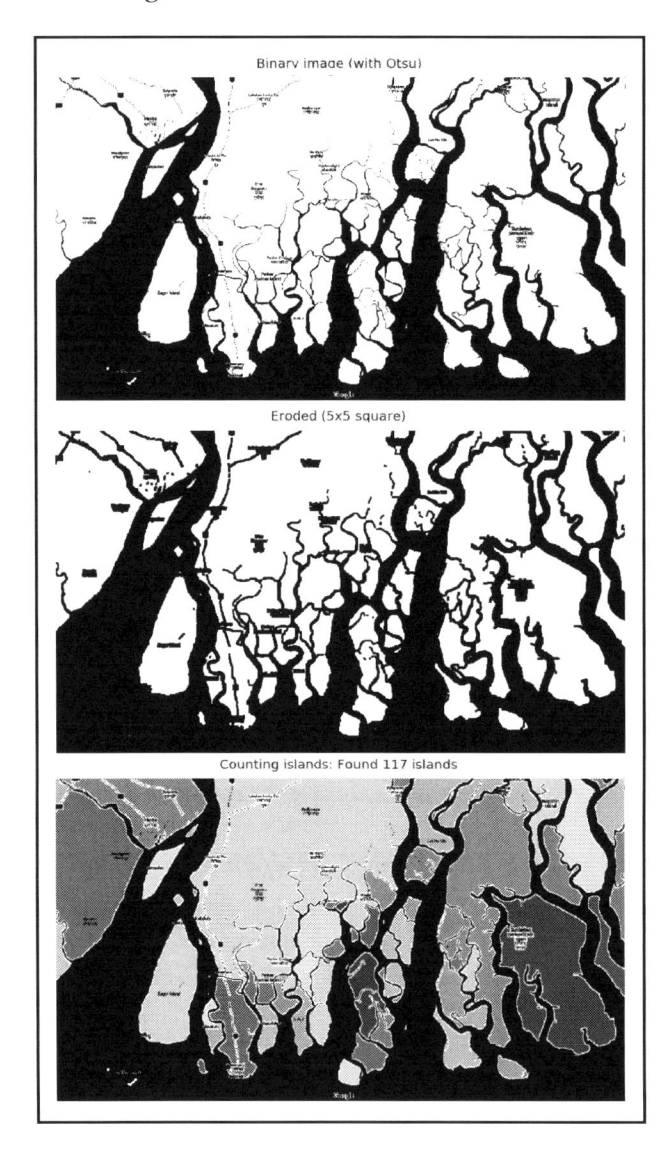

Binary image (with Otsu)

Eroded (5x5 square)

Counting islands: Found 117 islands

See also

Refer to the following articles to learn more about this recipe:

- `https://docs.opencv.org/3.0-beta/doc/py_tutorials/py_imgproc/py_morphological_ops/py_morphological_ops.html`
- `https://docs.opencv.org/trunk/d4/d86/group__imgproc__filter.html#ga67493776e3ad1a3df63883829375201f`
- `https://www.pyimagesearch.com/2015/11/02/watershed-opencv/`

5
Image Registration

Image registration refers to an image processing task where the objective is to align a target image with a source image. In more general terms, it aims to compute the spatial transform (function) that maps (some) points from one image to the corresponding points in the other image. Often, finding a transformation from one image to another is referred to as alignment and then actually performing the image warping procedure using the estimated transform is called **registration**. There are three general philosophies to compare to determine alignment:

- Intensity-based (compare actual pixel values from one image to another, for example, with mutual information)
- Segmentation-based (register the binary segmentation)
- Landmark (or feature)-based (mark key points in both images and derive a transform that makes every pair of landmarks match)

The transformations that we will estimate (to register the images) may be any of the following types:

- Rigid (rotate, translate)
- Affine (rigid + scale and shear/skew)
- Deformable (free-form = affine + vector field)

Many other types of transformations are also possible.

In this chapter, we will concentrate on intensity- and feature-based image registration techniques and their applications, and we will go through the following recipes:

- Medical image registration with SimpleITK
- Image alignment with ECC algorithm and warping
- Face alignment with dlib
- Robust matching and homography with the RANSAC algorithm
- Image mosaicing (panorama)

- Face morphing
- Implementing an image search engine

Medical image registration with SimpleITK

As discussed, the objective of registration is to estimate the transformation that associates the points in given input images. The transformation estimated via registration is said to map points from the **fixed** to the **moving** image coordinate system. SimpleITK provides a configurable multi-resolution registration framework, implemented in the `ImageRegistrationMethod` class. To create a specific registration instance using `ImageRegistrationMethod`, you need to select several components that together define the registration instance:

- Transformation
- Similarity metric
- Optimizer
- Interpolator

The following diagram shows the components of the registration framework in SimpleITK:

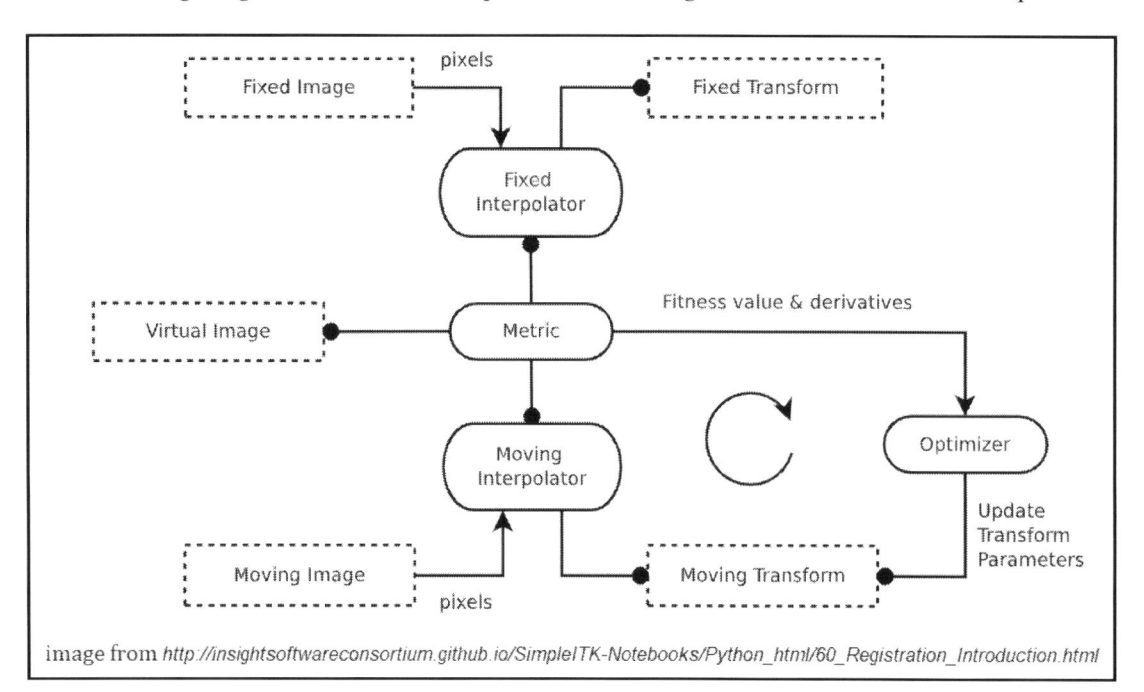

Image registration is done using optimization in the parameter space (the transform to be applied to the moving image to align with the fixed image is defined by the parameters); these parameters are tweaked using an optimization algorithm to optimize a similarity metric computed between the images.

Getting ready

We are going to use a CT-scan image and an MRI-T1 image for the demonstration of image-registration using `SimpleITK`. These images were extracted from the raw (`.mhd`) files downloaded from https://www.insight-journal.org/rire/download.php (download the ZIP and extract the files after agreeing to the license). Let's start by loading the required libraries, as you always do:

```
%matplotlib inline
import SimpleITK as sitk
import numpy as np
import matplotlib.pyplot as plt
```

How to do it...

Execute the following steps to implement image registration with `SimpleITK`:

1. First, read the images to be aligned, a CT-scan image as the fixed (target) image, and an MRI-T1 image as the moving (source) image:

    ```
    fixed_image = sitk.ReadImage("images/ct_scan_11.jpg", \
                                  sitk.sitkFloat32)
    moving_image = sitk.ReadImage("images/mr_T1_06.jpg", \
                                   sitk.sitkFloat32)
    ```

2. Convert the `SimpleITK` Image objects into NumPy arrays to display the images using `matplotlib`:

    ```
    fixed_image_array = sitk.GetArrayFromImage(fixed_image)
    moving_image_array = sitk.GetArrayFromImage(moving_image)
    print(fixed_image_array.shape, moving_image_array.shape)
    # (512, 512) (512, 512)
    ```

Image Registration

The following screenshot shows the fixed and the moving images and their initial alignment (as you can see they are not properly aligned):

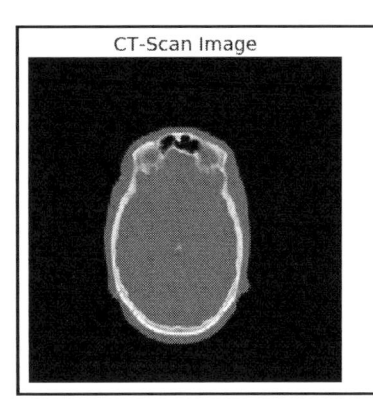

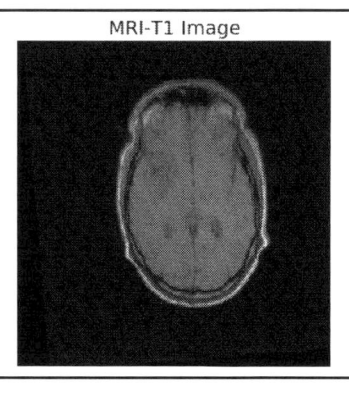

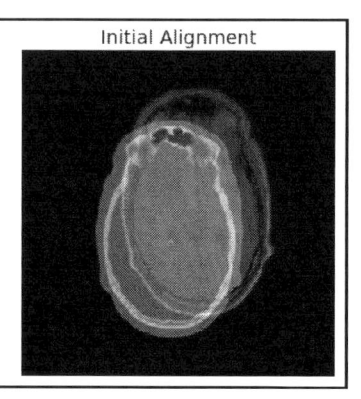

3. Create an instance of the `ImageRegistrationMethod` class, which implements a configurable multi-resolution registration framework in `SimpleITK`:

   ```
   registration_method = sitk.ImageRegistrationMethod()
   ```

4. Use the `CenteredTransformInitializer()` method to align the centers of the input images and define the center of the fixed image as the center of rotation:

   ```
   initial_transform = sitk.CenteredTransformInitializer(fixed_image, \
                       moving_image, sitk.Similarity2DTransform())
   ```

5. Set the similarity metric as the `MattesMutualInformation` metric and the interpolator as a simple linear interpolator using the following code lines of code:

   ```
   registration_method.SetMetricAsMattesMutualInformation(numberOfHistogramBins=50)
   registration_method.SetInterpolator(sitk.sitkLinear)
   ```

6. Set the optimizer as a gradient descent optimizer with the learning rate parameter initialized to `1.0` and the number of iterations set to `100`:

   ```
   registration_method.SetOptimizerAsGradientDescent(learningRate=1.0,
   numberOfIterations=100, convergenceMinimumValue=1e-6,
   convergenceWindowSize=10)
   ```

7. Apply the initial transformation and then perform registration with the settings from the preceding steps to obtain the estimated final transform:

   ```
   registration_method.SetInitialTransform(initial_transform,
   inPlace=False)
   final_transform =
   registration_method.Execute(sitk.Cast(fixed_image,
   sitk.sitkFloat32),
    sitk.Cast(moving_image, sitk.sitkFloat32))
   ```

8. Resample the moving (source) image according to the final transformation obtained in the last step to obtain an image aligned to the fixed (target) image:

   ```
   resampler = sitk.ResampleImageFilter()
   resampler.SetReferenceImage(fixed_image)
   resampler.SetInterpolator(sitk.sitkLinear)
   resampler.SetDefaultPixelValue(100)
   resampler.SetTransform(final_transform)
   out = resampler.Execute(moving_image)
   ```

9. Finally, combine the target image with the transformed (aligned) source image (to visualize the alignment):

   ```
   simg1 = sitk.Cast(sitk.RescaleIntensity(fixed_image), \
                    sitk.sitkUInt8)
   simg2 = sitk.Cast(sitk.RescaleIntensity(out), sitk.sitkUInt8)
   cimg = sitk.Compose(simg1, simg2, simg1//2.+simg2//2.)
   ```

   If you run the preceding code snippets and plot the target (CT-scan) image, aligned source (MRI-T1) image, and combined image, you will get an output like the following screenshot:

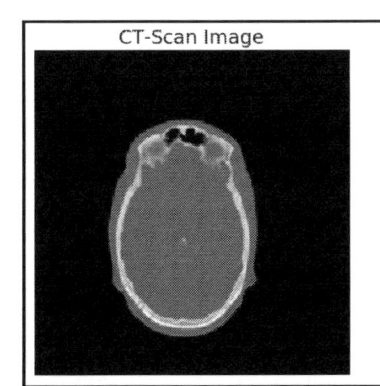

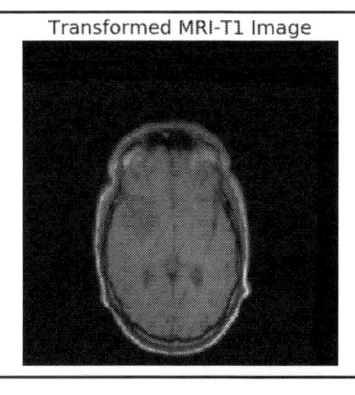

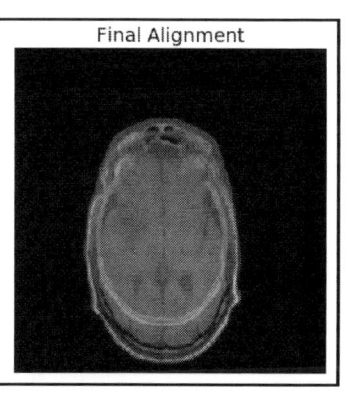

Image Registration

How it works...

The `ImageRegistrationMethod` class provides an interface method to the modular `SimpleITK` (v4) registration framework. This class captures all of the necessary elements required to execute a simple image registration between two images.

Registration will done using optimization; the `SetOptimizerAsGradientDescent()` method implements a simple gradient descent optimizer. At each iteration, the current parameter is updated according to the following equation (where *f* is the objective function for the optimization and p_n represents the value of a parameter, *p*, at iteration *n*, with a parameter that can be initialized with a small random value):

$$p_n + 1 = p_n - \text{learningRate} \frac{\delta f(p_n)}{\delta p_n}$$

The parameters passed to the gradient descent function are `learningRate` (defaults to `1.0`), `numberOfIterations` (the number of iterations to run the gradient descent algorithm), `convergenceMinimumValue` (when the convergence value reaches this value, the algorithm is treated as converged), and `convergenceWindowSize`.

The `SetMetricAsMattesMutualInformation()` method is used to register two images with the mutual information between them using the method of Mattes et al.

There's more

Plot the metric value during the gradient descent iterations (using the `SimpleITK` observers); it should look like the following curve (the metric value should increase with iterations in general since the mutual information is being maximized and the local maxima obtained need to be highlighted):

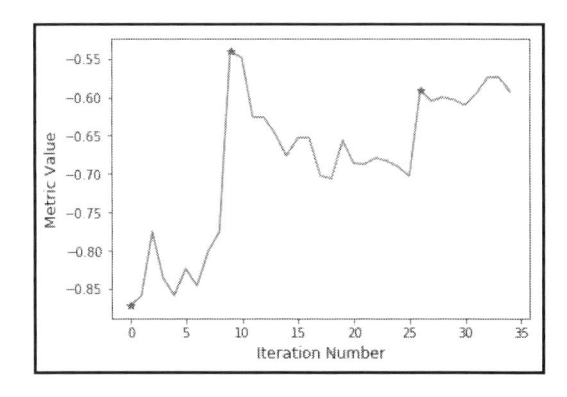

Start with an MRI-T1 image and its shifted (translated) version, as shown in the following image, and register the images using SimpleITK. Use two different similarity metrics (for example, mean-squared and mutual information metrics) and the gradient descent optimizer. You should obtain an output like the following screenshot (notice that mutual information can be used to output better alignment):

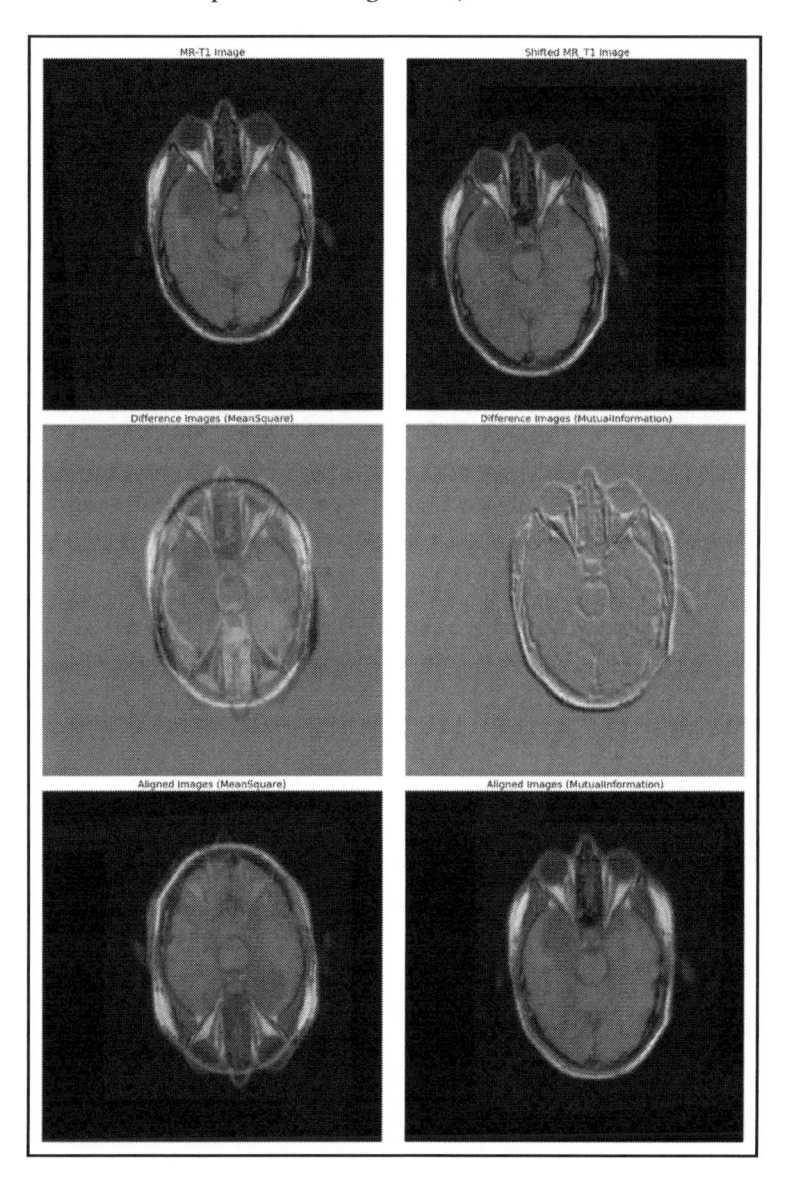

Image Registration

Use checkerboard visualization (hint: use a `SimpleITK` filter) to display the images before and after registration (by combining the pixels from the two input/output images in a checkerboard pattern):

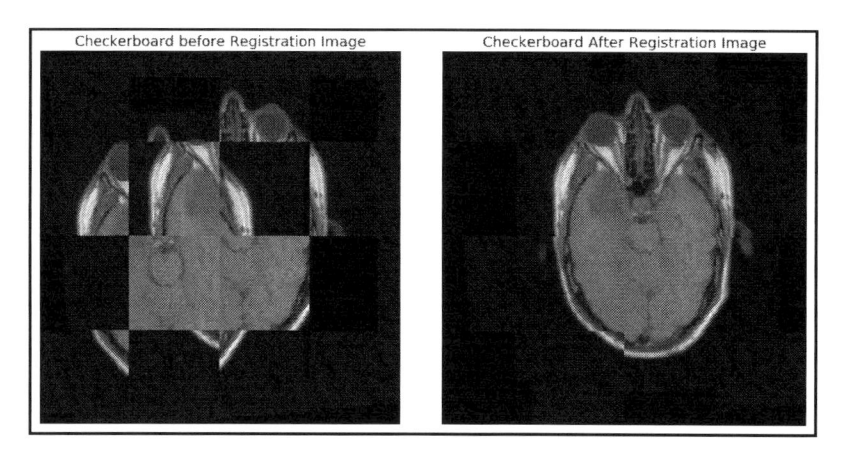

Use SimpleITK's Registration framework to register two images using deformable (non-affine) transformation (for example, elastic transform).

See also

Refer to the following links to learn more about this recipe:

- `https://www.cs.cmu.edu/~galeotti/methods_course/ITK_Registration.pdf`
- `https://buildmedia.readthedocs.org/media/pdf/simpleitk/master/simpleitk.pdf`
- `http://insightsoftwareconsortium.github.io/SimpleITK-Notebooks/Python_html/60_Registration_Introduction.html`
- `https://simpleitk.readthedocs.io/en/master/Documentation/docs/source/registrationOverview.html`
- `https://stackoverflow.com/questions/41692063/what-is-the-difference-between-image-registration-and-image-alignment`
- `https://www.youtube.com/watch?v=MaFiP6RerpM`

Image alignment with ECC algorithm and warping

The parametric image alignment problem involves finding a transformation that aligns two images. In this recipe, you will learn how to estimate the geometric transform (in terms of a warp matrix) between two images using the ECC criterion with OpenCV-Python library's implementation. Given a pair of image profiles (intensities), $I_r(x)$ (the reference image) and $I_w(y)$ (the warped image), and a set of coordinates $T=\{x_k, k=1,..,K\}$ (known as the **target area**), the alignment problem is to find the corresponding coordinate set in the warped image. Assuming φ is the given transformation model, the alignment problem can be extrapolated to the problem of estimating the parameters, *p*, as shown in the following screenshot:

$$\text{Estimate } p: \quad I_r(\mathbf{x}) = I_w(\phi(\mathbf{x};\mathbf{p})), \quad \forall \mathbf{x} \in \mathcal{T}$$

$$\text{Optimization problem: } \min_{\mathbf{p},\alpha} E(\mathbf{p},\alpha) = \min_{\mathbf{p},\alpha} \sum_{\mathbf{x}\in\mathcal{T}} |I_r(\mathbf{x}) - \Psi(I_w(\phi(\mathbf{x};\mathbf{p})),\alpha)|^p$$

$$\text{reference vector:} \quad \mathbf{i}_r = [I_r(\mathbf{x}_1)\ I_r(\mathbf{x}_2)\cdots I_r(\mathbf{x}_K)]^t$$

$$\text{warped vector:} \quad \mathbf{i}_w(\mathbf{p}) = [I_w(\mathbf{y}_1(\mathbf{p}))\ I_w(\mathbf{y}_2(\mathbf{p}))\cdots I_w(\mathbf{y}_K(\mathbf{p}))]^t$$

$$\text{(minimize) ECC criterion:} \quad E_{ECC}(\mathbf{p}) = \left\| \frac{\bar{\mathbf{i}}_r}{\|\bar{\mathbf{i}}_r\|} - \frac{\bar{\mathbf{i}}_w(\mathbf{p})}{\|\bar{\mathbf{i}}_w(\mathbf{p})\|} \right\|^2$$

$$\text{(maximize) enhanced correlation coefficient:} \quad \rho(\mathbf{p}) = \frac{\bar{\mathbf{i}}_r^t \bar{\mathbf{i}}_w(\mathbf{p})}{\|\bar{\mathbf{i}}_r\|\|\bar{\mathbf{i}}_w(\mathbf{p})\|} = \hat{\mathbf{i}}_r^t \frac{\bar{\mathbf{i}}_w(\mathbf{p})}{\|\bar{\mathbf{i}}_w(\mathbf{p})\|}$$

Taken from http://xanthippi.ceid.upatras.gr/people/evangelidis/george_files/PAMI_2008.pdf

ρ(p) is maximized with gradient-based approaches. The ECC criterion does not depend on the changes in contrast/brightness. An approximation to the non-linear objective function is iteratively optimized instead to make the optimizer computationally simple.

Getting ready

In this recipe, we will use a colored (RGB) image whose color channels are not properly aligned (resulting in an improper visualization of the colored image). You will align the color channels using the ECC algorithm and then render the colored image to improve its visualization. Let's start by importing the required libraries as usual:

```
import cv2
import numpy as np
import matplotlib.pylab as plt
```

Image Registration

How to do it...

Follow these steps to implement the **ECC** algorithm using OpenCV-Python:

1. Since the color channels of an image are correlated more strongly in the gradient than in the intensity domain, we will run the ECC algorithm in the gradient domain. Define the `get_gradient()` function, which you will use shortly:

   ```
   def get_gradient(im) :
     grad_x = cv2.Sobel(im,cv2.CV_32F,1,0,ksize=3)
     grad_y = cv2.Sobel(im,cv2.CV_32F,0,1,ksize=3)
     grad = cv2.addWeighted(np.absolute(grad_x), 0.5, \
                  np.absolute(grad_y), 0.5, 0)
     return grad
   ```

2. Read the input RGB image and plot the original image and its unaligned color channels:

   ```
   im_unaligned = cv2.imread("images/me_unaligned.jpg")
   height, width = im_unaligned.shape[:2]
   print(height, width)
   # 992 610
   channels = ['B', 'G', 'R']

   plt.figure(figsize=(30,12))
   plt.gray()
   plt.subplot(1,4,1), plt.imshow(cv2.cvtColor(im_unaligned, \
               cv2.COLOR_BGR2RGB)), plt.axis('off'), \
               plt.title('Unaligned Image (ECC)', size=20)
   for i in range(3):
     plt.subplot(1,4,i+2), plt.imshow(im_unaligned[...,i]), \
               plt.axis('off')
     plt.title(channels[i], size=20)
   plt.suptitle('Unaligned Image and Color Channels', size=30)
   plt.show()
   ```

   If you run the preceding code snippet, you will get an output like the following screenshot:

![Unaligned Image and Color Channels showing four panels: Unaligned Image, B, G, R]

3. Initialize the output image with a copy of the input image:

   ```
   im_aligned = im_unaligned.copy()
   ```

4. Initialize `wrap_mode` to choose a motion model to be estimated:

   ```
   warp_mode = cv2.MOTION_HOMOGRAPHY
   ```

5. Initialize the `warp_matrix` (for example, to the identity matrix) to store the motion model:

   ```
   warp_matrix = np.eye(3, 3, dtype=np.float32)
       # if warp_mode == cv2.MOTION_HOMOGRAPHY
   ```

6. Define the criteria of termination for the iterative algorithm:

   ```
   criteria = (cv2.TERM_CRITERIA_EPS | cv2.TERM_CRITERIA_COUNT, 500,
   1e-6)
   ```

7. Let's say you want to align the B and G channels to the R channel; compute the gradient of R channel first with the following line of code:

   ```
   im_grad2 = compute_gradient(im_unaligned[...,2])
   ```

8. Estimate warp matrices for the first two channels (green and blue) to the red (third) channel using the `findTransformECC()` function. Keep in mind that OpenCV-Python uses the BGR format for an RGB image:

```
for i in range(2) :
    (cc, warp_matrix) = cv2.findTransformECC(im_grad2, \
                       get_gradient(im_unaligned[...,i]), \
                       warp_matrix, warp_mode, criteria)
```

9. Apply `warp_matrix` to the green and blue channels to align it with the red channel (use `warpPerspective` since it is a homography transformation):

```
im_aligned[...,i] = cv2.warpPerspective (im_unaligned[...,i], \
                    warp_matrix, (width,height), \
                    flags=cv2.INTER_LINEAR + cv2.WARP_INVERSE_MAP)
```

If you run the preceding code snippets and then plot the output aligned RGB image and its color channels, you will get an output like the following screenshot:

How it works...

Weighted Sobel horizontal and vertical gradients were used in the `get_gradient()` function to compute the gradient of a color channel. The `findTransformECC()` function from OpenCV-Python was used for the ECC algorithm. The first two parameters accepted by this function were the (single-channel) template image and the input image.

The red color channel was used as a template (reference) and the green/blue color channels were used as inputs. The third parameter passed to the function was `warp_matrix`, which was initialized to the 3x3 identity matrix.

The fourth parameter is the motion model; here, `MOTION_HOMOGRAPHY` was used as the motion model (8 parameters are estimated in the 3x3 warp matrix). The following table lists all possible motion models in OpenCV-Python that can be passed as the value of the parameter, `MOTION_AFFINE` being the default motion model:

Motion Model	Warp Matrix Dimension	Number of parameters to estimate
`MOTION_TRANSLATION`	2x3	2
`MOTION_EUCLIDEAN`	2x3	3
`MOTION_AFFINE`	2x3	6
`MOTION_HOMOGRAPHY`	3x3	8

This function estimates the optimum warp matrix for transformation, with respect to the ECC criterion, as shown here:

$$\text{warpMatrix} = \arg\max_{w} \text{ECC}(\text{templateImage}(x, y), \text{inputImage}(x', y'))$$

$$\text{where } \begin{bmatrix} x' \\ y' \end{bmatrix} = W \cdot \begin{bmatrix} x \\ y \\ 1 \end{bmatrix}$$

The function returns the final enhanced correlation coefficient, computed between the warped input image and the template image. The `findTransformECC()` function uses similarities in intensity to implement an alignment based on area. It updates the initial transformation, aligning the images roughly.

> If the images pass through strong displacements/rotations, an additional transformation needs to be applied a prior to roughly align the images (for example, a simple Euclidean transform resulting in the images with approximately the same content).

The `warpPerspective()` function was used along with the `cv2.WARP_INVERSE_MAP` input flag and the estimated warp matrix to apply an inverse warping on the input image to take the input green/blue color channels close to the reference red color channel.

There is more

Reconstruct the *Prokudin-Gorskii Collection* (it can be found here: `https://www.learnopencv.com/image-alignment-ecc-in-opencv-c-python`) of color images with the ECC algorithm. Use two images that have strong displacements/rotations and use the ECC algorithm to align them with properly initializing `warp_matrix`.

See also

Refer to the following links to learn more about this recipe:

- `http://xanthippi.ceid.upatras.gr/people/evangelidis/george_files/PAMI_2008.pdf`
- `https://docs.opencv.org/3.0-beta/modules/video/doc/motion_analysis_and_object_tracking.html`
- `https://stackoverflow.com/questions/45997891/cv2-motion-euclidean-for-the-warp-mode-in-ecc-image-alignment-method`
- `https://www.learnopencv.com/image-alignment-ecc-in-opencv-c-python/`

Face alignment with dlib

Face alignment can be thought of as an image processing task consisting of the following steps:

1. Identify the *facial landmarks* (or the *facial geometric structure*).
2. Compute a *canonical alignment* by estimating a *geometric transformation* (for example, an *affine transform*) of the face to be *aligned* using the *landmarks*.

Face alignment is a data normalization process—an essential pre-processing step for many facial recognition algorithms. In this recipe, you will first learn how to use the `dlib` library's face detector to detect the faces from an image containing face(s) and then use the shape predictor to extract the facial landmarks from the detected faces. After that, we will warp the input face (using the estimated transformation) to the output face using the facial landmarks extracted.

The key facial attributes of a face (for example, the corners of the mouth, left/right eyes/eyebrows, tip of the nose, jaw, and so on) are identified and labeled with the facial landmarks. The `dlib` library's face detector uses a pre-trained ensemble of regression trees to label the landmarks from input face image's pixel intensities directly (without any feature extraction), with high precision. Next, we will use the `FaceAligner` class from the `imutil` library to align the faces by first estimating and then applying an affine transform between the landmarks extracted from the candidate faces to be aligned.

Getting ready

Import the following libraries to start working on this recipe:

```
from imutils.face_utils import FaceAligner
from imutils.face_utils import rect_to_bb
import imutils
import dlib
import cv2
import matplotlib.pylab as plt
```

How to do it...

Run the following steps to implement facial alignment using the `imutil` library (from PyImagesearch):

1. First, initialize the face detector from `dlib`. Load the pre-trained model as a facial landmark predictor and, finally, instantiate a `FaceAligner` object from `imutils`:

    ```
    detector = dlib.get_frontal_face_detector()
    predictor = dlib.shape_predictor('models/shape_predictor_68_face_landmarks.dat')
    face_aligner = FaceAligner(predictor, desiredFaceWidth=256)
    ```

2. Read the input image from disk, resize the image, and convert it into grayscale:

    ```
    image = cv2.imread('images/scientists.png')
    image = imutils.resize(image, width=800)
    gray = cv2.cvtColor(image, cv2.COLOR_BGR2GRAY)
    ```

Image Registration

Now, if you plot the original image, you will get an output like the following screenshot:

Original Image: Famous Indian Scientists

3. Detect faces in the grayscale image using the following lines of code.

```
rects = detector(gray, 2)
print('Number of faces detected:', len(rects))
# 17
```

Chapter 5

4. Loop over the faces detected; for each of the faces extract the ROI, use facial landmarks to estimate the affine transformation for alignment, and apply the transform to align the face:

```
for rect in rects:
    (x, y, w, h) = rect_to_bb(rect)
    face_original = imutils.resize(image[y:y + h, x:x + w], width=256)
    face_aligned = face_aligner.align(image, gray, rect)
```

Now, if you run the preceding code snippets and plot the detected and aligned faces, you will get an output like the following screenshot (only four faces are shown):

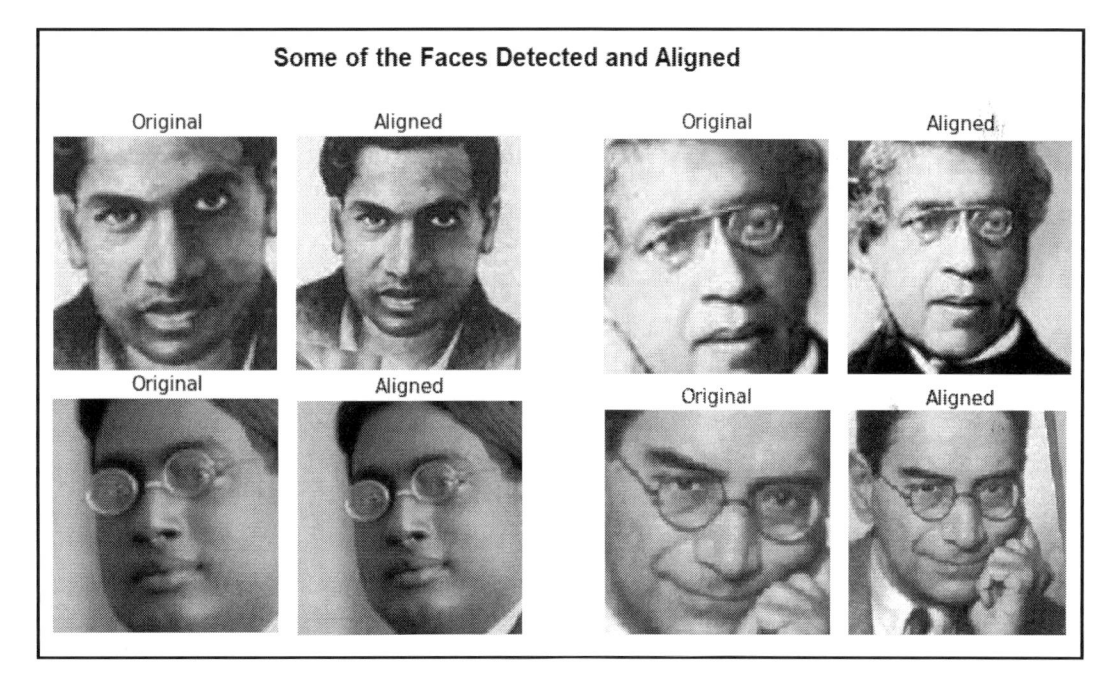

How it works...

The `get_frontal_face_detector()` function (**histogram of oriented gradients** (HOG) feature-based) from the `dlib` library was used to detect the faces. The `shape_predictor()` function from `dlib` was invoked with the serialized *pre-trained facial landmark detector* (the data file) to estimate the (x, y) coordinates of sixty-eight key points that map to facial landmarks (structures) from a given detected face (the `dlib` shape predictor internally implements *Kazemi and Sullivan*'s algorithm, which uses an ensemble of regression trees to estimate the facial landmarks directly from input face pixels without any feature extraction). The landmarks extracted from a face look like as shown in the following screenshot:

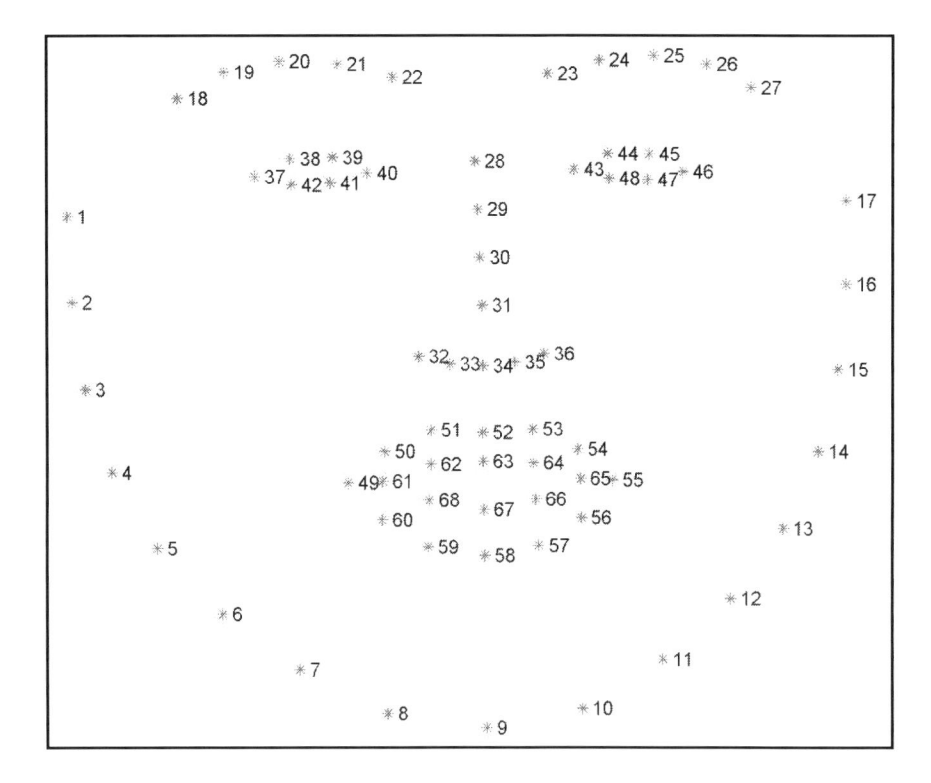

An object of the `FaceAligner` class from the `imutils` library was instantiated with the `shape_predictor` object as an input parameter (since it is required to access the facial landmarks extracted). Its `align()` method was used to align a given detected face.

The `align()` method does the following operations on facial landmarks to align a given face. The angle of rotation between the *eyes* is computed, which allows correcting for rotation. Next, it calculates the scale of the new output image.

Finally, it uses the `warpAffine()` function from the OpenCV-Python library along with the rotation matrix computed and the desired output size as parameters to the function to obtain the aligned output image.

There is more

Start with the following screenshot (obtained from https://www.needpix.com/photo/801551/mona-lisa-painting-leonardo-da-vinci-portrait-young-face-substitution) with the Mona Lisa face present twice in two different orientations and use the `dlib` library's face detector and shape predictor to detect the faces along with the facial landmarks:

Now, use the facial landmarks extracted to estimate an affine transformation (using scikit-image) and then warp the left face on the right face. You should get a figure like the following screenshot if you plot the detected faces and the warped face, along with the facial landmarks extracted:

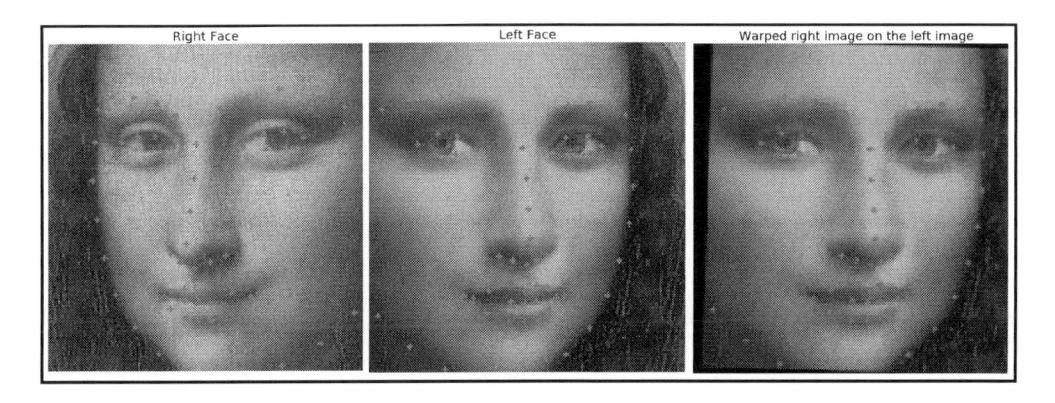

Image Registration

You can use deep learning to align faces too. Try to use `DeepLearningNetwork` and the `face_alignment` library provided in the links in the following *See also* section to align faces. You can also use the `face_alignment` library functions to obtain 2D and 3D facial landmarks (compare with `dlib`), as shown (this is left as an exercise for you to carry out on your own) with Swami Vivekananda's image:

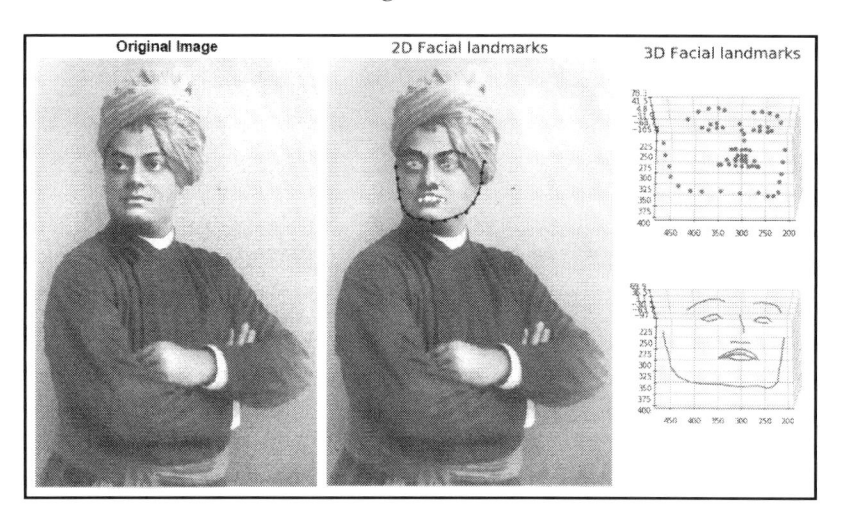

See also

Refer to the following links to learn more about this recipe:

- https://www.pyimagesearch.com/2017/05/22/face-alignment-with-opencv-and-python/
- https://ibug.doc.ic.ac.uk/resources/facial-point-annotations/
- https://www.pyimagesearch.com/2017/05/22/face-alignment-with-opencv-and-python/
- https://github.com/jrosebr1/imutils/tree/master/imutils/face_utils
- https://github.com/MarekKowalski/DeepAlignmentNetwork
- https://github.com/1adrianb/face-alignment/
- http://www.nada.kth.se/~sullivan/Papers/Kazemi_cvpr14.pdf
- https://ieeexplore.ieee.org/document/6909637

Chapter 5

Robust matching and homography with the RANSAC algorithm

Random Sample Consensus (RANSAC) is an iterative non-deterministic algorithm for the robust estimation of parameters of a mathematical model from several random subsets of inliers from the complete dataset (containing outliers). In this recipe, we will use the `skimage.measure` module's implementation of the RANSAC algorithm. Each iteration of the RANSAC algorithm does the following:

1. It selects a random sample of a size of `min_samples` from the original data (hypothetical inliers) and ensures that the sample dataset is valid for fitting the model.

2. It fits a model (that is, estimate the model parameters) to the sampled dataset and ensures that the estimated model is valid.

3. It checks whether the estimated model fits to all of the other data points. Computes the consensus set (`inliers`) and the outliers from all of the data points by computing some model-specific loss function (for example, the residuals) to the estimated model. `inliers` are defined to be the data points that have the smaller residuals than the specified residual threshold.

4. It saves the model (defined by the *estimated model parameters*) as the best model (seen so far) if the number of samples in the consensus set (`inliers`) is *maximal*. If there is a tie (in terms of the number of `inliers`), the model that has fewer *residuals* is considered the best model.

The preceding steps are repeatedly executed either for a maximum number of times (defined by `max_trials`) or until one of the stopping criteria (specified using `stop_sample_num`, `stop_probability`, and so on) is met. The final model is obtained using all `inlier` samples corresponding to the best model found so far. The number of required trials (or random samples chosen) N, so that, with probability p, at least one random sample is free from outliers, is given by the expression shown in the following diagram (a typical value of p we want to have is 0.99 or higher):

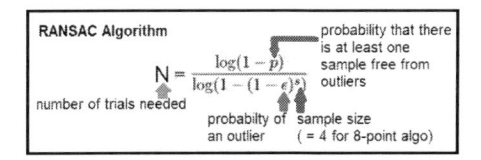

$$N = \frac{\log(1-p)}{\log(1-(1-\varepsilon)^s)}$$

RANSAC Algorithm
- N = number of trials needed
- p = probability that there is at least one sample free from outliers
- ε = probability of an outlier
- s = sample size (= 4 for 8-point algo)

[189]

Getting ready

In this recipe, we will use the RANSAC algorithm to compute a robust match (feature-based alignment) between two images (of the Victoria Memorial Hall in Kolkata) with Harris Corner keypoints and **Binary Robust Independent Elementary Features (BRIEF)** binary descriptors and estimate a robust homography matrix (use the matrix to warp the second image on the first one, with/without using RANSAC). Let's start by importing the libraries required:

```
from skimage.feature import (corner_harris, corner_peaks, BRIEF, match_descriptors, plot_matches)
from skimage.transform import ProjectiveTransform, warp
from skimage.measure import ransac
from skimage.io import imread
from skimage.color import rgb2gray
import numpy as np
import matplotlib.pylab as plt
```

How to do it...

Run the following code segments to see how the RANSAC algorithm makes model fitting robust:

1. Set a random seed using `numpy` (for the sake of reproducible results):

    ```
    np.random.seed(2)
    ```

2. Read the input images to be matched:

    ```
    img1 = rgb2gray(imread('images/victoria3.png'))
    img2 = rgb2gray(imread('images/victoria4.png'))
    ```

3. Extract the Harris Corner keypoints (features) from the input images using the following couple of lines of code:

    ```
    keypoints1 = corner_peaks(corner_harris(img1), min_distance=1)
    keypoints2 = corner_peaks(corner_harris(img2), min_distance=1)
    ```

4. Extract the binary BRIEF descriptors for the keypoints found for both of the input images:

   ```
   extractor = BRIEF(patch_size=10)
   extractor.extract(img1, keypoints1)
   descriptors1 = extractor.descriptors
   extractor.extract(img2, keypoints2)
   descriptors2 = extractor.descriptors
   ```

5. Match the descriptors from the two images and select the keypoints from the images that only match:

   ```
   matches = match_descriptors(descriptors1, descriptors2)
   src_keypoints = keypoints1[matches[:,0]]
   dst_keypoints = keypoints2[matches[:,1]]
   ```

6. Compute the homography matrix of the two images using all of the matched keypoints from the source and the destination images. As you can see, there are 39 matched keypoints:

   ```
   homography = ProjectiveTransform()
   homography.estimate(src_keypoints, dst_keypoints)
   print(len(matches))
   # 39
   ```

7. Now, use the RANSAC algorithm to compute the robust match with the highest number of inliers using the ProjectiveTransform class. You will obtain a different homography matrix this time. As you can see, with the RANSAC algorithm, the number of keypoint matches decreased to 6 (only robust matches survived):

   ```
   homography_robust, inliers = ransac((src_keypoints, dst_keypoints),
                           ProjectiveTransform, min_samples=4,
                           residual_threshold=2, max_trials=500)
   robust_matches = match_descriptors(descriptors1[matches[:,0]]
                           [inliers], descriptors2[matches[:,1]][inliers])
   print(len(robust_matches))
   # 6
   ```

Image Registration

8. Warp the second image onto the first image using the `ProjectiveTransform` objects obtained with/without RANSAC and plot them:

    ```
    img2_proj_with_homography = warp(img2, homography,
    output_shape=img2.shape)
    img2_proj_with_robust_homography = warp(img2, homography_robust,
    output_shape=img2.shape)
    ```

How it works...

If you run the preceding code snippets and plot the matches starting from the keypoints and descriptors obtained with/without RANSAC algorithm and then plot the second image warped onto the first one using the estimated `homography` matrix, you will get an output like the following screenshot:

As you can see from the next screenshot, using the RANSAC algorithm removes all of the wrong matches and generates a much better projective transform.

The `corner_harris()` and `corner_peaks()` functions from `skimage.feature` are used to obtain the Harris Corner keypoints from the input images (it finds points with a large corner response function R, by picking the local maxima in R, as shown in the next screenshot):

$$M_{2\times 2} = \sum_{x,y} w(x,y) \begin{bmatrix} I_x^2 & I_x I_y \\ I_x I_y & I_y^2 \end{bmatrix}$$

where $w(x,y)$ is the window function and the matrix contains image derivatives.

$$R_{corner\ response} = \frac{\det M}{\text{Trace } M}$$

The `skimage.feature` module's `BRIEF` class was instantiated and its `extract()` method was used to compute the binary descriptors corresponding to the keypoints for both images. BRIEF is an efficient binary feature descriptor that is often very discriminative. Hamming distance is often used with a binary descriptor (such as BRIEF) for feature matching, leading to lower computational cost (no floating-point operation is needed) than the L2 norm.

> For the copyright of BRIEF, please refer to the following link:
> https://scikit-image.org/docs/dev/license.html

Again, the `skimage.feature` module's `match_descriptors()` function was used to match the corresponding keypoints and the matched keypoints are only returned. The `skimage.feature` module's `ranac()` function was used to fit a homography model for the transformation with the RANSAC algorithm.

The parameters of the `ransac()` function were the source/destination images, the model class (`ProjectiveTransform`), the number of `min_samples` (set to 4 since the minimum number of data points to estimate `homography` is 8, using the 8-point algorithm), `residual_threshold` (maximum distance for a data point to be classified as an `inlier`), and `max_trials` (maximum number of iterations for the algorithm).

Image Registration

Finally, the `warp()` function was used to apply the projective transform on the destination image (with the `homography` object as the `inverse_map` argument to the function, for using the inverse of the homography matrix estimated with/without RANSAC). The following diagram explains it in detail:

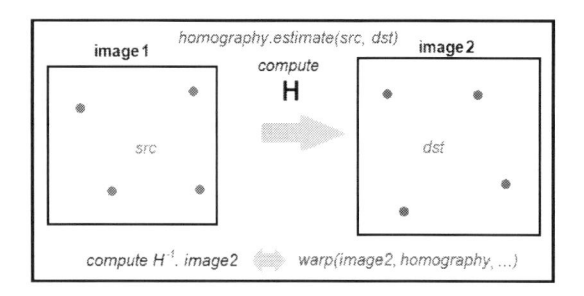

See also

Refer to the following links to learn more about this recipe:

- `https://scikit-image.org/docs/dev/api/skimage.feature.html`
- `https://scikit-image.org/docs/dev/api/skimage.measure.html`
- `https://sandipanweb.wordpress.com/2017/10/22/feature-detection-with-harris-corner-detector-and-matching-images-with-feature-descriptors-in-python/`
- `https://www.cs.ubc.ca/~lowe/525/papers/calonder_eccv10.pdf`
- `https://www.youtube.com/watch?v=l7pna8xYC4I`
- *Chapter 7* of the book, *Hands-on Image Processing with Python*

Image mosaicing (panorama)

Image stitching (also called **image mosaicing**) refers to the image processing task of combining multiple overlapping images to create a (segmented) **panorama** image (alternatively called an **image mosaic**). There are three major components of image stitching:

- Register images (so their features align)
- Determine overlap
- Blend

[194]

In this recipe, you will learn how to implement image stitching by registering a bunch of overlapped images using **Scale-Invariant Feature Transform** (**SIFT**) features (using OpenCV-Python), warping them to match the overlapped regions, and iteratively adding new regions not present in the image mosaic so far. You will also learn how to use OpenCV-Python library's stitch class method to create image mosaic with a single method invocation.

Getting ready

In this recipe, we will use a few (overlapping) images of Victoria Memorial Hall, Kolkata and stitch them using OpenCV-Python library functions. Let's start by importing the required libraries, as usual:

```
import cv2
import numpy as np
from matplotlib import pyplot as plt
import math
import glob
```

How to do it...

The following are the steps that you will follow (you will have to implement a few functions) to implement image stitching/mosaicing:

1. First, implement the `compute_homography()` function, which computes the homography matrix, h, from two given input images:

    ```
    def compute_homography(image1, image2, bff_match=False):
    ```

2. Similar to the previous recipe, first compute keypoints/descriptors (this time use `SIFT`):

    ```
    sift = cv2.xfeatures2d.SIFT_create(edgeThreshold=10, sigma=1.5, \
                                      contrastThreshold=0.08)
    kp1, des1 = sift.detectAndCompute(image1, None)
    kp2, des2 = sift.detectAndCompute(image2, None)
    ```

3. Match the descriptors using brute-force `knnMatch()` and then select the good matches using Lowe's ratio test:

    ```
    bf = cv2.BFMatcher()   # Brute force matching
    matches = bf.knnMatch(des1, trainDescriptors=des2, k=2)
    good_matches = []
    ```

Image Registration

```
for m, n in matches:
    if m.distance < 0.75 * n.distance:  # Lowes Ratio
        good_matches.append(m)
```

4. Estimate the homography matrix, H, using the keypoints corresponding to the good matches and return H:

```
src_pts = np.float32([kp1[m.queryIdx].pt for m in \
                    good_matches]).reshape(-1, 1, 2)
dst_pts = np.float32([kp2[m.trainIdx].pt for m in \
                    good_matches]).reshape(-1, 1, 2)
if len(src_pts) > 4:
    H, mask = cv2.findHomography(dst_pts, src_pts, cv2.RANSAC, 5)
else:
    H = np.array([[0, 0, 0], [0, 0, 0], [0, 0, 0]])
return H
```

5. Next, implement the `warp_image()` function, which warps an image using a homography matrix, H (as you did in the previous recipe):

```
def warp_image(image, H):
    image = cv2.cvtColor(image, cv2.COLOR_BGR2BGRA)
    h, w, _ = image.shape
```

6. Find the minimum and maximum of *x* and *y* for the new image:

```
p = np.array([[0, w, w, 0], [0, 0, h, h], [1, 1, 1, 1]])
p_prime = np.dot(H, p)
yrow = p_prime[1] / p_prime[2]
xrow = p_prime[0] / p_prime[2]
ymin, xmin, ymax, xmax = min(yrow), min(xrow), max(yrow), \
    max(xrow)
```

7. Create a new matrix that removes the offset and multiply it by the homography matrix, H:

```
new_mat = np.array([[1, 0, -1 * xmin], [0, 1, -1 * ymin], \
                    [0, 0, 1]])
H = np.dot(new_mat, H)
```

8. Compute `height` and `width` of the new image frame:

```
height, width = int(round(ymax - ymin)), int(round(xmax - xmin))
size = (width, height)
```

9. Create a spherical warp of the input image using the homography matrix, H, and return the warped image:

   ```
   warped = cv2.warpPerspective(src=image, M=H, dsize=size)
   return warped, (int(xmin), int(ymin))
   ```

10. Next, implement a function that creates a cylindrical warp of an input image given a homography matrix, H, using the following code snippet:

    ```
    def cylindrical_warp_image(img, H):
        h, w = img.shape[:2]
    ```

11. Convert the pixel coordinates into homogeneous coordinates:

    ```
    y_i, x_i = np.indices((h, w)) # pixel coordinates
    X = np.stack([x_i,y_i,np.ones_like(x_i)],axis=-1).reshape(h*w,3)
    # to homogeneous
    ```

12. Normalize the coordinates:

    ```
    Hinv = np.linalg.inv(H)
    X = Hinv.dot(X.T).T # normalized coords
    ```

13. Calculate the *cylindrical coordinates* ($sin\theta, h, cos\theta$) and convert back into pixel coordinates from the homogeneous coordinates using the following code snippet:

    ```
    A = np.stack([np.sin(X[:,0]),X[:,1],np.cos(X[:,0])],\
                 axis=-1).reshape(w*h,3)
    B = H.dot(A.T).T # project back to image-pixels plane
    B = B[:,:-1] / B[:,[-1]] # back from homogeneous coordinates
    ```

14. Make sure to warp coordinates only within the image bounds:

    ```
    B[(B[:,0] < 0) | (B[:,0] >= w) | (B[:,1] < 0) | \
      (B[:,1] >= h)] = -1
    B = B.reshape(h, w, -1)
    ```

15. Warp the image according to cylindrical coordinates and return `cv2.remap`:

    ```
    return cv2.remap(img_rgba, B[:,:,0].astype(np.float32), \
                     B[:,:,1].astype(np.float32), cv2.INTER_AREA, \
                     borderMode=cv2.BORDER_TRANSPARENT)
    ```

Image Registration

16. Implement a function to create an image mosaic given a set of input images and the corresponding origins as parameters:

    ```
    def create_mosaic(images, origins):
    ```

17. Find the central image and the corresponding origin first:

    ```
    for i in range(0, len(origins)):
        if origins[i] == (0, 0):
            central_index = i
            break

    central_image = images[central_index]
    central_origin = origins[central_index]
    ```

18. Zip `origins` and `images` together and sort by distance from the origin (highest to lowest):

    ```
    zipped = list(zip(origins, images))
    # sort by distance from origin
    func = lambda x: math.sqrt(x[0][0] ** 2 + x[0][1] ** 2)
    dist_sorted = sorted(zipped, key=func, reverse=True)
    x_sorted = sorted(zipped, key=lambda x: x[0][0])
    # sort by x value
    y_sorted = sorted(zipped, key=lambda x: x[0][1])
    # sort by y value
    ```

19. Determine the coordinates in the new frame of the central image:

    ```
    if x_sorted[0][0][0] > 0: cent_x = 0
        # leftmost image is central image
    else:   cent_x = abs(x_sorted[0][0][0])
    if y_sorted[0][0][1] > 0: cent_y = 0
        # topmost image is central image
    else:   cent_y = abs(y_sorted[0][0][1])
    ```

20. Create a new list of the starting points in a new frame of each image:

    ```
    spots = []
    for origin in origins:
        spots.append((origin[0]+cent_x, origin[1] + cent_y))
    zipped = zip(spots, images)
    # get height and width of new frame
    total_height = 0
    total_width = 0
    for spot, image in zipped:
        total_width = max(total_width, spot[0]+image.shape[1])
        total_height = max(total_height, spot[1]+image.shape[0])
    ```

[198]

Chapter 5

21. Create a new frame for the output stitched image with the following line of code:

    ```
    stitch = np.zeros((total_height, total_width, 4), np.uint8)
    ```

22. Stitch the images into the frame created, in order of distance, and return the image mosaic obtained:

    ```
    for image in dist_sorted:
        offset_y = image[0][1] + cent_y
        offset_x = image[0][0] + cent_x
        end_y = offset_y + image[1].shape[0]
        end_x = offset_x + image[1].shape[1]
        stitch_cur = stitch[offset_y:end_y, offset_x:end_x, :4]
        stitch_cur[image[1]>0] = image[1][image[1]>0]
    return stitch
    ```

23. Now, implement a function that will create the output panorama image using the `create_mosaic()` function, given the input images to be stitched and the index of the central image (as center):

    ```
    def create_panorama(images, center):
        h,w,_ = images[0].shape
        f = 1000 # 800
        H = np.array([[f, 0, w/2], [0, f, h/2], [0, 0, 1]])
        for i in range(len(images)):
            images[i] = cylindrical_warp_image(images[i], H)
    ```

24. First, stitch all of the images on the left side of the central image using the following code snippet:

    ```
    panorama = None
    for i in range(center):
        print('Stitching images {}, {}'.format(i+1, i+2))
        image_warped, image_origin = warp_image(images[i], \
                            homography(images[i + 1], images[i]))
        panorama = create_mosaic([image_warped, images[i+1]], \
                            [image_origin, (0,0)])
        images[i + 1] = panorama
    #print('Done left part')
    ```

25. Stitch all of the images on the right side of the central image using the following code snippet. Return the panorama obtained:

    ```
    for i in range(center, len(images)-1):
        print('Stitching images {}, {}'.format(i+1, i+2))
        image_warped, image_origin = warp_image(images[i+1], \
                            homography(images[i], images[i + 1]))
        panorama = create_mosaic([images[i], image_warped], \
    ```

[199]

Image Registration

```
                                [(0,0), image_origin])
        images[i + 1] = panorama
    #print('Done right part')

    return panorama
```

26. Finally, call the `create_panorama()` function to obtain the output image mosaic:

    ```
    center = len(images) // 2
    panorama = create_panorama(images, center)
    ```

    If you plot the input images, you will get an output like the following screenshot:

    If you plot the output panorama image, you will get an output like the following screenshot:

Chapter 5

Panorama with OpenCV-Python

You can implement image-stitching directly with the OpenCV-Python library's `Stitcher` class methods (without explicitly performing the stitching steps, for example, feature extraction/matching/blending). Just run the following steps:

1. First, ensure that the version of OpenCV you are using is <= 3.4.2 (until the `SIFT` patent expires):

   ```
   print(cv2.__version__)
   # 3.4.2
   ```

2. Initialize the list of the images to be stitched:

   ```
   images = [ cv2.cvtColor(cv2.imread(img), cv2.COLOR_BGR2RGB) for \
                       img in glob.glob('images/victoria*.png')]
   print('Number of images to stitch: {}'.format(len(images)))
   # Number of images to stitch: 7
   ```

3. Instantiate OpenCV-Python library's image `stitcher` object and then use the `stitch()` method to generate the image mosaic:

   ```
   stitcher = cv2.createStitcher()
   (status, stitched) = stitcher.stitch(images)
   #print(status)
   ```

4. Finally, plot the panorama image:

   ```
   plt.figure(figsize=(20,10))
   plt.imshow(stitched), plt.axis('off'), plt.title('Final Panorama
   Image', size=20)
   plt.show()
   ```

[201]

You will obtain the final panorama image, like the following one:

Final Panorama Image

How it works...

The SIFT descriptor was used to register/align images. The OpenCV-Python function findHomography() was used to compute the homography matrix between two images. The opencv-python function, warpPerspective(), was used to warp an image on its adjacent one using the homography matrix obtained.

The stitch() method of the Stitcher class from opencv-python was directly used to create the image mosaic. It has its own pipeline, as illustrated in the following screenshot:

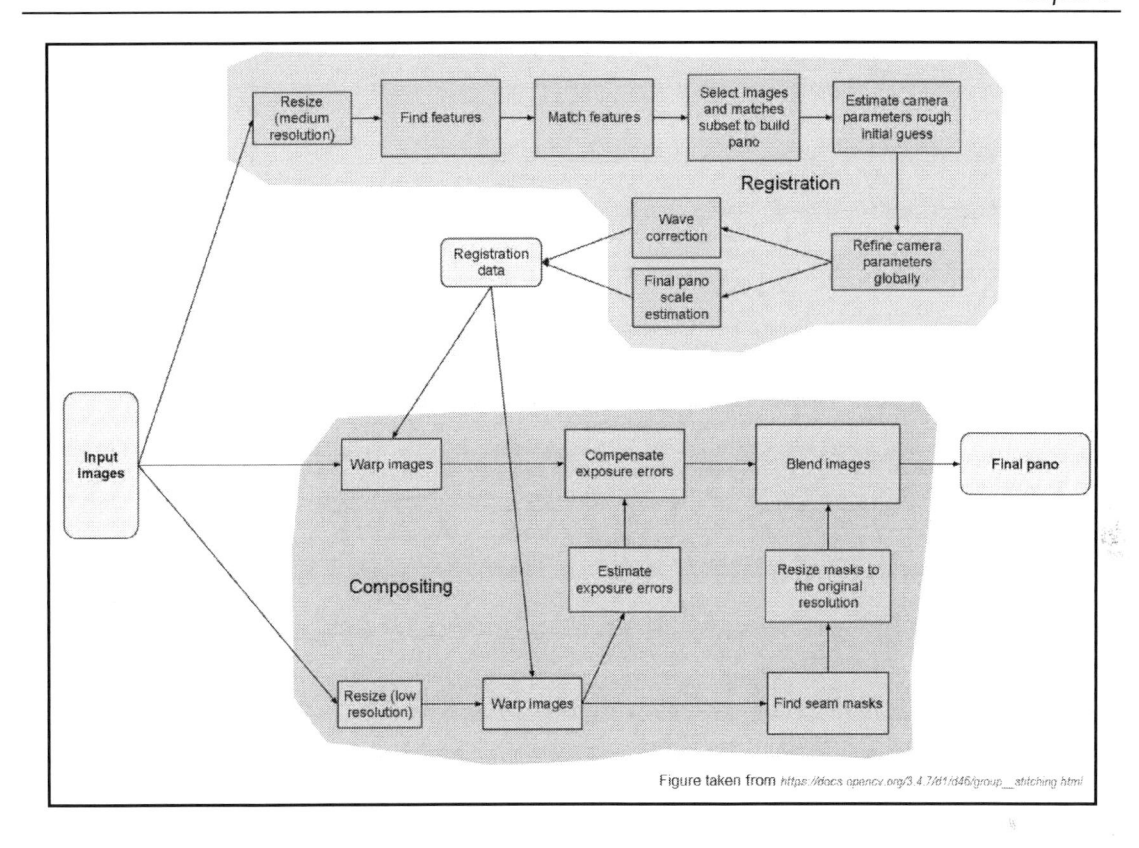

Figure taken from https://docs.opencv.org/3.4.7/d1/d46/group__stitching.html

There is more

Use pyramid blending or gradient (Poisson) blending to blend the images (hint: change in the `create_mosaic()` function) while stitching them to make the output panorama image look like a single real image (the borders of the stitched images should disappear).

See also

Refer to the following links to learn more about this recipe:

- http://www.cs.toronto.edu/~kyros/courses/2530/papers/Lecture-14/Szeliski2006.pdf
- http://6.869.csail.mit.edu/fa15/lecture/6.869-Lec5-ImageFeatures-web.pdf

- https://www.microsoft.com/en-us/research/wp-content/uploads/2004/10/tr-2004-92.pdf
- http://matthewalunbrown.com/papers/ijcv2007.pdf
- https://en.wikipedia.org/wiki/Image_stitching
- https://docs.opencv.org/3.4.7/d1/d46/group__stitching.html
- https://www.youtube.com/watch?v=UpUdj9rbQ_0

Face morphing

The goal of image/face morphing is to find the average of two objects/faces in the images. It is not an average of two images of objects (faces); rather, it is an image of the average object (face). The very first idea that might come to mind is a two-step process:

1. Globally align two face images (warping with an affine transformation).
2. Cross-dissolve (a linear combination of the images with alpha-blending) to create the output image.

But this often does not work. We can again resort to (local) feature matching. For example, to do face morphing, the matching can take place between keypoints such as nose to nose, eye to eye, and so on—this is a local (non-parametric) warp.

Here are the steps of the face morphing implementation with the *mesh-warping* algorithm:

1. **Defining correspondences**: The face morphing algorithm transforms the source face into the target face using a set of feature points common to both faces, either created manually or using facial landmarks generated automatically using facial feature detection for each face. You need to find point-correspondences between the faces to be aligned (for example, label the feature points consistently using the same ordering of keypoints in the two faces).
2. **Delaunay triangulation**: You need to provide a triangulation of the points to be used for morphing. A Delaunay triangulation doesn't output very skinny triangles, hence, this algorithm is commonly used. Compute the Delaunay triangulation on either of the point sets (not both) and the triangulation must be the same throughout the morphing.

3. **Computing the mid-way (morphed) face**: Before computing the whole morph sequence, compute the mid-way face of your source and destination images. This involves computing the average shape (that is, the average of each keypoint location in the two faces): compute the location of feature points in the morphed image, *M*. For each triangle in the source image, compute the affine transform that maps three corners of the triangle to the corresponding corner points of a triangle in the morphed image, and then transform all pixels inside the triangle to the morphed image using the affine transform just computed. Finally, alpha-blend these two images and this is your final morphed image.

In this recipe, you will learn how to implement face morphing between a human and a lion face, where the facial landmarks for the human face are obtained automatically using the `dlib` library's facial landmark extraction, and the corresponding feature points in the lion's face are manually created.

Getting ready

Let's first start by importing all of the required libraries that you will need to implement face morphing:

```
from scipy.spatial import Delaunay
from skimage.io import imread
import scipy.misc
import cv2
import dlib
import numpy as np
from matplotlib import pyplot as plt
```

Image Registration

How to do it...

Follow the steps listed for the face morphing implementation:

1. First, use the `dlib` library's face detector and shape predictor (as you did in the *Face alignment with dlib* recipe) to automatically compute the facial landmarks from the human face by implementing the `get_face_landmarks()` function. It takes the input image, a Boolean flag indicating whether to add the boundary points or not, and the `dlib` library's `shape_predictor` model's path:

   ```
   def get_face_landmarks(img, add_boundary_points=True,
   predictor_path = 'images/shape_predictor_68_face_landmarks.dat'):
     detector = dlib.get_frontal_face_detector()
     predictor = dlib.shape_predictor(predictor_path)
   ```

2. Compute 68 facial landmarks (keypoints) using `dlib` for each face detected (in this case, there will be just one face) using the shape `predictor` object for the human face image and return the landmark points:

   ```
   dets = detector(img, 1)
   points = np.zeros((68, 2))
   for k, d in enumerate(dets):
      shape = predictor(img, d) # get the landmarks for the face \
       in box d.
      for i in range(68):
         points[i, 0] = shape.part(i).x
         points[i, 1] = shape.part(i).y
   points = points.astype(np.int32)
   return points
   ```

3. The corresponding landmarks on the lion's face are manually defined in a text file. Read the landmarks with the following function:

   ```
   def read_lion_landmarks():
       with open("images/lion_face_landmark.txt") as key_file:
           keypoints = [list(map(int, line.split())) for line in \
                        key_file]
       return(keypoints)
   ```

4. Compute alpha-blending of two sets of points (pixels) and two images using the following functions:

   ```
   def weighted_average_points(start_points, end_points, percent=0.5):
       if percent <= 0: return end_points
       elif percent >= 1: return start_points
       else: return np.asarray(start_points*percent + \
   ```

[206]

```
                end_points*(1-percent), np.int32)

    def weighted_average(img1, img2, percent=0.5):
        if percent <= 0: return img2
        elif percent >= 1: return img1
        else: return cv2.addWeighted(img1, percent, img2, \
            1-percent, 0)
```

5. Implement a `bilinear_interpolate()` function, which interpolates over every image channel:

```
def bilinear_interpolate(image, coords):
    int_coords = coords.astype(np.int32)
    x0, y0 = int_coords
    dx, dy = coords - int_coords
    q11, q21, q12, q22 = image[y0, x0], image[y0, x0+1], \
                    image[y0+1, x0], image[y0+1, x0+1]
    btm = q21.T * dx + q11.T * (1 - dx)
    top = q22.T * dx + q12.T * (1 - dx)
    interpolated_pixels = top * dy + btm * (1 - dy)
    return interpolated_pixels.T
```

6. Implement the `get_grid_coordinates()` function to generate an array of all possible (x, y) grid coordinates within the **Region Of Interest** (ROI) of input points:

```
def get_grid_coordinates(points):
    xmin, xmax = np.min(points[:, 0]), np.max(points[:, 0]) + 1
    ymin, ymax = np.min(points[:, 1]), np.max(points[:, 1]) + 1
    return np.asarray([(x, y) for y in range(ymin, ymax)
            for x in range(xmin, xmax)], np.uint32)
```

7. Implement the `process_warp()` function to warp the triangles from `src_img`—the ones that are inside the ROI of `result_img` (corresponding to the points in `dst_points`):

```
def process_warp(src_img, result_img, tri_affines, dst_points,
delaunay):
    roi_coords = grid_coordinates(dst_points)
    roi_tri_indices = delaunay.find_simplex(roi_coords)
    for simplex_index in range(len(delaunay.simplices)):
        coords = roi_coords[roi_tri_indices == simplex_index]
        num_coords = len(coords)
        out_coords = np.dot(tri_affines[simplex_index],
                np.vstack((coords.T, np.ones(num_coords))))
        x, y = coords.T
        result_img[y, x] = bilinear_interpolate(src_img, \
```

Image Registration

```
                                out_coords)
            return None
```

8. Implement a Python generator function,
   `gen_triangular_affine_matrices()`, to compute the affine transformation matrix for each triangle vertices from `dest_points` to the corresponding vertices in `src_points`:

   ```
   def gen_triangular_affine_matrices(vertices, src_points,
   dest_points):
       ones = [1, 1, 1]
       for tri_indices in vertices:
           src_tri = np.vstack((src_points[tri_indices, :].T, ones))
           dst_tri = np.vstack((dest_points[tri_indices, :].T, ones))
           mat = np.dot(src_tri, np.linalg.inv(dst_tri))[:2, :]
           yield mat
   ```

9. Now, implement a `warp_image()` function that takes the sources/destination images and the corresponding control points and uses the defined functions to compute the morphed output image and the corresponding Delaunay triangulation of the control points (face landmarks):

   ```
   def warp_image(src_img, src_points, dest_points, dest_shape):
     num_chans = 3
     src_img = src_img[:, :, :3]
     rows, cols = dest_shape[:2]
     result_img = np.zeros((rows, cols, num_chans), np.uint8)
     delaunay = Delaunay(dest_points)
     tri_affines =
   np.asarray(list(gen_triangular_affine_matrices(delaunay.simplices,
                                   src_points, dest_points)))
     process_warp(src_img, result_img, tri_affines, dest_points,
   delaunay)
       return result_img, delaunay
   ```

10. Read the source (human face), destination (lion face), and the lion face landmarks from the file. Resize the source image to match the destination image size. Compute the human face landmarks using the `get_face_landmarks()` function:

    ```
    src_path = 'images/me.png'
    dst_path = 'images/lion.png'
    src_img = imread(src_path)
    dst_img = imread(dst_path)
    size = dst_img.shape[:2]
    src_img = cv2.resize(src_img[...,:3], size)
    src_points = get_face_landmarks(src_img)
    ```

```
dst_points = read_lion_landmarks()
```

If you plot the source and destination face images along with the landmarks, you will get an output like the following screenshot:

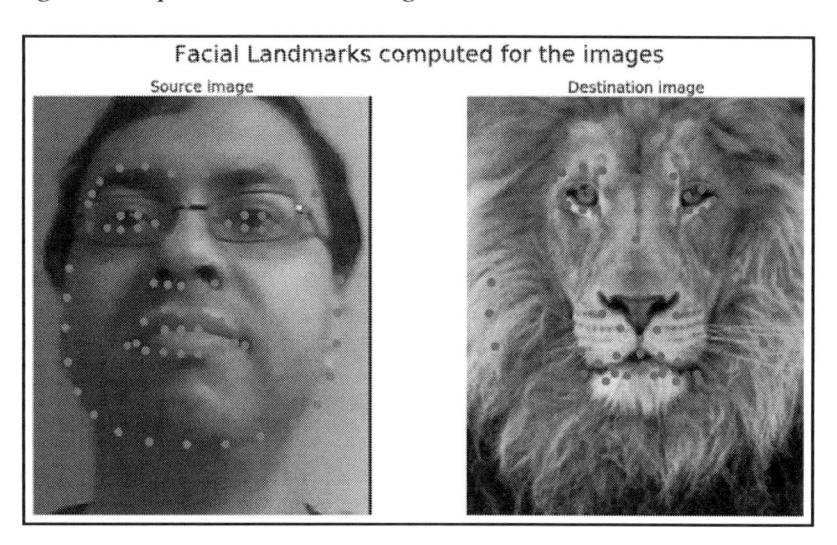

Facial Landmarks computed for the images
Source image | Destination image

11. Run the following code to visualize the faces with the triangles obtained using Delaunay triangulation with the facial landmarks as vertices of the triangles:

```
fig = plt.figure(figsize=(20,10))
plt.subplot(121), plt.imshow(src_img)
plt.triplot(src_points[:,0], src_points[:,1],
src_d.simplices.copy())
plt.plot(src_points[:,0], src_points[:,1], 'o', color='red')
plt.title('Source image', size=20), plt.axis('off')
plt.subplot(122), plt.imshow(dst_img)
plt.triplot(dst_points[:,0], dst_points[:,1],
end_d.simplices.copy())
plt.plot(dst_points[:,0], dst_points[:,1], 'o')
plt.title('Destination image', size=20), plt.axis('off')
plt.suptitle('Delaunay triangulation of the images', size=30)
fig.subplots_adjust(wspace=0.01, left=0.1, right=0.9)
plt.show()
```

Image Registration

If you run the preceding code snippet, you will get the following screenshot as output:

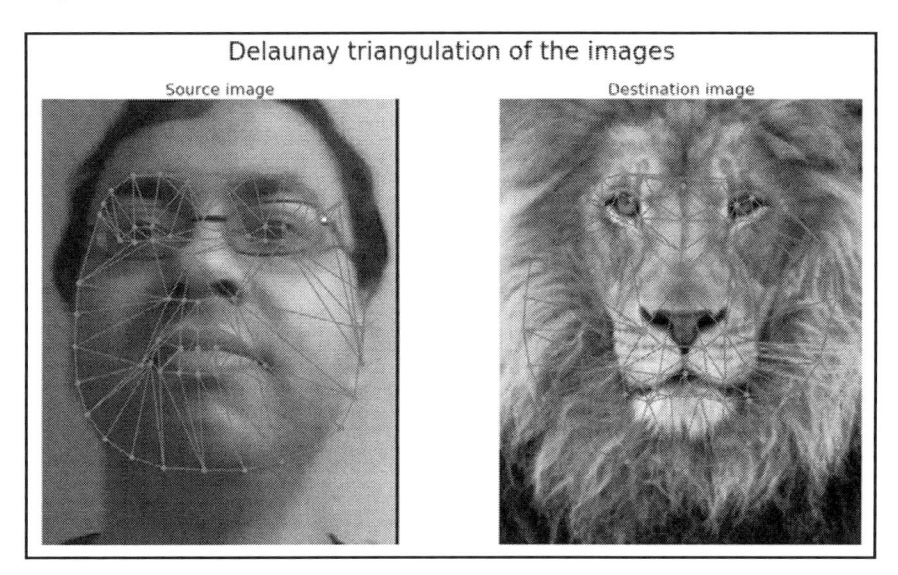

Delaunay triangulation of the images

Source image | Destination image

12. Finally, compute the morphed image with increasing `alpha` values (from 0 to 1) to the obtained morphed images with different blending proportions and animate them to observe a smooth transition from the source to the destination image:

```
fig = plt.figure(figsize=(18,20))
fig.subplots_adjust(top=0.925, bottom=0, left=0, right=1, \
                    wspace=0.01,  hspace=0.08)
i = 1
for percent in np.linspace(1, 0, 16):
 points = weighted_average_points(src_points, dst_points, percent)
 src_face, src_d = warp_image(src_img, src_points, points, size)
 end_face, end_d = warp_image(dst_img, dst_points, points, size)
 average_face = weighted_average(src_face, end_face, percent)
 plt.subplot(4,4,i), plt.imshow(average_face)
 plt.title('alpha=' + str(round(percent,4)), size=20), \
          plt.axis('off')
 i += 1
plt.suptitle('Face morphing', size=30)
plt.show()
```

If you run the preceding code block, you will get a screenshot like the following screenshot as output:

[210]

Face morphing

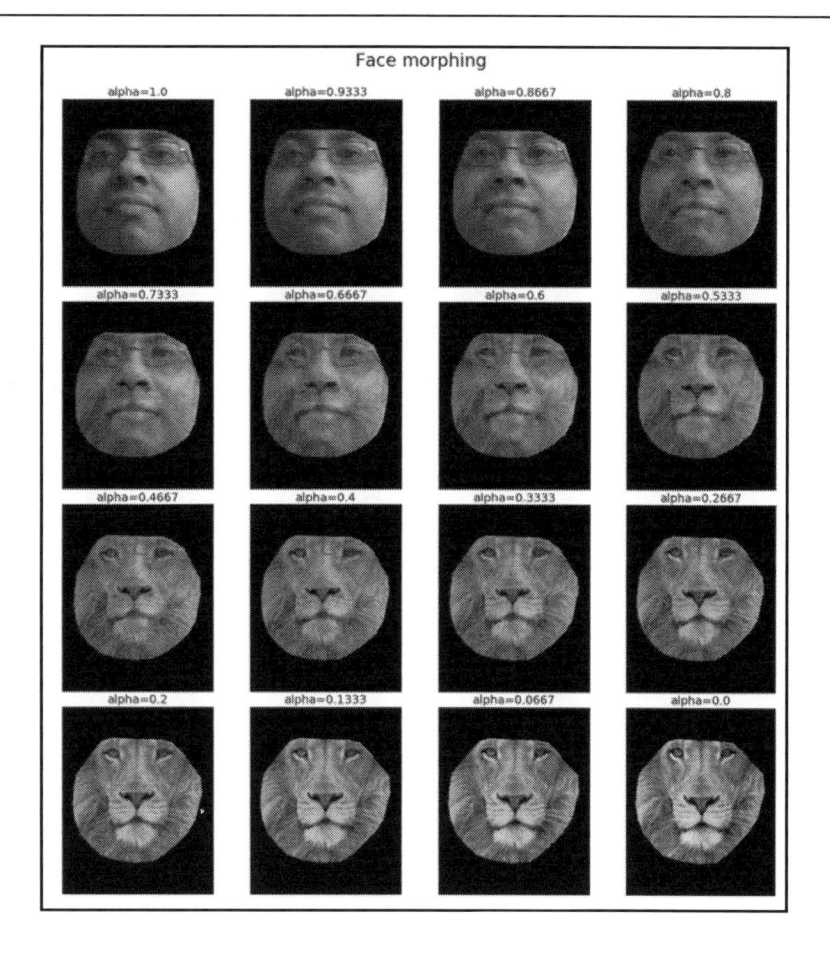

[Sequence of morphing images from alpha=1.0 to alpha=0.0, transitioning from a human face to a lion face]

How it works

To morph a source image, I_S, into a destination image, I_D, first, the pixel correspondence between the two images needs to be established. For every pixel in image I_S, the corresponding pixel in image I_D is to be found. Once these correspondences are found, the images can be blended in two steps:

1. Compute the location of the pixel in the morphed image (it was computed using the `weighted_average_points()` function).
2. Compute the intensity of the pixel at that location in the morphed image (it was computed using the `weighted_average()` function).

Image Registration

It's very computationally expensive to find a corresponding pixel in destination image for every pixel in the source image and it isn't really necessary; instead, a handful of control points will suffice. The equation to compute the location of a control pixel in I_M given the location of the pixel in I_S and I_D is shown in the following screenshot:

$$x_i^M = (1-\alpha)x_i^S + \alpha x_i^D$$
$$y_i^M = (1-\alpha)y_i^S + \alpha y_i^D \qquad \forall (x_i, y_i) \in P_C$$
$$\text{Control Points}$$

$$\underbrace{I_M(x_i, y_i)}_{\text{Morph Image}} = (1-\alpha)\underbrace{I_S(x_i, y_i)}_{\text{Source Image}} + \alpha \underbrace{I_D(x_i, y_i)}_{\text{Destination Image}}$$

Both the `weighted_average_points()` and `weighted_average()` functions accept α (or the percent), a third argument.

The `bilinear_interpolate()` function accepts a couple of input parameters, the first one being the input image (maximum number of channels in the image is assumed to be three) and the second one being the input coordinates, `coords` (an *np array* with two rows; the first and second rows represent the *x* and *y* coordinates of the input point, respectively). This function returns the interpolated pixels corresponding to the ones specified by the input, `coords`.

The `gen_triangular_affine_matrices()` function is a Python generator function that accepts three input parameters, the first one (`vertices`) being the NumPy array of *triplet indices* corresponding to the corners of a triangle, the second one (`src_points`) being the NumPy array of (x, y) points corresponding to the facial landmarks for the source image, and the third one (`dest_points`) being the NumPy array of (x, y) points corresponding to the landmarks for the destination image. The function yields an estimated 2x3 affine transformation matrix for each triangle.

There is more

Depending on the source and destination face sizes, you may need to implement a `resize_crop()` function that centralizes the faces in the images and extracts the bounding rectangle of the control points to be used as the input images; otherwise, while iterative blending, the area of the morphed face may keep on increasing/decreasing.

You just implemented the *mesh warping* algorithm for face morphing. Alternatively, you can implement the *Beier-Neely field morphing* algorithm too for face morphing. Implement this algorithm from the references/links provided in the following section, *See also*.

See also

Refer to the following links to learn more about this recipe:

- `https://www.studocu.com/en/document/university-of-pennsylvania/computer-vision-computational-photography/lecture-notes/cis581-morph-2018-morphing-lecture-notes/3317837/view`
- `https://www.seas.upenn.edu/~cse399b/Lectures/CSE399b-07-triangle.pdf`
- `http://alumni.media.mit.edu/~maov/classes/comp_photo_vision08f/lect/07_Image%20Morphing.pdf`
- `http://en.wikipedia.org/wiki/Bilinear_interpolation`
- `https://www.cs.toronto.edu/~mangas/teaching/320/slides/CSC320T12.pdf`
- `https://www.cs.princeton.edu/courses/archive/fall00/cs426/papers/beier92.pdf`
- `https://inst.eecs.berkeley.edu/~cs194-26/fa18/hw/proj4/index.html`
- `https://www.learnopencv.com/face-morph-using-opencv-cpp-python`
- `http://davis.wpi.edu/~matt/courses/morph/2d.htm`
- `https://www.youtube.com/watch?v=i_tG7XRLPmU`

Implementing an image search engine

In this recipe, you will learn how to implement a simple image **search engine** (SE). It will be a search by example system, relying only on the image contents, known as **content-based image retrieval** (CBIR) systems. The images along with the features extracted are stored so that the system can return similar images (based on the features) during a search. The following describes the four steps of any CBIR system:

1. Defining an image descriptor (descriptive features of an image)
2. Indexing search images (for quick retrieval of the images with similar descriptors to the query image. Use an efficient data structure for fast retrieval)
3. Defining the similarity metric to be used (Euclidean/cosine/chi-squared distance, and so on)
4. Searching (the user submits a query image to the SE, and the SE extracts features from this query image and uses the indexed features of the images stored to quickly return the most relevant images using the similarity metric— retrieval should be fast using the efficient data structure for indexing)

You will first learn how to compute the similarity of a query image with a set of search images and then you will extend the idea to implement a simple SE.

Getting ready

Let's start by importing all of the required libraries using the following code snippet:

```
import cv2
import matplotlib.pylab as plt
from collections import defaultdict
from skimage.feature import hog
from scipy.spatial.distance import cdist
from sklearn.neighbors import BallTree
from skimage.io import imread
from skimage.exposure import import rescale_intensity
import pickle
import numpy as np
from matplotlib.pylab import plt
from glob import glob
import time, os
```

How to do it...

Let's first learn how to compute feature-based similarity between a query image and a set of search images. Then, you will learn how to implement a simple search engine by extending the idea.

Finding similarity between an image and a set of images with SIFT

You will use `SIFT` keypoints/descriptors to compute the similarity between two images (using `opencv-python`). Here are the steps that you will need to follow:

1. First, read the `query` image. Also, read all of the images from the search directory to find the best possible matches:

    ```
    query = cv2.imread("images/query.jpg")
    matched_images = defaultdict(list)
    for image_file in glob.glob('images/search/*.jpg'):
        search_image = cv2.imread(image_file)
    ```

    The query image is shown here:

2. Extract the SIFT keypoints and descriptors for the query image and all of the search images using the following code:

   ```
   sift = cv2.xfeatures2d.SIFT_create()
   kp_1, desc_1 = sift.detectAndCompute(query, None)
   kp_2, desc_2 = sift.detectAndCompute(search_image, None)
   ```

3. Use an *approximate nearest neighbors* based match for fast matching of the descriptors (you can use your own data structure for fast retrieval, for example, use kd-trees from scikit-learn):

   ```
   index_params = dict(algorithm=FLANN_INDEX_KDTREE, trees=5)
   search_params = dict()
   flann = cv2.FlannBasedMatcher(index_params, search_params)
   matches = flann.knnMatch(desc_1, desc_2, k=2)
   ```

4. Again, use the *ratio test* (as in the earlier recipes) to find good matches:

   ```
   good_points = []
   ratio = 0.6
   for m, n in matches:
     if m.distance < ratio*n.distance:
       good_points.append(m)
   num_good_points = len(good_points)
   ```

Image Registration

5. Draw a few very good matches (> 300 good matchings) representing the top similar images and a few very poor matches (< 10 good matchings) representing very dissimilar images using the following code. Update the `matched_images` dictionary to have a key with value *k* and all of the search images having exactly *k* matches with the `query` image:

```
if (num_good_points > 300) or (num_good_points < 10):
    result = cv2.drawMatches(query, kp_1, search_image, kp_2, \
                             good_points, None)
    matched_images[len(good_points)].append(search_image)
```

If you plot the keypoint matches of search images (corresponding to some good and some poor matches) with the query image, you will get an output like the following screenshot:

Chapter 5

Finally, if you rank the search images with regards to the number of good matches with the `query` image (using the `matched_images` dictionary), you will get an output like the following screenshot (this is just some parts of the output):

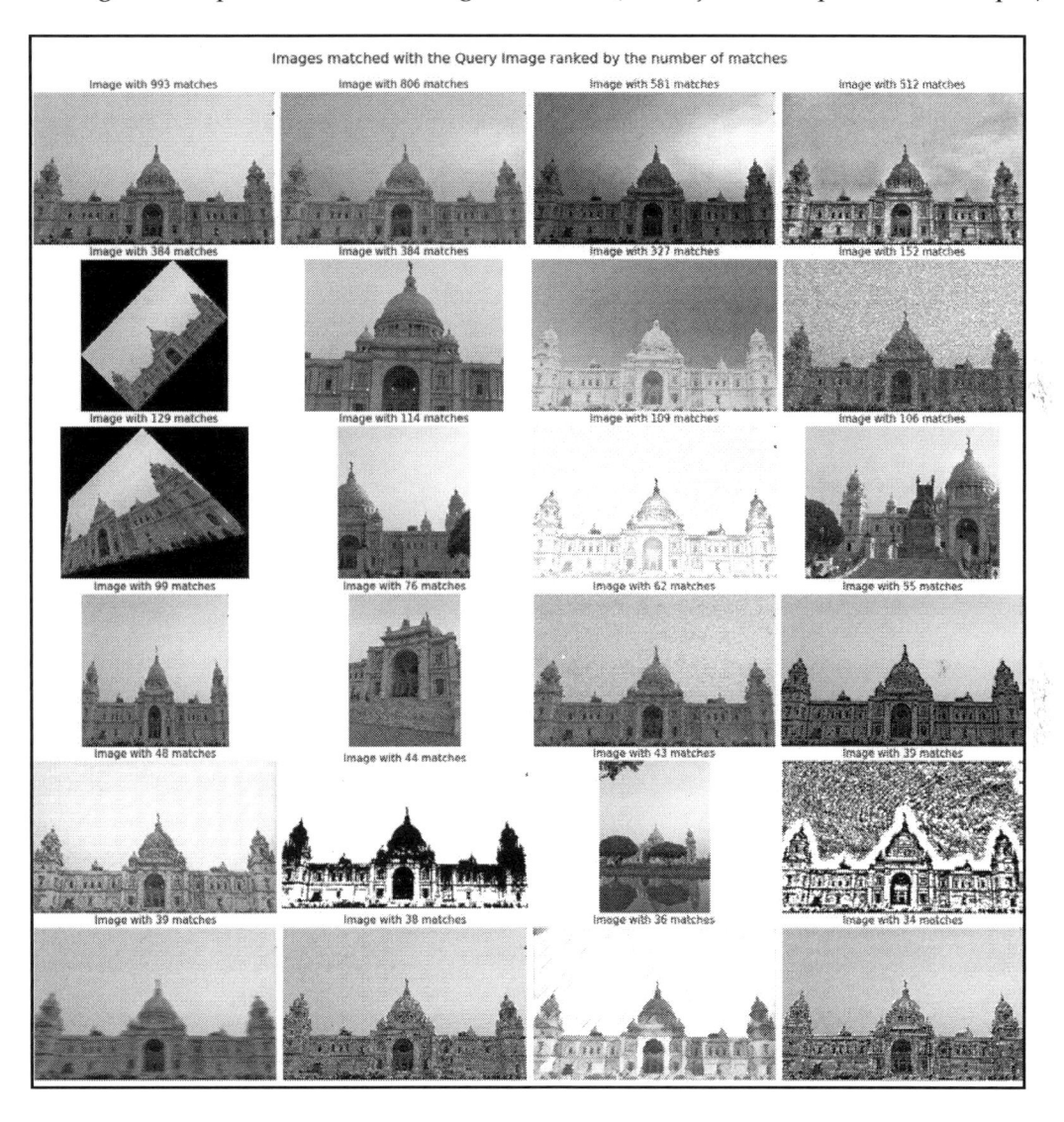

[217]

Image Registration

Steps to implement a simple image search engine

Execute the steps listed to implement your simple search engine:

1. First, download a set of images to build your search database (for example, from `https://www.open-tour.org/en/dataset.html` with ~250 images or `http://www.robots.ox.ac.uk/~vgg/data/oxbuildings/` with ~5,000 images).

2. Implement the `SimpleSearchEngine` class, which has the following members (initialize them in the constructor or the `__init__()` method):

- `search_dir` (where you save the search images)
- `save_dir` (where you save search image descriptors)
- `search_ds` (the data structure in which the search images are stored for fast retrieval of the search image descriptors most similar with the query descriptor)

```python
class SimpleSearchEngine:

    def __init__(self, search_dir, save_dir):
        self.search_dir = search_dir
        self.save_dir = save_dir
        self.search_ds = None
```

3. Implement the `read_preprocess()` method to convert every image into the `HSV` color space:

```python
def read_preprocess(self, imfile):
    return cv2.cvtColor(cv2.imread(imfile), cv2.COLOR_BGR2HSV)
```

4. Implement the `compute_descriptor()` method to extract and return the descriptors of an image (we will use region-based `HSV` histograms here for 5 regions in the image, with the area of each region being a quarter of that of the image, namely, the top-left quarter, the top-right quarter, the bottom-right quarter, and the bottom-left quarter, along with the center quarter region of the image. You are encouraged to use any other feature descriptor, for example, `SIFT`, and compare the search results and develop some intuition):

```python
def compute_descriptor(self, im):
    bins = (8, 12, 3)
    (h, w) = im.shape[:2]
    (c_x, c_y) = (int(w * 0.5), int(h * 0.5))
    regions = [(c_x, 0, 0, c_y), (c_x, 0, w, c_y), \
               (0, c_y, c_x, h), (c_x, c_y, w, h)]
    descriptor = []
    for (start_x, start_y, endX, endY) in regions:
```

[218]

```
                region_mask = np.zeros(im.shape[:2], dtype=np.uint8)
                cv2.rectangle(region_mask, (start_x, start_y), (endX, \
                                endY), 255, -1)
                hist = cv2.calcHist([im], [0, 1, 2], region_mask, \
                                bins, [0, 180, 0, 256, 0, 256])
                hist = cv2.normalize(hist, np.zeros(hist.shape[:0], \
                                dtype="float")).flatten()
                descriptor += list(hist)
        return np.array(descriptor)
```

5. Implement the `cosine_cdist()` method to compute the cosine distances between the query image and the search images database:

```
def cosine_cdist(self, descriptor):
    descriptor = descriptor.reshape(1, -1)
    return cdist(self.search_ds, descriptor, 'cosine').reshape(-1)
```

6. Implement the `store_ds()` method for storing the search image descriptors in an efficient data structure:

```
def store_ds(self, descriptors):
    #self.search_ds = BallTree(descriptors)
    self.search_ds = descriptors
```

7. Implement the `query_ds()` method to query the search image data structure with the query image descriptor and return the top `k` most similar images according to the cosine distance measure:

```
def query_ds(self, descriptor, k):
    img_distances = self.cosine_cdist(descriptor)
    return np.argsort(img_distances)[:k].tolist()
```

8. Implement the `build_index()` method to build an index on the search image database, that is, create a data structure for efficient storage (with `store_ds()`) and retrieval (with `query_ds()`) of the search images according to the similarity to the query image:

```
def build_index(self):
    t_before = time.time()
    descriptors = np.array([])
    search_pat = self.search_dir + '*.jpg'
    i = 0
    for imfile in glob(search_pat):
        print(i, imfile)
        im = self.read_preprocess(imfile)
        descriptor = self.compute_descriptor(im)
        descriptors = np.hstack((descriptors, descriptor)) if i==0
```

Image Registration

```
                            else np.vstack((descriptors, descriptor))
        i += 1
    self.store_ds(descriptors)
    t_after = time.time()
    t_build = t_after - t_before
    print("Time to build SE model (seconds): ", t_build)
    with open(self.save_dir + 'SE.pkl', 'wb') as pickle_file:
        pickle.dump(self.search_ds, pickle_file, \
                    pickle.HIGHEST_PROTOCOL)
```

9. Implement the `query_search_engine()` method, which takes a query image file as input and a number, `k` (the number of top similar images to output). It returns the top `k` most similar images to the query image from the search database:

```
def query_search_engine(self, imfile, k=10):
    if self.search_ds is None:
        if not os.path.exists(self.save_dir + 'SE.pkl'):
            self.build_index()
        with open(self.save_dir + 'SE.pkl', 'rb') as pickle_file:
            self.search_ds = pickle.load(pickle_file)
    im = self.read_preprocess(imfile)
    descriptor = self.compute_descriptor(im)
    t_before = datetime.datetime.now() #time.time()
    neighbors = self.query_ds(descriptor, k)
    t_after = datetime.datetime.now() #time.time()
    t_search = (t_after - t_before).microseconds/1000
    print("Time to query SE (milliseconds): ", t_search)
    imfiles = glob(self.search_dir + '*.jpg')
    return [cv2.imread(imfiles[id]) for id in neighbors]
```

10. Finally, instantiate the search engine and build an index once at the very outset (or periodically if new images get added to the search engine). Select a query image and ask the search engine to find images similar to this image. Retrieve the top `k=10` most similar images with the query image by using the `query_search_engine()` method:

```
se = SimpleSearchEngine('images/oxford_buildings/', 'models/')
#db_milano
query_image = 'images/oxford_buildings/all_souls_000051.jpg'
# First build index then search the index with the query
# se.build_index()
knbrs = se.query_search_engine(query_image, 10)
```

Search the engine with the following query image, using the preceding code snippets:

Image Registration

You will get the top 10 images returned by the search engine, as shown in the following screenshot:

There is more

For feature-based similarity comparison between two images, you could use the proportion (percentage) of matches as the ranking criterion too (for example, have the percentage of a match in the keypoints as key in the `matched_images` dictionary). Also, for scalability and reusability, you should serialize the descriptors for all of the search images you have in your search directory (for example, use pickle) and load/deserialize all of the descriptors when you want to match with a query image descriptor—it is also left for you as an exercise. You can use SURF, KAZE, or any other feature for matching and any distance/similarity metric between the descriptors. For production, use an algorithm for fast computation of the similarities between millions of images (for example, try Annoy Index, which is simple to use and pretty fast—searching 1,000,000 images takes ~2 ms).

Use different features (SIFT/SURF/KAZE), different similarity metrics (cosine/Euclidean), and different storage data structures (kd-tree/ball-tree) to implement your search engine and compare the top 10 search results. If you have a ground truth available (in terms of which top 10 images should be returned), you can compare different search engines' performance with `precision10` (defined as out of the top 10 search results, what proportion was in the top 10 ground truth) / `recall10` (defined as out of top 10 ground truth, what proportion was returned in the top 10 search results). Also, compare the speed of retrieval.

See also

Refer to the following links to learn more about this recipe:

- https://www.pyimagesearch.com/2014/12/01/complete-guide-building-image-search-engine-python-opencv/
- https://www.pyimagesearch.com/2019/08/26/building-an-image-hashing-search-engine-with-vp-trees-and-opencv/
- https://medium.com/machine-learning-world/feature-extraction-and-similar-image-search-with-opencv-for-newbies-3c59796bf774

6
Image Segmentation

Image segmentation refers to the partitioning of an image into distinct regions or categories, with each region containing pixels with similar attributes and each pixel in an image being allocated to one of these categories.

Image segmentation is usually done to simplify the representation of an image into segments that are more meaningful and easier to analyze. If segmentation is done well, then all other stages in image analysis are made simpler, which means that the quality and reliability of segmentation dictates whether the analysis of an image will be successful. But to partition an image into correct segments is often a very challenging problem.

In this chapter, we will look at the following recipes:

- Thresholding with Otsu and Riddler–Calvard
- Image segmentation with self-organizing maps
- RandomWalk segmentation with scikit-image
- Skin color segmentation with the GMM–EM algorithm
- Medical image segmentation
- Deep semantic segmentation
- Deep instance segmentation

Thresholding with Otsu and Riddler–Calvard

Thresholding refers to a family of algorithms that use a pixel value as a threshold to create a binary image (an image with only black-and-white pixels) from a grayscale image (this is the simplest possible method, segmenting foreground objects from the background in an image). The threshold can be chosen manually (by looking at the histogram of pixel values) or automatically using an algorithm. Image segmentation techniques may be noncontextual (without considering spatial relationships between the features in an image and grouping pixels only with regard to certain global attributes—for example, color/gray level) or contextual (additionally exploiting spatial relationships). In this recipe, you will learn how to use a couple of popular histogram-based thresholding methods known as Otsu's (with the assumption of a bimodal histogram) and Riddler–Calvard's methods using `mahotas` library functions. Using the Otsu method, for every possible value of the threshold, the weighted within-class variance between two classes of pixels (being separated by that threshold value) is computed. The optimal threshold is the one that minimizes this variance, as shown in the following diagram:

Otsu Thresholding

$$q_1(t) = \sum_{i=0}^{t} P(i) \qquad q_2(t) = \sum_{i=t+1}^{L-1} P(i)$$

$$\mu_1(t) = \sum_{i=0}^{t} \frac{iP(i)}{q_1(t)} \qquad \mu_2(t) = \sum_{i=t+1}^{L-1} \frac{iP(i)}{q_2(t)}$$

$$\sigma_1^2(t) = \sum_{i=0}^{t} [i - \mu_1(t)]^2 \frac{P(i)}{q_1(t)} \qquad \sigma_2^2(t) = \sum_{i=t+1}^{L-1} [i - \mu_2(t)]^2 \frac{P(i)}{q_2(t)}$$

variance of class with pixel values $\leq t$ $\qquad$ variance of class with pixel values $> t$

$$\sigma_w^2(t) = q_1(t)\sigma_1^2(t) + q_2(t)\sigma_2^2(t)$$

Weighted within-class variance

$$t_{otsu} = \arg\min_{0 \leq t \leq L-1} \sigma_w^2(t)$$

The Riddler–Calvard method, on the contrary, chooses the (optimum) threshold automatically as a result of an iterative process that provides progressively cleaner extractions of the object region after a series of iterations.

Getting ready

We are going to use a grayscale image of a statue of Subhas Chandra Bose for the demonstration of binary image segmentation using `mahotas`. Let's start by loading the required libraries, as we always do:

```
%matplotlib inline
import mahotas as mh
import numpy as np
import matplotlib.pylab as plt
```

How to do it...

Go through the following steps to implement the thresholding algorithms using `mahotas`:

1. First, read the image and use the `mahotas` library functions to obtain the optimum thresholds for the input grayscale image using the following code snippet. As you can see, the thresholds obtained with the two aforementioned algorithms are pretty close to each other for the given input image:

    ```
    image = mh.imread('images/netaji.png')
    thresh_otsu, thresh_rc = mh.otsu(image), mh.rc(image)
    print(thresh_otsu, thresh_rc)
    # 161 161.5062276206947
    ```

2. Perform the binary segmentation of the input image using the optimum thresholds obtained for the pixel values. You will obtain two different binary output images, corresponding to the algorithms:

    ```
    binary_otsu, binary_rc = image > thresh_otsu, image > thresh_rc
    ```

Image Segmentation

3. Finally, plot the input image, the histogram of the input image, the thresholds computed, and the output images obtained using the following code:

```
fig, axes = plt.subplots(nrows=2, ncols=2, figsize=(20, 15))
axes = axes.ravel()
axes[0].imshow(image, cmap=plt.cm.gray)
axes[0].set_title('Original', size=20), axes[0].axis('off')
axes[1].hist(image.ravel(), bins=256, normed=True)
axes[1].set_title('Histogram', size=20)
axes[1].axvline(thresh_otsu, label='otsu', color='green', lw=3)
axes[1].axvline(thresh_rc, label='rc', color='red', lw=2)
axes[1].legend(loc='upper left', prop={'size': 20}), axes[1].grid()
axes[2].imshow(binary_otsu, cmap=plt.cm.gray)
axes[2].set_title('Thresholded (Otsu)', size=20),
axes[2].axis('off')
axes[3].imshow(binary_rc, cmap=plt.cm.gray)
axes[3].set_title('Thresholded (Riddler-Calvard)', size=20),
axes[3].axis('off')
plt.tight_layout()
plt.show()
```

How it works...

Thresholding functions have a trivial interface in `mahotas`: they take an image and return a value.

The `otsu()` function was used to compute the optimum Otsu threshold for the input image.

Similarly, the `rc()` function was used to compute the Riddler–Calvard threshold for the given input image.

Finally, on running the code blocks, you will get a figure like the following as your output:

Chapter 6

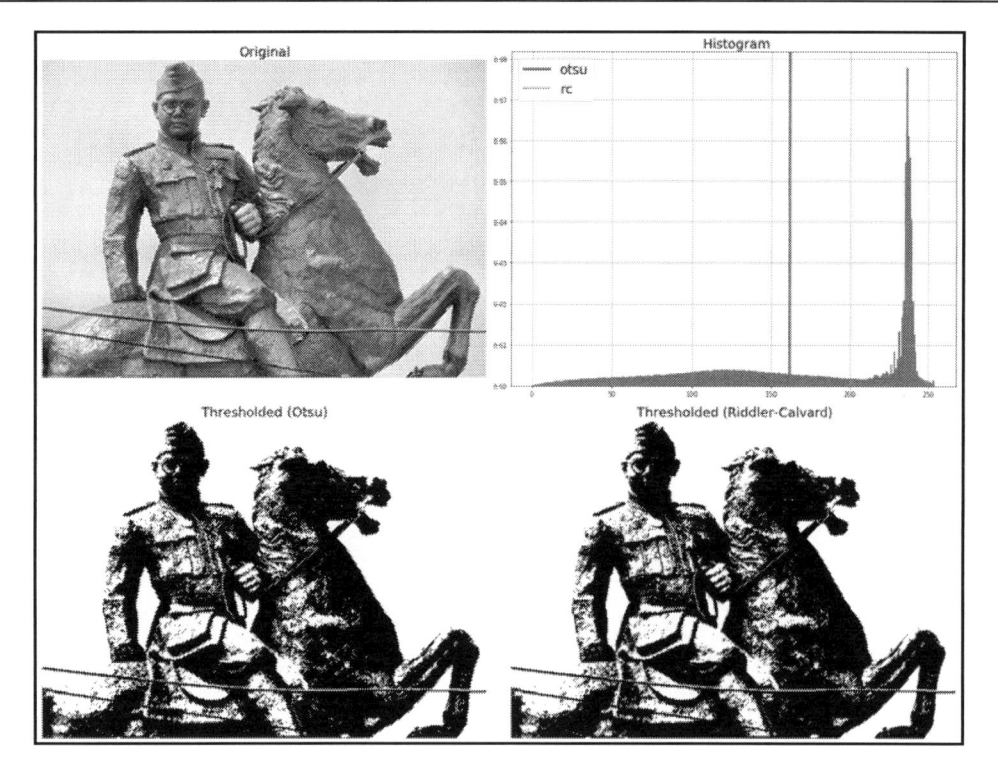

All the pixels with values less than or equal to the optimum threshold are assigned a value of zero (black foreground object) and those with values above it are assigned a value of one (white background), in order to obtain the output binary image for each of the two algorithms.

There's more...

There are many thresholding algorithms for binary segmentation; the scikit-image library provides implementations of some of them. You can also evaluate the algorithms and select the one that gives the best result for your image. For each of the algorithms, you must specify a radius if you want to use the local version; otherwise, the global version will be invoked by default. The following figure shows how different (global) thresholding functions perform on an input grayscale blackboard image from a statistics course at MIT. Implement it on your own; maybe also try using different radii to implement the local versions for different algorithms and see the impact of the radius on the binary output image. As you can see from the following output figure, the Isodata and Otsu perform better than the other methods for binary segmentation based on the thresholding for the given input image:

[229]

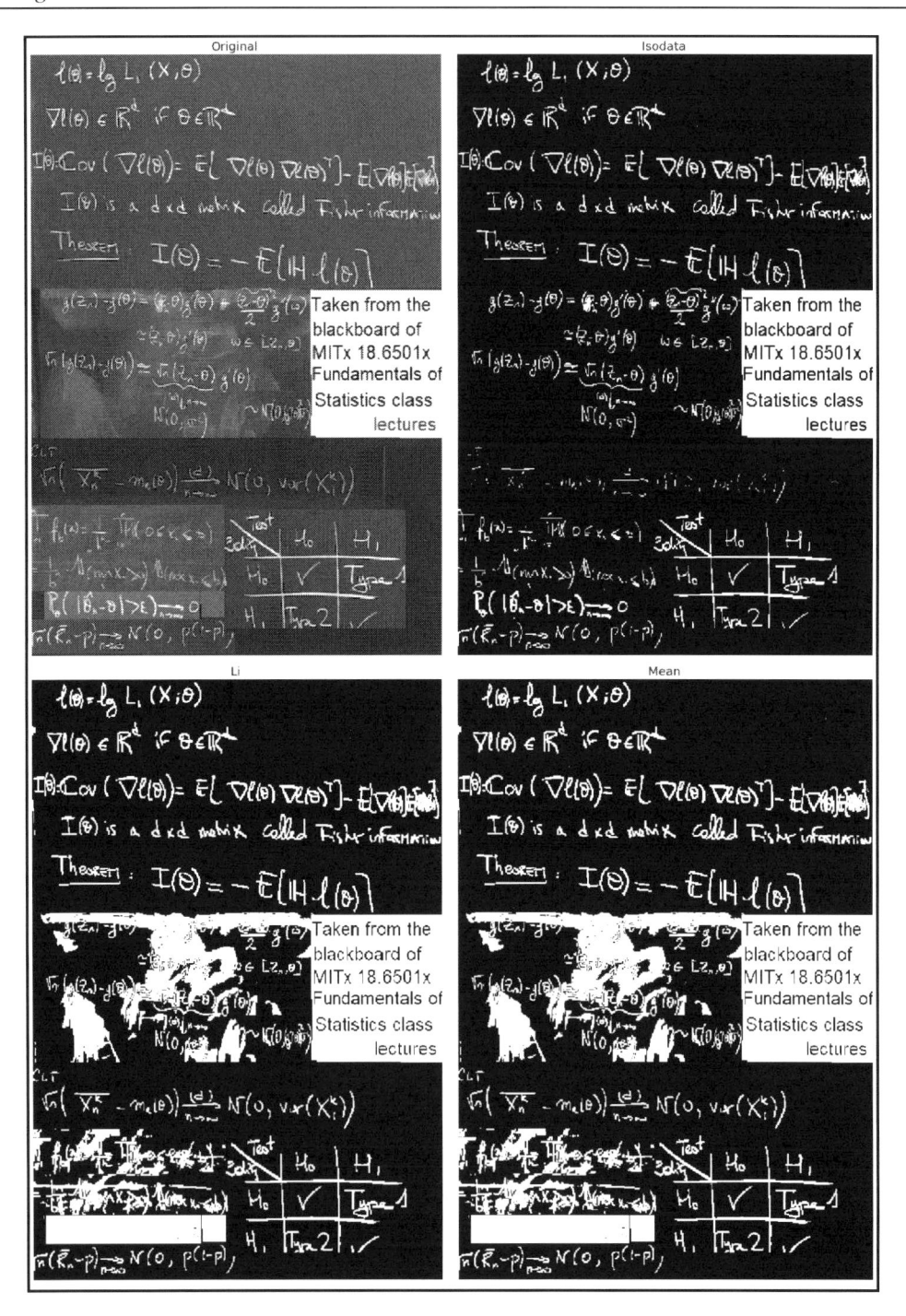

Image Segmentation

See also

Refer to the following articles to learn more about this recipe:

- https://ieeexplore.ieee.org/stamp/stamp.jsp?arnumber=4310039
- https://engineering.purdue.edu/kak/computervision/ECE661.08/OTSU_paper.pdf
- https://scikit-image.org/docs/dev/api/skimage.filters.html#skimage.filters.try_all_threshold
- https://mahotas.readthedocs.io/en/latest/thresholding.html
- *Chapter 8, Image Segmentation*, from the Packt Publishing book *Hands-On Image Processing with Python*.

Image segmentation with self-organizing maps

A **self-organizing map** (SOM) is a competitive learning network (an interesting class of unsupervised machine learning), and it is one of the most popular neural network models. In this network, only one neuron gets activated at a given time, so the output neurons compete among themselves to be activated. This activated neuron is called the **winning neuron**. When one neuron fires, its closest neighbors tend to get more excited than ones that are further away (defining a topological neighborhood with decaying distance). As a result, the neurons are forced to organize themselves (through an adaptive or learning process) and a feature map between inputs and outputs is created. That's why this network is known as a self-organizing map.

The adaptive process of the SOM algorithm takes place in the following two steps:

1. **Ordering (self-organizing) phase**: The topological ordering of the weight vectors happens in this phase. Typically, this takes around 1,000 iterations.
2. **Convergence phase**: In this phase, the feature map is fine-tuned and forms an accurate statistical quantification of the input space. Typically, it takes at least as many iterations as 500 times the number of neurons.

Image Segmentation

SOM can be used for clustering data when the class labels are not available. It's also known as the **self-organizing feature map (SOFM)** since it can be used to detect features that are inherent to the problem. Map units (neurons) typically form a two-dimensional lattice, and this provides a topology-preserving mapping from the high-dimensional space onto a plane. The SOM model also has a generalization ability, where a new input datapoint is assimilated by the neuron it's mapped to.

> To know the steps for the SOM algorithm and how it can be used for image segmentation through the quantization of colors, refer to the following links:
> - http://www.math.le.ac.uk/people/ag153/homepage/AkindukoMirkesGorbanInfTech2016.pdf
> - https://genome.tugraz.at/MedicalInformatics2/SOM.pdf
> - http://www.cs.bham.ac.uk/~jxb/NN/l16.pdf

In this recipe, you will learn to implement image segmentation by color quantization using SOM with the Python library `minisom`.

Getting ready

In this recipe, we are going to use an *RGB* image of apples and orange and segment the image with SOM. Let's first start by importing the required packages:

```
!pip install MiniSom
from minisom import MiniSom
import numpy as np
import matplotlib.pyplot as plt
from matplotlib.gridspec import GridSpec
from pylab import pcolor
from collections import defaultdict
from sklearn import datasets
from sklearn.preprocessing import scale
```

How to do it...

Go through the following steps to implement the image color quantization with SOM:

1. Let's define the following function to segment an RGB color image with SOM. The function accepts the input image along with the dimension of the SOM grid ($n_x \times n_y$) and the parameters σ and n (the number of random pixels to be chosen to *train* the network—that is, learn the weight vectors at the neurons). The image needs to be flattened (that is, each row should represent the RGB values for a single pixel) before the SOM is trained:

   ```
   def segment_with_SOM(image, nx, ny, sigma=1., n=500):

       pixels = np.reshape(image, (image.shape[0]*image.shape[1], 3))

       # SOM initialization and training
       som = MiniSom(x=nx, y=ny, input_len=3, sigma=sigma, \
           learning_rate=0.2) # nx x ny final colors
       som.random_weights_init(pixels)
       starting_weights = som.get_weights().copy() # saving \
           the starting weights
       som.train_random(pixels, n)
   ```

2. Once the training finishes, use the SOM to quantize all the pixels in the image (using the weight vectors at each neuron) with the following code snippet.

   ```
   # quantization
   qnt = som.quantization(pixels)
   ```

3. Replace the original pixel values by the quantized values with the following code and return the quantized image along with the weights at the neurons:

   ```
   clustered = np.zeros(image.shape)
   for i, q in enumerate(qnt): # place the quantized values into \
           a new image
       clustered[np.unravel_index(i, dims=(image.shape[0], \
           image.shape[1]))] = q
   final_weights = som.get_weights()
   return clustered, starting_weights, final_weights
   ```

Image Segmentation

4. Read the input image and call the function to segment the image into two clusters (with an 1 x 2 SOM grid), using SOM quantization. Plot the segmented binary image:

```
image = plt.imread('images/apples.png')
clustered, starting_weights, final_weights = \
                            segment_with_SOM(image, 1, 2, .1)
colors = np.unique(clustered.reshape(-1,3), axis=0)
clustered_binary = np.zeros_like(clustered)
clustered_binary[np.where((clustered[...,0]==colors[1][0]) & \
    (clustered[...,1]==colors[1][1]) & \
    (clustered[...,2]==colors[1][2]))] = 1.
```

5. If you run this code block and plot the input/output images (with two clusters), you will get a figure like the following one:

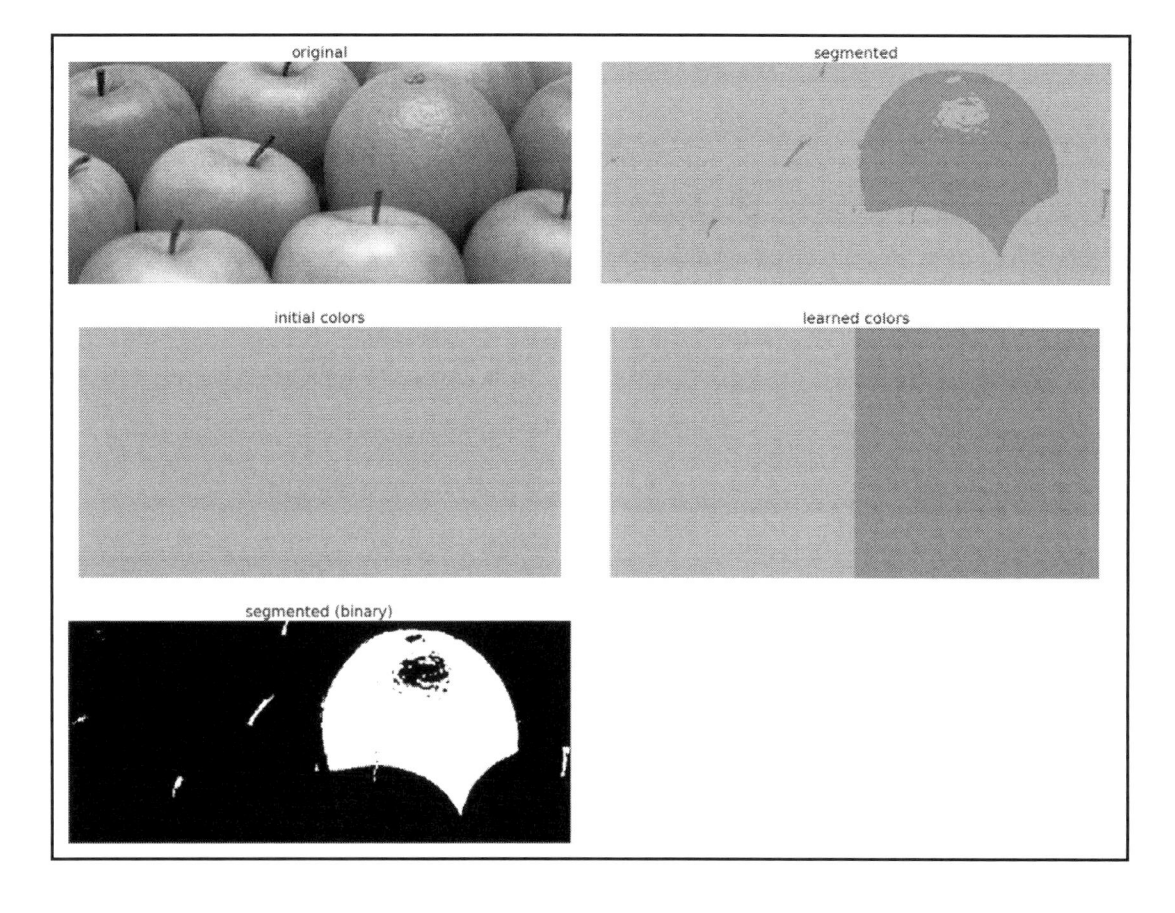

[234]

Chapter 6

6. If you run the following line of code and plot the input/output images (with 25 clusters, a using 5 x 5 SOM grid), you will get a figure like the following one:

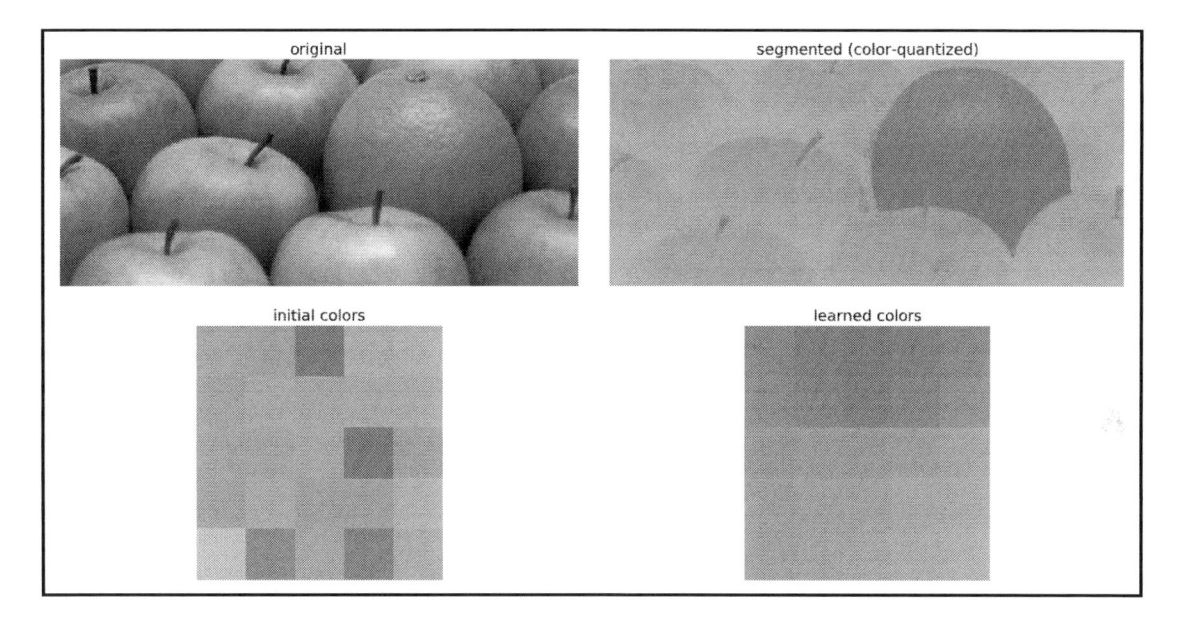

How it works...

We used the `train_random()` function to train the SOM by picking pixel samples at random from (flattened) image data. Along with the input image, it accepts a second parameter, `num_iteration`, that denotes the maximum number of iterations (one iteration per sample pixel).

We then used the function quantization to assign a code book (the weights vector of the winning neuron) to each pixel and thereby perform color quantization.

There's more...

We can use SOM for clustering images, too. Now you will learn how to cluster handwritten digit images using SOM.

Clustering handwritten digit images with SOM

Go through the following steps to cluster the digits images from the scikit-image dataset:

1. Load the digits and scale:

   ```
   digits = datasets.load_digits(n_class=10)
   data = digits.data # matrix where each row is a vector that represent a digit.
   data = scale(data)
   num = digits.target # num[i] is the digit represented by data[i]
   ```

2. Create a SOM grid with 900 (30 x 30) neurons. Initialize the neurons with PCA weights:

   ```
   som = MiniSom(30, 30, 64, sigma=4, learning_rate=0.5,
   neighborhood_function='triangle')
   som.pca_weights_init(data)
   ```

3. Train the SOM by choosing 5,000 randomly chosen digits using the following line of code:

   ```
   som.train_random(data, 5000) # random training
   ```

3. Finally, plot the distance map of the weights (each cell is the normalized sum of the distances between a neuron and its neighbors) and overlay the images of the digits on the cells (neurons):

   ```
   plt.figure(figsize=(15, 12))
   pcolor(som.distance_map().T, cmap='coolwarm')
   plt.colorbar()
   wmap = defaultdict(list)
   im = 0
   for x, t in zip(data, num): # scatterplot
       w = som.winner(x)
       wmap[w].append(im)
       plt.text(w[0]+.5, w[1]+.5, str(t),
                 color=plt.cm.Dark2(t / 10.), fontdict={'weight': \
                           'bold', 'size': 11})
       im = im + 1
   plt.axis([0, som.get_weights().shape[0], 0,
   som.get_weights().shape[1]])
   plt.show()
   ```

If you run this code block, you will get a figure like the following. From the distance map and the colorbar (to its right), note that the cells (neurons) that have different digits assigned to their neighbors have high values on the distance map (and the cells that have the same digits assigned to all their neighbors typically have low values on the distance map), as expected:

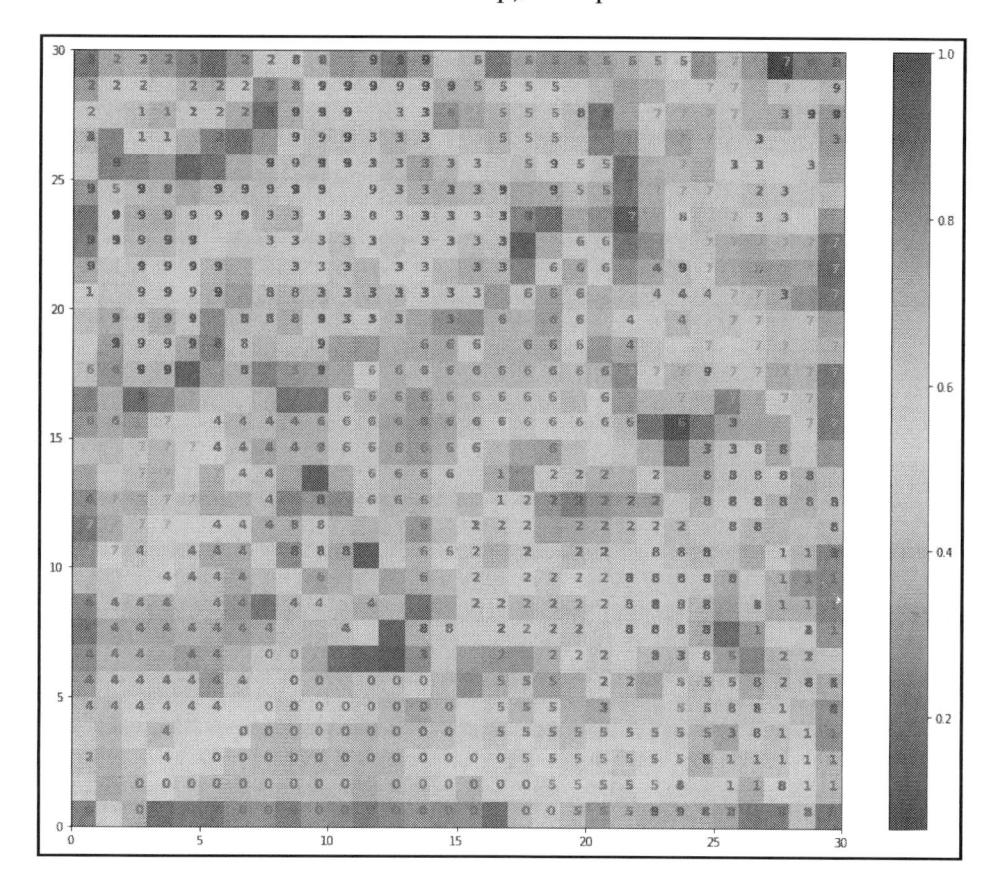

4. Plot the digits that are mapped to a particular cell at the coordinates (23,15) on the grid using the following code:

```
print(wmap[23,15])
# [581, 598, 1361] # 3 digits assigned to node (23,15)
plt.gray()
for index in wmap[23,15]:
 plt.figure(figsize=(1,1))
 plt.imshow(np.reshape(digits.images[index], (8,-1))), \
     plt.title(digits.target[index]), plt.axis('off')
 plt.show()
```

Image Segmentation

You will get the following output:

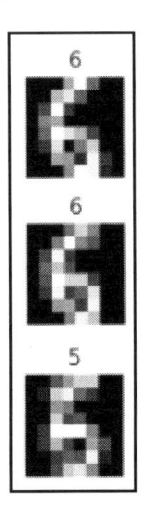

As you can see, three digits were assigned to the same neuron.

See also

Refer to the following articles to learn more about this recipe:

- `http://www.cs.bham.ac.uk/~jxb/NN/l16.pdf`
- `https://genome.tugraz.at/MedicalInformatics2/SOM.pdf`
- `https://github.com/JustGlowing/minisom`
- `http://www.math.le.ac.uk/people/ag153/homepage/AkindukoMirkesGorbanInfTech2016.pdf`
- `https://www.youtube.com/watch?v=-_d0h3VhpAs`

RandomWalk segmentation with scikit-image

RandomWalk segmentation is an interactive, multilabel image-segmentation method. It starts with a few seed pixels with user-defined labels and then, for each unlabeled pixel, the probability that a random walker starting at that particular pixel will first reach one of the prelabeled pixels is computed. Then the unlabeled pixel is assigned the label corresponding to the higher of the probability values (denoting the probability of reaching first). This results in a high-quality image segmentation. The following figure describes the algorithm steps:

Random Walk for Image Segmentation	Combinatorial Dirichlet problem
Algorithm 1) Map the image intensities to edge weights in the lattice $$w_{ij} = \exp(-\beta(g_i - g_j)^2),$$ g_i = image intensity at pixel i 2) Obtain a set, V_M, of marked (labeled) pixels with K labels, either interactively or automatically. 3) Solve for the potentials $$L_U x^s = -B^T m^s$$ for each label except the final one, f (for computational efficiency). Set $x_i^f = 1 - \sum_{s<f} x_i^s$. 4) Obtain a final segmentation by assigning to each node, v_i, the label corresponding to $\max_s (x_i^s)$.	The **Dirichlet integral** $D[u] = \frac{1}{2}\int_\Omega \|\nabla u\|^2 d\Omega$ **harmonic function** $\nabla^2 u = 0$ **Laplace equation** combinatorial Laplacian matrix $$L_{ij} = \begin{cases} d_i & \text{if } i = j, \\ -w_{ij} & \text{if } v_i \text{ and } v_j \text{ are adjacent nodes,} \\ 0 & \text{otherwise,} \end{cases}$$ x_i^s = probability (potential) at node, v_i, for label, s $Q(v_j) = s, \forall v_j \in V_M, \sum_s x_i^s = 1, \forall v_i \in V$ set of labels seed for seed points points $$m_j^s = \begin{cases} 1 & \text{if } Q(v_j) = s, \\ 0 & \text{if } Q(v_j) \neq s. \end{cases} \quad s \in \mathbb{Z}, 0 < s \leq K$$

Ref: http://vision.cse.psu.edu/people/chenpingY/paper/grady2006random.pdf

In this recipe, you will learn how to use the scikit-image segmentation module's random walker segmentation implementation function to segment an image, starting from a few seed pixels marking the foreground and background of the image.

Image Segmentation

Getting ready

In this recipe, we are going to use the first image of the Earth by the MCC of the Mars Orbiter Spacecraft from the ISRO public images gallery (https://www.isro.gov.in/pslv-c25-mars-orbiter-mission/pictures-mars-colour-camera-mcc-onboard-india%E2%80%99s-mars-orbiter), and we will try to segment the land (foreground) from the sea (background) using random walker segmentation (a binary segmentation). Let's import all the required libraries first:

```
import numpy as np
import matplotlib.pyplot as plt
from skimage.segmentation import random_walker
from skimage import img_as_float
from skimage.exposure import rescale_intensity
from skimage.io import imread
from skimage.color import rgb2gray
```

How to do it...

Go through the following steps to implement the random walker segmentation with scikit-image functions:

1. Again, you first need to create a mask for the input image by (manually) picking a few seed pixels from the foreground (object) and background. For this implementation, the foreground/background seed pixels are marked green and red, respectively. A mask image with the seed pixels marked is provided for the input image to be segmented. First, read the input and mask images:

    ```
    img = imread('images/earth_by_MCC.png')
    mask = imread('images/earth_by_MCC_mask.png')
    ```

2. Extract the object and background seed pixels from the mask image with the following code and create a new marker image in the way that the `random_walker` function expects (that is, mark the seed pixels with distinct positive labels for each segment and leave the unlabeled pixels as zero labels):

```
markers = np.zeros(img.shape[:2],np.uint8)
markers[(mask[...,0] >= 200) & (mask[...,1] <= 20) & (mask[...,2] <= 20)] = 1
markers[(mask[...,0] <= 20) & (mask[...,1] >= 200) & (mask[...,2] <= 20)] = 2
```

3. Run the random walker algorithm to segment the images in order to obtain the binary segmentation and the full probabilities assigned to the pixels using the following lines of code:

```
labels = random_walker(img, markers, beta=9, mode='bf', multichannel=True)
labels2 = random_walker(img, markers, beta=9, mode='bf', multichannel=True, return_full_prob = True)
```

4. Finally, plot the input images and the results obtained:

```
fig, ((ax1, ax2), (ax3, ax4)) = plt.subplots(2, 2, figsize=(20, 18), sharex=True, sharey=True)
fig.subplots_adjust(0,0,1,0.95,0.01,0.01)
ax1.imshow(mask, interpolation='nearest'), ax1.axis('off')
ax1.set_title('Original Image with Markers', size=25)
ax2.imshow(img, interpolation='nearest'), ax2.contour(labels, linewidths=5, colors='r'), ax2.axis('off')
ax2.set_title('Segmentation Contour', size=25)
ax3.imshow(labels, cmap='gray', interpolation='nearest'), ax3.axis('off')
ax3.set_title('Segmentation', size=25)
prob = ax4.imshow(labels2[1,...], cmap='inferno', interpolation='nearest')
ax4.axis('off'), ax4.set_title('Segmentation Probabilities', size=25)
fig.colorbar(prob, ax=ax4)
plt.show()
```

Image Segmentation

How it works...

If you run these code blocks, you will get the following output:

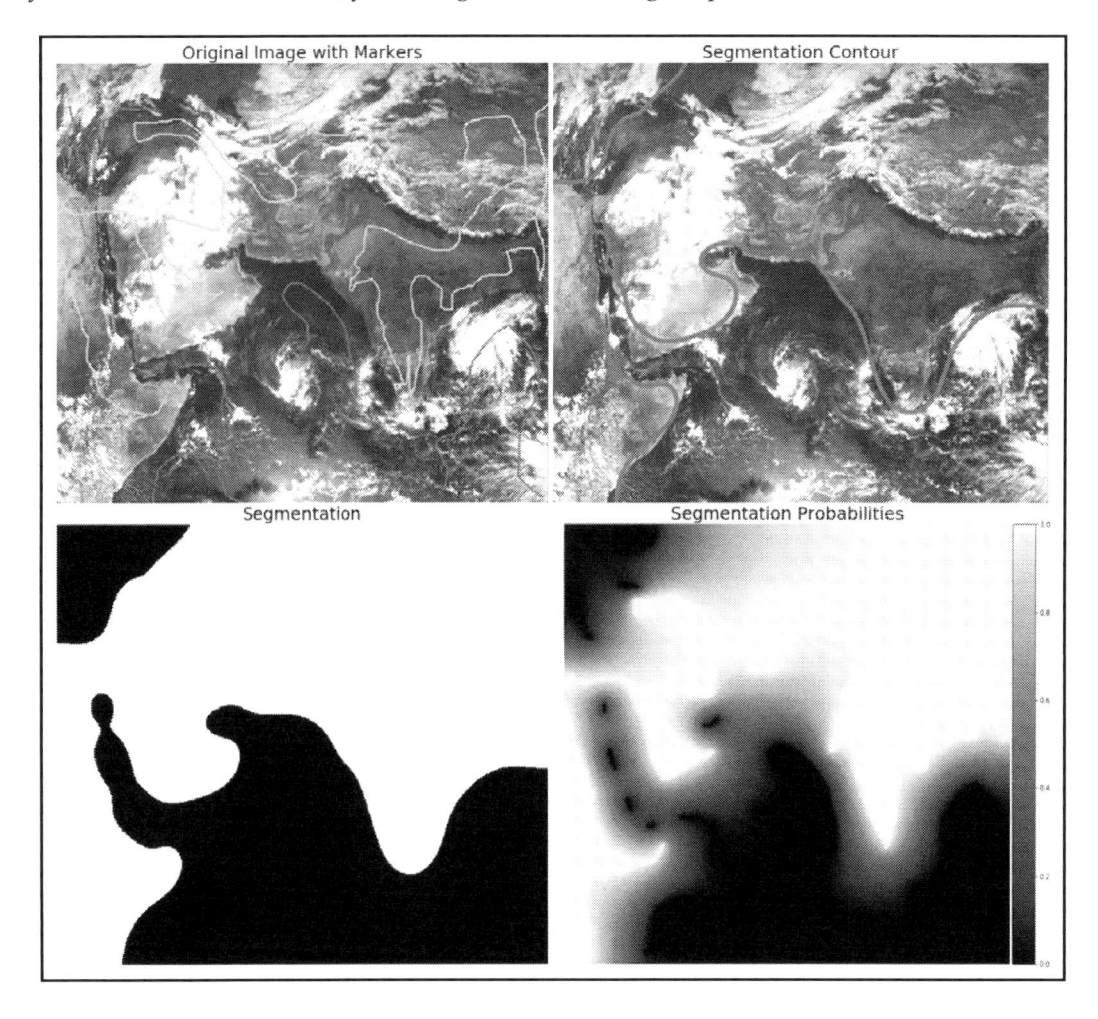

The `random_walker()` function from scikit-image segmentation was used to implement the random walker algorithm for segmentation from the markers. We used a colored input image, so we set the multichannel parameter to `True`.

The `return_full_prob` parameter to the same function was assigned to `True` in order to obtain all the probability values of a pixel belonging to each label. When this parameter is `False` (which is the default case), it returns only the most likely label.

The algorithm solves the infinite time diffusion equation, with the sources placed on the markers of each of the phases (known as labels). The phase (label) that has the highest probability to diffuse to an unlabeled pixel first is the one the pixel gets labeled with.

The diffusion equation is solved by minimizing the weighted graph Laplacian $x^T L x$ of the image, x being the probability that a marker of the given phase (label) first reaches a pixel by diffusion.

There's more...

Try the multilabel segmentation with more than two labels using random walker segmentation. For example, if you segment the bones image with the appropriate seed pixel markers, run segmentation, and plot all the input/output images, you should get an output like the following with the input image taken from `https://www.rsipvision.com/ct-segmentation-orthopedic-surgery/`:

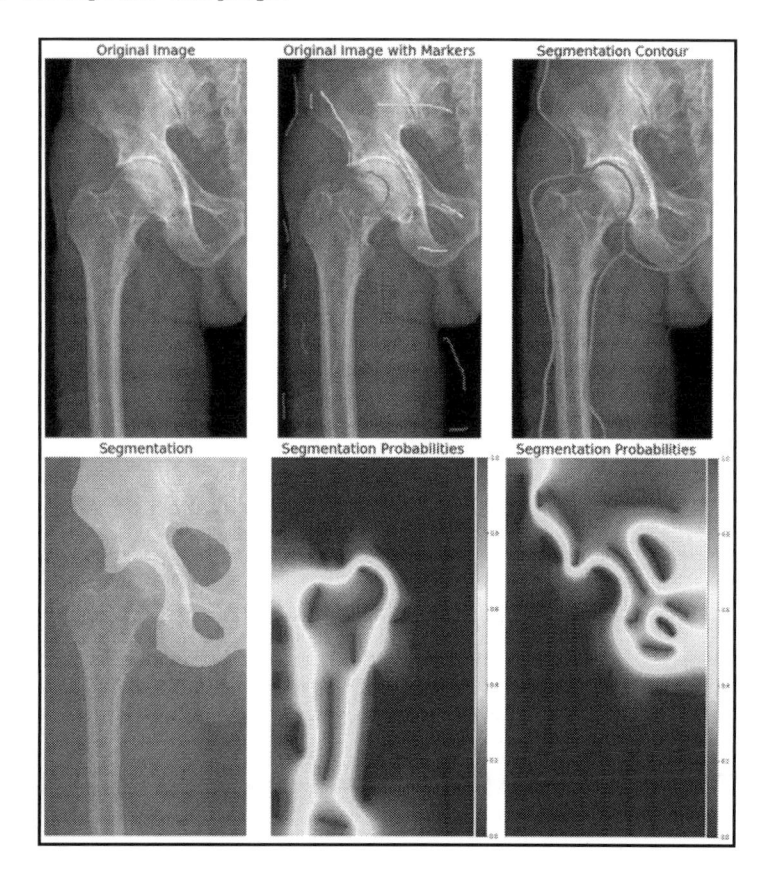

See also

Refer to the following articles to learn more about this recipe:

- http://vision.cse.psu.edu/people/chenpingY/paper/grady2006random.pdf
- https://scikit-image.org/docs/dev/api/skimage.segmentation.html#skimage.segmentation.random_walker
- https://www.rsipvision.com/ct-segmentation-orthopedic-surgery/

Human skin segmentation with the GMM-EM algorithm

In this recipe, you will learn how to use a parametric model (namely, a Gaussian mixture model) to detect color and segment the pixels corresponding to human skin in an image. You will be given a dataset containing a set of RGB pixel values and their labels (whether they correspond to human skin or not). This dataset is from the UCI Machine Learning Repository, and it is collected by randomly sampling R, G, and B values from images of the faces of different age groups (young, middle-aged, old), regions, and genders. The following table shows the size of the samples in the dataset to be used:

Total learning sample size	Skin sample size	Non-skin sample size
245057	50859	194198

> We shall use the YCbCr colorspace instead of RGB, since it separates the luminance from chrominances in RGB values using a linear transform. Then we will train a parametric model on the given dataset, but only using the chrominance channels.

The color-channel values of human skin/non-skin samples from our dataset can be thought of being generated using a mixture of distributions of multimodal random variables from multiple sources. We will use a finite **Gaussian mixture model** (**GMM**) to estimate the **probability density function** (**pdf**) as the skin color samples in our dataset generate multimodal random variables. Here, we assume that a (2D) Gaussian form is sufficient for each single source. Hence, you will train a Gaussian mixture model on the given dataset and estimate the parameters of the mixture model using the **expectation-maximization** (**EM**) algorithm. Once the parameters are learned, you will use the model to predict which pixels from a new test image belong to human skin.

> To learn about the EM algorithm to be used to estimate the GMM parameters go to https://courses.edx.org/courses/course-v1:ColumbiaX+CSMM.102x+2T2017/course/.

We will fit a GMM on the positive (skin) examples and another one on the negative (nonskin) examples. For each pixel in an image, we will compute the score (for example, log-likelihood) that it is human skin, using the trained GMMs. In this recipe, you will learn how to use scikit-learn's implementation of the Gaussian mixture model for skin-color detection and segmentation.

Getting ready

First, download the skin segmentation dataset from the UCI Machine Learning Repository at https://archive.ics.uci.edu/ml/datasets/skin+segmentation. This dataset has the dimensions of 245057 x 4 and the first three columns are B, G, R values (corresponding to the variables $x1$, $x2$, and $x3$, respectively) and the fourth column is the class label (decision variable y, where $y = 1$ is a positive (that is, a skin example) and $y = 2$ is a nonskin example). Let's start by importing all the required libraries:

```
import numpy as np
import matplotlib as mpl
import matplotlib.pyplot as plt
from sklearn.mixture import GaussianMixture
import pandas as pd
import seaborn as sns
from skimage.io import imread
from skimage.color import rgb2ycbcr, gray2rgb
```

How to do it...

Go through the following steps to segment the skins using scikit-learn's `GaussianMixture`:

1. Read the training dataset that you downloaded as a pandas DataFrame:

    ```
    df = pd.read_csv('images/Skin_NonSkin.txt', header=None,
    delim_whitespace=True)
    df.columns = ['B', 'G', 'R', 'skin']
    ```

Image Segmentation

The next screenshot shows what the first few rows of the data look like:

B	G	R	skin
74	85	123	1
73	84	122	1
72	83	121	1
70	81	119	1
70	81	119	1

2. Plot the distribution of the RGB values for skin and nonskin examples separately, using boxplot:

```
g = sns.factorplot(data=pd.melt(df, id_vars='skin'), \
    x='variable', y='value', hue='variable', col='skin', \
    kind='box', palette=sns.color_palette("hls", 3)[::-1])
plt.show()
```

If you run the code snippet, you will obtain a figure like the following one:

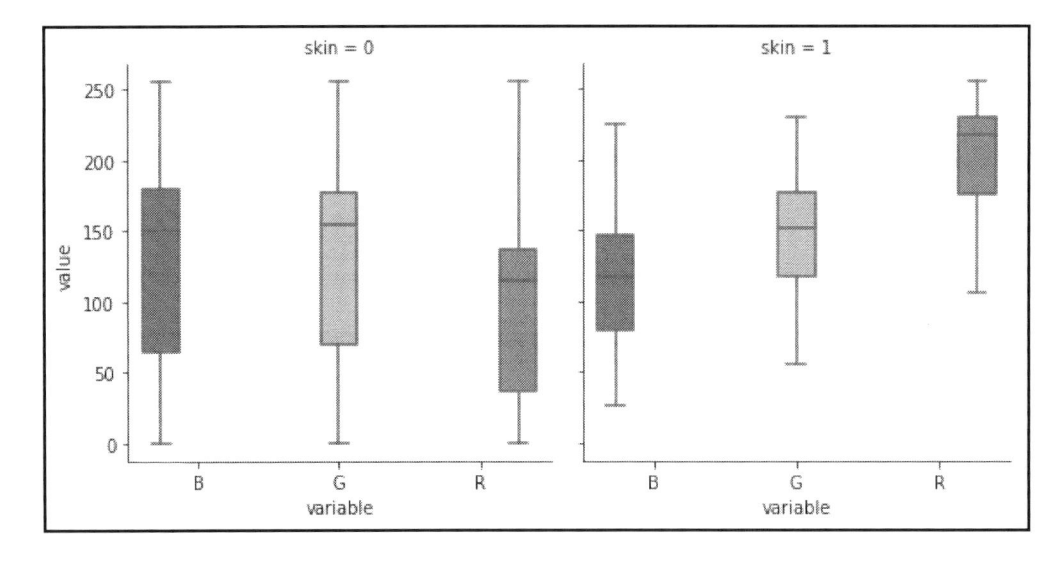

[246]

3. Obtain C_b and C_r channel values from the RGB values of pixels and plot their distribution for skin and nonskin examples separately, using boxplot:

```
#Y = .299*r + .587*g + .114*b # not needed
df['Cb'] = np.round(128 -.168736*df.R -.331364*df.G + \
                    .5*df.B).astype(int)
df['Cr'] = np.round(128 +.5*df.R - .418688*df.G - \
                    .081312*df.B).astype(int)
df.drop(['B','G','R'], axis=1, inplace=True)
g = sns.factorplot(data=pd.melt(df, id_vars='skin'), \
        x='variable', y='value', hue='variable', \
        col='skin', kind='box')
plt.show()
```

If you run this code snippet, you will obtain a figure like the following one:

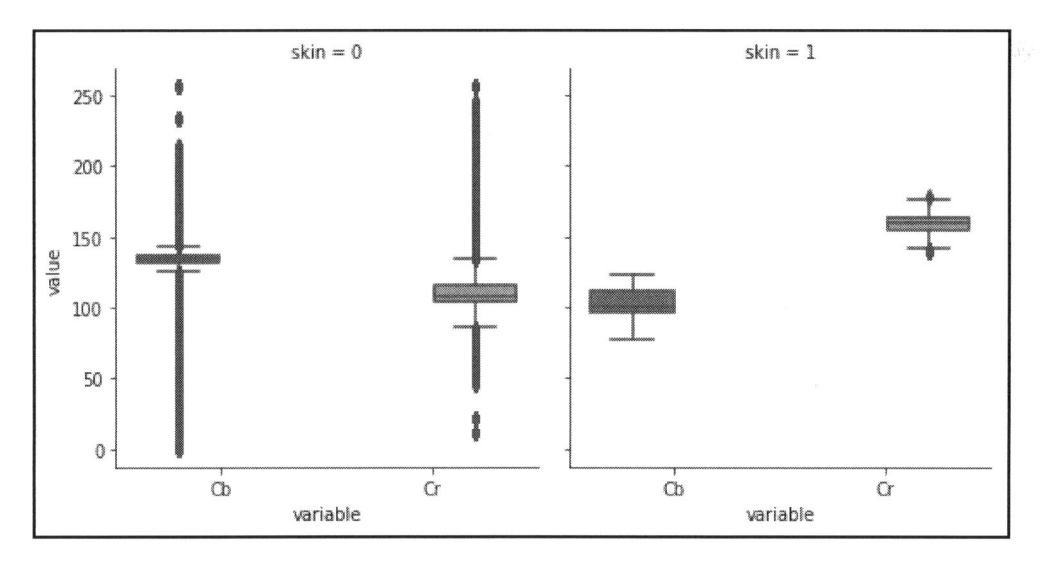

4. Now, using the following code block, separate the skin and nonskin training examples and fit two Gaussian mixture models, one on the skin examples and another on the nonskin examples, each using 4 Gaussian components:

```
skin_data = df[df.skin==1].drop(['skin'], axis=1).to_numpy()
not_skin_data = df[df.skin==2].drop(['skin'], axis=1).to_numpy()
skin_gmm = GaussianMixture(n_components=4,
covariance_type='full').fit(skin_data)
not_skin_gmm = GaussianMixture(n_components=4,
covariance_type='full').fit(not_skin_data)
colors = ['navy', 'turquoise', 'darkorange', 'gold']
```

Image Segmentation

5. Define the following function to visualize the Gaussian mixture models fitted for skin and nonskin:

```
def draw_ellipses(gmm, ax):
 for n, color in enumerate(colors):
 covariances = gmm.covariances_[n][:2, :2]
 v, w = np.linalg.eigh(covariances)
 u = w[0] / np.linalg.norm(w[0])
 angle = np.arctan2(u[1], u[0])
 angle = 180 * angle / np.pi # convert to degrees
 v = 2. * np.sqrt(2.) * np.sqrt(v)
 ell = mpl.patches.Ellipse(gmm.means_[n, :2], v[0], v[1], \
         180 + angle, color=color)
 ell.set_clip_box(ax.bbox)
 ell.set_alpha(0.5)
 ax.add_artist(ell)
 ax.set_aspect('equal', 'datalim')
```

If you run the code block to plot the skin and nonskin GMMs fitted, you will get an output like the following image:

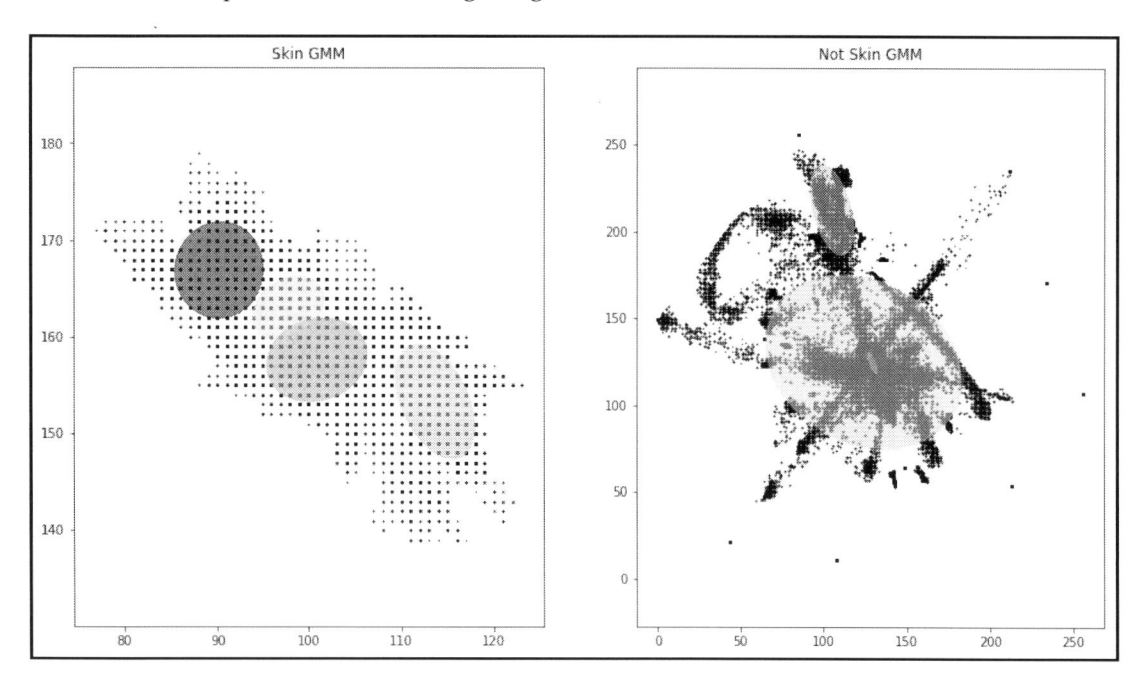

[248]

6. Now load the input image that you want to segment (containing human faces/skins), convert it to the *YCbCr* colorspace, and score each pixel in the image with both the mixture models. Mask out the pixels where the score predicted by the skin GMM is lower (that is, the pixels that were predicted to be nonskin) and obtain the final segmentation result:

```
image = imread('images/skin.png')[...,:3]
proc_image = np.reshape(rgb2ycbcr(image), (-1, 3))
skin_score = skin_gmm.score_samples(proc_image[...,1:])
not_skin_score = not_skin_gmm.score_samples(proc_image[...,1:])
result = skin_score > not_skin_score
result = result.reshape(image.shape[0], image.shape[1])
result = np.bitwise_and(gray2rgb(255*result.astype(np.uint8)), image)
```

How it works...

If you run the code snippets and plot the input and result images, you will get a figure like the following one:

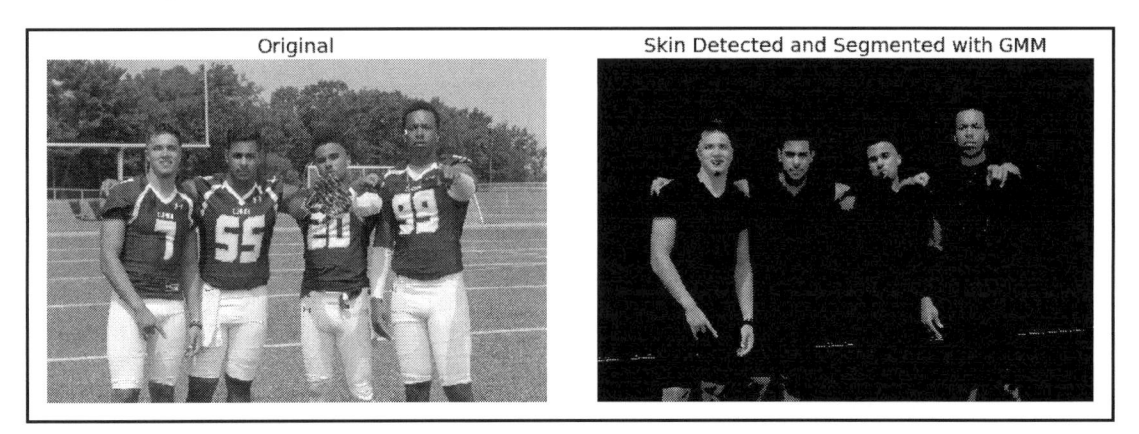

The `GaussianMixture` class from scikit-learn's mixture module was used to implement the GMM. The parameters of a Gaussian mixture distribution can be estimated (with MLE) using this class.

We created two instances of the `GaussianMixture` class: one for the skin (fitted on the skin samples) another for the `NonSkin` (fitted on the nonskin samples).

The `fit()` method of this class was used to estimate the parameters of the GMM with the EM algorithm.

The `score()` method of this class was used to compute the log-likelihood of each pixel in the input image.

See also

Refer to the following articles to learn more about this recipe:

- https://ce-publications.et.tudelft.nl/publications/465_adaptive_gaussian_mixture_model_for_skin_color_segmentation.pdf
- http://www.jatit.org/volumes/Vol95No17/28Vol95No17.pdf
- https://archive.ics.uci.edu/ml/datasets/skin+segmentation
- http://people.csail.mit.edu/dsontag/courses/ml12/slides/lecture21.pdf

Medical image segmentation

Medical image segmentation aims to detect the boundaries separating different objects from the background inside a two-dimensional or three-dimensional medical image. Medical images are highly variable in nature, and this makes the medical image segmentation difficult. The variations arise because of major modes of variation in human anatomy and because of different modalities of the images being segmented (for example, X-ray, MRI, CT, microscopy, endoscopy, OCT, and so on) used to obtain medical images. Further diagnostic insights can be obtained from segmentation results to help doctors make decisions. Regions with missing edges, the absence of texture contrast, and so on create major issues, and many segmentation approaches have been proposed to fix them. The automatic measurement of organs, cell counting, and simulations based on the extracted boundary information are some applications of medical segmentation. In this recipe, you will learn how to use Python libraries, such as SimpleITK, and deep learning libraries, such as Keras, to segment a few medical images.

Getting ready

Let's import the required libraries, using the following code snippet:

```
import SimpleITK as sitk
import numpy as np
import matplotlib.pylab as plt
from scipy.stats import norm
from sklearn.mixture import GaussianMixture
```

How to do it...

Let's start by segmenting an MRI image using a GMM-EM with scikit-learn.

Segmentation with GMM-EM

Run the following steps to segment an MR T1 brain image using GMM–EM, this time using scikit-learn library functions:

1. First, download the atlas image from `atlas_slicez90.nii.gz` (this is a high-quality image, obtained by registering and averaging interpatient T1 brain images) from `https://github.com/curiale/Medical-Image-Analysis-IPython-Tutorials/tree/master/tutorial_3/data`. Read the brain slice image with the following code snippet:

    ```
    max_int_val = 512;
    image = sitk.ReadImage("images/atlas_slicez90.nii.gz",
    sitk.sitkFloat32)
    image = sitk.RescaleIntensity(image,0.0,max_int_val)
    image_data = sitk.GetArrayFromImage(image)
    ```

2. Compute the parameters for the Gaussian mixture model:

    ```
    g = GaussianMixture(n_components=4, covariance_type='diag',
        tol=0.01, max_iter=100, n_init=1, init_params='kmeans')
    ```

3. Estimate the GMM model parameters (using MLE) with the **expectation maximization (EM)** algorithm:

    ```
    g.fit(image_data[0].flatten().reshape(-1, 1))
    ```

Image Segmentation

4. Define the following function to plot the pdf of each Gaussian model:

```
def plot_pdf_models(x, g):
    we = g.weights_
    mu = g.means_
    si = np.sqrt(g.covariances_)
    for ind in range(0,we.shape[0]):
        plt.plot(x,we[ind]*norm.pdf(x, mu[ind], si[ind]),linewidth=4)
```

5. Plot the Class pdf:

```
x = np.linspace(0,max_int_val,500)
plt.figure(figsize=(16, 5), dpi=100)
plot_pdf_models(x,g)
plt.hist(image_data.flatten(), bins=int(max_int_val/6), range=(0, max_int_val), normed=True)
plt.title('Class specific probability distribution functions',fontsize=20)
plt.show()
```

If you run the code block, you will get the following figure as the output:

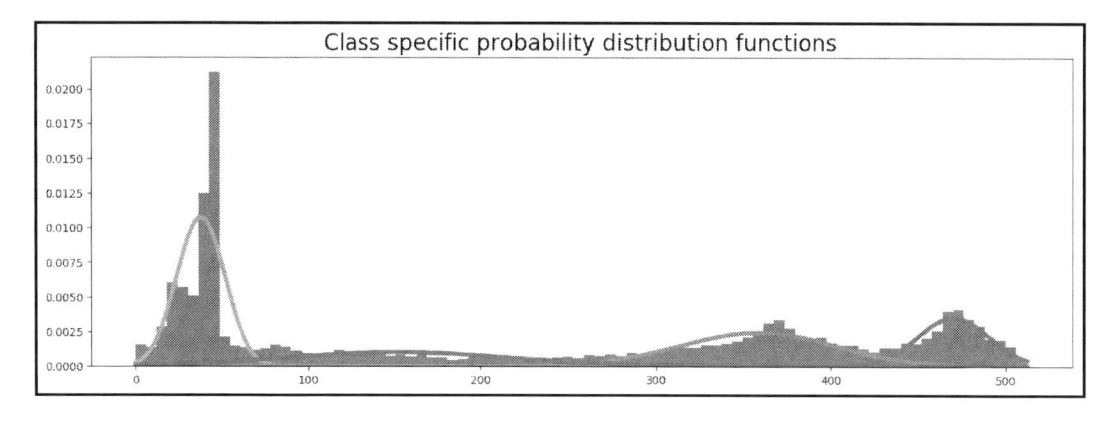

6. Compute and plot the class posterior probabilities for each Gaussian in the model:

```
plt.figure(figsize=(16, 3), dpi=100)
print(x.shape, g.predict_proba(x.reshape(-1,1)).shape)
plt.plot(x,g.predict_proba(x.reshape(-1,1)), linewidth=4)
plt.title('Class posterior probability under each Gaussian in the model',fontsize=20)
plt.show()
```

[252]

Chapter 6

Class posterior probability under each Gaussian in the model

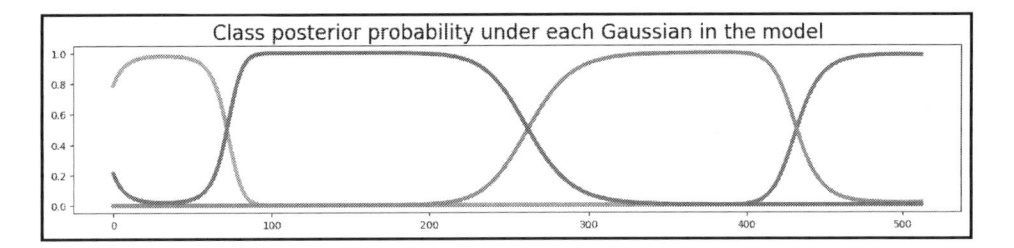

7. Finally, compute the label image obtained after segmentation with GMM:

```
label_data = g.predict(image_data[0].flatten().reshape(-1, 1))
#.flatten())
label_data = label_data.reshape(image_data[0].shape)
```

If you plot the input and the segmented (label) image with GMM–EM, you should get the following figure:

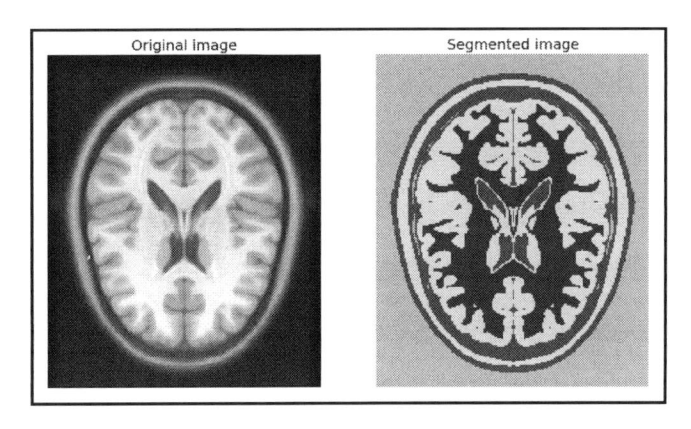

Brain tumor segmentation using deep learning

Run the following steps to segment an MR T2/flair brain image, this time using a pretrained deep learning model in Keras:

1. Start by importing the required libraries:

```
import keras
from keras.models import model_from_json
from keras.utils.vis_utils import plot_model
from skimage.transform import resize
from keras.utils.vis_utils import model_to_dot
keras.utils.vis_utils.pydot = pydot
```

[253]

Image Segmentation

2. First, download the pretrained weights for the deep learning (Unet) model from `https://drive.google.com/file/d/1hE9It0ZOOeIuSFvt6GdiR_0cq9inWdTy/view` (uploaded to the GitHub repository at `https://github.com/polo8214/Brain-tumor-segmentation-using-deep-learning/`). Load the model structure from the `.json` file and the (pretrained) weights from the `weights-full-best.h5` file. Plot the Unet deep learning model architecture:

```
loaded_model_json = open('models/model.json', 'r').read()
model = model_from_json(loaded_model_json)
model.load_weights('models/weights-full-best.h5')
plot_model(model, to_file='images/model_plot.png',
    show_shapes=True, show_layer_names=True)
```

If you run the code snippet, the weights will get loaded into the model. Part of the Unet model architecture is shown here:

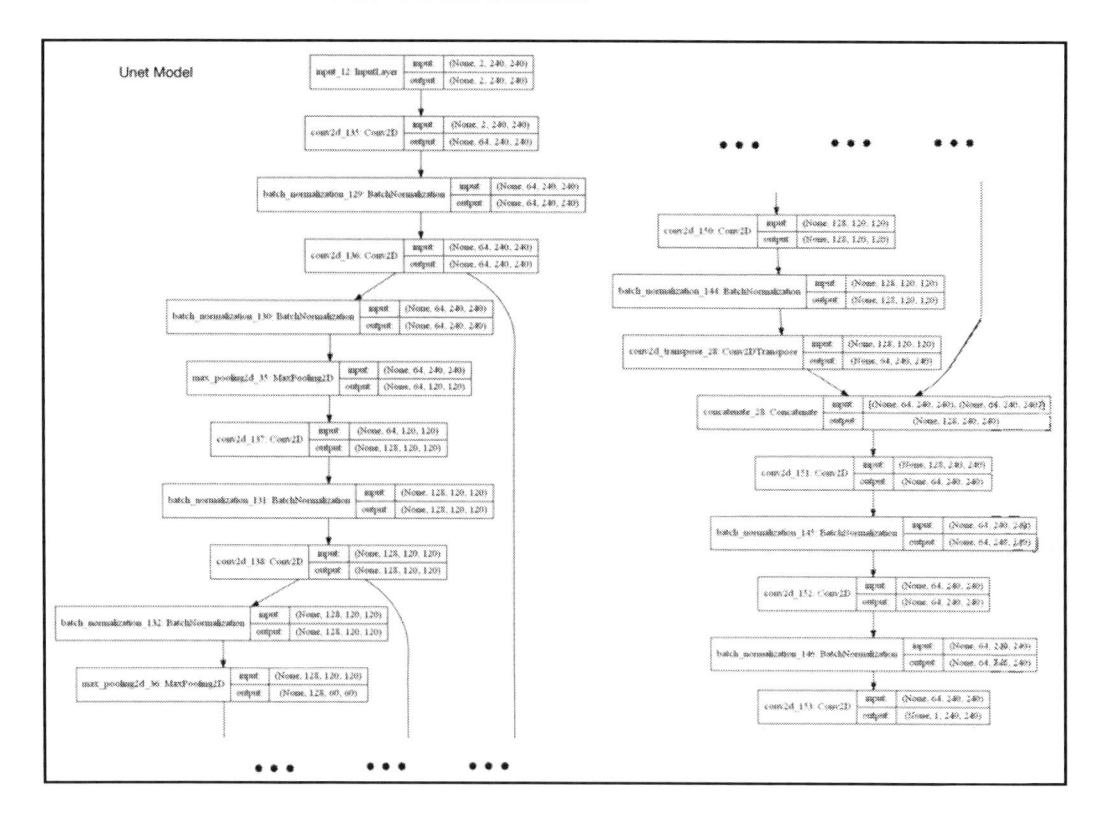

[254]

3. Use the MRI flair and T2 images (both the input images must be of size 240 x 240) as input images for full brain tumor segmentation. Preprocess the input images (for example, resize, z-score normalize, reshape, and so on) using the following code snippet to prepare the input for the deep learning model:

```
x = np.zeros((1,2,240,240),np.float32)
Flair =
resize((rgb2gray(imread('images/Flair.png')).astype('float32')),
(240,240))
T2 = resize((rgb2gray(imread('images/T2.png'))).astype('float32'),
(240,240))
ground_truth = resize(rgb2gray(imread('images/ground_truth.png')),
(240,240))
T2 = (T2-T2.mean()) / T2.std()
Flair = (Flair-Flair.mean()) / Flair.std()
x[:,:1,:,:] = np.reshape(Flair, (1,1,240,240))
x[:,1:,:,:] = np.reshape(T2, (1,1,240,240))
```

4. Finally, predict the tumor from the input by running a Unet forward pass on it:

```
pred_full = model.predict(x)
pred_full = np.reshape(pred_full, (240,240))
```

5. If you run the code blocks and plot the input images, the ground truth (shown in red), and the predicted tumor (shown in yellow patch), then you will get a figure like the following one:

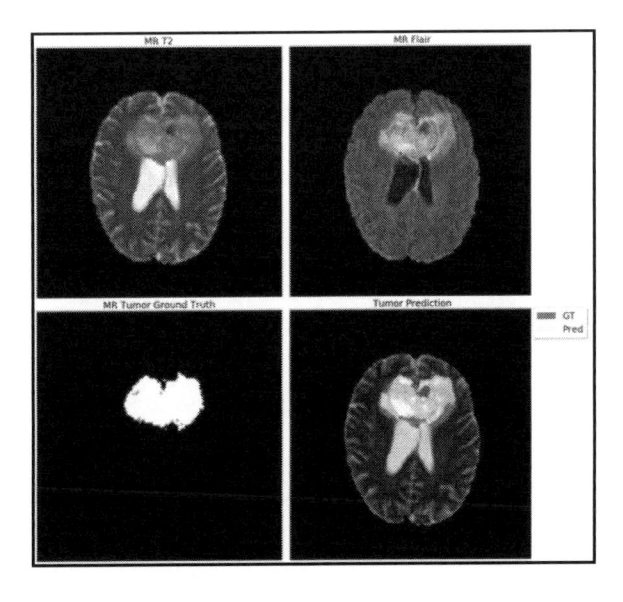

Segmentation with watershed

In this example, you will learn how to use the `SimpleITK` library functions to segment bacteria from a three-dimensional focused ion beam-scanning electron microscopy (FIB-SEM) image. The name of the bacterium is *bacillus subtilis*—it is a rod-shaped organism and is naturally found in plants and soil. Here are the steps involved:

1. Read the bacteria image and separate the foreground (bacteria) from the background (resin) using thresholding with a manually chosen threshold. Use morphological opening and closing to get rid of small components/holes with the following code block:

   ```
   img = sitk.ReadImage('images/fib_sem_bacillus_subtilis_slice_118.png', sitk.sitkFloat32)
   f = sitk.RescaleIntensityImageFilter()
   img = f.Execute(img, 0, 255)
   thresh_value = 120
   thresh_img = img>thresh_value
   cleaned_thresh_img = sitk.BinaryOpeningByReconstruction(thresh_img, [10, 10, 10])
   cleaned_thresh_img = sitk.BinaryClosingByReconstruction(cleaned_thresh_img, [10, 10, 10])
   ```

2. Compute the distance map. Seeds with a distance ≥ 10 from the object boundary are labeled uniquely. Relabel the seed objects with consecutive object labels when getting rid of all of the seeds with size ≤ 15 pixels:

   ```
   dist_img = sitk.SignedMaurerDistanceMap(cleaned_thresh_img != 0, \
                  insideIsPositive=False, squaredDistance=False, \
                  useImageSpacing=False)
   radius = 10
   seeds = sitk.ConnectedComponent(dist_img < -radius)
   seeds = sitk.RelabelComponent(seeds, minimumObjectSize=15)
   ```

3. Run the watershed segmentation algorithm on the distance map computed, with the seeds as markers:

   ```
   ws = sitk.MorphologicalWatershedFromMarkers(dist_img, seeds, markWatershedLine=True)
   ws = sitk.Mask( ws, sitk.Cast(cleaned_thresh_img, ws.GetPixelID()))
   ```

Chapter 6

If you run these code snippets and plot all the images obtained, you should get a figure like the following one:

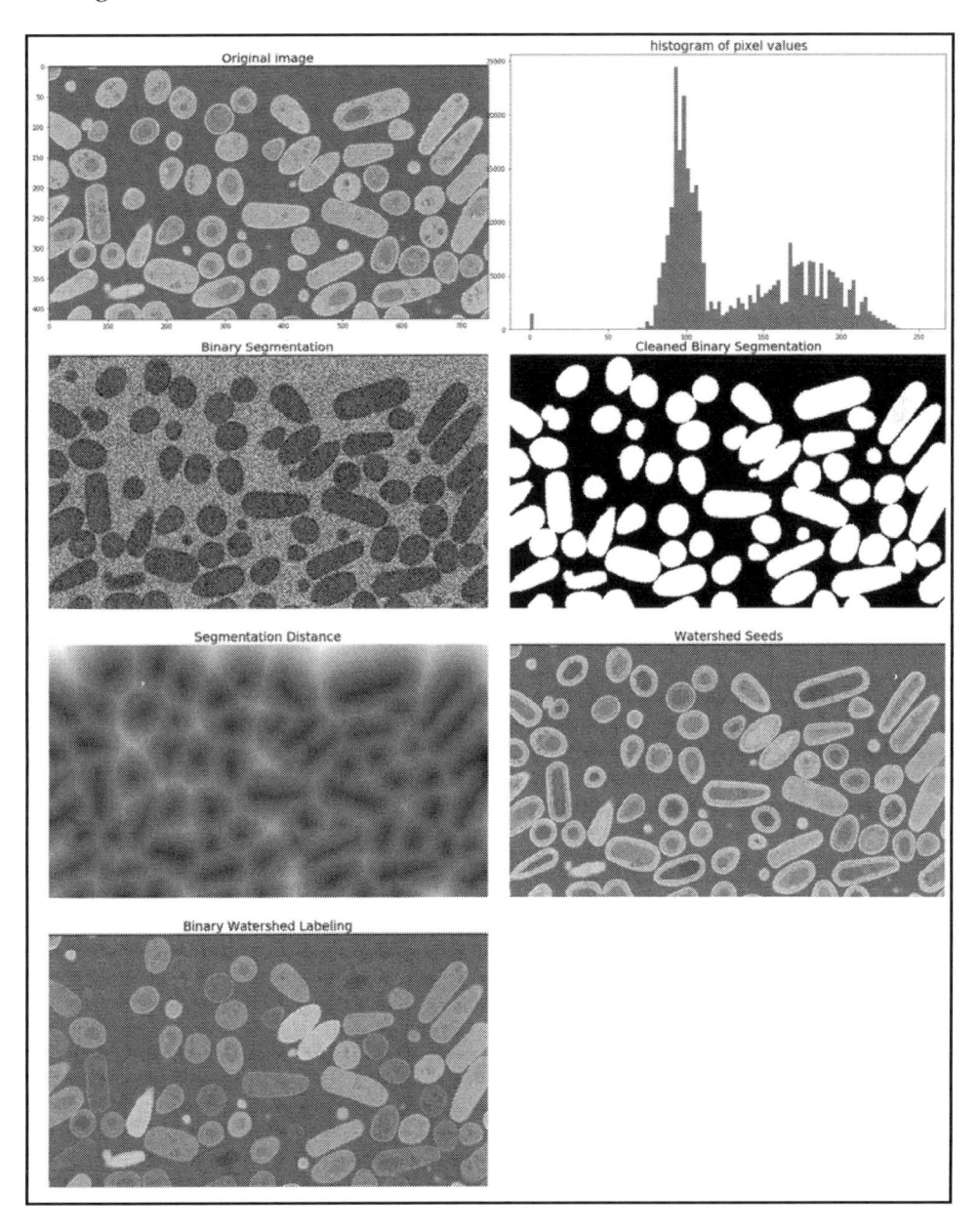

[257]

Image Segmentation

How it works...

We used SimpleITK's `MorphologicalWatershedFromMarkers` class for watershed segmentation implementation with morphological operators.

Watershed pixels were labeled 0. Output image labels were reordered in a way that the object labels became consecutive. Then those objects were sorted with respect to the object size with a `RelabelComponent` image filter.

There's more...

Use connected-component labeling to segment the MRI image (obtained from `https://github.com/loli/medpy/tree/master/notebooks/scripts/resources`). You should get a figure like the following one:

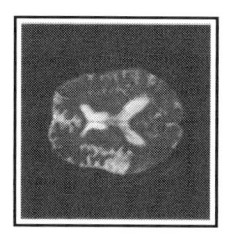

Implement region-growing segmentation with SimpleITK to segment an MR T1 image like the following figure:

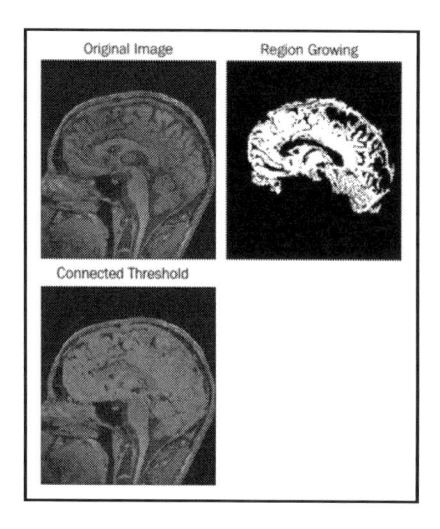

See also

Refer to the following articles to learn more about this recipe:

- https://github.com/curiale/Medical-Image-Analysis-IPython-Tutorials
- https://www5.cs.fau.de/research/groups/medical-image-segmentation/
- https://www.sciencedirect.com/topics/engineering/medical-image-segmentation
- http://yanivresearch.info/writtenMaterial/simpleITKNotebooks.pdf
- https://link.springer.com/epdf/10.1007/s10278-017-0037-8?author_access_token=yinJkOXIy1CDH5qFryMpife4RwlQNchNByi7wbcMAY7nZiB2CrLz3lP8Z25z8a70zrQ5n2yqVseS4BZxRjmiywgPJheGzjIWwgaNNDOjYBtsruXKIaTRDTIL4Ik2OSejaIJvtA9KgG0s0zbeOADArw%3D%3D
- https://stackoverflow.com/questions/47568515/simpleitk-installation-in-anaconda
- https://electron.nci.nih.gov/
- https://www.insight-journal.org/browse/publication/92
- https://www.youtube.com/watch?v=3zobt4O4ibs
- Chapter 8, *Image Segmentation*, from the Packt Publishing book *Hands-On Image Processing with Python*.

Deep semantic segmentation

Semantic segmentation refers to an understanding of an image at pixel level, that is, when we want to assign each pixel in the image an object class (a semantic label). It is a process to obtain coarse-to-fine inference. It achieves fine-grained inference by making dense predictions that infer labels for every pixel. Each pixel is assigned to a label with the class of its surrounding object/region. In this recipe, you will learn how to use a couple of deep learning (pretrained) models to perform semantic segmentation of images, using DeepLab V3+ and Caffe FCN.

Image Segmentation

Getting ready

First, download the pretrained model from `deeplabv3_pascal_trainval_2018_01_04.tar.gz` at `https://github.com/tensorflow/models/blob/master/research/deeplab/g3doc/model_zoo.md`. Import all the required libraries (the `tensorflow` and `keras` library modules) using the following code block:

```
from PIL import Image
import tensorflow as tf
from tensorflow.python.platform import gfile
from keras.models import import *
from keras.layers import *
from keras.optimizers import *
from keras.callbacks import ModelCheckpoint, LearningRateScheduler
from keras.preprocessing.image import ImageDataGenerator
from keras import backend as keras
import numpy as np
import skimage.io as io
import skimage.transform as trans
import matplotlib.pylab as plt
import imutils
from glob import glob
import os, time
```

How to do it...

Let's use the pretrained DeepLab V3 model and then an FCN for semantic segmentation.

Semantic segmentation with DeepLabV3

Run the following steps to implement semantic segmentation with DeepLabV3:

1. Define the following function to load the pretrained DeepLab V3 model (frozen-inference graph) and run a forward pass with `tensorflow` to obtain the segmentation map:

```
def run_semantic_segmentation(image, model_path):

    input_tensor_name = 'ImageTensor:0'
    output_tensor_name = 'SemanticPredictions:0'
    input_size = 513

    graph = tf.Graph()
```

```
graph_def = None
with gfile.FastGFile(model_path, 'rb') as f:
    graph_def = tf.GraphDef()
    graph_def.ParseFromString(f.read())
if graph_def is None:
  raise RuntimeError('Cannot find inference graph in tar \
                    archive.')
with graph.as_default():
  tf.import_graph_def(graph_def, name='')

sess = tf.Session(graph=graph)
width, height = image.size
resize_ratio = 1.0 * input_size / max(width, height)
target_size = (int(resize_ratio * width), \
              int(resize_ratio * height))
resized_image = image.convert('RGB').resize(target_size, \
                Image.ANTIALIAS)
batch_seg_map = sess.run(
    output_tensor_name,
    feed_dict={input_tensor_name: [np.asarray(resized_image)]})
seg_map = batch_seg_map[0]
return resized_image, seg_map
```

2. Define the following function to create a pascal label, `colormap`:

```
def create_pascal_label_colormap():
  colormap = np.zeros((256, 3), dtype=int)
  ind = np.arange(256, dtype=int)
  for shift in reversed(range(8)):
    for channel in range(3):
      colormap[:, channel] |= ((ind >> channel) & 1) << shift
    ind >>= 3
  return colormap
```

3. Next, define a function to convert the labels of the segmented image to the colors from the desired colormap:

```
def label_to_color_image(label):
  colormap = create_pascal_label_colormap()
  if np.max(label) >= len(colormap):
    raise ValueError('label value too large.')
  return colormap[label]
```

[261]

Image Segmentation

4. Define the following function to visualize the segmented image:

```python
def visualize_segmentation(image, seg_map):
    plt.figure(figsize=(20, 15))
    plt.subplots_adjust(left=0, right=1, bottom=0, top=0.95, \
        wspace=0.05, hspace=0.05)
    plt.subplot(221), plt.imshow(image), plt.axis('off'), \
        plt.title('input image', size=20)
    plt.subplot(222)
    seg_image = label_to_color_image(seg_map).astype(np.uint8)
    plt.imshow(seg_image), plt.axis('off'), \
        plt.title('segmentation map', size=20)
    plt.subplot(223), plt.imshow(image), plt.imshow(seg_image, \
        alpha=0.7), plt.axis('off')
    plt.title('segmentation overlay', size=20)
    unique_labels = np.unique(seg_map)
    ax = plt.subplot(224)
    plt.imshow(full_color_map[unique_labels].astype(np.uint8), \
        interpolation='nearest')
    ax.yaxis.tick_right(), plt.yticks(range(len(unique_labels)), \
        label_names[unique_labels])
    plt.xticks([], [])
    ax.tick_params(width=0.0, labelsize=20), plt.grid('off')
    plt.show()
```

5. Read the input image, run semantic segmentation using DeepLab V3, and visualize the results using the following code snippet:

```python
label_names = np.asarray([
    'background', 'aeroplane', 'bicycle', 'bird', 'boat', 'bottle',
    'bus', 'car', 'cat', 'chair', 'cow', 'diningtable', 'dog',
    'horse', 'motorbike', 'person', 'pottedplant', 'sheep', 'sofa',
    'train', 'tv'
])

full_label_map =
np.arange(len(label_names)).reshape(len(label_names), 1)
full_color_map = label_to_color_image(full_label_map)
image, seg_map =
run_semantic_segmentation(Image.open('images/pets.png'),
    'models/frozen_inference_graph.pb')
visualize_segmentation(image, seg_map)
```

If you run this code block, you will get the following figure. Note the difference between this and the instance segmentation from the last recipe:

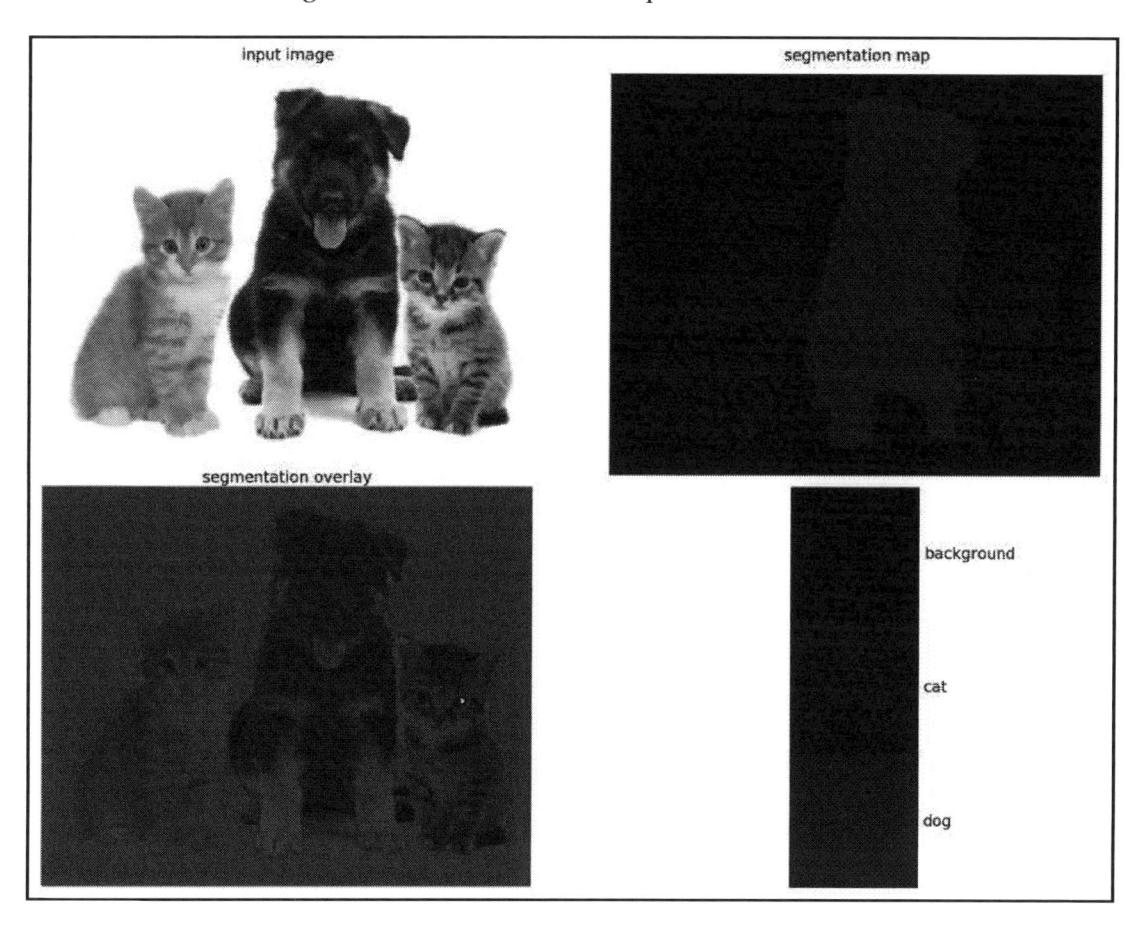

Run the same function with another (road) image. You will get the following output:

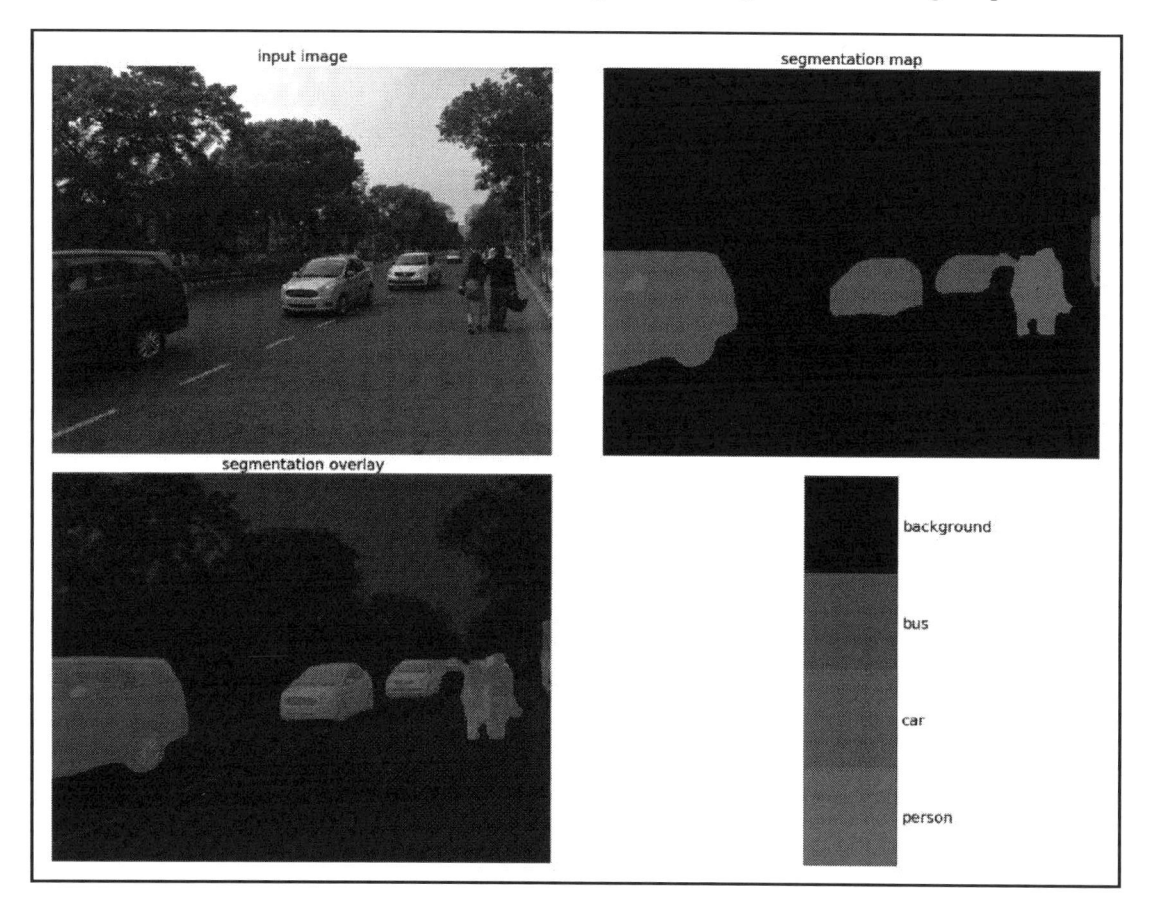

Semantic segmentation with FCN

Run the following steps to implement semantic segmentation with a pretrained **fully convolutional network (FCN)** model:

1. Download the pretrained Caffe FCN model from `http://dl.caffe.berkeleyvision.org/fcn8s-heavy-pascal.caffemodel` and save it to the `models` folder. Load the class label names and initialize the legend visualization using the following code block:

    ```
    lines = open('models/pascal-
    classes.txt').read().strip().split("\n")
    classes, colors = [], []
    ```

```
for line in lines:
    words = line.split(' ')
    classes.append(words[0])
    colors.append(list(map(int, words[1:])))
colors = np.array(colors, dtype="uint8")
legend = np.zeros(((len(classes) * 25) + 25, 300, 3),
dtype="uint8")

# iterate over the class names and colors and draw
for (i, (className, color)) in enumerate(zip(classes, colors)):
    color = [int(c) for c in color]
    cv2.putText(legend, className, (5, (i * 25) + 17), \
            cv2.FONT_HERSHEY_SIMPLEX, 0.5, (0, 0, 255), 2)
    cv2.rectangle(legend, (100, (i * 25)), (300, (i * 25) + 25), \
            tuple(color), -1)
```

2. Load the serialized FCN model from the disk, set the input image `blob` as the model input, and run a forward pass on it using `opencv-python` functions:

```
model = cv2.dnn.readNetFromCaffe \
    ('models/fcn8s-heavy-pascal.prototxt', \
    'models/fcn8s-heavy-pascal.caffemodel')
image = cv2.imread('images/cycling.jpeg')
image = cv2.cvtColor(image, cv2.COLOR_BGR2RGB)
image = imutils.resize(image, width=500)
blob = cv2.dnn.blobFromImage(image, 1, (image.shape[1], \
        image.shape[0]))
model.setInput(blob)
output = model.forward()
```

3. Obtain the total number of classes and the mask image shape from the output obtained. For each pixel coordinate in the image, find the class label with the maximum probability. Find the color (with which the pixel will be represented in the output mask image) corresponding to the label. Resize the mask and class map to the input image size:

```
(num_classes, height, width) = output.shape[1:4]
labels = output[0].argmax(0)
mask = colors[labels]
mask = cv2.resize(mask, (image.shape[1], image.shape[0]), \
        interpolation=cv2.INTER_NEAREST)
labels = cv2.resize(labels, (image.shape[1], image.shape[0]), \
        interpolation=cv2.INTER_NEAREST)
```

Image Segmentation

4. Compute a weighted linear combination of the input and mask image to create a segmentation overlay (for example, `output = 0.3 * image + 0.7 * mask`) and plot the images. You will get an output like the following one:

[266]

See also

Refer to the following articles to learn more about this recipe:

- `http://brainiac2.mit.edu/isbi_challenge/`
- `http://dl.caffe.berkeleyvision.org/`
- `https://github.com/tensorflow/models/blob/master/research/object_detection/g3doc/detection_model_zoo.md`
- `https://github.com/zhixuhao/unet`
- `https://www.youtube.com/watch?v=nLuYZAcuhrU`
- `https://www.youtube.com/watch?v=fh6AQN_0uDU`

Deep instance segmentation

Similar to deep semantic segmentation, deep instance segmentation also assigns a label to each pixel in an image. The labels collectively produce pixel-based masks for each object in an input image. The difference between these two techniques is that even if multiple objects have the same class label (for example, two cats and a dog in the input image shown in the following figure), the instance segmentation should report each object instance as a unique one (for example, a total of three unique objects: two cats and a dog), as opposed to the semantic segmentation that reports the total number of unique class labels found (for example, two unique classes, namely a cat and dog), as shown in the following screenshot:

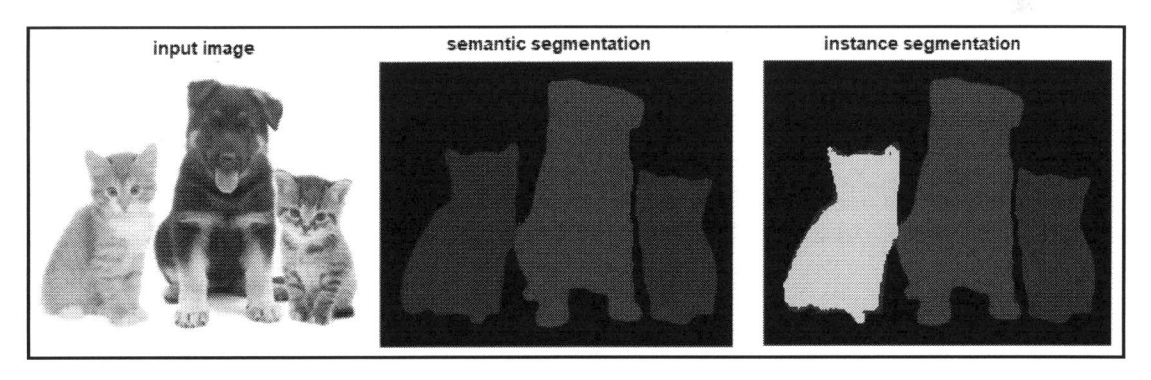

In this recipe, you will learn how to use a pretrained mask R-CNN deep learning model to perform instance segmentation.

Image Segmentation

The region-based CNN (R-CNN) is a model that pioneered deep learning-based object detection. This algorithm has the following four steps:

1. An image is input into the network.
2. Region proposals (image regions that can potentially contain objects) are computed using an algorithm such as selective search.
3. Features (an ROI) are extracted for each proposal using a pretrained CNN.
4. Each proposal is classified with a **support-vector machine** (**SVM**) classifier (using the features extracted).

However, since the R-CNN model is very slow in practice, the fast R-CNN model can be introduced with an end-to-end trainable network, using the following algorithm steps:

1. An image and the corresponding ground-truth bounding boxes are input.
2. The feature map is extracted.
3. ROI pooling is introduced and the ROI feature vector is extracted.
4. Two sets of fully connected layers are used to predict class labels and compute bounding boxes corresponding to the objects classified for each proposal.

> For more detailed coverage on fast R-CNN and mask R-CNN, please read through the article at `https://www.pyimagesearch.com/2018/11/19/mask-r-cnn-with-opencv/`.

Getting ready

First, download the pretrained mask-RCNN model from the model zoo (`http://download.tensorflow.org/models/object_detection/mask_rcnn_inception_v2_coco_2018_01_28.tar.gz`), extract the `frozen_inference_graph.pb` file, and save it to the `models` folder. Import all the required libraries to start with:

```
import numpy as np
import time
import cv2
import os
import random
import matplotlib.pylab as plt
print(cv2.__version__)
# 4.1.0
```

How to do it...

Go through the following steps to implement deep instance segmentation using `opencv-python` functions:

1. Define the following function to generate N random (bright) colors using the HSV colorspace:

   ```
   def random_colors(N, bright=True):
    brightness = 1.0 if bright else 0.7
    hsv = [(i / N, 1, brightness) for i in range(N)]
    colors = list(map(lambda c: colorsys.hsv_to_rgb(*c), hsv))
    random.shuffle(colors)
    return 256*np.array(colors)
   ```

2. Initialize the model constants and the path that you have used to download the model:

   ```
   model_path = 'models\\'
   conf = 0.5
   thresh = 0.3
   ```

3. Read the COCO class labels on which the mask R-CNN (pretrained) model was trained:

   ```
   labels_path = os.path.sep.join([model_path,
   "object_detection_classes_coco.txt"])
   labels = open(labels_path).read().strip().split("\n")
   ```

4. Initialize the paths to the pretrained mask R-CNN model weights and configuration files:

   ```
   weights_path = os.path.sep.join([model_path,
   "frozen_inference_graph.pb"])
   config_path = os.path.sep.join([model_path,
   "mask_rcnn_inception_v2_coco_2018_01_28.pbtxt"])
   ```

5. Load the pretrained mask R-CNN model from the disk:

   ```
   net = cv2.dnn.readNetFromTensorflow(weights_path, config_path)
   ```

Image Segmentation

6. Now, read the input image to be segmented, set it as the loaded model input, and run a forward pass on the model with it to get the object masks and the bounding boxes:

```
image = cv2.imread('images/pets.jpg')
blob = cv2.dnn.blobFromImage(image, swapRB=True, crop=False)
net.setInput(blob)
(boxes, masks) = net.forward(["detection_out_final",
"detection_masks"])
num_classes = masks.shape[1]
num_detections = boxes.shape[2]
print('# instances: {}'.format(num_detections))
# instances: 4
colors = random_colors(num_detections)
print("# classes: {}".format(num_classes))
# classes: 90
```

7. For each of the objects detected, if the score is higher than the confidence-threshold value, compute the bounding box corners:

```
h = image.shape[0]
w = image.shape[1]

for i in range(num_detections):
  box = boxes[0, 0, i]
  mask = masks[i]
  score = box[2]
  if score > conf:
    class_id = int(box[1])
    left, top, right, bottom = int(w * box[3]), int(h * box[4]), \
                               int(w * box[5]), int(h * box[6])
    left, top = max(0, min(left, w - 1)), max(0, min(top, h - 1))
    right, bottom = max(0, min(right, w - 1)), \
                    max(0, min(bottom, h - 1))
    class_mask = mask[class_id]
```

8. Extract the mask for each object detected by the model, colorize the mask with the corresponding class label's color, and blend the mask with the input image (to create an overlay):

```
label = labels[class_id]
class_mask = cv2.resize(class_mask, (right - left + 1, \
                        bottom - top + 1))
mask = (class_mask > thresh)
roi = image[top:bottom+1, left:right+1][mask]
color_index = np.random.randint(0, len(colors)-1)
color = np.array(colors[color_index])
```

```
image[top:bottom+1, left:right+1][mask] = (0.4*color + \
                         0.6 * roi).astype(np.uint8)
```

9. Draw the object boundaries (with contours) on the segmentation overlay image using the following code block:

```
mask = mask.astype(np.uint8)
contours, hierarchy = cv2.findContours(mask, cv2.RETR_TREE, \
                                  cv2.CHAIN_APPROX_SIMPLE)
cv2.drawContours(image[top:bottom+1, left:right+1], contours, \
            -1, color, 3, cv2.LINE_8, hierarchy, 100)
label_size, _ = cv2.getTextSize(label, \
            cv2.FONT_HERSHEY_SIMPLEX, 0.5, 1)
top = max(top, label_size[1])
cv2.putText(image, label, ((left + right)//2, top), \
                  cv2.FONT_HERSHEY_SIMPLEX, 0.75, (0,0,0), 2)
cv2.imwrite('images/instance_seg_out.png', image)
```

How it works...

If you run the code blocks and plot the input and output the segmented images, you will obtain the following figure:

Mask R-CNN can detect 90 classes, including people, animals, vehicles, signs, food, and so on (refer to the `object_detection_classes_coco.txt` file to see the supported classes).

The `cv2.dnn.blobFromImage()` function was used to construct a blob from the input image and then pass it to the deep-neural-net model.

The input image needs to be preprocessed before it can be fed to the deep learning model (this was also done by the same `cv2.dnn.blobFromImage()` function). Preprocessing steps normally involve mean subtraction, scaling, and optional channel swapping.

The class label and confidence of each detected object was extracted from the model output. The weak predictions were filtered out (the ones with low confidence, that is with a confidence less than the confidence threshold).

The mask image was extracted from the model output. It was thresholded to obtain a binary image, and for each object detected, the ROI was extracted.

Finally, the masked region was blended with the ROI to create the segmentation overlay image—the output of deep instance segmentation.

See also

Refer to the following articles to learn more about this recipe:

- https://arxiv.org/pdf/1311.2524.pdf
- https://arxiv.org/pdf/1504.08083.pdf
- https://arxiv.org/pdf/1506.01497.pdf
- https://arxiv.org/pdf/1703.06870.pdf
- https://www.pyimagesearch.com/2018/11/19/mask-r-cnn-with-opencv/
- http://cocodataset.org/

7
Image Classification

In this chapter, we will learn about the image classification problem, which is a supervised machine learning task of assigning (the most likely) label to an input image from a fixed set of labels (categories). We will also learn how to classify images using different Python libraries. This is one of the core problems in image processing that has a large variety of practical applications. Moreover, many other seemingly different image-processing tasks (such as object detection and segmentation) can be reduced to image classification. Image classification refers to the process of assigning a label to (that is, classifying) an image based on its visual content. For example, a binary image classification algorithm (model) may be developed to predict whether a human is in an image.

In this chapter, you will primarily learn how to implement two types of image classifiers. The first one is feature-based, where a feature generation (preprocessing) algorithm extracts a set of image features that are used to represent an image. An algorithm for image classification (a classical supervised machine learning algorithm) is then used to classify the image using the features. The following diagram shows a feature-based image classification:

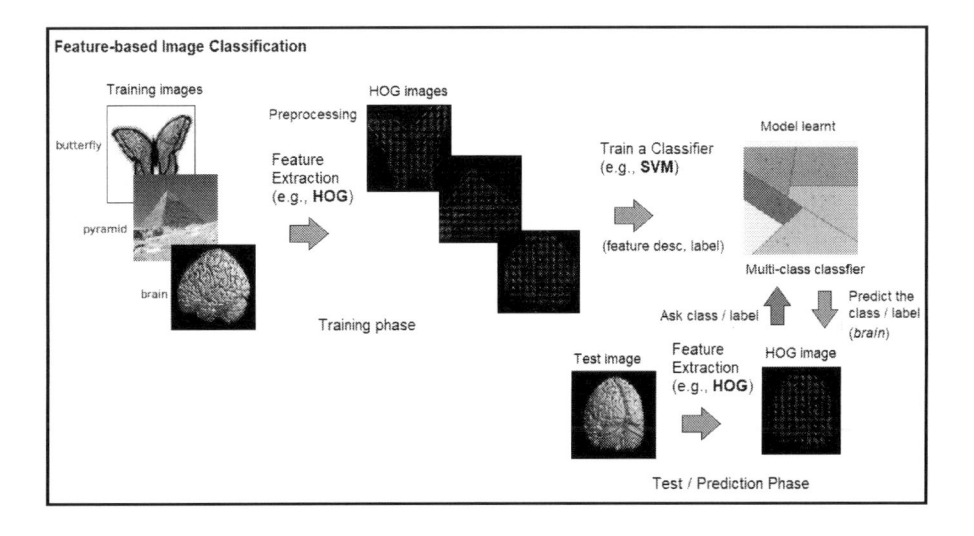

Image Classification

The second type of classifier is a deep learning classifier where no preprocessing step (such as feature extraction) is implemented, and an end-to-end deep neural network is trained to perform the classification task. The following diagram shows deep learning-based (end-to-end) image classification:

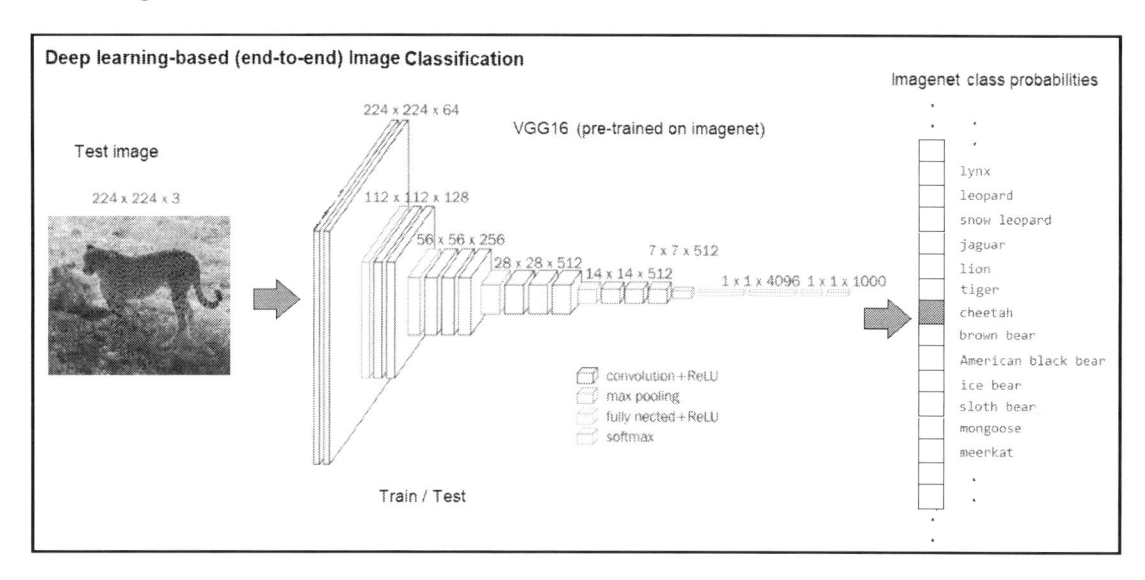

Image classification is a supervised machine learning task that consists of two phases: training and testing. In the training phase, a set of labeled input images (with known class labels) is provided to the classification algorithm, which trains a classification model using the input (typically, the model parameters are learned). Often, a set of validation (held-out) images is used to evaluate the current performance of the model on unseen images. Once the training is over, the learned model can be used to classify or predict the label of new (test) images—this is known as the testing phase. The predicted label can be compared with the ground-truth label to compare the accuracy of a classifier.

In this chapter, we are going to look at the following recipes:

- Classifying images with scikit-learn (HOG and logistic regression)
- Classifying textures with Gabor filter banks
- Classifying images with VGG19/Inception V3/MobileNet/ResNet101 (with PyTorch)
- Fine-tuning (with transfer learning) for image classification
- Classifying traffic signs using a deep learning model (with PyTorch)
- Estimating a human pose using a deep learning model

Classifying images with scikit-learn (HOG and logistic regression)

In this recipe, you are going to implement a feature-based image classifier using the scikit-image and scikit-learn library functions. A multiclass logistic regression (softmax regression) classifier will be trained on the **histogram of oriented gradients** (**HOG**) descriptors extracted from the training images. The following equations show how the parameters for a *K*-class softmax regression classifier are estimated in the training phase (for example, with stochastic gradient descent) and then the model that is learned is used to predict the probability of a class label given an input image in the testing phase:

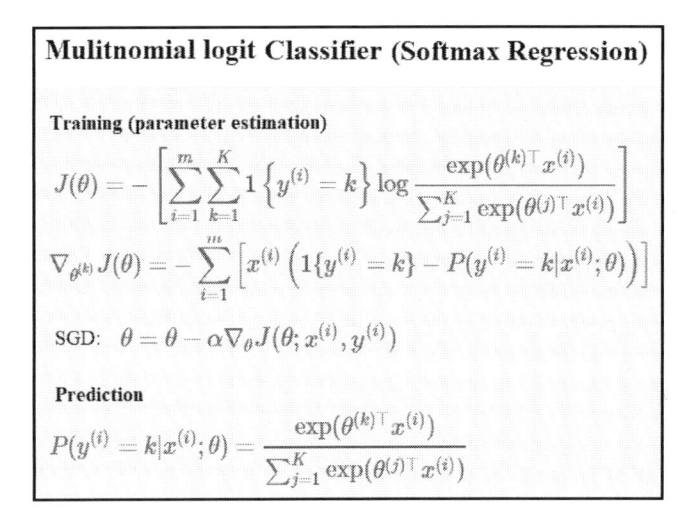

Mulitnomial logit Classifier (Softmax Regression)

Training (parameter estimation)

$$J(\theta) = -\left[\sum_{i=1}^{m}\sum_{k=1}^{K} 1\{y^{(i)} = k\} \log \frac{\exp(\theta^{(k)\top} x^{(i)})}{\sum_{j=1}^{K} \exp(\theta^{(j)\top} x^{(i)})}\right]$$

$$\nabla_{\theta^{(k)}} J(\theta) = -\sum_{i=1}^{m}\left[x^{(i)}\left(1\{y^{(i)} = k\} - P(y^{(i)} = k | x^{(i)}; \theta)\right)\right]$$

SGD: $\theta = \theta - \alpha \nabla_\theta J(\theta; x^{(i)}, y^{(i)})$

Prediction

$$P(y^{(i)} = k | x^{(i)}; \theta) = \frac{\exp(\theta^{(k)\top} x^{(i)})}{\sum_{j=1}^{K} \exp(\theta^{(j)\top} x^{(i)})}$$

Getting ready

In this recipe, we will classify images using scikit-learn's implementation of the multiclass logistic regression classifier with the HOG features extracted from the images. Let's start by importing all the required libraries using the following code snippet:

```
%matplotlib inline
import numpy as np
from skimage.io import imread
from skimage.color import gray2rgb
from skimage.transform import resize
from skimage.feature import hog
from sklearn.linear_model import LogisticRegression
from sklearn.model_selection import train_test_split
```

Image Classification

```
from sklearn.metrics import classification_report, accuracy_score
from glob import glob
from matplotlib import pyplot as plt
```

How to do it...

Execute the following steps for this recipe:

1. First, download the Caltech101 images from http://www.vision.caltech.edu/Image_Datasets/Caltech101/ and decompress it. There are image objects corresponding to 101 classes, although we have used a subset of them, corresponding to only 12 class labels (namely brain, butterfly, Buddha, chair, elephant, laptop, piano, pigeon, pizza, pyramid, rhino, sunflower) to speed up the preprocessing and training phases, but, you can train using all the classes if you want.

2. Read the images corresponding to the 10 different classes (they get extracted in separate folders) from the respective folders and extract the HOG images/descriptors from the images using the following code. Print the number of images present for each class label:

```
images, hog_images = [], []
X, y = [], []
ppc = 16
sz = 200
for dir in glob('images/Caltech101_images/*'):
    image_files = glob(dir + '/*.jpg')
    label = dir.split('\\')[-1]
    print(label, len(image_files))
    for image_file in image_files:
        image = resize(imread(image_file), (sz,sz))
        if len(image.shape) == 2: # if a gray-scale image
            image = gray2rgb(image)
        fd,hog_image = hog(image, orientations=8, \
                    pixels_per_cell=(ppc,ppc),
                    cells_per_block=(4, 4), \
                    block_norm= 'L2',visualize=True)
        images.append(image)
        hog_images.append(hog_image)
        X.append(fd)
        y.append(label)

# brain 98
# butterfly 91
# buddha 85
```

```
# chair 62
# elephant 64
# laptop 81
# piano 99
# pigeon 45
# pizza 53
# pyramid 57
# rhino 59
# sunflower 85
```

3. If you plot a few input images using `matplotlib`, then you will get an image along the lines of the following:

Image Classification

4. Plot the HOG images created from the preceding images using the preceding code snippet. You will get an image like the following:

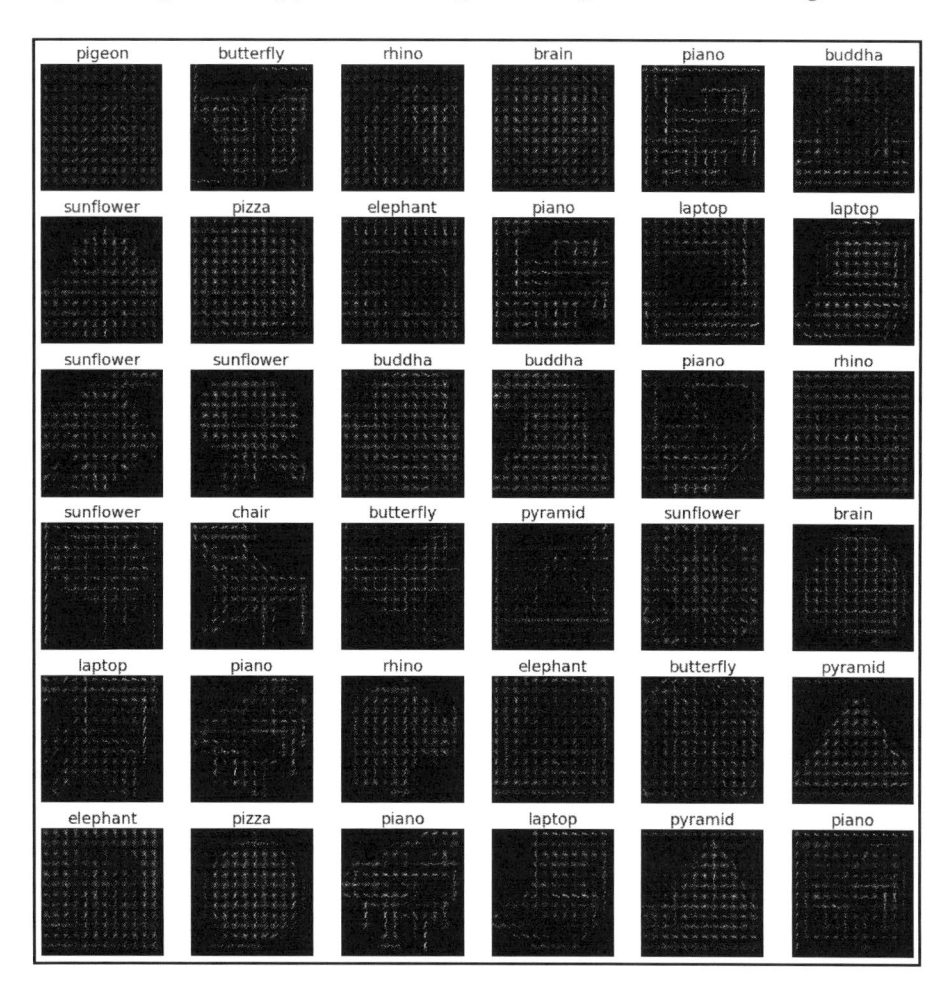

5. Create the image dataset to be used by the classifier using the HOG descriptor and the label for each image. Split the image dataset into two parts: 90% as the training and 10% as the test dataset. Finally, instantiate a `LogisticRegession` class for the multiclass classification and train the classifier on the training dataset created:

```
X = np.array(X)
y = np.array(y)
indices = np.arange(len(X))
X_train, X_test, y_train, y_test, id_train, id_test =
```

Chapter 7

```
train_test_split(X, y, indices,
test_size=0.1, random_state=1)
clf = LogisticRegression(C=1000, random_state=0, solver='lbfgs',
multi_class='multinomial')
clf.fit(X_train, y_train)
```

6. Predict the labels of the images in the test dataset created and compute the accuracy of the prediction on the test dataset (which is not seen by the model when it is being trained):

```
y_pred = clf.predict(X_test)
print("Accuracy: " + str(accuracy_score(y_test, y_pred)))
print('\n')
# Accuracy: 0.7439024390243902
print(classification_report(y_test, y_pred))
```

You will get a classification report like the following, showing the accuracy of the image classification on the test dataset using the current model. As you can see, we could get around 80.6% accuracy on the test image dataset:

```
Accuracy: 0.8068181818181818
              precision    recall  f1-score   support

       brain       0.90      0.75      0.82        12
      buddha       0.75      0.60      0.67         5
   butterfly       0.88      0.78      0.82         9
       chair       1.00      0.25      0.40         4
    elephant       0.78      0.88      0.82         8
      laptop       0.88      1.00      0.93         7
       piano       1.00      1.00      1.00        12
      pigeon       1.00      0.60      0.75         5
       pizza       0.38      0.75      0.50         4
     pyramid       0.60      0.75      0.67         4
       rhino       0.70      1.00      0.82         7
   sunflower       0.90      0.82      0.86        11

    accuracy                           0.81        88
   macro avg       0.81      0.76      0.76        88
weighted avg       0.85      0.81      0.81        88
```

7. Finally, plot all the test images along with the actual (ground-truth) labels and the labels predicted by the image classifier:

```
plt.figure(figsize=(20,20))
j = 0
for i in id_test:
    plt.subplot(10,10,j+1), plt.imshow(images[i]), plt.axis('off')
    plt.title('{}/{}'.format(y_test[j], y_pred[j]))
```

[279]

Image Classification

```
            j += 1
plt.suptitle('Actual vs. Predicted Class Labels', size=20)
plt.show()
```

How it works...

If you run the preceding code block and plot the result of the prediction, along with the actual labels of the images in the test dataset, you will get an image like the following:

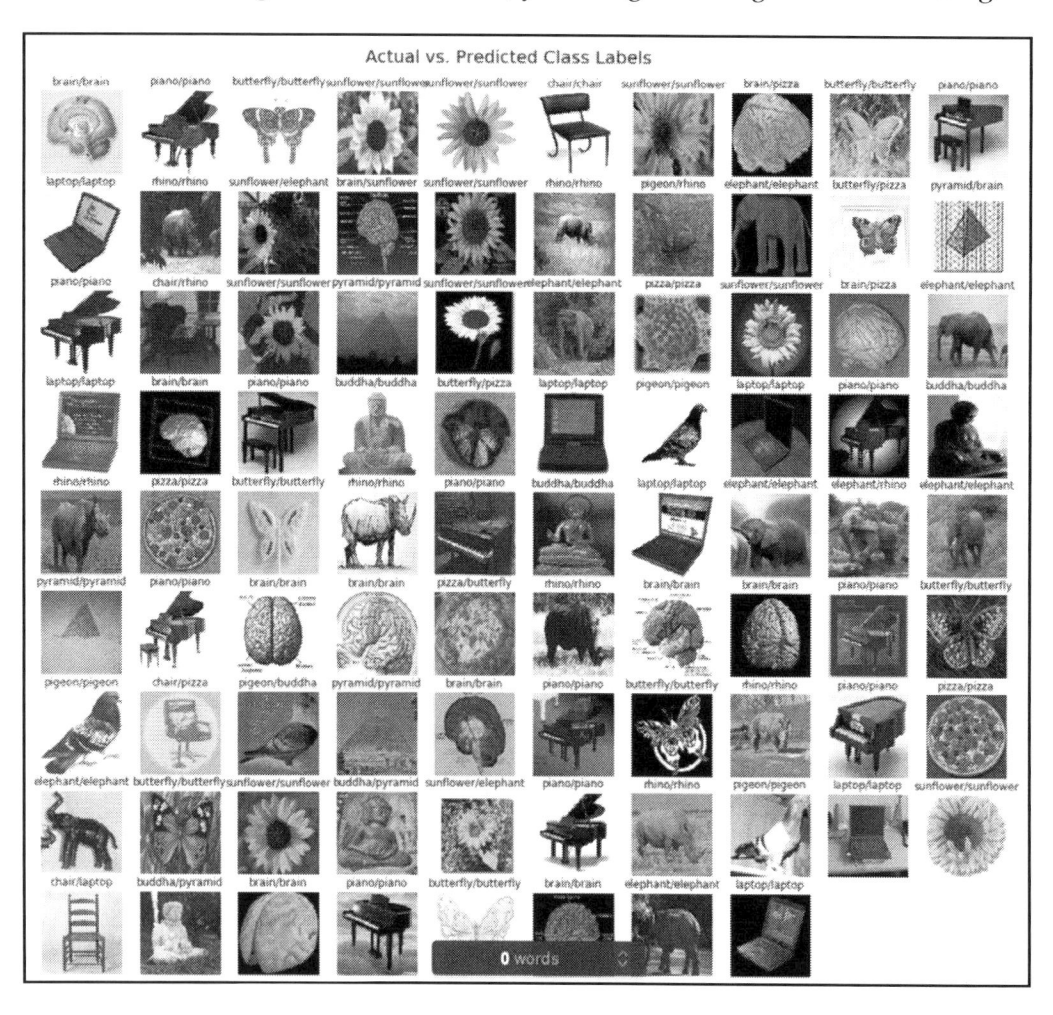

[280]

The `hog()` function from the scikit-image `feature` module was used to extract the HOG for a given image. It uses the following steps to compute a HOG:

1. (Optional) Normalize the image globally.
2. Compute the gradient image.
3. Compute gradient histograms.
4. Perform block normalization.
5. Flatten into a vector of features (feature descriptor).

The `multichannel` parameter of the function is set to `True` since the last image dimension is to be considered as a color (RGB) channel. Some of the images were grayscale (two dimensional); to convert each of them to a three-dimensional array, the `gray2rgb()` function from scikit-image `color` module was used.

The function returns the HOG descriptor for an input image and a HOG image. A flattened one-dimensional array is returned as the feature vector when the parameter `feature_vector` is `True`. A visualization of the HOG image is also returned if the visualize parameter is set to `True`.

The `train_test_split()` function from the `sklearn.model_selection` module was used to split the image dataset into random train and test subsets (90% train and 10% test) by setting the `test_size` parameter to `0.1`.

The `LogisticRegression` class from `sklearn.linear_model` was instantiated to fit a logistic regression (`logit`) classifier model with the training dataset. In this case of multiclass classification, when the `multi_class` parameter is set to multinomial, the cross-entropy loss is used (which is supported by the `lbfgs` solver that we used).

The `predict()` method was used to predict the class of a test image. The `sklearn.metric` functions `classification_report()` and `accuracy_score()` were used to evaluate the model performance on the test dataset (against the ground-truth labels).

There's more...

Use the **support-vector machine (SVM)** classifier (using the `svm.SVC()` and `svm.LinearSVC()` functions from `scikit-learn`) instead of the logistic-regression classifier with the HOG features. Does it improve the accuracy on the test images? Now use transfer learning/fine-tuning (hint: refer to the next few recipes to see how this is done) to increase the accuracy of classification.

See also

For more information, read through the following sources:

- https://scikit-learn.org/stable/modules/generated/sklearn.linear_model.LogisticRegression.html#sklearn.linear_model.LogisticRegression
- https://scikit-learn.org/stable/modules/generated/sklearn.model_selection.train_test_split.html
- http://www.vision.caltech.edu/Image_Datasets/Caltech101/
- https://www.sciencedirect.com/topics/computer-science/image-classification
- http://deeplearning.stanford.edu/tutorial/supervised/SoftmaxRegression/
- Chapter 8, *Object Detection in Images*, and Chapter 9, *Face Recognition, Image Captioning, and More*, from the Packt Publishing book *Hands-On Image Processing with Python*.

Classifying textures with Gabor filter banks

In this recipe, you will learn how to classify textures using Gabor filter banks with scikit-image's filter module's functions. Frequency and orientation are two key parameters of the Gabor filter, which detects the presence of a given frequency content in an image in a given direction around the ROI neighborhood. The Gabor kernel has both a real and an imaginary part, where the real part is used to filter images. The features to be used for (texture) classification are the mean and variance (often based on LSE) of a filtered image. The Gabor filter's impulse response is a product of a sinusoidal function and a Gaussian function, as shown in the following image:

$$g(x, y; \lambda, \theta, \psi, \sigma, \gamma) = \exp\left(-\frac{x'^2 + \gamma^2 y'^2}{2\sigma^2}\right) \exp\left(i\left(2\pi\frac{x'}{\lambda} + \psi\right)\right)$$

where $x' = x\cos\theta + y\sin\theta$
$y' = -x\sin\theta + y\cos\theta$

λ wavelength of the sinusoidal factor

θ orientation of the normal to the parallel stripes of a Gabor function

ψ phase offset

σ standard deviation of the Gaussian envelope

γ spatial aspect ratio

Getting ready

Download the texture images from `http://slazebni.cs.illinois.edu/research/uiuc_texture_dataset.zip` and unzip the data to get the texture images. There are 25 texture classes, each of which has separate folders and 41 images inside each folder. For demonstration purposes, we shall use 4 texture classes and rename the classes as `woods`, `stones`, `bricks`, and `checks`. First, let's import the required libraries using the following code snippet:

```
import numpy as np
import matplotlib.pyplot as plt
from skimage.io import imread
from skimage.color import rgb2gray
from skimage.filters import gabor_kernel
import scipy.ndimage as ndi
```

How to do it...

The following are the steps to implement texture classification using the Gabor filter with `scikit-learn`:

1. First, prepare the Gabor filter bank kernels with the following code snippet:

   ```
   kernels = []
   for theta in range(4):
       theta = theta / 4. * np.pi
       for sigma in (1, 3):
           for frequency in (0.05, 0.25):
               kernel = np.real(gabor_kernel(frequency, \
                           theta=theta, sigma_x=sigma, sigma_y=sigma))
               kernels.append(kernel)
   ```

2. Define the following function to convolve an input image with the Gabor kernel (with the real and imaginary parts):

   ```
   def power(image, kernel):
       # Normalize images for better comparison.
       image = (image - image.mean()) / image.std()
       return np.sqrt(ndi.convolve(image, np.real(kernel), \
                   mode='wrap')**2 + ndi.convolve(image, \
                   np.imag(kernel), mode='wrap')**2)
   ```

Image Classification

3. For each of the four texture classes, we shall use two images—one as a reference and the other as a test image. Let's first load the reference images for each of the four classes we selected using the following code snippet:

```
image_names = ['images/UIUC_textures/woods/T04_01.jpg',
 'images/UIUC_textures/stones/T12_01.jpg',
 'images/UIUC_textures/bricks/T15_01.jpg',
 'images/UIUC_textures/checks/T25_01.jpg']
labels = ['woods', 'stones', 'bricks', 'checks']

images = []
for image_name in image_names:
    images.append(rgb2gray(imread(image_name)))
```

4. Create four filter bank kernels with different values of parameters (theta and frequency):

```
results = []
kernel_params = []
for theta in (0, 1):
    theta = theta / 4. * np.pi
    for frequency in (0.1, 0.4):
        kernel = gabor_kernel(frequency, theta=theta)
        params = 'theta=%d,\nfrequency=%.2f' % \
                    (theta * 180 / np.pi, frequency)
        kernel_params.append(params)
        results.append((kernel, [power(img, kernel) for img \
                    in images]))
```

5. If you run the preceding code snippets and plot the original input images, Gabor filter banks, and their responses (the convolved images), you will get an output like the following screenshot:

Chapter 7

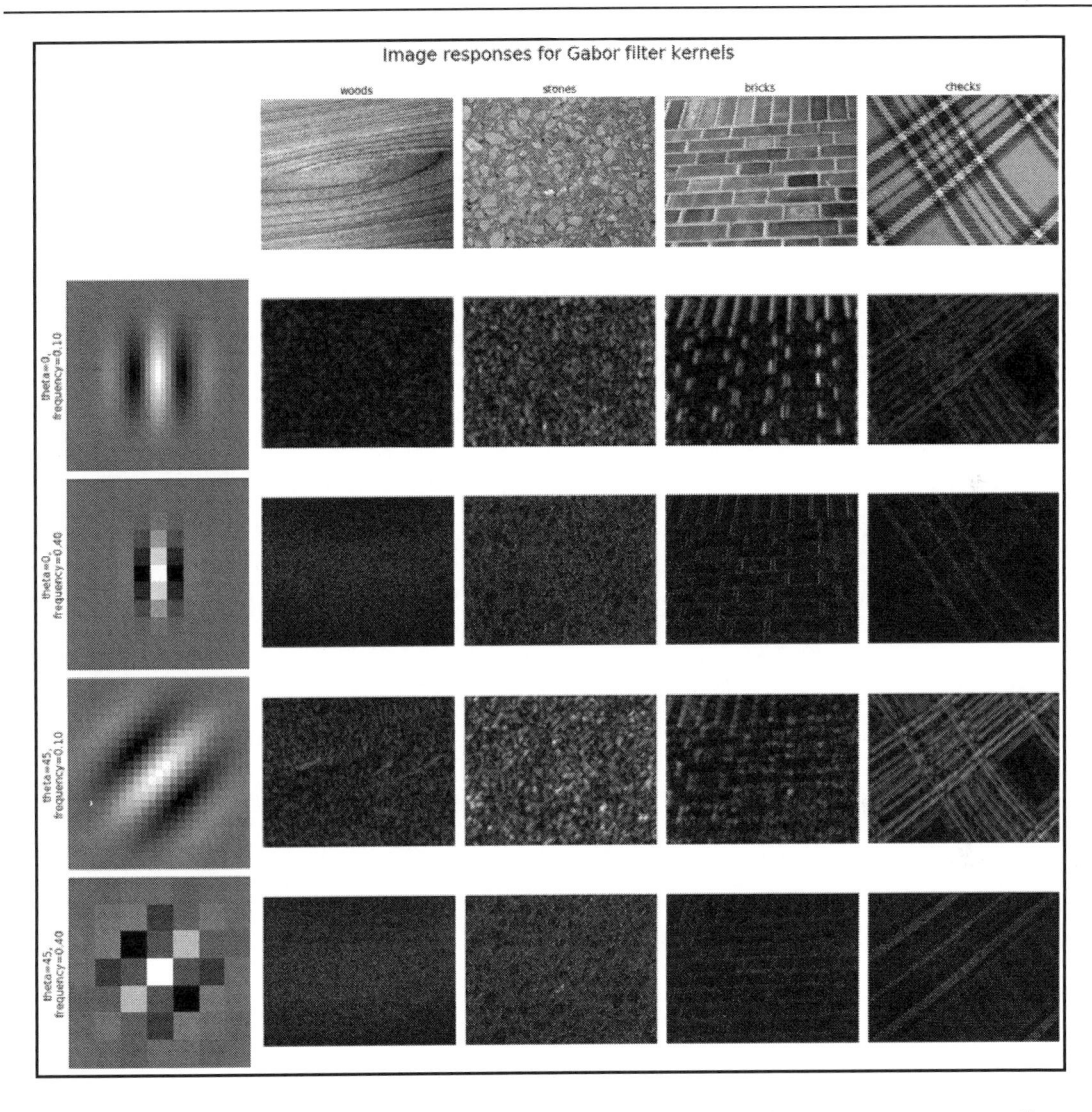

6. Now, implement the function to extract the features of an image corresponding to the Gabor filter bank kernels:

```
def compute_feats(image, kernels):
    feats = np.zeros((len(kernels), 2), dtype=np.double)
    for k, kernel in enumerate(kernels):
        filtered = ndi.convolve(image, kernel, mode='wrap')
        feats[k, 0] = filtered.mean()
        feats[k, 1] = filtered.var()
    return feats
```

[285]

Image Classification

7. Implement a function match that performs the classification task—that is, it accepts the extracted features of a new image along with the features of the reference images as parameters, then matches the new image with the reference images and returns the index of the reference image that is the nearest in feature space (let's use Euclidean distance, here):

```
def match(feats, ref_feats):
    min_error = np.inf
    min_i = None
    for i in range(ref_feats.shape[0]):
        error = np.sum((feats - ref_feats[i, :])**2)
        if error < min_error:
            min_error = error
            min_i = i
    return min_i
```

8. Now, extract the reference image's features and the new test image's features. Classify the test images—that is, match each new (test) image with the nearest reference image and label the test image with the class of the reference image:

```
ref_feats = np.zeros((4, len(kernels), 2), dtype=np.double)
for i in range(4):
 ref_feats[i, :, :] = compute_feats(images[i], kernels)

print('Images matched against references using Gabor filter banks:')

new_image_names = ['images/UIUC_textures/woods/T04_02.jpg',
                   'images/UIUC_textures/stones/T12_02.jpg',
                   'images/UIUC_textures/bricks/T15_02.jpg',
                   'images/UIUC_textures/checks/T25_02.jpg',
                  ]

for i in range(4):
    image = rgb2gray(imread(new_image_names[i]))
    feats = compute_feats(image, kernels)
    mindex = match(feats, ref_feats)
    print('original: {}, match result: {}'.format(labels[i], labels[mindex]))
```

If you run the preceding code blocks and plot the original test images and the reference images identified for those images side by side, you will get the following output of the classes:

[286]

Chapter 7

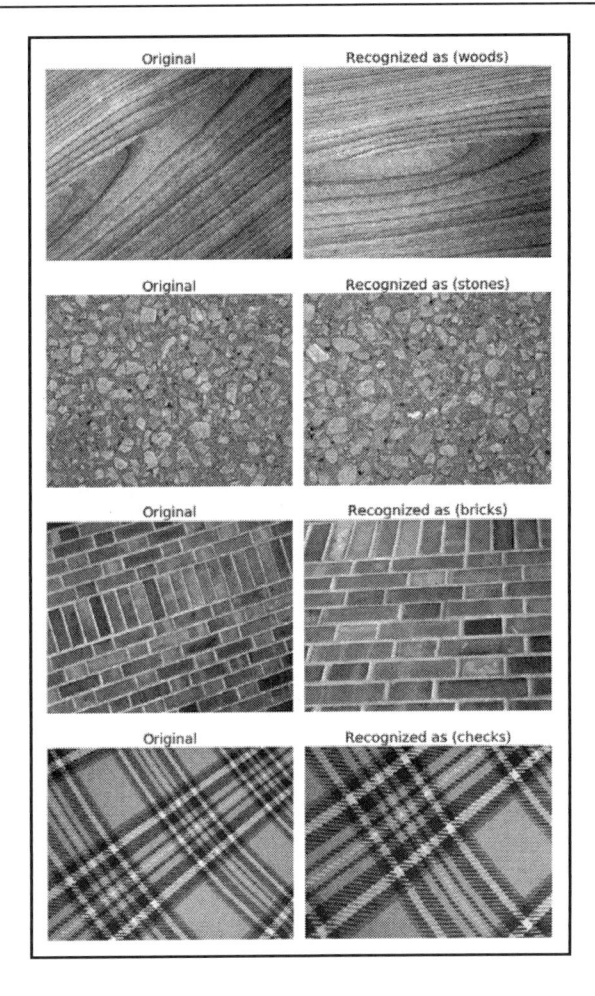

We can see that a test image is matched as the nearest image to a reference image.

How it works...

From `skimage.filters`, use the `gabor_kernel()` function to return the complex two-dimensional Gabor filter kernel.

The Gabor kernel is a Gaussian kernel multiplied (modulated) by a (complex) harmonic function, consisting of a real cosine and an imaginary sine term.

The `frequency` parameter to the function represents the spatial frequency of the harmonic (in pixels).

Image Classification

The frequency is ∞ 1/wavelength and is also inversely proportional to σ. Similarly, the bandwidth is ∞ 1/σ, where σ is the standard deviation of a Gaussian kernel.

The θ parameter represents the orientation in radian (for example, θ =0 implies that the harmonic is oriented toward the *x* direction).

The `bandwidth` parameter represents the bandwidth that the Gabor filter captures. For a given bandwidth, σ*x* and σ*y* decreases when the frequency increases.

The (optional) parameters σ*x* and σ*y* denote the standard deviations in the *x* and *y* directions. For example, when θ = π/2, then the kernel undergoes a 90-degree rotation and σ*x* controls the vertical direction.

The `match()` function finds the best possible match for a test image by computing the distance of the test image that Gabor features with each of the reference image's Gabor features and returning the reference image that is the closest.

There's more...

The **local binary pattern** (**LBP**) and Haralick features (using the GLCM matrices) can also be used for texture classification (use the `local_binary_pattern()` function from the `skimage.feature` and the `haralick()` function from `mahotas.features`). Implement texture classification using these features.

See also

For more information, read through the following sources:

- http://slazebni.cs.illinois.edu/research/uiuc_texture_dataset.zip
- https://scikit-image.org/docs/dev/auto_examples/features_detection/plot_gabor.html
- https://scikit-image.org/docs/dev/api/skimage.filters.html#skimage.filters.gabor_kernel
- https://dsp.stackexchange.com/questions/14714/understanding-the-gabor-filter-function
- https://en.wikipedia.org/wiki/Gabor_filter
- https://web.archive.org/web/20180127125930/http://mplab.ucsd.edu/tutorials/gabor.pdf

Classifying images with VGG19/Inception V3/MobileNet/ResNet101 (with PyTorch)

In this recipe, you are going to learn how to use torchvision's pretrained (on Imagenet) deep learning models for a few famous models. ImageNet is an image database organized as per the WordNet hierarchy. Hundreds/thousands of images belong to each node in the hierarchy.

The following plot shows the top-1 accuracy achieved by a few popular deep neural nets participated in the ImageNet challenge, starting from AlexNet (Krizhevsky et al., 2012) on the far left, to the best performing Inception-v4 (Szegedy et al., 2016) on the far right:

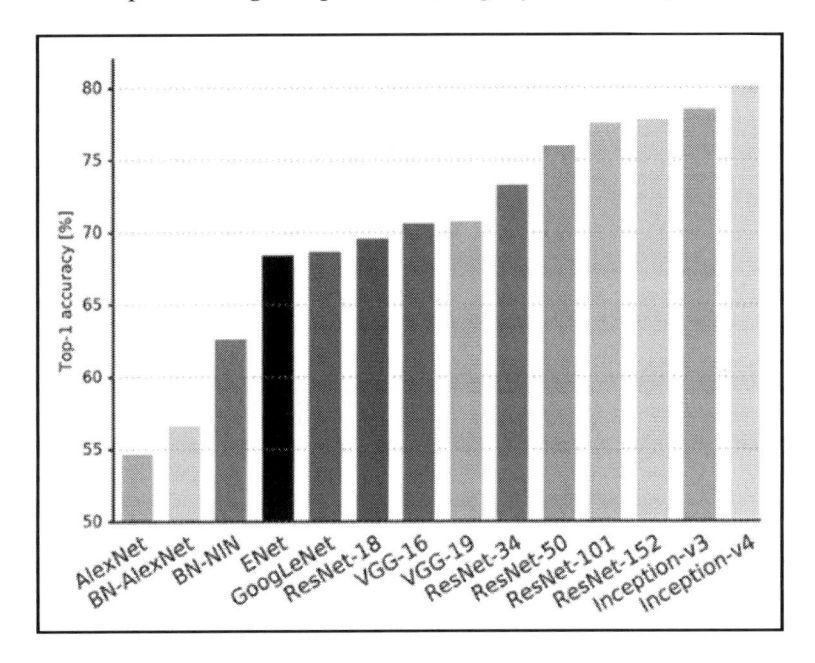

The top-1 accuracy is defined as the average number of times the correct label for an image was the highest probability class predicted by the CNN for that image. At the other end of the scale, the top-1 error shows the error that occurs when the model-predicted class (the class label to which the model ascribes the highest confidence) is different from the actual class (ground-truth).

Getting ready

First, import the required libraries using the following code block:

```
import torch
from torchvision import models, transforms
from PIL import Image, ImageDraw, ImageFont
import matplotlib.pylab as plt
```

How to do it...

Go through the following steps to classify an image using pretrained deep neural net models with PyTorch/torchvision:

1. Implement a `classify()` function that accepts an input image and a pretrained model (on ImageNet), along with the model name and the ImageNet class labels, returning the classifier corresponding to the highest-predicted probability:

    ```
    def classify(img, model_index, model_name, model_pred, labels):
        _, index = torch.max(model_pred, 1)
        model_pred, indices = torch.sort(model_pred, dim=1,\
            descending=True)
        percentage = torch.nn.functional.softmax(model_pred, dim=1)\
            [0] * 100
        draw = ImageDraw.Draw(img)
        font = ImageFont.truetype(r'arial.ttf', 50)
        draw.text((5, 5+model_index*50),'{}, pred: \
            {},{}%'.format(model_name, labels[index[0]], \
            round(percentage[0].item(),2)),(255,0,0),font=font)
        return indices, percentage
    ```

2. Read the ImageNet classes (there are 1,000 classes) and list the available models in torchvision:

    ```
    with open('models/imagenet_classes.txt') as f:
      labels = [line.strip() for line in f.readlines()]
    print(dir(models))

    # ['AlexNet', 'DenseNet', 'GoogLeNet', 'Inception3', 'MNASNet',
    'MobileNetV2', 'ResNet', 'ShuffleNetV2', 'SqueezeNet', 'VGG',
    '__builtins__', '__cached__', '__doc__', '__file__', '__loader__',
    '__name__', '__package__', '__path__', '__spec__', '_utils',
    'alexnet', 'densenet', 'densenet121', 'densenet161', 'densenet169',
    'densenet201', 'detection', 'googlenet', 'inception',
    'inception_v3', 'mnasnet', 'mnasnet0_5', 'mnasnet0_75',
    ```

```
'mnasnet1_0', 'mnasnet1_3', 'mobilenet', 'mobilenet_v2', 'resnet',
'resnet101', 'resnet152', 'resnet18', 'resnet34', 'resnet50',
'resnext101_32x8d', 'resnext50_32x4d', 'segmentation',
'shufflenet_v2_x0_5', 'shufflenet_v2_x1_0', 'shufflenet_v2_x1_5',
'shufflenet_v2_x2_0', #'shufflenetv2', 'squeezenet',
'squeezenet1_0', 'squeezenet1_1', 'utils', 'vgg', 'vgg11',
'vgg11_bn', 'vgg13', 'vgg13_bn', 'vgg16', 'vgg16_bn', 'vgg19',
'vgg19_bn', 'video', 'wide_resnet101_2', 'wide_resnet50_2']
```

3. Compose the transformations that are to be applied to the input image as a preprocessing step (for example, resize, center-crop, and z-score normalize transforms, and then convert the image to a tensor) using the following code block:

```
transform = transforms.Compose([
 transforms.Resize(256),
 transforms.CenterCrop(224),
 transforms.ToTensor(),
 transforms.Normalize(
 mean=[0.485, 0.456, 0.406],
 std=[0.229, 0.224, 0.225]
 )])
```

4. Read the input images that are to be classified using the pretrained deep neural networks. Apply the preprocessing transformation defined earlier to the images:

```
for imgfile in ["images/cheetah.png", "images/swan.png"]:
 img = Image.open(imgfile).convert('RGB')
 img_t = transform(img)
 batch_t = torch.unsqueeze(img_t, 0)
```

5. Instantiate a few pretrained (with ImageNet weights) famous deep learning models (for example, VGG16, MobileNetV2, InceptionV3, and ResNet101), using the following code snippets. Run a forward pass on the input image and obtain the prediction (along with the probability values corresponding to each of the 1,000 classes in ImageNet) for the probable image class:

```
vgg19 = models.vgg19(pretrained=True)
vgg19.eval()
pred = vgg19(batch_t)
classify(img, 0, 'vgg19', pred, labels)

mobilenetv2 = models.mobilenet_v2(pretrained=True)
mobilenetv2.eval()
pred = mobilenetv2(batch_t)
classify(img, 1, 'mobilenetv2', pred, labels)
```

Image Classification

```
inceptionv3 = models.inception_v3(pretrained=True)
inceptionv3.eval()
pred = inceptionv3(batch_t)
classify(img, 2, 'inceptionv3', pred, labels)

resnet101 = models.resnet101(pretrained=True)
resnet101.eval()
pred = resnet101(batch_t)
indices, percentages = classify(img, 3, 'resnet101', pred, labels)
```

How it works...

While running the preceding code blocks, plot the input image along with the most probable class (along with the probability of each of the 1,000 class labels). As you can see, the input **Cheetah** image is classified correctly by all of the four pretrained models with a high probability of success:

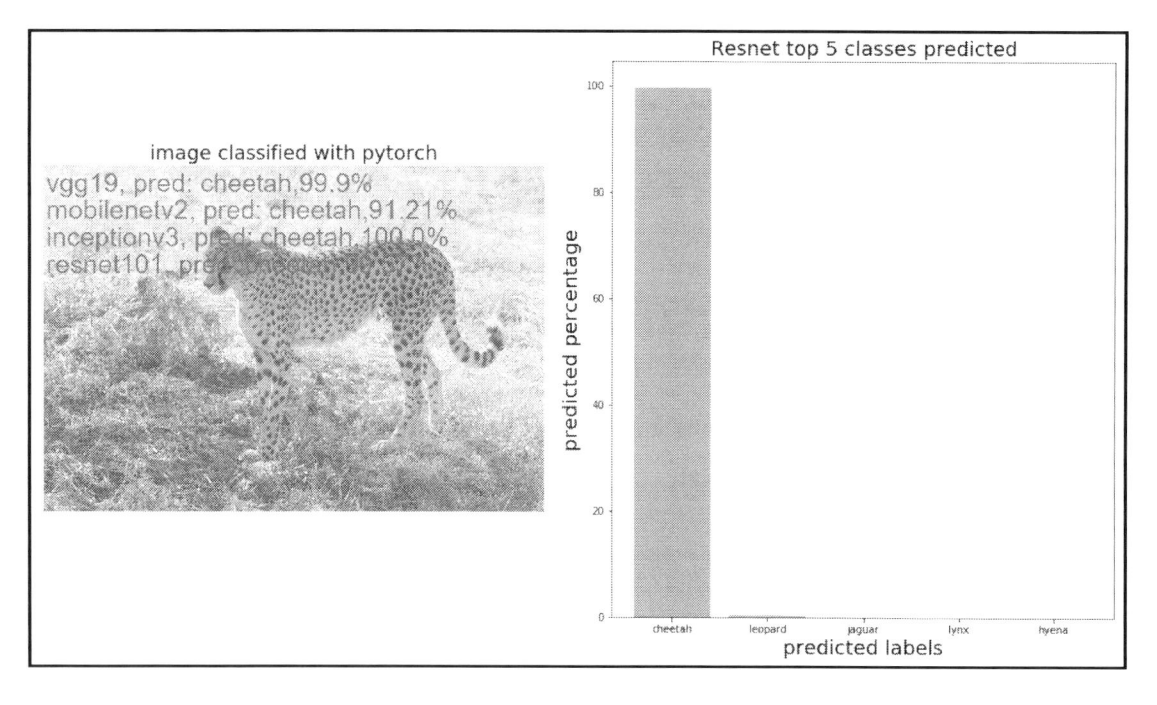

If you used the image of the swans as input, then all models except `mobilenetv2` classified the image as `goose`, while `mobilenetv2` classified the image as an American egret, as shown in the following screenshot:

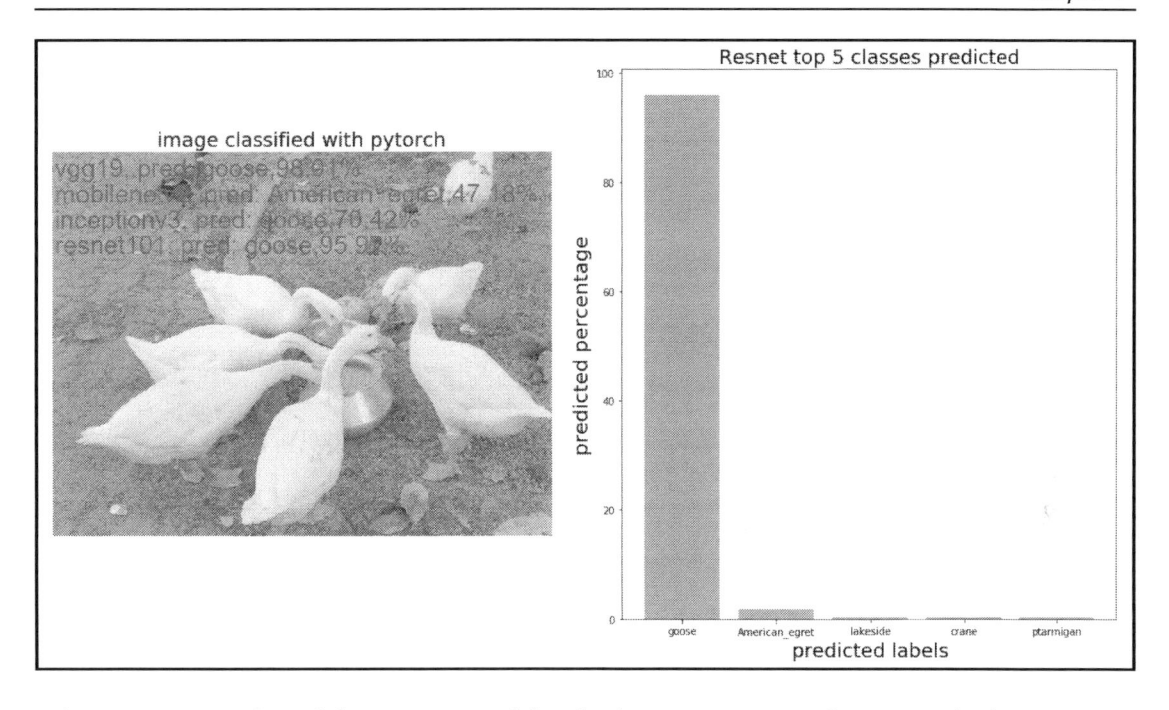

![Image showing geese classified by pytorch with predictions from vgg19, mobilenet, inception v3, and resnet101, alongside a bar chart of Resnet top 5 classes predicted: goose, American_egret, lakeside, crane, ptarmigan]

When a pretrained model is instantiated for the first time, its weights are cached to a directory that can be set using the `TORCH_MODEL_ZOO` environment variable (using `torch.utils.model_zoo.load_url()` functions).

> Note that there is one entry called **ResNet** (which refers to the Python class) and one called resnet (a convenience function instantiating a ResNet). Also note that each of the convenience functions `resnet50`, `resnet101`, and `resnet152` instantiate ResNet class, but the number of layers is different (for example, 50, 101, and 152, respectively). The number of parameters for ResNet101 is around 44.5.

First, the input image was loaded and preprocessed (so that it has the shape and mean or standard deviation expected by the corresponding model) in order to ensure that the model outputs meaningful results.

The input image was transformed using `torchvision.transforms` and the `Compose()` function is used to group a series of image transformations (a variable transform is created as a combination of all the transformations that are to be applied to the input image as a preprocessing step; for example, resizing, center-cropping, and normalizing).

An instance of a deep neural network was created by loading the model weights from a pretrained model (on ImageNet). For example, with `models.vgg19(pretrained=True)`, the weights of the model are downloaded for the first time and then cached (a PyTorch model commonly has extension the `.pt/.pth`).

The model was set to its eval mode using the `resnet101.eval()` method (for the model ResNet101, for example).

To run inference (that is, to run a forward pass through the pretrained model with the input image), the `resnet101()` method was called (for the `ResNet101` model, for example) it outputted a 1,000-element (class) vector, where each element value represents the probability that the input image belongs to a particular class (according to the pretrained model).

Finally, we needed to find out the index of the class corresponding to the maximum score (using the `np.argmax()` function) from the output vector. This class index is used to extract the name of the predicted class from the list of classes. We can get the probability corresponding to the predicted class from the output probability vector (for example, the `ResNet101` predicted the cheetah image correctly with 99.57% confidence).

The performance of the pretrained models can be compared using the following evaluation criteria: top-1/top-5 error, inference time on CPU/GPU, model size. A good model needs to have small values of top-1/top-5 error, inference time, and model size.

There's more...

Use the pretrained models from Keras to perform the image classification task. Compare the top-1 versus top-5 accuracy for different models. Also, use a pretrained model from Caffe to classify an image. Finally, train your own image dataset and learn the weights of a model (for example, VGG19) and then use it to predict unseen images.

See also

For more information, read through the following sources:

- http://cs231n.github.io/classification/
- https://pytorch.org/docs/stable/torchvision/models.html
- https://arxiv.org/pdf/1512.00567.pdf
- https://arxiv.org/pdf/1801.04381.pdf
- https://arxiv.org/pdf/1512.03385.pdf

- https://arxiv.org/pdf/1409.1556.pdf
- https://www.learnopencv.com/pytorch-for-beginners-image-classification-using-pre-trained-models/
- http://www.image-net.org/
- https://www.researchgate.net/publication/331980242_A_Deep_Learning-Based_Intelligent_Medicine_Recognition_System_for_Chronic_Patients/figures?lo=1utm_source=googleutm_medium=organic
- https://ai.googleblog.com/2018/04/mobilenetv2-next-generation-of-on.html
- https://www.researchgate.net/publication/328017644_Benchmark_Analysis_of_Representative_Deep_Neural_Network_Architectures/figures

Fine-tuning (with transfer learning) for image classification

A generic definition of transfer learning is that it is a deep learning technique that reuses knowledge gained from solving one problem by applying it to a related but different problem. Let's understand this by looking at an example. Let's say that we have three types of flowers—namely, a rose, a sunflower, and a tulip. We can use the standard pretrained models, such as VGG16/19, ResNet50, or InceptionV3 models (pretrained on ImageNet with 1,000 output classes, listed at https://gist.github.com/yrevar/942d3a0ac09ec9e5eb3a) to classify the flower images, but our model won't correctly classify them since these flower categories were not there in the ground-truth classes that the model was trained on. In other words, they are classes that the model is not aware of. The following image shows how the flower images are classified wrongly by the pretrained VGG16 model (use pretrained models from keras for the classification):

Image Classification

When a deep neural network is trained from scratch, a huge set of data (along with powerful computing resources) is required to train the network (since the neural net has millions of parameters and we aim to obtain an optimal set of parameters through training). It creates a problem when we have small datasets that are not sufficient to train the deep network. Here, transfer learning comes to the rescue.

Since standard models, such as VGG-16/19, are quite large and are trained on many images, they are capable of learning many different features for different classes. We can simply reuse the convolutional layers as a feature extractor that learns low- and high-level image features, and train only the **fully connected** (**FC**) layer weights (parameters). This is what transfer learning is. But if you use transfer learning with only the FC layers being trainable (and the convolutional layers fixed, with the ImageNet-pretrained VGG16 deep neural network) to classify a small dataset consisting of rose, sunflower, and tulip images, you will see that the accuracy of the prediction on the test dataset with transfer learning is not good. In this recipe, you will learn how to use fine-tuning (similar to transfer learning, but with more trainable layers) to train a model that has better accuracy on the test dataset.

Fine-tuning a deep neural net again tries to modify the parameters (by partially training only a few chosen layers) of a pretrained network to make it adapt to the new task (for example, classifying the flowers with new class labels). Since the initial layers of a deep neural network learn very general features (for example, edges in an image) and the deeper layers learn more specific patterns (with respect to the task it is being trained for), with fine-tuning, the initial layers are kept intact (by freezing) and a few of the deeper layers are retrained for the new task. The amount of data required for this partial training is not much since the entire network is not trained and we don't need to train from scratch (hence a lower number of parameters need to be updated, with less time required for retraining).

Getting ready

First, download the input images from the TensorFlow sample image dataset, available at `http://download.tensorflow.org/example_images/flower_photos.tgz`. Let's use 600 images for each of the three classes, making a total of 1,800 images, which is a small number of images and the right time to use transfer learning. We'll use 500 images from each class for training, reserving the remaining 100 images from each class to test the trained model. Let's also create a folder called `flower_photos`, with two subfolders called `train` and `test` inside it, and save our training and test images inside those folders, respectively. The folder structure should look like the following:

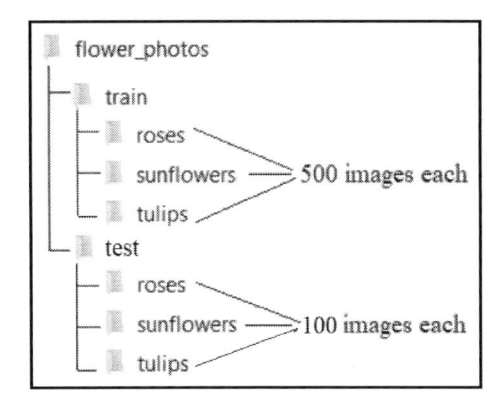

```
flower_photos
├── train
│   ├── roses
│   ├── sunflowers      ──> 500 images each
│   └── tulips
└── test
    ├── roses
    ├── sunflowers      ──> 100 images each
    └── tulips
```

Let's import all the required libraries using the following code block:

```
from keras.applications import VGG16
from keras.preprocessing.image import ImageDataGenerator
from keras import models, layers, optimizers
from keras.layers.normalization import BatchNormalization
from keras.preprocessing.image import load_img
from keras import models
from keras import layers
from keras import optimizers
import pydot_ng as pydot
from keras.utils import plot_model
import matplotlib.pylab as plt
import numpy as np
```

How to do it...

Run the following steps to implement fine-tuning (with transfer learning) using keras.

1. Define the train and test directories along with the size that the input images will get resized to before training:

   ```
   train_dir = 'images/flower_photos/train'
   test_dir = 'images/flower_photos/test'
   image_size = 224
   ```

2. Load the pretrained VGG16 network, but without the top FC layers:

   ```
   vgg_conv = VGG16(weights='imagenet', include_top=False,
   input_shape=(image_size, image_size, 3))
   ```

3. Freeze all the convolutional layers except the last two convolutional layers, along with the FC layers, to reuse the pretrained weights for those layers (without retraining them):

   ```
   for layer in vgg_conv.layers[:-2]:
       layer.trainable = False
   ```

4. Now let's verify the status (trainable or not) of each the layers using the following code:

   ```
   for layer in vgg_conv.layers:
       print(layer, layer.trainable)
   ```

5. Now create a sequential model with Keras and add the VGG16 base model (with convolutional layers) to it. Then add a couple of new FC layers. Print the model summary to see the model structure, along with the number of trainable parameters:

   ```
   model = models.Sequential()
   model.add(vgg_conv)
   model.add(layers.Flatten())
   model.add(layers.Dense(1024, activation='relu'))
   model.add(layers.Dropout(0.5))
   model.add(layers.Dense(3, activation='softmax'))
   model.summary()
   # Total params: 40,408,899
   # Trainable params: 25,694,211
   # Non-trainable params: 14,714,688
   ```

6. Load the training and test input images. Set the validation split as 0.2—that is, 20% of the training images will be held out (as a validation dataset) to evaluate the classifier model that is trained on the remaining 80% of the training images (validation is a popular machine learning technique that helps improve the generalizability of the model by reducing model variance; the model then becomes more likely to achieve higher accuracy on unseen test images). Define the train batch size (that is, the number of training images to be passed in one forward/backward pass):

   ```
   train_datagen = ImageDataGenerator(rescale=1./255,
   validation_split=0.2) # set validation split
   test_datagen = ImageDataGenerator(rescale=1./255)
   train_batchsize = 100
   ```

7. Define the training, validation, and test data generators to read/generate batches of images and labels from the appropriate directories. Configure the model created previously for training:

```
train_generator = train_datagen.flow_from_directory(
    train_dir,
    target_size=(image_size, image_size),
    batch_size=train_batchsize,
    class_mode='categorical',
    subset='training')

validation_generator = train_datagen.flow_from_directory(
    train_dir,
    target_size=(image_size, image_size),
    batch_size=train_batchsize,
    class_mode='categorical',
    classes = ['roses', 'sunflowers', 'tulips'],
    subset='validation') # set as validation data

test_generator = test_datagen.flow_from_directory(
    test_dir,
    target_size=(image_size, image_size),
    batch_size=1,
    class_mode='categorical',
    classes = ['roses', 'sunflowers', 'tulips'],
    shuffle=False)

model.compile(loss='categorical_crossentropy',
              optimizer=optimizers.RMSprop(lr=1e-5),
              metrics=['acc'])
```

8. Plot the model architecture using the following line of code:

```
plot_model(model, to_file='images/model.png')
```

Image Classification

If you run the preceding line of code, the model structure will be saved to the `.png` file provided. The model architecture saved will look like the one shown in the following diagram:

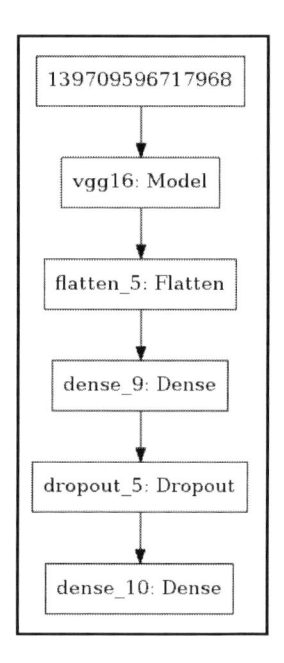

```
139709596717968
      │
      ▼
  vgg16: Model
      │
      ▼
 flatten_5: Flatten
      │
      ▼
  dense_9: Dense
      │
      ▼
 dropout_5: Dropout
      │
      ▼
 dense_10: Dense
```

9. Train the model with the following code snippet. Save the weights obtained:

```
history = model.fit_generator(
    train_generator,
    steps_per_epoch=train_generator.\
        samples/train_generator.batch_size,
    epochs=20,
    validation_data=validation_generator,
    validation_steps=validation_generator.\
        samples/validation_generator.batch_size,
    verbose=1)
model.save('all_freezed.h5')
```

Chapter 7

10. Extract the accuracy and loss values from the training history:

    ```
    acc = history.history['acc']
    val_acc = history.history['val_acc']
    loss = history.history['loss']
    val_loss = history.history['val_loss']
    ```

11. Get the test filenames and the corresponding ground truths from the generator and map the class indices to labels:

    ```
    test_generator.reset()
    fnames = test_generator.filenames
    ground_truth = test_generator.classes
    label2index = test_generator.class_indices
    index2label = dict((v,k) for k,v in label2index.items())
    ```

12. Finally, predict the labels of the test images using the test-data generator. Get the predictions from the model using the generator using the following code snippets, compare them with the corresponding ground truths, and compute the number of mistakes (errors) made by the model:

    ```
    predictions = model.predict_generator(test_generator,
    steps=len(fnames))
    predicted_classes = np.argmax(predictions,axis=-1)
    predicted_classes = np.array([index2label[k] for k in
    predicted_classes])
    ground_truth = np.array([index2label[k] for k in ground_truth])
    errors = np.where(predicted_classes != ground_truth)[0]
    print("No of errors =
    {}/{}".format(len(errors),test_generator.samples))
    # No of errors = 45/300
    ```

[301]

Image Classification

How it works...

If you run the preceding code snippets and plot how the accuracy and loss changes for the training and validation image dataset over the number of epochs, you will get an output as shown in the following screenshot:

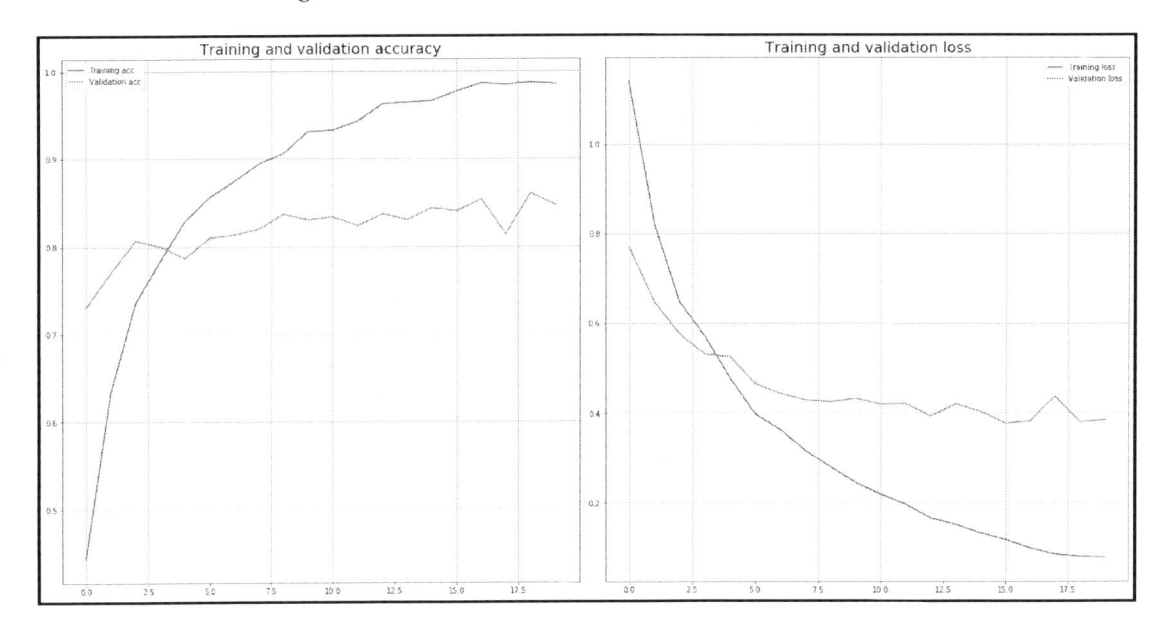

This time, 45 test images (out of 300 images) were classified wrongly (that is, the predicted label ≠ ground-truth label) by the fine-tuning model; a few of them are shown in the following screenshot. The prediction accuracy was increased:

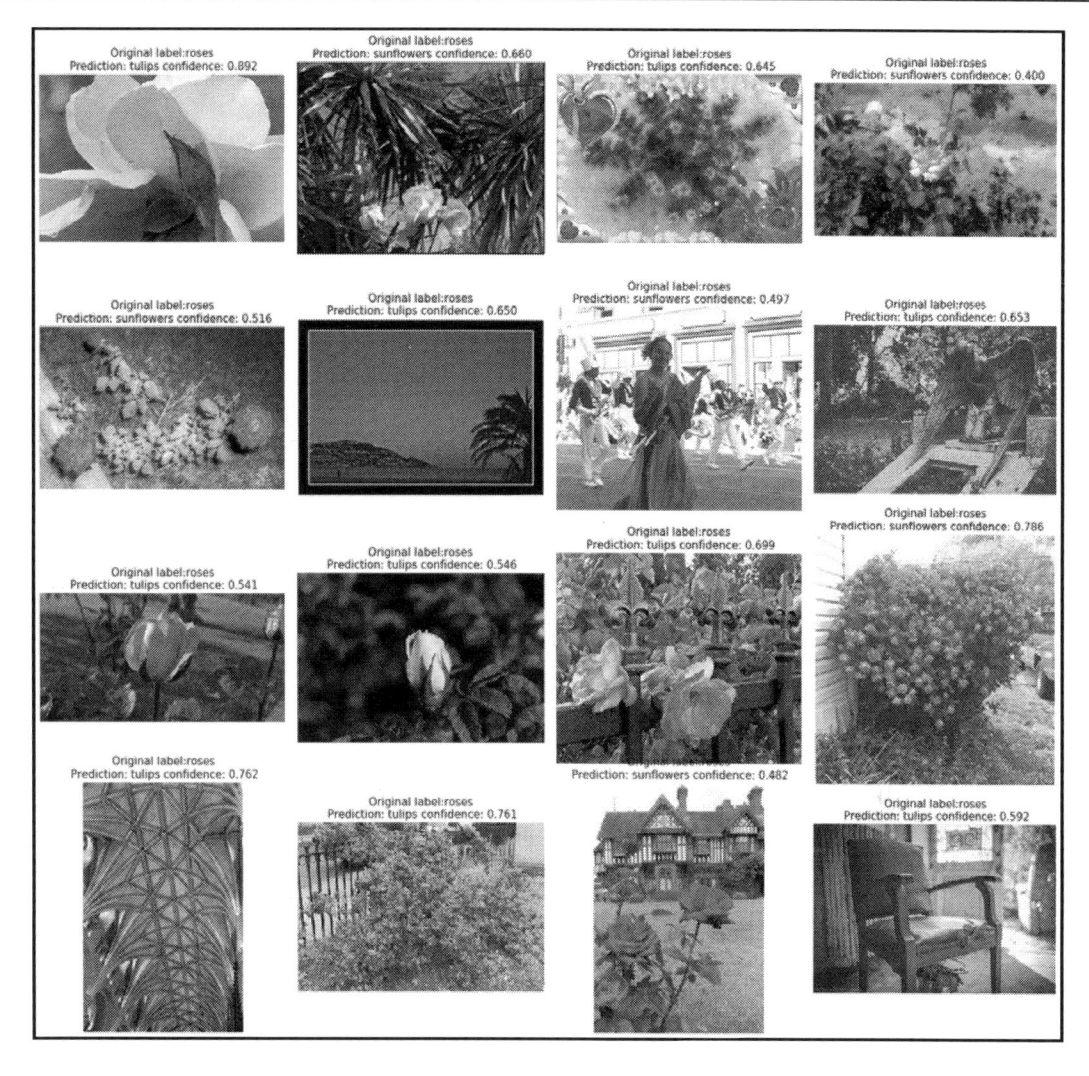

Only the weights of the convolutional layers were loaded for the pretrained VGG16 model (with `include_top=False`, the weights corresponding to the last two FC layers were not loaded); this model was used as the classifier model. Note that the size of the last layer was 7 x 7 x 512.

A couple of new FC layers were added on top of the pretrained convolutional layers (the weights for these layers are to be trained on the training image partition using forward/backward propagation), followed by a softmax output layer that has three classes.

The `ImageDataGenerator` class was used to load the images and the `flow_from_directory()` function was used for the generation of batches of images and labels. The model was configured with the `model.compile()` function using the categorical cross-entropy loss (since we have three classes) and the `RMSProp` optimizer with a learning rate of 10-5.

The `model.fit_generator()` method was used to train the model.

The fine-tuning implemented with Keras trained the VGG16 model partially—that is, it only learned the weights for the FC layers and the last two convolutional layers from the training partition.

The `model.predict_generator()` method was used to predict the labels of the test images.

In Keras, each layer of a network has a trainable parameter. To freeze (that is, stop training) any given layer, the parameter corresponding to that layer needs to be set to `False`.

We went over each layer to select the layers to be retrained.

There's more...

What is likely to happen if you select more convolutional layers to retrain (fine-tune)? For example, what if you select the last four (or six) convolutional layers and retrain them by tweaking the preceding code? What is the impact on the test accuracy? Does it improve? Change the optimizer to Adam and tune the (hyper-) parameters' epoch, learning rate, and `batch_size`. Note the impact of the hyperparameter tuning on test accuracy. Can you get a model with better accuracy only by using transfer learning? Try to implement transfer learning/fine-tuning using PyTorch and TensorFlow as well.

See also

For more information, read through the following sources:

- https://www.learnopencv.com/keras-tutorial-fine-tuning-using-pre-trained-models/
- https://www.learnopencv.com/image-classification-using-convolutional-neural-networks-in-keras/#cnn-hierachical

Classifying traffic signs using a deep learning model (with PyTorch)

In this recipe, you will learn how to train a custom neural network from scratch using PyTorch and use the model's predictions to classify traffic signs. We shall use the **German Traffic Sign Recognition Benchmark (GTSRB)** dataset (https://sid.erda.dk/public/archives/daaeac0d7ce1152aea9b61d9f1e19370/published-archive.html) as the input images for training/testing. The images are labeled with 43 different traffic signs. The dataset contains 39,209 training and 12,630 test images. For this recipe, it is also recommended that you use a computer with GPU(s) in it to make the training process faster.

Getting ready

First, download the compressed pickled dataset from https://s3-us-west-1.amazonaws.com/udacity-selfdrivingcar/traffic-signs-data.zip. Extract it to the `traffic_signs` folder inside the `images` folder (it contains three pickled files, with the images for training, validation, and testing, respectively). Here is the summary of the pickled dataset:

- 34,799 training images
- 4,410 validation images
- 12,630 testing images
- Image size = (32, 32)
- 43 unique classes

Import the following packages to start with:

```
import pickle
import numpy as np
import pandas as pd
import matplotlib.pylab as plt
import seaborn as sns
import cv2
import torch
from torch.utils.data.dataset import Dataset
from torch.utils.data import DataLoader
import torchvision.transforms as transforms
from torchvision.utils import make_grid
import torch.utils.data.sampler as sampler
from torch import nn, optim
```

Image Classification

```
from livelossplot import PlotLosses
import torch.nn.functional as F
import os
```

How to do it...

Go through the following the steps for training a deep neural net on the GTSRB images for traffic sign classification:

1. Load the pickle files corresponding to the training, validation, and test datasets:

   ```
   training_file = "traffic_signs/train.p"
   validation_file = "traffic_signs/valid.p"
   testing_file = "traffic_signs/test.p"
   with open(training_file, mode='rb') as f: train = pickle.load(f)
   with open(validation_file, mode='rb') as f: valid = pickle.load(f)
   with open(testing_file, mode='rb') as f: test = pickle.load(f)
   ```

2. Extract the features (the images) and the labels (the traffic signs) from the training, validation, and test images using the following code snippet:

   ```
   X_train, y_train = train['features'], train['labels']
   X_valid, y_valid = valid['features'], valid['labels']
   X_test, y_test = test['features'], test['labels']
   n_signs = len(np.unique(y_train))
   print(X_train.shape, X_valid.shape, X_test.shape, n_signs)
   # (34799, 32, 32, 3) (4410, 32, 32, 3) (12630, 32, 32, 3) 43
   ```

3. Load the signal names `.csv` file and create a map between traffic signal class IDs and names:

   ```
   signal_names = pd.read_csv('images/signal_names.csv')
   signal_names.head()
   ```

4. The first few rows of the data frame with the `ClassId` and `SignName` of the traffic signals are shown in the following image:

	ClassId	SignName
0	0	Speed limit (20km/h)
1	1	Speed limit (30km/h)
2	2	Speed limit (50km/h)
3	3	Speed limit (60km/h)
4	4	Speed limit (70km/h)

5. If you plot the ID of the traffic signal classes against their frequencies, you will get a diagram along the lines of the following (note that the data is very imbalanced):

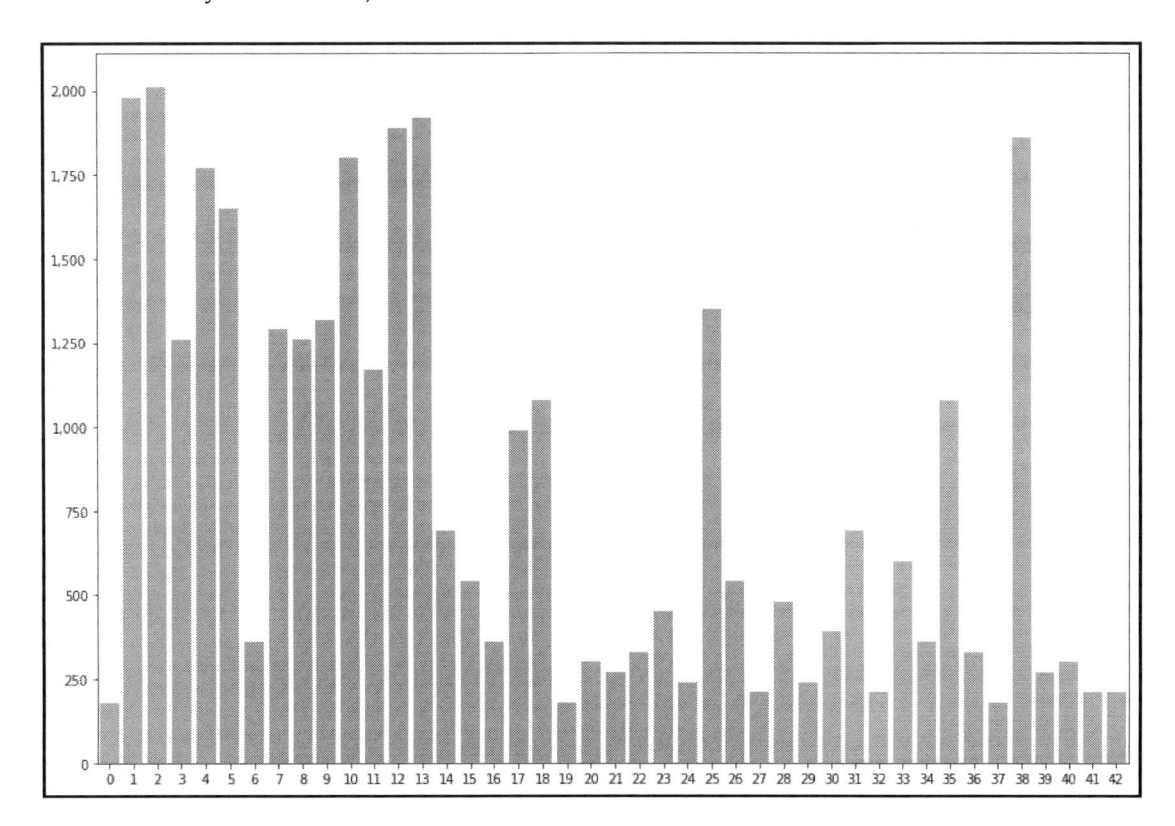

Image Classification

6. If you select a few samples from the training images and plot them along with their labels, you will get a diagram along the lines of the following:

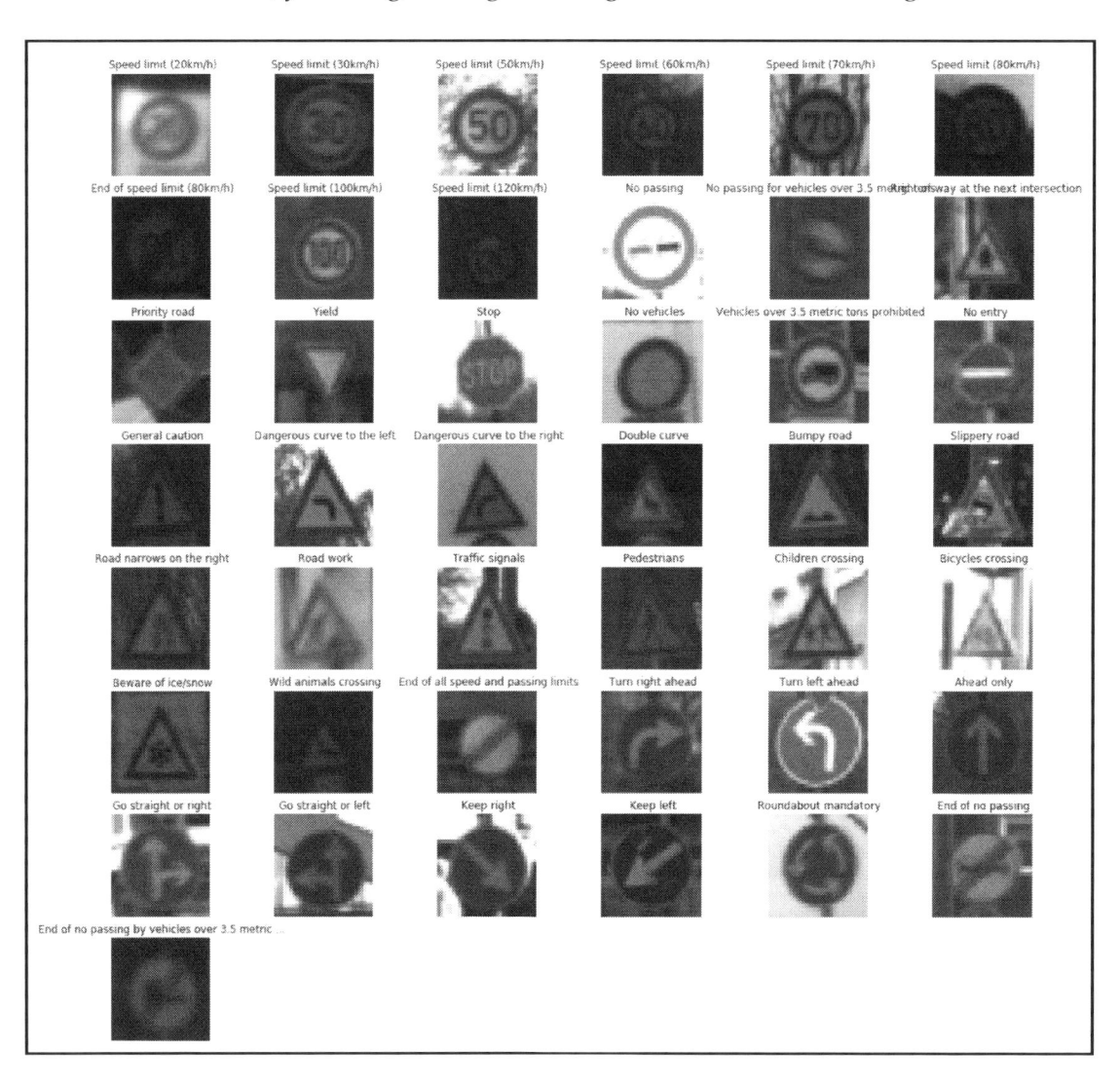

7. Implement the IDSIA MCDNN model by defining a `TrafficNet` class (inheriting from the `nn.Module`). Use the constructor (the `__init__()` method) to define the neural network (with convolution, pooling, and fully connected layers) and implement the forward pass in the neural net with the `forward()` method using the following code snippet:

```
class TraffficNet(nn.Module):

  def __init__(self, gray=False):
    super(TraffficNet, self).__init__()
    input_chan = 1 if gray else 3
    self.conv1 = nn.Conv2d(input_chan, 6, 5)
    self.pool = nn.MaxPool2d(2, 2)
    self.conv2 = nn.Conv2d(6, 16, 5)
    self.fc1 = nn.Linear(16 * 5 * 5, 120)
    self.fc2 = nn.Linear(120, 84)
    self.fc3 = nn.Linear(84, 43)

  def forward(self, x):
    x = self.pool(F.relu(self.conv1(x)))
    x = self.pool(F.relu(self.conv2(x)))
    x = x.view(-1, 16 * 5 * 5)
    x = F.relu(self.fc1(x))
    x = F.relu(self.fc2(x))
    x = self.fc3(x)
    return x
```

8. The input images have high contrast variations and use contrast normalization with the CLAHE transform (that is, they apply an adaptive histogram equalization to the images using the `opencv-python` function):

```
class ClaheTranform:
  def __init__(self, clipLimit=2.5, tileGridSize=(4, 4)):
    self.clipLimit = clipLimit
    self.tileGridSize = tileGridSize

  def __call__(self, im):
    img_y = cv2.cvtColor(im, cv2.COLOR_RGB2YCrCb)[:,:,0]
    clahe = cv2.createCLAHE(clipLimit=self.clipLimit, \
          tileGridSize=self.tileGridSize)
    img_y = clahe.apply(img_y)
    img_output = img_y.reshape(img_y.shape + (1,))
    return img_output
```

Image Classification

9. The input dataset you downloaded was serialized using pickle. Let's define the `PickledTrafficSignsDataset` class by inheriting it from the PyTorch dataset class:

   ```
   class PickledTrafficSignsDataset(Dataset):
     def __init__(self, file_path, transform=None):
       with open(file_path, mode='rb') as f:
       data = pickle.load(f)
       self.features = data['features']
       self.labels = data['labels']
       self.count = len(self.labels)
       self.transform = transform

     def __getitem__(self, index):
       feature = self.features[index]
       if self.transform is not None:
         feature = self.transform(feature)
       return (feature, self.labels[index])

     def __len__(self):
       return self.count
   ```

10. Define the `train()` function to implement the entire training process, starting from loading the data, applying the transforms, and then running the training epochs:

    ```
    def train(model, device):

      data_transforms = transforms.Compose([
        ClaheTranform(),
        transforms.ToTensor()
      ])
      liveloss = PlotLosses()
      torch.manual_seed(1)
      train_dataset = PickledTrafficSignsDataset(training_file, \
                    transform=data_transforms)
      valid_dataset = PickledTrafficSignsDataset(validation_file, \
                    transform=data_transforms)
      test_dataset = PickledTrafficSignsDataset(testing_file, \
                    transform=data_transforms)
      class_sample_count = np.bincount(train_dataset.labels)
      weights = 1 / np.array([class_sample_count[y] for y in \
                    train_dataset.labels])
      samp = sampler.WeightedRandomSampler(weights, 43 * 2000)
      train_loader = DataLoader(train_dataset, batch_size=64, \
                        sampler=samp)
      valid_loader = DataLoader(valid_dataset, batch_size=64, \
    ```

[310]

```
                         shuffle=False)
test_loader = DataLoader(test_dataset, batch_size=64, \
                         shuffle=False)
optimizer = optim.SGD(model.parameters(), lr=0.005, momentum=0.7)
train_epochs(model, device, train_loader, valid_loader, optimizer)
```

11. Define the following function that will run the actual training epochs (let's run for 20 epochs). For each epoch, run a forward pass on the model first with the training data loader and then with the validation data loader. Switch the mode of the model from `train` to `eval` to use the input training and validation dataset, respectively:

    ```
    def train_epochs(model, device, train_data_loader,
    valid_data_loader, optimizer):

      liveloss = PlotLosses()
      loss_function = nn.CrossEntropyLoss()
      running_loss = 0.0
      running_corrects = 0
      data_loaders = {'train': train_data_loader,
    'validation':valid_data_loader}

      for epoch in range(20):
       logs = {}
       for phase in ['train', 'validation']:
        if phase == 'train': model.train()
        else: model.eval()
        running_loss = 0.0
        running_corrects = 0
        total = 0
    ```

Image Classification

12. For the training phase, compute the training loss and run a backward pass (back propagation) to update the model weights. For the validation phase, just compute the validation loss (with the `loss_function()`, using the actual and the predicted class labels for a traffic signal instance):

    ```
    for batch_idx, (data, target) in enumerate(data_loaders[phase]):

        if phase == 'train':
          output = model(data.to(device))
          target = target.long().to(device)
          loss = loss_function(output, target)
          optimizer.zero_grad()
          loss.backward()
          optimizer.step()
        else:
          with torch.no_grad():
            output = model(data.to(device))
            target = target.long().to(device)
            loss = loss_function(output, target)

        if batch_idx % 100 == 0:
          print('Train Epoch: {} [{}/{} ({:.0f}%)]\t{} \
              Loss: {:.6f}'.format(epoch, batch_idx *
              len(data), len(data_loaders[phase].dataset),
              100. * batch_idx / len(data_loaders[phase]), phase,
              loss.item()))
    ```

13. Finally, compare the model-predicted class and the ground-truth label to compute the number of correctly predicted examples. Keep track of the running loss and use `livelossplot` to automatically plot the training and validation loss:

    ```
    pred = torch.argmax(output, dim=1)
    running_loss += loss.detach()
    running_corrects += torch.sum(pred == target).sum().item()
    total += target.size(0)
    epoch_loss = running_loss / len(data_loaders[phase].dataset)
    epoch_acc = running_corrects / total

    prefix = ''
    if phase == 'validation': prefix = 'val_'
    logs[prefix + 'log loss'] = epoch_loss.item()
    logs[prefix + 'accuracy'] = epoch_acc.item()
    liveloss.update(logs)
    liveloss.draw()
    ```

[312]

If you run the preceding code blocks and use `livelossplot` to automatically plot the log-loss/accuracy during the training, you will get an output along the lines of the following:

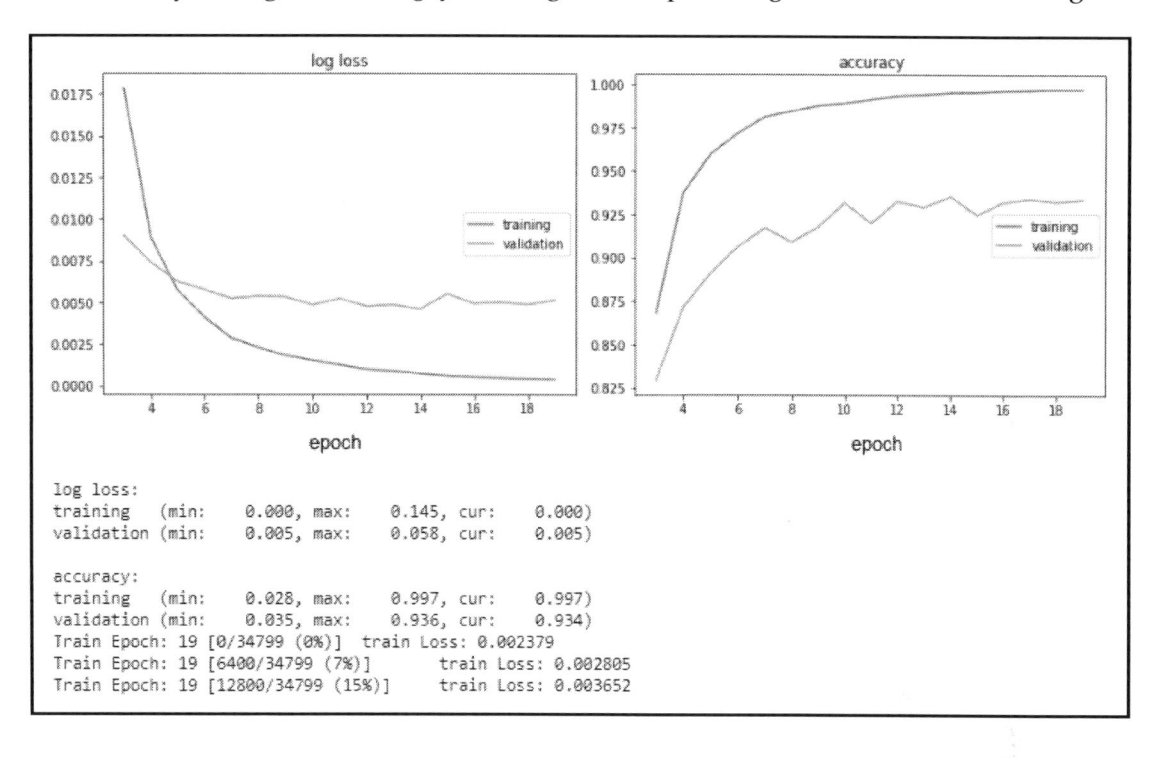

```
log loss:
training   (min:    0.000, max:    0.145, cur:    0.000)
validation (min:    0.005, max:    0.058, cur:    0.005)

accuracy:
training   (min:    0.028, max:    0.997, cur:    0.997)
validation (min:    0.035, max:    0.936, cur:    0.934)
Train Epoch: 19 [0/34799 (0%)]      train Loss: 0.002379
Train Epoch: 19 [6400/34799 (7%)]   train Loss: 0.002805
Train Epoch: 19 [12800/34799 (15%)] train Loss: 0.003652
```

Image Classification

If you run the preceding code block and plot a few images from the test dataset with their predicted labels, you will get an output along the lines of the following:

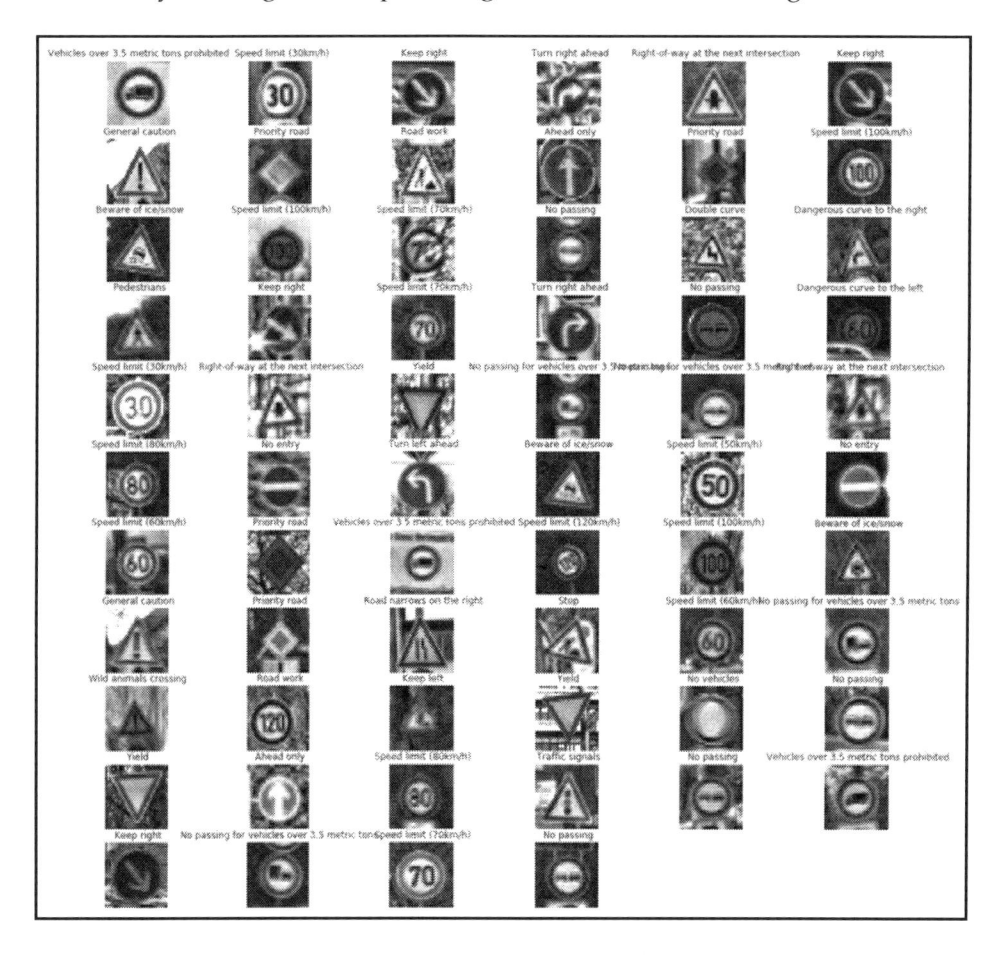

How it works...

As can be seen from the last barplot, the dataset is very imbalanced: some classes have as many as 2,000 sample images corresponding to it, whereas a few classes have as few as 200 sample images.

This class imbalance in the training dataset is likely to result in a biased model being learned, since the model simply sees images corresponding to some traffic-sign classes more often than others.

Sampling was used to resolve class imbalance and also to prevent overfitting.

The `WeightedRandomSampler()` was used to sample the images corresponding to all of the 43 classes with equal frequency (2,000 images per class, which increases the total number of input images too) and then they were passed to the PyTorch data loader.

The **contrast-limited adaptive histogram equalization** (**CLAHE**) algorithm was used to partition the images into contextual regions followed by an application of the histogram equalization to every region. The hidden features of the image appear to be more visible with CLAHE than with vanilla histogram equalization since the distribution of used gray values is evened out.

The input color images were converted to grayscale images by first transforming them from RGB to the YCbCr colorspace and then extracting the intensity channel Y from the YCbCr color space.

The abstract class `torch.utils.data.Dataset` represents a dataset that can be iterated over with `torch.utils.data.DataLoader`.

In order to prevent overfitting, dropout and batch normalization regularization techniques were used.

The `livelossplot` library was used to plot the live training loss.

The `torch.no_grad()` function stops the calculation of the gradients in the validation phase (since we just want to evaluate the model that we learned so far on the held-out validation dataset and don't want to update the weights in this phase).

There's more...

Compute the accuracy of the model trained on the test dataset and plot the confusion matrix. What is the test accuracy achieved? How can you improve it?

See also

For more information, read through the following sources:

- https://pytorch.org/tutorials/beginner/blitz/cifar10_tutorial.html
- https://medium.com/@wolfapple/traffic-sign-recognition-2b0c3835e104
- https://github.com/wolfapple/traffic-sign-recognition/blob/master/notebook.ipynb

- `https://sid.erda.dk/public/archives/daaeac0d7ce1152aea9b61d9f1e19370/published-archive.html`
- `https://github.com/mohamedameen93/German-Traffic-Sign-Classification-Using-TensorFlow`
- `https://github.com/vxy10/ImageAugmentation/blob/master/img_transform_NB.ipynb`
- `https://towardsdatascience.com/recognizing-traffic-signs-with-over-98-accuracy-using-deep-learning-86737aedc2ab`
- `https://people.lu.usi.ch/mascij/data/papers/2012_nn_traffic.pdf`

Estimating a human pose using a deep learning model

Human pose estimation is an image processing/computer vision task that predicts different keypoints' (joints/landmarks—for example, elbows, knees, neck, shoulder, hips, and chest) locations in the human skeleton, representing the pose (orientation) of a human (sets of coordinates are connected to find a person's overall pose). A limb/pair is defined by a valid connection between two parts; some combinations of two parts may not form valid pairs.

Multiperson pose estimation is harder than its single-person counterpart, as both the number of people in an image along with the locations are not known. As a bottom-up approach to solve this problem, all parts of the image for all the featured people are first detected and then those parts corresponding to individuals are associated/grouped. A popular bottom-up approach is the OpenPose network (from Carnegie Mellon University), which first extracts input image features (using the first few layers of VGG19, as shown in the following diagram) that are fed into two parallel branches of convolutional layers. The following three steps summarize how OpenPose works:

1. **Keypoints localization**: The first branch predicts all of the keypoints (a set of 18 confidence maps) with confidence scores, where each map denotes a specific part of the human skeleton.
2. **Part affinity fields (PAFs)**: The second branch predicts a two-dimensional vector field consisting of a set of 38 PAFs that represents the degree of association between the parts. Successive stages refine each branch's predictions.
3. **Greedy inference**: All the keypoints are connected using a greedy algorithm (with bipartite graphs constructed between pairs of parts and the weaker links in the graphs pruned using the PAF values):

Taken from *https://arxiv.org/pdf/1611.08050.pdf*

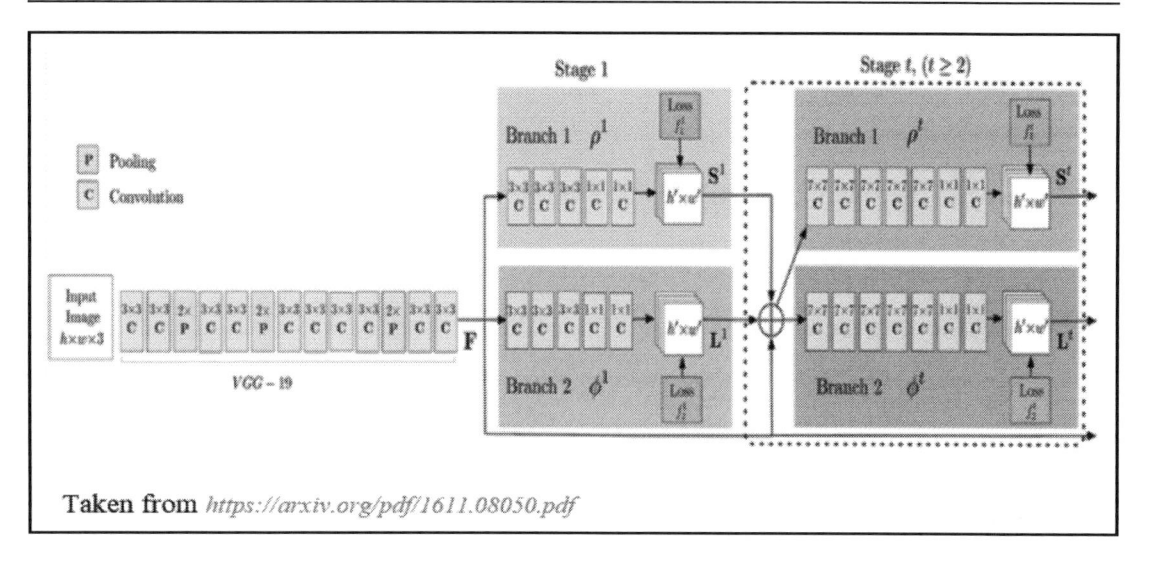

In this recipe, you will learn how to use the OpenPose deep neural net model for human pose estimation with a pretrained Caffe model using `opencv-python` library functions (it won the COCO Keypoints Challenge in 2016).

Getting ready

First, download the pretrained Caffe model from `http://posefs1.perception.cs.cmu.edu/OpenPose/models/pose/mpi/pose_iter_160000.caffemodel`—this model is trained on the **multi-person dataset** (**MPI**). Let's start by importing all the required libraries using the following code snippet:

```
import cv2
import time
import numpy as np
import matplotlib.pyplot as plt
print(cv2.__version__)
# 3.4.4
```

Image Classification

How to do it...

Run the following steps to implement human pose estimation with the pretrained Caffe model:

1. This MPI dataset has 15 keypoints corresponding to different parts of the human body—let's define them first. You will also need to define pose pairs for the limbs that connect the keypoints. The limbs are predicted using the pose affinity maps:

    ```
    n_points = 15
    body_parts = {"Head": 0, "Neck": 1, "RShoulder": 2, "RElbow": 3,
    "RWrist": 4, "LShoulder": 5, "LElbow": 6, "LWrist": 7, "RHip": 8,
    "RKnee": 9, "RAnkle": 10, "LHip": 11, "LKnee": 12, "LAnkle": 13,
    "Chest": 14, "Background": 15}

    pose_pairs = [ ["Head", "Neck"], ["Neck", "RShoulder"],
    ["RShoulder",
    "RElbow"], ["RElbow", "RWrist"], ["Neck", "LShoulder"],
    ["LShoulder",
    "LElbow"], ["LElbow", "LWrist"], ["Neck", "Chest"], ["Chest",
    "RHip"],
    ["RHip", "RKnee"], ["RKnee", "RAnkle"], ["Chest", "LHip"], ["LHip",
    "LKnee"], ["LKnee", "LAnkle"] ]
    ```

2. Next, load the pretrained model (trained on the Caffe deep learning framework) you downloaded. There are a couple of files that the Caffe models have—namely, a `.prototxt` file (describing the architecture of the neural net model) and a `.caffemodel` file (storing the weights of the trained model). Let's load the model into memory by reading these files using the following code snippet:

    ```
    proto_file = "models/pose_deploy_linevec_faster_4_stages.prototxt"
    weights_file = "models/pose_iter_160000.caffemodel"
    net = cv2.dnn.readNetFromCaffe(proto_file, weights_file)
    ```

3. Let's read the input image with the human(s) whose pose we will estimate. Prepare the input to be passed to the network using the following code snippet:

    ```
    image = cv2.imread("images/leander.jpg")
    height, width = image.shape[:2]
    blob = cv2.dnn.blobFromImage(image, 1.0 / 255, (368,368), (0, 0,
    0), swapRB=False, crop=False)
    net.setInput(blob)
    ```

4. The model predictions can be generated by just running a forward pass on the neural net model with the input image fed to the network:

```
output = net.forward()
```

The output is a matrix with four dimensions. The contents and the dimensions are as follows:

- The image ID (required when multiple images are input to the model).
- The indices of the keypoints. The model generates the concatenated confidence and part affinity maps as output. For the MPI model, it produces 44 points, corresponding to 15 keypoint confidence maps + 1 background + 14 x 2 part affinity maps. We shall use the first few points corresponding to keypoints.
- The output map's height.
- The output map's width.

5. Plot the keypoint confidence maps for the first five keypoints using the following code:

```
h, w = output.shape[2:4]

plt.figure(figsize=[14,10])
plt.imshow(cv2.cvtColor(image, cv2.COLOR_BGR2RGB))
prob_map = np.zeros((width, height))
for i in range(1,5):
  pmap = output[0, i, :, :]
  prob_map += cv2.resize(pmap, (height, width))
plt.imshow(prob_map, alpha=0.6)
plt.colorbar()
plt.axis("off")
plt.show()
```

Image Classification

If you run the preceding code block, then you will get the following heatmap as output:

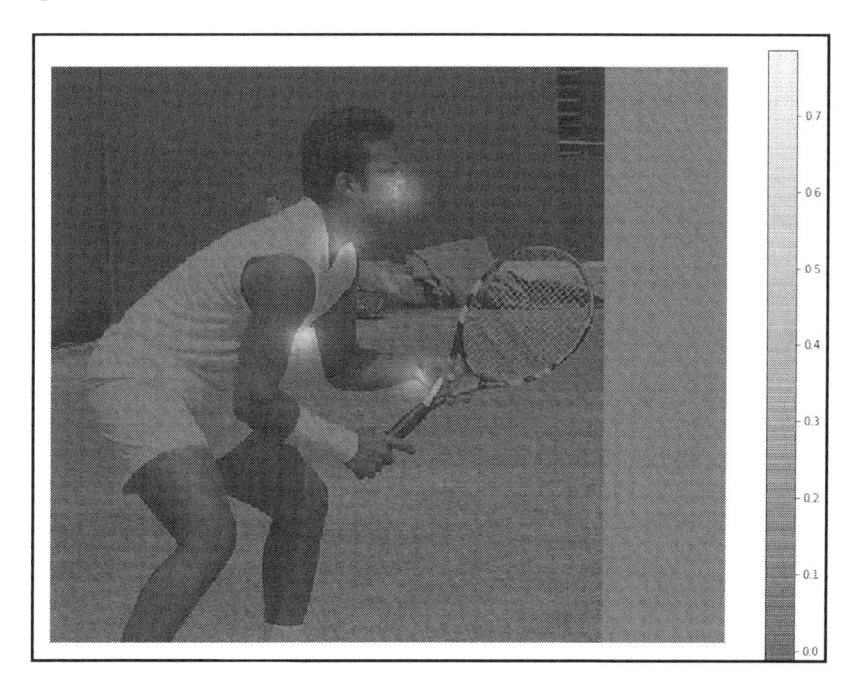

6. For each keypoint, check the presence of the keypoint in the image and retrieve the keypoint coordinates corresponding to the maximum of the confidence map from that keypoint (along with a threshold to be used to decrease false positives):

```
threshold = 0.1
image1 = image.copy()
points = []
for i in range(n_points):
 prob_map = output[0, i, :, :] #  confidence map of \
        corresponding body's part.
 min_val, prob, min_loc, point = cv2.minMaxLoc(prob_map)
 # scale the point to fit on the original image
 x = (width * point[0]) / w
 y = (height * point[1]) / h
 if prob > threshold :
  cv2.circle(image1, (int(x), int(y)), 8, (255, 0, 255), \
        thickness=-1, lineType=cv2.FILLED)
  cv2.putText(image1, "{}".format(i), (int(x), int(y)), \
        cv2.FONT_HERSHEY_SIMPLEX, 0.6, (0, 255, 0), 2, \
        lineType=cv2.LINE_AA)
  cv2.circle(image, (int(x), int(y)), 8, (255, 0, 255), \
```

[320]

```
                  thickness=-1, lineType=cv2.FILLED)
   points.append((int(x), int(y)))
  else :
   points.append(None)
```

7. Finally, since the indices of the keypoints are known beforehand, just join the pairs to draw the skeleton on the image:

```
for pair in pose_pairs:
 part_from = body_parts[pair[0]]
 part_to = body_parts[pair[1]]
 if points[part_from] and points[part_to]:
   cv2.line(image, points[part_from], points[part_to], \
       (0, 255, 0), 3)

plt.figure(figsize=[20,12])
plt.subplot(121), plt.imshow(cv2.cvtColor(image1,
cv2.COLOR_BGR2RGB)), plt.axis('off'), plt.title('Keypoints',
size=20)
plt.subplot(122), plt.imshow(cv2.cvtColor(image,
cv2.COLOR_BGR2RGB)), plt.axis('off'), plt.title('Pose', size=20)
plt.show()
```

If you run the preceding code block, you will get the following output:

How it works...

The `cv2.dnn.blobFromImage()` function was used to convert the image from the OpenCV format to Caffe blob format. First, the pixel values were normalized so that they were within the (0,1) range. Then the size of the resizing target image was provided. Finally, the mean value was subtracted. No color-channel swapping was required since both OpenCV and Caffe use the same color format of BGR.

The `cv2.minMaxLoc()` function was used to compute the local maxima of the confidence map.

See also

For more information, read through the following sources:

- https://www.learnopencv.com/deep-learning-based-human-pose-estimation-using-opencv-cpp-python/
- https://cv-tricks.com/pose-estimation/using-deep-learning-in-opencv/
- https://medium.com/beyondminds/an-overview-of-human-pose-estimation-with-deep-learning-d49eb656739b
- https://arxiv.org/pdf/1812.08008.pdf
- https://arxiv.org/pdf/1611.08050.pdf
- https://github.com/CMU-Perceptual-Computing-Lab/openpose

8
Object Detection in Images

Object detection is an image processing/computer vision task that detects (semantic) objects' instances corresponding to a given type (for example, faces, humans, vehicles, and buildings) in images. In this chapter, you will learn to implement a few state-of-the-art object detection techniques. The following image processing tasks are related to each other (although they refer to different tasks): image classification, object localization, and object detection. Image classification (discussed in the last chapter) aims to predict a class label for an image, whereas object localization deals with identifying the locations and drawing bounding boxes around an object in an image. Object detection combines these two tasks (classification + localization)—it draws a bounding box around each object (there can be multiple objects) of interest in the image and assigns each of them a class label. All of these problems are collectively known as object recognition. The following screenshot explains the difference between these techniques:

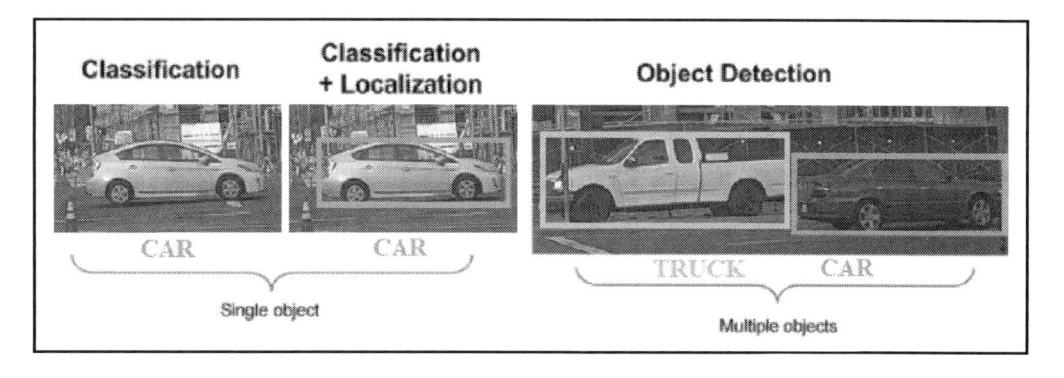

Object Detection in Images

In this chapter, we are going to cover the following recipes:

- Object detection with HOG/SVM
- Object detection with Yolo V3
- Object detection with Faster R-CNN
- Object detection with Mask R-CNN
- Multiple object tracking with `opencv-python`
- Text detection/recognition in images with EAST/Tesseract
- Face detection with Viola-Jones/Haar-like features

Object detection with HOG/SVM

A popular feature descriptor for object detection is the **Histogram of Oriented Gradients** (**HOG**). HOG descriptors can be computed from an image by first computing the horizontal and vertical gradient images, then computing the gradient histograms and normalizing across blocks, and finally flattening into a feature descriptor vector. These normalized block descriptors finally obtained are called HOG descriptors, a feature descriptor used in a variety of computer vision and image processing applications for object detection.

The use of HOG descriptors has been particularly successful for detecting humans, animals, faces, and text. We already described how to compute a HOG descriptor from an image. At first, a (linear) **Support Vector Machine** (**SVM**) binary classifier model is trained with several positive and negative training example images. Positive images are examples that contain the object we want to detect. The negative training set can be any images that do not contain the object we want to detect. Positive and negative source images are converted into HOG block descriptors. The SVM trainer selects the best hyperplane/decision boundary (defined using a set of support vectors) to separate the positive and negative examples in the training image dataset. The support vectors are used later by the SVM model to classify HOG-descriptor blocks from a test image to detect the presence/absence of an object.

Classification is traditionally performed by repeatedly stepping a sliding window of, say, 64 pixels wide by 128 pixels high across a test image and computing the HOG descriptors. As the HOG descriptor calculation does not have an intrinsic sense of scale and since the objects can occur at multiple scales within an image, the HOG description computation is repeated across each level of a scale pyramid. The scaling factor between each level in the scale pyramid is commonly between 1.05 and 1.2 and the image is repeatedly scaled down until the scaled source image can no longer accommodate a complete HOG window. If the SVM classifier predicts the detection of an object at any scale, the corresponding bounding box is returned. The following diagram shows a typical HOG object (human) detection workflow:

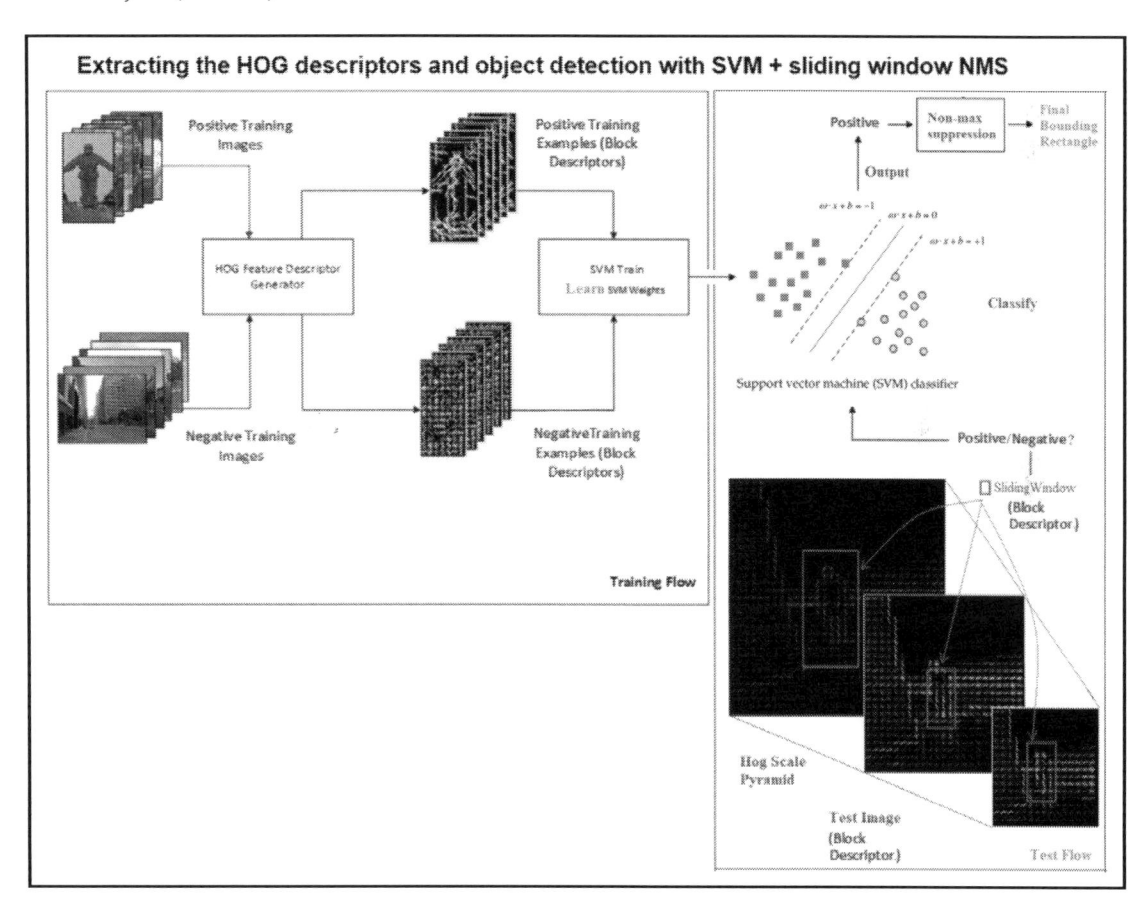

In this recipe, you will learn how to use OpenCV-Python library functions to detect human objects in an image.

Getting started

Let's start by importing the required libraries, using the following code snippet:

```
import numpy as np
import cv2
import matplotlib.pylab as plt
```

How to do it...

Perform the following steps to detect people in an image using `opencv-python library` functions:

1. First, read the image and initialize the HOG detector using the following lines of code:

    ```
    img = cv2.imread("images/walk.jpg")
    hog = cv2.HOGDescriptor()
    ```

2. Initialize the SVM detector to be the default people detector:

    ```
    hog.setSVMDetector(cv2.HOGDescriptor_getDefaultPeopleDetector())
    ```

3. Run the detection algorithm, with a spatial stride of 4 pixels (horizontal and vertical), a scale stride of 1.1, and no grouping of the rectangles (to notice that HOG detects the same object at multiple scales in the scale pyramid). As you can see, 314 potential bounding boxes were detected (with multiple detections of the same object):

    ```
    (found_bounding_boxes, weights) = hog.detectMultiScale(img, \
                            winStride=(4, 4), padding=(8, 8), \
                            scale=1.1, finalThreshold=0)
    print(len(found_bounding_boxes)) # number of bounding boxes
    # 314
    ```

4. Define the following function to implement non-maximum suppression to ignore redundant, overlapping bounding boxes:

    ```
    def non_max_suppression(boxes, scores, threshold):
        assert boxes.shape[0] == scores.shape[0]
        ys1, xs1, ys2, xs2 = boxes[:, 0], boxes[:, 1], boxes[:, 2], \
                            boxes[:, 3]
        areas = (ys2 - ys1) * (xs2 - xs1)
        scores_indexes = scores.argsort().tolist()
        boxes_keep_index = []
    ```

```
        while len(scores_indexes):
            index = scores_indexes.pop()
            boxes_keep_index.append(index)
            if not len(scores_indexes):
                break
            ious = compute_iou(boxes[index], boxes[scores_indexes], \
                                areas[index], areas[scores_indexes])
            filtered_indexes = set((ious > threshold).nonzero()[0])
            scores_indexes = [v for (i, v) in enumerate(scores_indexes) \
                                if i not in filtered_indexes]
        return np.array(boxes_keep_index)
```

5. Define the following function to compute the intersection over union (iou) metric for a given box against all other boxes:

```
    def compute_iou(box, boxes, box_area, boxes_area):
        assert boxes.shape[0] == boxes_area.shape[0]
        ys1 = np.maximum(box[0], boxes[:, 0])
        xs1 = np.maximum(box[1], boxes[:, 1])
        ys2 = np.minimum(box[2], boxes[:, 2])
        xs2 = np.minimum(box[3], boxes[:, 3])
        intersections = np.maximum(ys2 - ys1, 0) * \
                        np.maximum(xs2 - xs1, 0)
        unions = box_area + boxes_area - intersections
        ious = intersections / unions
        return ious
```

6. Detect people (pedestrians) in the input image using the detectMultiScale function and obtain the corresponding bounding boxes:

```
    (found_bounding_boxes, weights) = hog.detectMultiScale(img, \
                                    winStride=(4, 4), padding=(8, 8), \
                                    scale=1.1, finalThreshold=0)
    print(len(found_bounding_boxes)) # number of bounding boxes
    # 70
    found_bounding_boxes[:,2] = found_bounding_boxes[:,0] +
    found_bounding_boxes[:,2]
    found_bounding_boxes[:,3] = found_bounding_boxes[:,1] +
    found_bounding_boxes[:,3]
```

Object Detection in Images

7. Apply `non_max_suppression` to get rid of duplicate detection, using the following code snippet:

```
box_indices = non_max_suppression(found_bounding_boxes,
weights.ravel(), threshold=0.2)
found_bounding_boxes = found_bounding_boxes[box_indices,:]
found_bounding_boxes[:,2] = found_bounding_boxes[:,2] -
found_bounding_boxes[:,0]
found_bounding_boxes[:,3] = found_bounding_boxes[:,3] -
found_bounding_boxes[:,1]
print(len(found_bounding_boxes)) # number of boundingboxes
# 4
```

8. Alternatively, you can use meanshift-grouping to handle potential overlapping bounding boxes, as shown in the following code block:

```
(found_bounding_boxes, weights) = hog.detectMultiScale(img, \
                                    winStride=(4, 4), padding=(8, 8), \
                                    scale=1.01,
useMeanshiftGrouping=True)
print(len(found_bounding_boxes)) # number of boundingboxes
# 3
```

9. Finally, draw the final bounding boxes obtained (after applying non-maximum suppression or meanshift-grouping) on the image:

```
img_with_raw_boxes = img.copy()
for (hx, hy, hw, hh) in found_bounding_boxes:
    cv2.rectangle(img_with_raw_boxes, (hx, hy), (hx + hw, hy + hh),
(0, 0, 255), 2)
plt.figure(figsize=(20, 12))
img_with_raw_boxes = cv2.cvtColor(img_with_raw_boxes,
cv2.COLOR_BGR2RGB)
plt.imshow(img_with_raw_boxes, aspect='auto'), plt.axis('off')
plt.title('Boundingboxes found by HOG-SVM with meanshift grouping',
size=20)
plt.show()
```

If you run the preceding code block, you will get a diagram along the lines of the following output:

Boundingboxes found by HOG-SVM with meanshift grouping

How it works...

The HOG descriptors from the input image are computed and then fed into a pretrained SVM classifier (obtained using cv2's `HOGDescriptor_getDefaultPeopleDetector()`), which was used to predict the presence or absence of a person in or from an image block at multiple scales with the `detectMultiScale()` function from OpenCV-Python.

The object(s) were detected multiple times at different scales, and they were fused together using non-maximum suppression (additionally, we may see some false positives too).

The `non_max_suppression()` function was invoked to avoid the detection of the same object at multiple times and scales.

The IoU was used by non-maximum suppression to calculate the amount of overlap of two different bounding boxes, **B1** and **B2**. The IoU is defined as follows:

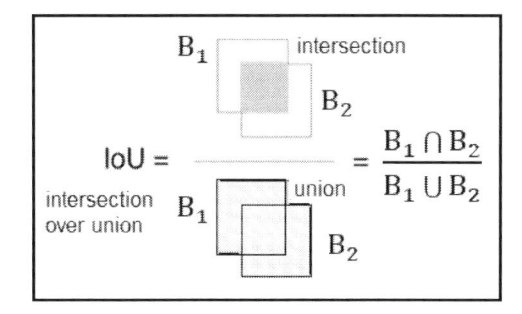

$$IoU = \frac{intersection}{union} = \frac{B_1 \cap B_2}{B_1 \cup B_2}$$

If the **IoU** is low (a threshold of 0.2 was used), that is, there is not much overlap, then there is a good probability that two different bounding boxes correspond to two different persons detected. None of the bounding box predictions are discarded by the non-maximum suppression algorithm; otherwise, one of the bounding boxes is discarded.

Final bounding boxes are drawn on top of the image and the objects (people) detected are indicated by bounding boxes (red rectangles).

There's more...

Compare the non-maximum suppression and meanshift-grouping post-processing approaches to avoid multiple detections of objects and false-positive detection. Use different values of `winStride`, scale, and such kinds of parameters to detect the `MultiScale()` function and observe the impact of parameter tuning on the output objects detected.

See also

Refer to the following links to learn more about this recipe:

- `https://gist.github.com/CMCDragonkai/1be3402e261d3c239a307a3346360506`
- `https://lear.inrialpes.fr/people/triggs/pubs/Dalal-cvpr05.pdf`
- `https://www.youtube.com/watch?v=kl6-NHxcn-k`
- `https://www.youtube.com/watch?v=qRouVgXb1G4`

Object detection with Yolo V3

The following screenshot (figure copyright: Ros Girshick) shows the improvement in mean average precision over years for object detection on the images from the **PASCAL VOC image dataset**. As you can see, up to **2012**, the performance for object detection started to stagnate and slow down a little bit. In **2013**, the deep learning approaches came around and performance received a boost from that time onward, getting better and better over time:

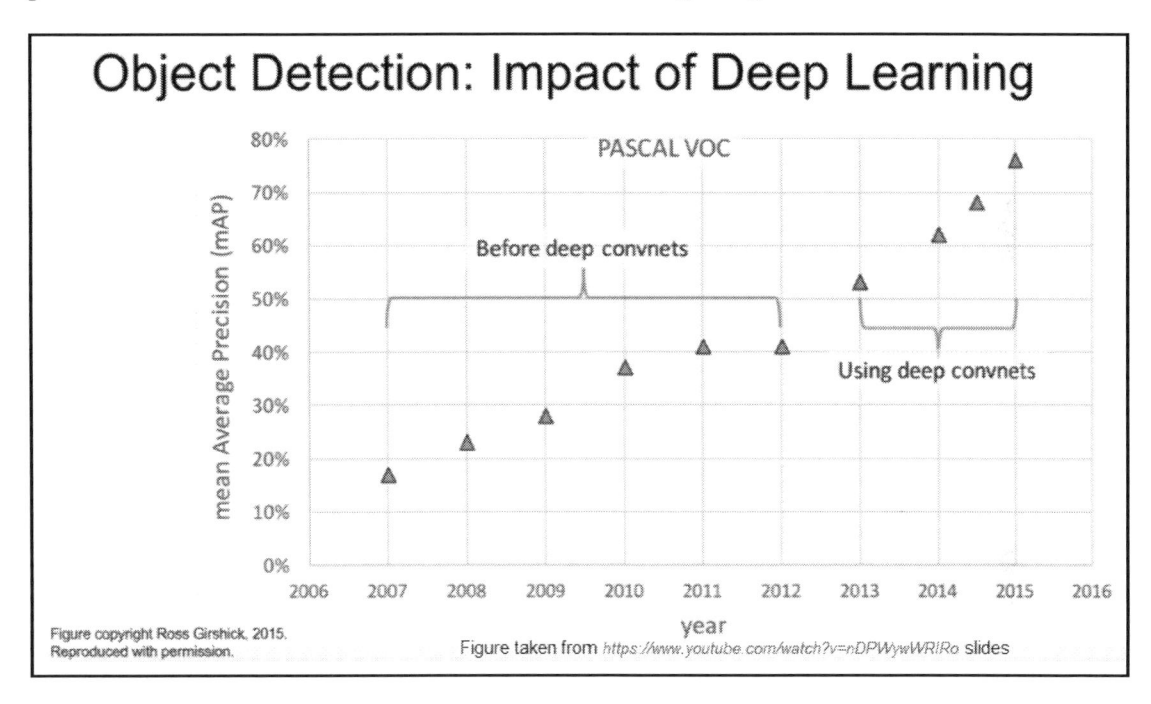

Algorithms such as Region-based-CNN (for example, Faster/Mask R-CNN) and YOLO have been developed to improve the precision of object detection drastically using deep learning. In this recipe, we will discuss a couple of popular fully convolutional network models for object detection, one of them being **YOLO** (You Only Look Once). This provides a high accuracy rate compared to other algorithms and runs in real time. As the name suggests, this algorithm looks only once at an image, meaning that it needs only a single forward propagation pass to compute accurate predictions for detecting the objects in the image.

Object Detection in Images

In this recipe, you will learn how to detect objects in images with a **Fully Convolutional Network** (**FCN**) deep learning model, **YOLO** (v3). Given an input image with some objects (for example, animals, and cars), we will aim to detect objects in the image with a pretrained *YOLO (v3)* model, with bounding boxes.

YOLO v3 has a number of incremental improvements over YOLO v2:

- YOLO v3 uses Darknet-53 (a deeper network with shortcut connections) instead of Darknet-19 used by YOLO v2.
- It has a more advanced feature extractor/object detector using feature map up sampling/concatenation.
- To detect small objects more efficiently, YOLO v3 performs detections at three different scales.
- YOLO v3 uses nine anchor boxes (three for each scale, instead of the total of five anchor boxes used by YOLO v2), predicting more bounding boxes than YOLO v2 given the same-sized image as input.
- YOLO v3 computes the object confidence scores and class labels with independent logistic regression classifiers instead of softmax (by computing cross-entropy error terms instead of the squared-loss functions).

In this recipe, you will learn how to use a pretrained YOLO v3 model to detect objects in an image using `opencv-python` library functions.

Getting started

First, download the pretrained YOLO v3 model files (for example, the `.cfg` and `.weights` files for YOLOv3-416, with input image sizes 416 x 416) from https://pjreddie.com/darknet/yolo/ and save the files inside the `models` folder. Let's now import all of the required libraries using the following code snippet:

```
import cv2
import numpy as np
import matplotlib.pylab as plt
from PIL import import Image, ImageDraw, ImageFont
import colorsys
from random import shuffle
```

How to do it...

Perform the following steps to implement object detection with a Yolo v3 pretrained model, using the `opencv-python library` functions:

1. First, initialize all of the parameters (for example, thresholds for non-maximum suppression and confidence for classification) with appropriate values:

    ```
    conf_threshold = 0.5 # Confidence threshold
    nms_threshold = 0.4 # Non-maximum suppression threshold
    width = 416 # Width of network's input image
    height = 416 # Height of network's input image
    ```

2. Load the names of the object classes (there are 80 classes corresponding to the MS-COCO dataset, including a person, bicycle, car, motorbike, and airplane) from the text file provided. Create unique colors corresponding to each object class (to distinguish the bounding boxes for the different objects detected). Also, initialize the model configuration and pretrained weight paths using the following code snippet:

    ```
    classes_file = "models/yolov3/coco_classes.txt";
    classes = None
    with open(classes_file, 'rt') as f:
        classes = f.read().rstrip('\n').split('\n')
    HSV_tuples = [(x/len(classes), x/len(classes), 0.8) for x in range(len(classes))]
    shuffle(HSV_tuples)
    colors = list(map(lambda x: colorsys.hsv_to_rgb(*x), HSV_tuples))
    model_configuration = "models/yolov3/yolov3.cfg"
    model_weights = "models/yolov3/yolov3.weights"
    ```

3. Load the pretrained deep neural net model with the `Darknet` model configuration and weight files:

    ```
    net = cv2.dnn.readNetFromDarknet(model_configuration, model_weights)
    net.setPreferableBackend(cv2.dnn.DNN_BACKEND_OPENCV)
    net.setPreferableTarget(cv2.dnn.DNN_TARGET_CPU)
    ```

4. Define the following function to obtain the names of the output layers in the network:

    ```
    def get_output_layers(net):
        layers_names = net.getLayerNames()
        return [layers_names[i[0] - 1] for i in net.getUnconnectedOutLayers()]
    ```

Object Detection in Images

5. To draw a bounding box around a predicted object (along with the predicted class label with the confidence of prediction), define the following function:

```
def draw_box(img, class_id, conf, left, top, right, bottom):
    label = "{}: {:.2f}%".format(classes[class_id], conf * 100)
    color = tuple([int(255*x) for x in colors[class_id]])
    top = top - 15 if top - 15 > 15 else top + 15
    pil_im = Image.fromarray(cv2.cvtColor(img,cv2.COLOR_BGR2RGB))
    thickness = (img.shape[0] + img.shape[1]) // 300
    font = ImageFont.truetype("arial.ttf", 25)
    draw = ImageDraw.Draw(pil_im)
    label_size = draw.textsize(label, font)
    text_origin = np.array([left,top-label_size[1]] if \
                    top-label_size[1] >= 0 else [left,top+1])
    for i in range(thickness):
        draw.rectangle([left + i, top + i, right - i, \
        bottom - i], outline=color)
    draw.rectangle([tuple(text_origin), tuple(text_origin + \
                    label_size)], fill=color)
    draw.text(text_origin, label, fill=(0, 0, 0), font=font)
    del draw
    img = cv2.cvtColor(np.array(pil_im), cv2.COLOR_RGB2BGR)
    return img
```

6. Use non-maximum suppression to get rid of the bounding boxes that have corresponding low confidence scores by means of the following code block:

```
def post_process(img, outs):
    img_height, img_width = img.shape[0], img.shape[1]
    class_ids = []
    confidences = []
    boxes = []
    for out in outs:
        for detection in out:
            scores = detection[5:]
            class_id = np.argmax(scores)
            confidence = scores[class_id]
            if confidence > conf_threshold:
                center_x, center_y = int(detection[0] * \
                    img_width), int(detection[1] * img_height)
                width, height = int(detection[2] * \
                    img_width), int(detection[3] * img_height)
                left, top = int(center_x - width / 2), \
                    int(center_y - height / 2)
                class_ids.append(class_id)
                confidences.append(float(confidence))
                boxes.append([left, top, width, height])
    indices = cv2.dnn.NMSBoxes(boxes, confidences, \
```

```
            conf_threshold, nms_threshold)
    for i in indices:
        i = i[0]
        box = boxes[i]
        left, top, width, height = box[0], box[1], box[2], box[3]
        img = draw_box(img, classIds[i], confidences[i], left, \
                       top, left + width, top + height)
    return img
```

7. Read the input image, get a blob from the input image (with preprocessing required), and run a forward pass on the YOLO v3 model with the image blob as input. Finally, invoke the `post_process()` function to draw the bounding boxes along with the object class for all of the objects detected using the model:

```
img = cv2.imread('images/mytable.png')
blob = cv2.dnn.blobFromImage(img, 1/255, (width, height), [0,0,0], 1, crop=False)
net.setInput(blob)
outs = net.forward(get_output_layers(net))
img = post_process(img, outs)
```

Run the preceding code blocks and plot the bounding boxes around the objects detected in the image along with the confidence corresponding to the predicted class. You will obtain output similar to the following:

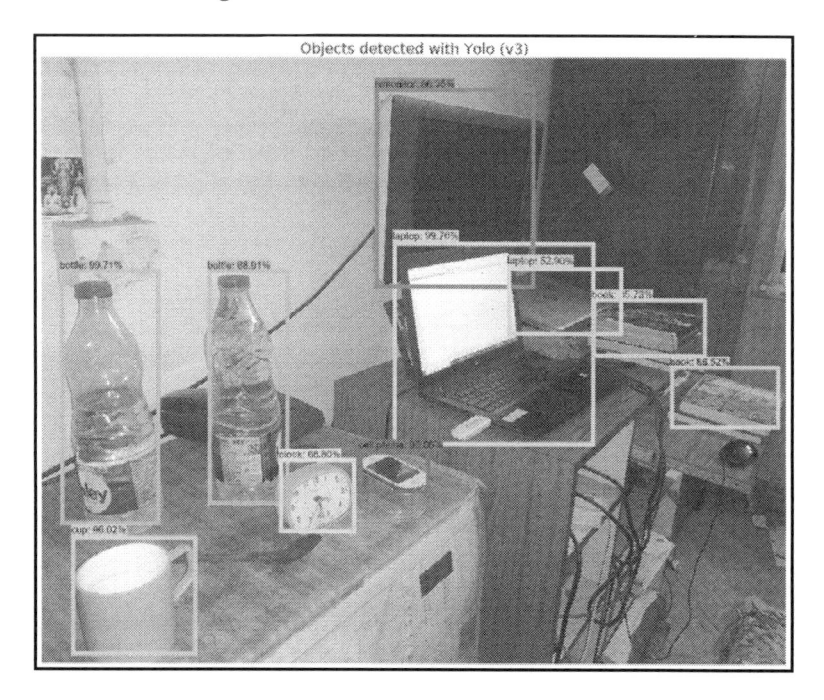

How it works...

In the `post_process()` function, all bounding boxes (returned by the model as output) were scanned through, subsequently discarding the ones with low confidence scores. The detected object's class label was the one corresponding to the highest probability score. The non-maximum suppression algorithm was run to prune overlapping/redundant bounding boxes.

The `opencv-python` function, `cv2.dnn.readNetFromDarknet()`, was used to read the pretrained Darknet model, using the paths to the provided `.cfg` file with a text description of the network architecture and the `.weights` file with a pretrained network as parameters.

The `cv2.dnn.blobFromImage()` function was used to create a 4D blob (the format in which the deep learning model expects its input) from the input image. The `net.setInput()` function was used to set the input to the network.

The `net.forward()` function was used to run the forward pass and obtain the outputs at the output layers.

Finally, the `post_process()` function was used to remove the overlapping bounding boxes and those bounding boxes with low confidence (less than the confidence threshold provided).

There's more...

The pretrained weights were obtained by training the model with the MS-COCO image dataset (get it from here: http://cocodataset.org/) as input. Try to train the model on your own and then use the model to detect objects in some unseen images.

See also

Refer to the following links to learn more about this recipe:

- https://pjreddie.com/darknet/yolo/
- https://arxiv.org/abs/1506.02640
- https://arxiv.org/abs/1612.08242
- https://arxiv.org/abs/1804.02767

- http://cocodataset.org/
- https://sandipanweb.wordpress.com/2018/03/11/autonomous-driving-car-detection-with-yolo-in-python/
- https://www.youtube.com/watch?v=nDPWywWRIRo
- https://www.youtube.com/watch?v=9s_FpMpdYW8
- https://www.youtube.com/watch?v=iSB_xbYA0wE
- https://www.youtube.com/watch?v=iSB_xbYA0wE
- *Chapter 10* of the book, *Hands-on Image Processing with Python*

Object detection with Faster R-CNN

As discussed in a previous Chapter 7, *Image Segmentation*, in the *Deep instance segmentation* recipe, region-based object detection methods (for example, R-CNN and Fast R-CNN) rely on region proposal algorithms (selective search) to guess object locations. Faster R-CNN is yet another region-based object detection model that was proposed as an improvement on R-CNN (2013) and Fast R-CNN (2015), by Girshick et al. again. Fast R-CNN decreases the execution time of detection (for example, for the slower R-CNN model) by introducing ROI Pooling, but still, region proposal computation becomes a bottleneck. Faster R-CNN introduces a Region Proposal Network (RPN). It achieves almost cost-free region proposals by sharing convolutional features with the detection network.

A **Region Proposal Network (RPN)** is an FCN that predicts regions that potentially contain an object with the object bounding boxes along with the objectness scores (that is, the probability that a region contains an object) at each position. End-to-end training of the RPN enables it to predict region proposals with high quality (using anchors and with recent attention mechanisms). Fast R-CNN then uses these regions for possible detection. The RPN and Fast R-CNN are concatenated to form a single network. The network is jointly trained with four losses:

- RPN provides a classification of object/not object (with an objectness score).
- RPN uses regression to compute box coordinates.
- A final classifier (from Fast R-CNN) classifies the object (with a classification score).
- Output bounding boxes corresponding to the object are computed with regression.

Object Detection in Images

The RPN implements a sliding window on top of the features of the CNN. For each location of the window, it computes a score and a (per-anchor) bounding box (if k is the number of anchors, $4k$ bounding box coordinates are needed to be computed). Thereby, the Faster R-CNN enables object detection in a test image to be performed in real time. The following diagram shows the architecture of the Faster R-CNN network:

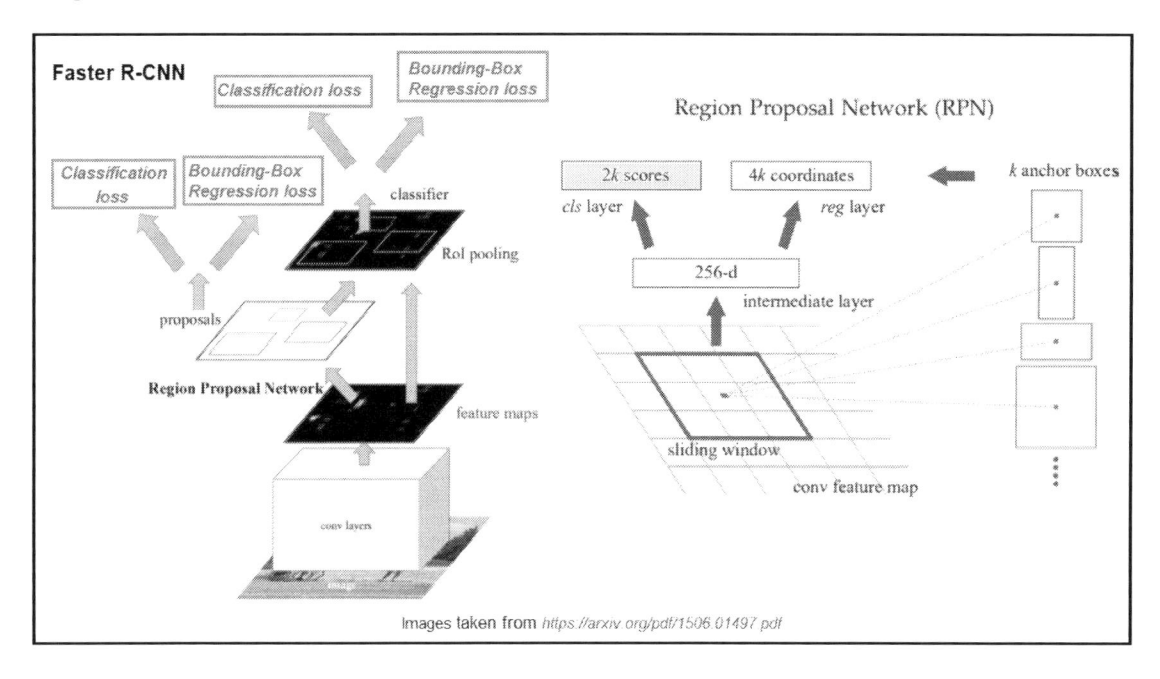

Images taken from https://arxiv.org/pdf/1506.01497.pdf

In this recipe, you will learn how to use a pretrained Faster-RCNN model in TensorFlow to detect objects in an image.

Getting started

First, download a pretrained model for the Faster R-CNN (for example, `faster_rcnn_resnet101_coco`, with **ResNet101** as the backbone and trained on the MS-COCO dataset) from the `tensorflow` object detection model zoo (https://github.com/tensorflow/models/blob/master/research/object_detection/g3doc/detection_model_zoo.md) and extract/save `.pb` of the model (frozen inference graph) inside the appropriate location in the `models` folder. Let's now import all of the required packages using the following code snippet:

```
import numpy as np
import cv2
from PIL import Image, ImageFont, ImageDraw
```

```
import json
import colorsys
import matplotlib.pylab as plt
import tensorflow as tf
print(tf.__version__)
# 2.0.0
```

How to do it...

Perform the following steps to implement object detection using the pretrained Faster R-CNN network in TensorFlow:

1. Initialize the list of class labels that the MobileNet SSD model was trained to detect:

    ```
    with open('models/image_info_test2017.json','r') as R: js = json.loads(R.read())
    labels = {i['id']:i['name'] for i in js['categories']}
    print(len(labels))
    # 80
    ```

2. Generate a set of unique colors for the bounding boxes for each class:

    ```
    HSV_tuples = [(x/len(labels), 0.8, 0.8) for x in range(len(labels))]
    colors = list(map(lambda x: colorsys.hsv_to_rgb(*x), HSV_tuples))
    ```

3. Read the input image and the pretrained TensorFlow model's frozen inference graph:

    ```
    img = cv2.imread('images/bus.jpg')
    with tf.io.gfile.GFile('models/faster_rcnn/frozen_inference_graph.pb', 'rb') as f:
        graph_def = tf.compat.v1.GraphDef()
        graph_def.ParseFromString(f.read())
    ```

Object Detection in Images

4. Preprocess the input image to feed into the model as input, restore the session, and run a forward pass on the model using the following code:

```
rows, cols = img.shape[:2]
conf = 0.2
with tf.compat.v1.Session() as sess:
  inp = cv2.resize(img, (300, 300))
  inp = inp[:, :, [2, 1, 0]]  # BGR2RGB
  sess.graph.as_default()
  tf.import_graph_def(graph_def, name='')
  out = sess.run([sess.graph.get_tensor_by_name('num_detections:0'),
            sess.graph.get_tensor_by_name('detection_scores:0'),
            sess.graph.get_tensor_by_name('detection_boxes:0'),
sess.graph.get_tensor_by_name('detection_classes:0')],
            feed_dict={'image_tensor:0': inp.reshape(1, \
                    inp.shape[0], inp.shape[1], 3)})
```

5. Draw the bounding boxes for the objects detected by the Faster R-CNN pretrained model (where the confidence level exceeds the threshold confidence) using the following code block:

```
for i in range(num_detections):
    idx = int(out[3][0][i])
    score = float(out[1][0][i])
    bbox = [float(v) for v in out[2][0][i]]
    if score > conf:
        x, y, right, bottom = bbox[1] * cols, bbox[0] * rows, \
                        bbox[3] * cols, bbox[2] * rows
        label = "{}: {:.2f}%".format(labels[idx], score * 100)
        color = tuple([int(255*x) for x in colors[idx]])
        y = y - 15 if y - 15 > 15 else y + 15
        thickness, font = (img.shape[0] + img.shape[1]) // 300, \
                    ImageFont.truetype("arial.ttf", 15)
        draw = ImageDraw.Draw(Image.fromarray(cv2.cvtColor\
                    (img, cv2.COLOR_BGR2RGB)))
        label_size = draw.textsize(label, font)
        text_origin = np.array([x, y - label_size[1]] if \
                    y - label_size[1] >= 0 else [x, y + 1])
        for i in range(thickness):
          draw.rectangle([x + i, y + i, right - i, bottom - i], \
                    outline=color)
        draw.rectangle([tuple(text_origin), tuple(text_origin + \
                    label_size)], fill=color)
        draw.text(text_origin, label, fill=(0, 0, 0), font=font)
```

If you run the preceding code, you will obtain a screenshot like the following:

How it works...

For each object detected in the image, the output (out) returned (by running the forward pass with the model) contains the following:

- Bounding box rectangle coordinates for the object (out[2][0][i], for the ith object)
- Class labels assigned to the object with confidence (out[3][0][i], the most probable class for the ith object)
- A probability (confidence) for each class label for the object (out[1][0][i], the confidence corresponding to the most probable class for the ith object)

Object Detection in Images

Graph (Computational Graph) is the core concept of `tensorflow` to present computation. GraphDef is a serialized version of a graph and the pretrained model's `GraphDef` object can be parsed using the `ParseFromString()` function.

The `import_graph_def()` function can be used to import a serialized TensorFlow `GraphDef` protocol buffer. It extracts individual `GraphDef` objects as `tf.Tensor`/`tf.Operation` objects. Once extracted, these objects are placed in the current default graph.

There's more...

Load the `tensorflow` pretrained model with `opencv-python` and run inference to detect objects in your images. Train your own Faster R-CNN model on Pascal-VOC images using a GPU (download the annotated image dataset from here: http://host.robots.ox.ac.uk/pascal/VOC/voc2012/VOCtrainval_11-May-2012.tar).

> **TIP**
> To train with Keras, refer to https://github.com/kbardool/keras-frcnn. Implement object detection using the vanilla R-CNN and Fast R-CNN models, and compare the speed and precision with Faster-RCNN on a test image.

See also

Refer to the following links to learn more about this recipe:

- https://arxiv.org/pdf/1506.01497.pdf
- https://papers.nips.cc/paper/5638-faster-r-cnn-towards-real-time-object-detection-with-region-proposal-networks.pdf
- https://github.com/tensorflow/models/blob/master/research/object_detection/g3doc/detection_model_zoo.md
- https://stackoverflow.com/questions/47059848/difference-between-tensorflows-graph-and-graphdef
- https://www.tensorflow.org/api_docs/python/tf/graph_util/import_graph_def
- http://host.robots.ox.ac.uk/pascal/VOC/voc2012/VOCtrainval_11-May-2012.tar
- https://www.youtube.com/watch?v=Z-CmHOoOJJA

Object detection with Mask R-CNN

The **Mask R-CNN algorithm** (2017), by Girshick et al., includes a number of improvements compared with the Faster R-CNN algorithm for region-based object detection, with the following two primary contributions:

- **ROI Pooling** is replaced with an **ROI Align module** (which is more accurate).
- An additional branch is inserted (which receives the output from ROI Align, subsequently feeding it into two successive convolution layers. Output from the last convolutional layer forms the object mask) at the output of the ROI Align module.

The `RoIAlign` module provides a more precise correspondence between the regions of the feature map selected and those of the input image. Much more fine-grained alignment is needed for pixel-level segmentation, rather than just computing the bounding boxes. The following screenshot shows the architecture of **Mask R-CNN**:

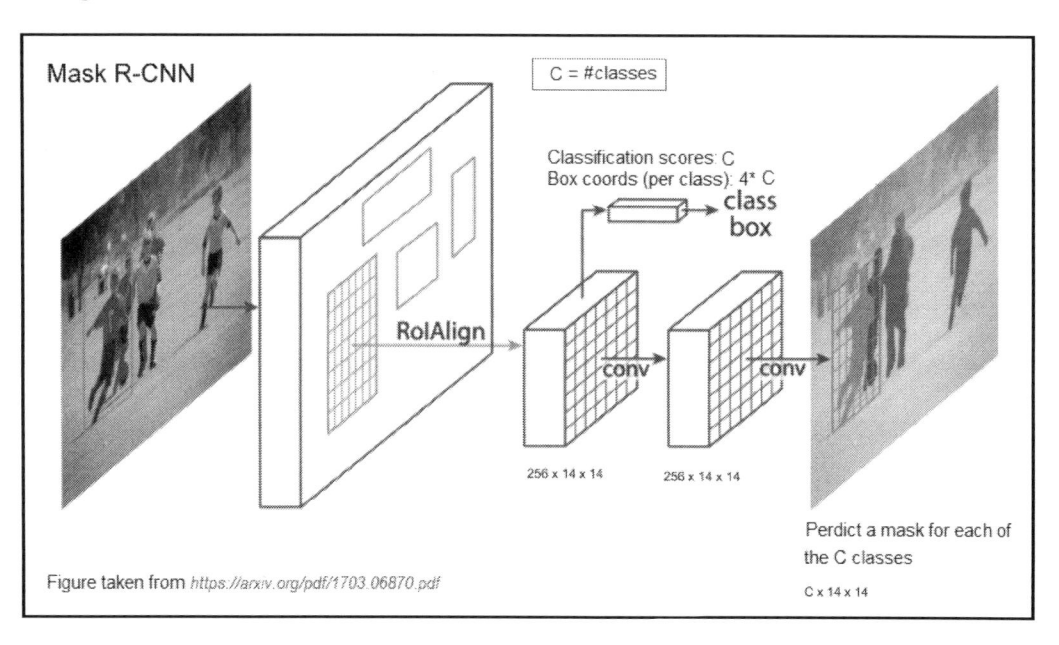

In this recipe, you will learn how to use a pretrained Mask R-CNN (`tensorflow`) model to detect objects in an image, this time using `opencv-python` library functions.

Object Detection in Images

Getting started

First, download the pretrained Mask R-CNN model from `http://download.tensorflow.org/models/object_detection/mask_rcnn_inception_v2_coco_2018_01_28.tar.gz` (the model being trained with `tensorflow` on the MS-COCO dataset again with Inception v2 as the backbone network), and extract the compressed model in the appropriate path inside the `models` folder. Import all of the necessary packages using the following command:

```
import cv2
print(cv2.__version__)
# 4.1.1
import numpy as np
import os.path
import sys
import random
import matplotlib.pylab as plt
```

How to do it...

Perform the following steps to implement object detection with the Mask R-CNN pretrained model using `opencv-python` functions:

1. Initialize the parameters (for example, thresholds for `Confidence` and `Mask`), using the following code snippet:

   ```
   conf_threshold = 0.5 # Confidence threshold
   mask_threshold = 0.3 # Mask threshold
   ```

2. Define the following function to plot the predicted bounding box for the detected object, colorize it as per the object's class predicted, and overlay the mask computed on top of the input image:

   ```
   def draw_box(img, class_id, conf, left, top, right, bottom, class_mask):
       cv2.rectangle(img, (left, top), (right, bottom), \
           (255, 178, 50), 3)
       label = '%.2f' % conf
       if classes:
           assert(class_id < len(classes))
           label = '%s:%s' % (classes[class_id], label)
       label_size, base_line = cv2.getTextSize(label, \
                   cv2.FONT_HERSHEY_SIMPLEX, 0.5, 1)
       top = max(top, label_size[1])
       cv2.rectangle(img, (left, top - round(1.5*label_size[1])), \
                   (left + round(1.5*label_size[0]), \
   ```

[344]

```
                    top + base_line), (255, 255, 255), cv2.FILLED)
        cv2.putText(img, label, (left, top),cv2.FONT_HERSHEY_SIMPLEX, \
                    0.75, (0,0,0), 1)
        class_mask = cv2.resize(class_mask, (right - left + 1, \
                    bottom - top + 1))
        mask = (class_mask > mask_threshold)
        roi = img[top:bottom+1, left:right+1][mask]
        # color = colors[class_id%len(colors)]
    # comment the above line and uncomment below two lines to generate
        different instance colors
        color_index = random.randint(0, len(colors)-1)
        color = colors[color_index]
        img[top:bottom+1, left:right+1][mask] = ([0.3*color[0], \
                                        0.3*color[1], 0.3*color[2]] + \
                                        0.7 *roi).astype(np.uint8)
        mask = mask.astype(np.uint8)
        contours, hierarchy = cv2.findContours(mask, \
                            cv2.RETR_TREE,cv2.CHAIN_APPROX_SIMPLE)
        cv2.drawContours(img[top:bottom+1, left:right+1], contours, \
                            -1, color, 3, cv2.LINE_8, hierarchy, 100)
```

3. Define the following function to post-process the output obtained from the network to extract the bounding boxes and masks corresponding to the objects detected:

```
        def post_process(boxes, masks):
            num_classes, num_deetections = masks.shape[1], boxes.shape[2]
            img_height, img_width = img.shape[0], img.shape[1]
            for i in range(num_deetections):
                box = boxes[0, 0, i]
                mask = masks[i]
                score = box[2]
                if score > conf_threshold:
                    class_id = int(box[1])
                    left,top,right,bottom = int(img_width*box[3]), \
                                            int(img_height*box[4]), \
                                            int(img_width*box[5]), \
                                            int(img_height*box[6])
                    left, top = max(0, min(left, img_width - 1)), \
                                            max(0, min(top, img_height - 1))
                    right, bottom = max(0, min(right, img_width - 1)), \
                                            max(0, min(bottom, img_height - 1))
                    class_mask = mask[class_id]
                    draw_box(img, class_id, score, left, top, right, \
                            bottom, class_mask)
```

4. Load the names of classes using the following code snippet from the label names file:

```
classes_file = "models/mask_rcnn/mscoco_labels.names";
classes = None
with open(classes_file, 'rt') as f:
    classes = f.read().rstrip('\n').split('\n')
```

5. Load the pretrained Mask R-CNN model by loading the `tensorflow` graph and the weight file for the model:

```
text_graph = "models/mask_rcnn/mask_rcnn_inception_v2_coco_2018_01_28.pbtxt"
model_weights = "models/mask_rcnn/frozen_inference_graph.pb"
net = cv2.dnn.readNetFromTensorflow(model_weights , text_graph)
net.setPreferableBackend(cv2.dnn.DNN_BACKEND_OPENCV)
net.setPreferableTarget(cv2.dnn.DNN_TARGET_CPU)
```

6. Prepare the colors to be used to draw the bounding boxes for the objects corresponding to the different classes:

```
colors_file = "models/mask_rcnn_inception_v2_coco_2018_01_28/colors.txt"
with open(colors_file, 'rt') as f:
    colors_str = f.read().rstrip('\n').split('\n')
colors = []
for i in range(len(colors_str)):
    rgb = colors_str[i].split(' ')
    color = np.array([float(rgb[0]), float(rgb[1]), float(rgb[2])])
    colors.append(color)
```

7. Read the input image, preprocess the image to create a blob as expected by the model, and set the blob as the input to the pretrained model using the next code snippet:

```
img = cv2.imread('images/road.png')
blob = cv2.dnn.blobFromImage(img, swapRB=True, crop=False)
net.setInput(blob)
```

8. Run a forward pass on the pretrained network with the input blob and then post-process the output obtained to draw the bounding boxes and masks around the objects detected using the following code block:

```
boxes, masks = net.forward(['detection_out_final', 'detection_masks'])
post_process(boxes, masks)
```

Chapter 8

If you run the code and plot the input image along with the output post-processed image, you will get the following output:

As you can see, Mask R-CNN correctly detects partially occluded objects (cars) for the input (test) image.

Object Detection in Images

How it works...

The `draw_box()` function does the following:

1. It draws a bounding box around a detected object.
2. It prints a label of the (most probable) class the object is assigned to.
3. It displays the label to the top-left corner of the bounding box.
4. Then, it resizes the mask, threshold, and color and applies it to the image.
5. Finally, it draws the contours on the image corresponding to the mask.

The `post_proress()` function extracts the bounding box along with the mask for every object detected for each image. Then, it chooses the right color (corresponding to the class label of the object) to draw the object bounding box and overlay the mask on the image.

There's more...

Train the Mask R-CNN network on the MS-COCO dataset (download the dataset from here: http://cocodataset.org/) and save the model trained (a GPU is highly recommended); use it to predict objects in your image.

See also

Refer to the following links to learn more about this recipe:

- https://arxiv.org/pdf/1703.06870.pdf
- https://www.pyimagesearch.com/2018/11/19/mask-r-cnn-with-opencv/
- https://github.com/facebookresearch/Detectron
- https://arxiv.org/pdf/1405.0312.pdf
- https://www.youtube.com/watch?v=g7z4mkfRjI4
- https://www.youtube.com/watch?v=FR25P1lMBY8
- https://www.youtube.com/watch?v=FR25P1lMBY8

Multiple object tracking with Python-OpenCV

Object tracking (in a video) is an image/video processing task that locates one or multiple moving objects over time. The goal of the task is to find an association between the target object(s) in the successive video frames. The task becomes difficult when the objects move faster relative to the frame rate or when the object to be tracked changes its orientation over time. The object tracking systems use a motion model taking into account how the target object may change for different possible motions of the object.

Object tracking is useful in human-computer interaction, security/surveillance, traffic control, and many more areas. Since it considers the appearance and the location of an object in the past frame, under certain circumstances, we may still be able to track an object despite the object detection fails. Few tracking algorithms that perform local searches are very fast. Hence, it's generally a good strategy to track an object indefinitely once it is detected for the first time. Most real-world applications implement tracking and detection simultaneously.

In this recipe, you will learn how to track multiple objects in a video using `opencv-python` functions, where the object locations in the very first frame will be provided to you in terms of bounding box coordinates.

Getting started

Let's start by importing the required libraries first. Note that the `opencv` version used for this recipe is 3.4.4:

```
#pip install opencv-python==3.4.4.19
#pip install opencv-contrib-python==3.4.4.19
import time
import cv2
import matplotlib.pylab as plt
from imutils import resize
print(cv2.__version__)
# 3.4.4
```

Object Detection in Images

How to do it...

Perform the following steps to implement multiple object tracking with `opencv-python` functions:

1. First, create a `MultiTracker` object using the following line of code:

   ```
   multi_tracker = cv2.MultiTracker_create()
   ```

2. You will track a couple of moving cars in a video. The location of the cars is provided to you for the very first frame in the video. You may try to extract the frames from the video and use your favorite object detection algorithm to obtain the bounding boxes of the cars in the very first frame:

   ```
   car_bbox = (141,175,45,29)
   car2_bbox = (295,170,55,39)
   bboxes = [car_bbox, car2_bbox]
   colors = [(0, 255, 255), (255, 255, 0)]
   ```

3. Read the first frame of the input video and start an OpenCV multi-object tracker by initializing it with the frame and the supplied bounding box coordinates (to locate the objects in the very first frame, to start with) using the following code snippet:

   ```
   vs = cv2.VideoCapture('images/road.mp4')
   _, frame = vs.read()
   frame = resize(frame, width=500)
   for bbox in bboxes:
       multi_tracker.add(cv2.TrackerCSRT_create(), frame, bbox)
   ```

4. Iteratively read frames from the video stream (read 3 frames in a second, for example, to reduce the number of frames to be read), until all of the frames are read, by using the following code block:

   ```
   j = 0
   while True:
       vs.set(cv2.CAP_PROP_POS_MSEC,(j*300)) # 1 sec read 3 frames
       _, frame = vs.read()
       if frame is None:
           break
   ```

5. Resize the frame (so we can process it faster) and grab the frame dimensions. Get the updated location of objects in subsequent frames. Check to see whether the tracking was a success and, if it was successful, draw the tracked objects:

```
frame = resize(frame, width=500)
success, boxes = multi_tracker.update(frame)
if success:
    for i, box in enumerate(boxes):
        p1 = (int(box[0]), int(box[1]))
        p2 = (int(box[0] + box[2]), int(box[1] + box[3]))
        cv2.rectangle(frame, p1, p2, colors[i], 2, 1)
j += 1
```

If you run the preceding code snippet and plot the updated locations (that is, bounding boxes) of the objects for different frames, you will end up with the following output:

How it works...

The `MultiTracker` class from OpenCV was used to implement multi-object tracking. The multi-object tracker (which is implemented simply as a collection of single-object trackers) processes the tracked objects independently.

A multi-object tracker needs two inputs, namely, a reference video frame (we used the first video frame as reference) and locations (to be specified in terms of bounding boxes) of all of the objects (in the reference frame) that we want to track. Then, the tracker simultaneously tracks the locations of the target objects in the succeeding frames.

OpenCV has eight different object trackers (types): BOOSTING, MIL, KCF, TLD, MEDIANFLOW, GOTURN, MOSSE, and CSRT. The **KCF** tracker is fast and accurate, the **CSRT** tracker is more accurate than KCF but slower, whereas the **MOSSE** tracker is extremely fast but not as accurate as either KCF or CSRT.

In this recipe, the CSRT tracker was used; its implementation is based on a discriminative correlation filter with spatial and channel reliability.

There's more...

Track multiple objects using the KCF, MOSSE, and GOTURN trackers (the last one is a deep learning-based object tracker), and compare the results obtained with the CSRT tracker.

See also

Refer to the following links to learn more about this recipe:

- https://en.wikipedia.org/wiki/Video_tracking
- https://www.learnopencv.com/multitracker-multiple-object-tracking-using-opencv-c-python/
- https://docs.opencv.org/3.4/d9/df8/group__tracking.html
- https://www.youtube.com/watch?v=GPTlMZQ6f8o

Text detection/recognition in images with EAST/Tesseract

Text detection refers to an image processing task that detects and localizes the bounding box coordinates of texts contained in an image. Extracting and understanding textual information contained in images has become important and popular. Text detection serves as a preprocessing task for it. In this recipe, you will first learn to detect text in an image with a pretrained deep learning model (called EAST) and then recognize text using `pytesseract` and `opencv-python` library functions.

The **EAST** (which stands for **Efficient and Accuracy Scene Text detection**) text detector is a powerful pipeline for accurate and fast text detection. The model is an FCN (a single deep neural net) that directly predicts the bounding boxes for the words/text lines present in the input image (with arbitrary orientations), thereby eliminating unnecessary preprocessing steps (such as candidate aggregation and word partitioning). It's only required to apply thresholding and NMS on predicted geometric shapes, as the post-processing steps. The following diagram shows the EAST pipeline:

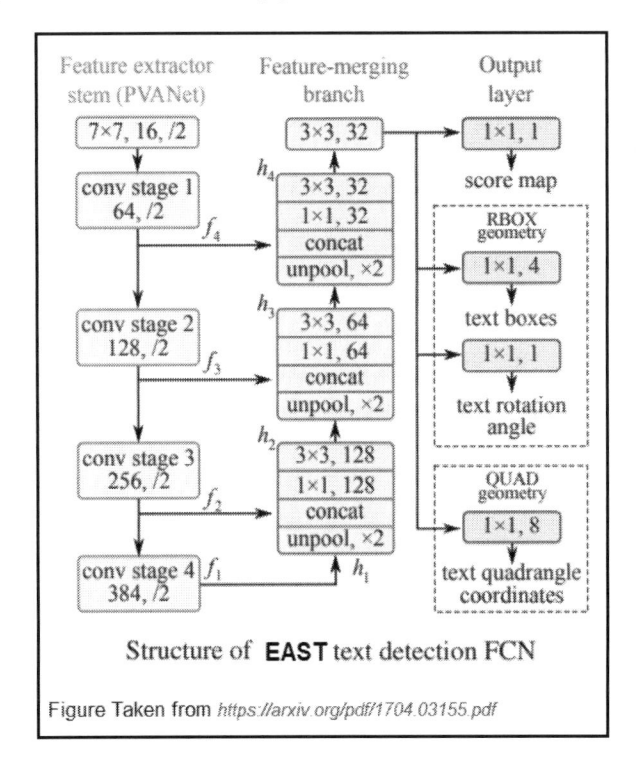

Structure of **EAST** text detection FCN

Figure Taken from https://arxiv.org/pdf/1704.03155.pdf

[353]

Object Detection in Images

Optical Character Recognition (OCR)/text recognition refers to the task of extracting text from images. In this recipe, we will use Tesseract v4 for text recognition. Tesseract v4, by default, uses an LSTM-based recognition engine. The `pytesseract` module just provides a wrapper over the Tesseract command-line tool (we can specify the command-line arguments with the `config` argument). The following screenshot shows the entire pipeline for text detection and recognition processes:

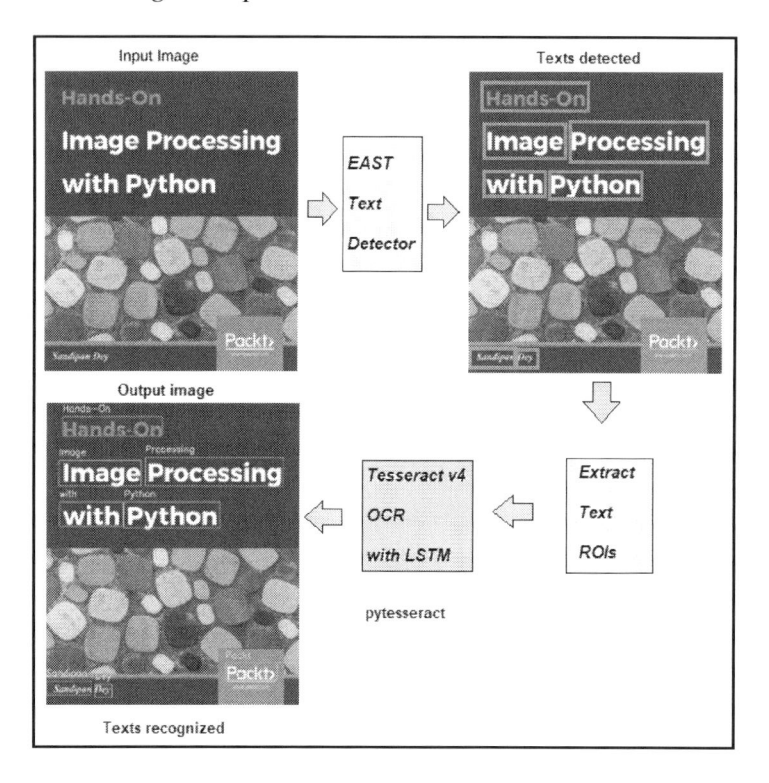

Getting started

First, download the pretrained EAST text detector model from `https://codeload.github.com/ZER-0-NE/EAST-Detector-for-text-detection-using-OpenCV/zip` and extract the compressed model in the appropriate path inside the `models` folder. Install Tesseract (v4) from `http://emop.tamu.edu/Installing-Tesseract-Windows8`, for example, and the `pytesseract` package with `pip`. Import the required libraries using the following code snippet:

```
import pytesseract
from imutils.object_detection import non_max_suppression
```

```
import cv2
import numpy as np
```

How to do it...

Perform the following steps to implement text detection and recognition using the `opencv-python` functions:

1. Define the following function to decode the predictions by EAST and extract the bounding boxes (locations of the texts detected) and associated confidences:

    ```
    min_confidence = 0.5

    def decode_predictions(scores, geometry):
        (num_rows, num_cols) = scores.shape[2:4]
        rects, confidences = [], []
        for y in range(0, num_rows):
            scores_data = scores[0, 0, y]
            x_data0, x_data1 = geometry[0, 0, y], geometry[0, 1, y]
            x_data2, x_data3 = geometry[0, 2, y], geometry[0, 3, y]
            angles_data = geometry[0, 4, y]
            for x in range(0, num_cols):
                if scores_data[x] < min_confidence: continue
                (offset_x, offset_y) = (x * 4.0, y * 4.0)
                angle = angles_data[x]
                cos, sin = np.cos(angle), np.sin(angle)
                h, w = x_data0[x] + x_data2[x], x_data1[x] + x_data3[x]
                end_x = int(offset_x + (cos * x_data1[x]) + \
                        (sin * x_data2[x]))
                end_y = int(offset_y - (sin * x_data1[x]) + \
                        (cos * x_data2[x]))
                start_x, start_y = int(end_x - w), int(end_y - h)
                rects.append((start_x, start_y, end_x, end_y))
                confidences.append(scores_data[x])
        return (rects, confidences)
    ```

2. Read the input image and obtain the shape of the image. Obtain a new image by resizing the original image to 320 x 320, and determine the ratio of the original versus the new image's width and height by using the following code snippet:

    ```
    im = 'images/book_cover.png'
    image = cv2.imread(im)
    orig = image.copy()
    (orig_height, orig_width) = image.shape[:2]
    width = height = 32*10
    (w, h) = (width, height)
    ```

Object Detection in Images

```
         r_width, r_height = orig_width / float(w), orig_height / float(h)
         image = cv2.resize(image, (w, h))
         (h, w) = image.shape[:2]
```

3. Load the pretrained EAST text detector model. Define a couple of output layer names of the model that we are interested in (the output probabilities and the coordinates of the bounding box for the detected text, respectively):

```
         layer_names = ["feature_fusion/Conv_7/Sigmoid",
         "feature_fusion/concat_3"]
         net =
         cv2.dnn.readNet('models/text_detection/frozen_east_text_detection.p
         b')
```

4. Transform the input image to a blob and run a forward pass on the model to get the output predictions:

```
         b, g, r = np.mean(image[...,0]), np.mean(image[...,1]),
         np.mean(image[...,2])
         blob = cv2.dnn.blobFromImage(image, 1.0, (w, h), (b, g, r),
         swapRB=True, crop=False)
         net.setInput(blob)
         (scores, geometry) = net.forward(layer_names)
```

5. Next, decode the predictions to obtain the bounding boxes of the texts detected and finally, use non-maximum suppression to get rid of weak, overlapping bounding boxes:

```
         (rects, confidences) = decode_predictions(scores, geometry)
         boxes = non_max_suppression(np.array(rects), probs=confidences)
```

6. For each location (bounding box) detected by EAST, extract the corresponding ROI, and then use `pytessearct` to extract the text inside the ROI, using the following code snippet:

```
         padding = 0.001 #0.01 #0.5
         results = []
         # loop over the bounding boxes
         for (start_x, start_y, end_x, end_y) in boxes:
             start_x, start_y = int(start_x*r_width), int(start_y*r_height)
             end_x, end_y = , int(end_x*r_width), int(end_y*r_height)
             d_x, d_y = int((end_x - start_x) * padding), \
                        int((end_y - start_y) * padding)
             start_x, start_y = max(0, start_x - d_x*2), \
                                max(0, start_y - d_y*2)
             end_x, end_y = min(orig_width, end_x + (d_x * 2)), \
                            min(orig_height, end_y + (d_y * 2))
```

[356]

```
roi = orig[start_y:end_y, start_x:end_x]
config = ("-l eng --oem 1 --psm 11")
text = pytesseract.image_to_string(roi, config=config)
results.append(((start_x, start_y, end_x, end_y), text))
results = sorted(results, key=lambda r:r[0][1])
```

7. Finally, iterate over the extracted texts from the detected ROIs and draw the texts at the appropriate locations of the image:

```
output = orig.copy()
for ((start_x, start_y, end_x, end_y), text) in results:
    # strip out non-ASCII text so we can draw the text on the image
    text = "".join([c if ord(c) < 128 else "" for c \
        in text]).strip()
    cv2.rectangle(output, (start_x, start_y), (end_x, end_y), \
                  (0, 255, 0), 2)
    cv2.putText(output, text, (start_x, start_y-20), \
                cv2.FONT_HERSHEY_SIMPLEX, 1.2, (0,255,0), 3)
```

If you run the preceding code blocks and plot the original image with the *detected texts* in it, you will get something similar to the following screenshot:

Object Detection in Images

How it works...

Running a forward pass on the pretrained EAST model returns scores and geometry that are decoded using the `decode_predictions()` function to obtain the bounding boxes (ROIs) predicted to be containing text. Next, the texts inside these ROIs are to be extracted with the `pytesseract image_to_string()` method.

To extract texts as strings using Tesseract v4 OCR, the command-line arguments are needed to be passed as a configuration to the `image_to_string()` method of `pytesseract` (for example, we used "`-l eng --oem 1 --psm 11`" as the configuration):

- A language (English, configuration)
- An OEM flag=1 (use an **LSTM(Long Short-Term Memory**) model for OCR)
- An OEM value=11 (treat as sparse text, that is, find as much text as possible in no particular order)

See also

Refer to the following links to learn more about this recipe:

- `https://stackoverflow.com/questions/44619077/pytesseract-ocr-multiple-config-options`
- `https://github.com/tesseract-ocr/tesseract/wiki/Command-Line-Usage`
- `https://github.com/ZER-0-NE/EAST-Detector-for-text-detection-using-OpenCV/`
- `https://www.learnopencv.com/deep-learning-based-text-recognition-ocr-using-tesseract-and-opencv/`
- `https://arxiv.org/pdf/1704.03155.pdf`
- `https://pdfs.semanticscholar.org/d933/a6d0049f53344c5384c0905afe463a086bdb.pdf?_ga=2.137491379.201554747.1577481675-754696371.1577481675`

Face detection with Viola-Jones/Haar-like features

Haar-like features are very useful image features used in object detection. They were introduced in the very first real-time face detector by **Viola** and **Jones**. Using integral images, **Haar-like features** of any size (scale) can be efficiently computed in constant time. The computation speed is the key advantage of a Haar-like feature over most other features. Using the **Viola-Jones** face detection algorithm, faces can be detected in an image using these Haar-like features. Each Haar-like feature acts as just a weak classifier, and hence a huge number of these features are required to detect a face with good accuracy. Therefore, a large number of features are computed for all possible locations and sizes of each Haar-like kernel, using the integral images. Then, an **AdaBoost** ensemble classifier is used to select important features from the huge number of features and combine them into a strong classifier model during the training phase. The model learned is then used to classify a face region with the selected features and can be used as a face detector.

In this recipe, you will learn how to use OpenCV's pretrained classifiers (that is, detectors) for face and eyes, to detect human faces in an image. These pretrained classifiers are serialized as XML files and come with an OpenCV installation (this can be found in the `'opencv/data/haarcascades/'` folder). You may need to download the pretrained classifier for smile detection—if it's not already there, it can be found here: https://github.com/opencv/opencv/blob/master/data/haarcascades/haarcascade_smile.xml.

Getting ready

Let's start by importing the required libraries, as usual, using the following code snippet:

```
import cv2
import numpy as np
import matplotlib.pylab as plt
```

Object Detection in Images

How to do it...

Perform the following steps to implement face detection with pretrained Haar-Cascade classifiers with `opencv-python`:

1. First, load the pretrained classifiers to detect the face, eyes, and smile, respectively, from the corresponding `xml` files:

    ```
    face_cascade =
    cv2.CascadeClassifier('models/haarcascade_frontalface_alt2.xml')
    eye_cascade = cv2.CascadeClassifier('models/haarcascade_eye.xml')
    #haarcascade_eye_tree_eyeglasses.xml
    smile_cascade =
    cv2.CascadeClassifier('models/face_detect/haarcascade_smile.xml')
    ```

2. Read the input image (containing seven faces) and convert it into grayscale. Detect the faces present in the image using the face cascade classifier model:

    ```
    img = cv2.imread('images/all.png')
    gray = cv2.cvtColor(img, cv2.COLOR_BGR2GRAY)
    faces = face_cascade.detectMultiScale(gray, 1.01, 8) #
    scaleFactor=1.2, minNbr=5
    print(len(faces)) # number of faces detected
    # 7
    ```

3. Inside each face bounding box, detect the eyes and smile using the corresponding pretrained models loaded. Draw the bounding boxes corresponding to the faces, eyes, and the smiles detected on top of the image, using the following code snippet:

    ```
    for (x,y,w,h) in faces:
        img = cv2.rectangle(img, (x,y), (x+w,y+h), (255,0,0),2)
        roi_gray = gray[y:y+h, x:x+w]
        roi_color = img[y:y+h, x:x+w]
        eyes = eye_cascade.detectMultiScale(roi_gray, 1.04, 10)
        for (ex,ey,ew,eh) in eyes:
            cv2.rectangle(roi_color, (ex,ey), (ex+ew,ey+eh), (0,255,0),2)
        smile = smile_cascade.detectMultiScale(roi_gray, 1.38, 6)
        for (mx,my,mw,mh) in smile:
            cv2.rectangle(roi_color, (mx,my), (mx+mw,my+mh), (0,0,255),2)
    ```

[360]

If you run the preceding code, you will obtain an output similar to the following:

How it works...

The faces in the image can be found using the cv2.detectMultiScale() function, with the pretrained face cascade classifier. This function accepts the following parameters:

- scaleFactor: This is a parameter that specifies the extent to which the image size is decreased for each image scale and used to create a scale pyramid (for example, a scale factor of 1.2 means reducing the size by 20%). The smaller the scaleFactor parameter, the higher the chance that a matching size is found (for detection, with the model).

Object Detection in Images

- `minNeighbors`: This is a parameter that specifies the number of neighbors each candidate rectangle needs to keep. This parameter affects the quality of the detected faces—a larger value enables detection with higher quality, but smaller in numbers.
- `minSize` and `maxSize`: These are the minimum and maximum possible object sizes, respectively. Objects of sizes beyond these values will be ignored.

When faces are detected, the positions the faces are returned by the function as a list of *Rect(x, y, w,h)*.

Once a face bounding box is obtained, it defines the ROI for the face, and then the eye/smile detection on this ROI can be applied (since the eyes/smile are always to be found on the face).

There's more...

Use the `dlib` HOG-based frontal face detector and OpenCV's Single Shot MuliBox Detector (SSD) pretrained deep learning model to detect faces in images. Compare different face detectors' performances (in terms of accuracy and time complexity). Try with face images with different angles/orientations and with eye glasses. Detect eyes with the `dlib` facial landmark detection.

See also

Refer to the following links to learn more about this recipe:

- https://www.cs.cmu.edu/~efros/courses/LBMV07/Papers/viola-IJCV-01.pdf
- https://www.learnopencv.com/face-detection-opencv-dlib-and-deep-learning-c-python/
- https://arxiv.org/abs/1512.02325
- https://github.com/opencv/opencv_extra/blob/master/testdata/dnn/
- https://github.com/opencv/opencv/blob/master/data/haarcascades/haarcascade_smile.xml
- https://docs.opencv.org/3.4/d1/de5/classcv_1_1CascadeClassifier.html#a90fe1b7778bed4a27aa8482e1eecc116
- *Chapter 7* of the book, *Hands-on Image Processing with Python*

9
Face Recognition, Image Captioning, and More

In this chapter, we will discuss the application of a few advanced machine learning and deep learning techniques to solve a few advanced image processing problems. We will start with a face recognition problem that tries to match a set of faces detected in an image with a fixed set of known faces using deep face embedding representations. You will then learn how to use a few deep learning models to solve problems, such as the age or gender recognition of a human face and automatically colorizing a grayscale image. Another interesting problem we will look at is automatically captioning images with a deep learning model called **im2txt**. Finally, we will concentrate on a few techniques for image generation. In particular, we will focus on generative models in image processing (for example, a GAN, a VAE, and an RBM), which is a hot topic in image processing. The term **generative models** (often contrasted with **discriminative models**, such as SVMs/logistic regression) refers to the class of machine learning/deep learning models that tries to model the generation or distribution of input data (for example, images) by learning a probabilistic model. The goal is to generate new data (images) by sampling from the model learned.

In this chapter, you will learn about the following recipes:

- Face recognition using FaceNet (a deep learning model)
- Age, gender, and emotion recognition using deep learning models
- Image colorization with deep learning
- Automatic image captioning with a CNN and an LSTM
- Image generation with a GAN
- Using a variational autoencoder to reconstruct and generate images
- Using a restricted Boltzmann machine to reconstruct Bangla MNIST images

Face recognition using FaceNet

Face recognition is an image processing/computer vision task that tries to identify and verify a person based on an image of their face. Face recognition problems can be categorized into two different types:

- **Face verification** *(is this the claimed person?)*: This is a 1:1 matching problem (for example, a mobile phone that unlocks using a specific face uses face verification).
- **Face identification** *(who is this person?)*: This is a 1:K matching problem (for example, an employee entering an office can be identified by face identification).

FaceNet is a unified system for face recognition (for both verification and identification). It is sometimes called a **Siamese network**. It is based on learning a Euclidean embedding per image using a deep convolutional network that encodes an image of a face into a vector of 128 numbers. The network is trained (via a **triplet loss function**) in a way that the square of the **L2** distances in the embedding space directly relates to the facial similarities. In this recipe, we will use a set of face images of six mathematicians—Bayes, Erdos, Euler, Gauss, Markov, and Turing (around 12 images for each of them in the training dataset and around 6 images for each of them in the test dataset). Although we are not going to train you in how to use FaceNet, the following diagram shows you how the system works (if it was trained from scratch with the triplet loss function). FaceNet learns an embedding $f(x)$, where x is an input image. The model learns the parameters in such a way that the $||f(x(i)) - f(x(j))||2$ L_2 norm is small when $x(i)$ and $x(j)$ are faces of the same person (positive) and large when the faces correspond to different people (negative), where $f(.)$ represents the encoding (embedding) function presented by the deep CNN, as in the following diagram:

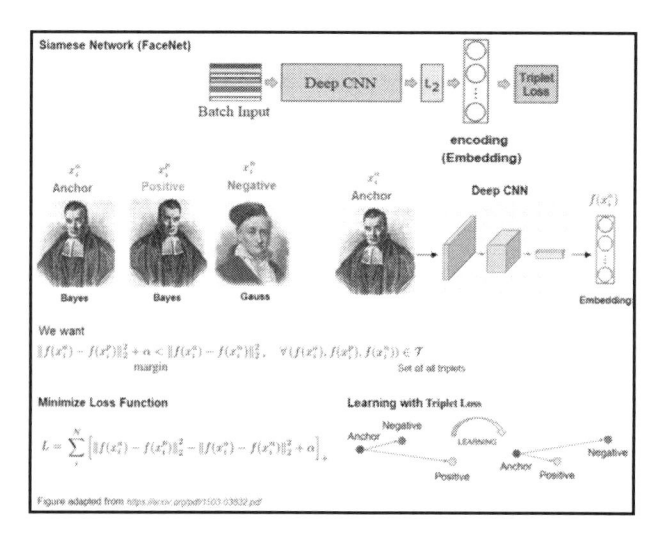

In this recipe, you will learn how to use a pre-trained FaceNet model (in Keras) for face identification in order to identify a given face in an image as one of the six mathematicians' faces. You will convert the face recognition problem into a multi-class classification problem in the embedding space.

Getting ready

First, download the pre-trained FaceNet model from `https://drive.google.com/drive/folders/12aMYASGCKvDdkygSv1yQq8ns03AStDO_`. Then, extract the model to the `models` folder. Download the images of the six mathematicians from the internet (you can use an automated script from `https://github.com/hardikvasa/google-images-download`). Download 20 images for each mathematician and for each mathematician, put 12 images in the `train` folder and the other 8 images in the `test` folder, as in the following screenshot (the `test` folder will also contain sub-folders with the mathematicians' names):

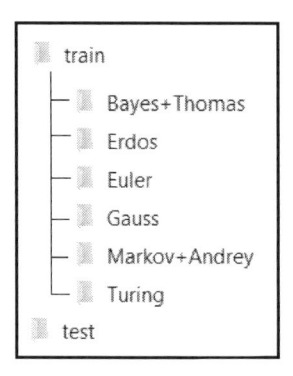

```
train
    ├── Bayes+Thomas
    ├── Erdos
    ├── Euler
    ├── Gauss
    ├── Markov+Andrey
    └── Turing
test
```

Import the necessary Python libraries using the following code block:

```
from tensorflow.keras.models import load_model
#!pip install mtcnn
import mtcnn
print(mtcnn.__version__)
# 0.1.0
from mtcnn.mtcnn import MTCNN
from sklearn.metrics import accuracy_score
from sklearn.preprocessing import LabelEncoder
from sklearn.preprocessing import Normalizer
from sklearn.svm import SVC
from skimage.io import imread
from skimage.color import rgb2gray, gray2rgb
from skimage.transform import resize
import numpy as np
```

```
import matplotlib.pylab as plt
import os
```

How to do it...

Run the following steps to implement face recognition with the pre-trained FaceNet model you downloaded:

1. Load the pre-trained model using the following line of code:

   ```
   model = load_model('models/facenet_keras.h5')
   ```

2. Define the following function to extract a single face from a given image. First, use the face detector module from the mtcnn library to detect the first face in the image (extract the bounding box corresponding to it) and then extract the face, resize it to the required size, and return it:

   ```
   def extract_face(image_file, required_size=(160, 160)):
       image = imread(image_file)
       image = gray2rgb(image) if len(image.shape) < 3 else \
               image[...,:3]
       detector = MTCNN()
       results = detector.detect_faces(image)
       x1, y1, width, height = results[0]['box']
       x2, y2 = abs(x1) + width, abs(y1) + height
       # extract the face
       face = image[y1:y2, x1:x2]
       return resize(face, required_size)
   ```

3. Define the following function to load all the face images from a given folder, extract the faces, and return them as a list:

   ```
   def load_faces(folder):
       faces = []
       for filename in os.listdir(folder):
           face = extract_face(folder + filename)
           faces.append(face)
       return faces
   ```

4. Define the following function to load the training dataset that contains one sub-folder for each class (that is, for each mathematician) and contains images corresponding to that class. Load all the faces from each sub-folder and label the images with the name of the class (that is, the mathematician) corresponding to each face:

```
def load_dataset(folder):
    X, y = [], []
    for sub_folder in os.listdir(folder):
        path = folder + sub_folder + '/'
        if not os.path.isdir(path): continue
        faces = load_faces(path)
        labels = [sub_folder for _ in range(len(faces))]
        print('>loaded %d examples for class: %s' % (len(faces), \
            sub_folder))
        X.extend(faces)
        y.extend(labels)
    return np.array(X), np.array(y)
```

5. Load the training and the `test` image datasets. Save all the images as a single compressed file (this whole process is time-consuming; you only need to do this once and from then onward, you can use the compressed dataset directly for training):

```
X_train, y_train = load_dataset('images/mathematicians/train/')
print(X_train.shape, y_train.shape)
# (72, 160, 160, 3) (72,)
X_test, y_test = load_dataset('images/mathematicians/test/')
print(X_test.shape, y_test.shape)
# (36, 160, 160, 3) (36,)
np.savez_compressed('images/6-mathematicians.npz', X_train,
y_train, X_test, y_test)
```

6. Uncompress the training and `test` datasets created in the previous step:

```
data = np.load('images/6-mathematicians.npz')
X_train, y_train, X_test, y_test = data['X_train'], \
                                   data['y_train'], \
                                   data['X_test'], \
                                   data['y_test']
```

Face Recognition, Image Captioning, and More

If you plot some of the training images chosen randomly from the training dataset, you will obtain an output, as in the following screenshot:

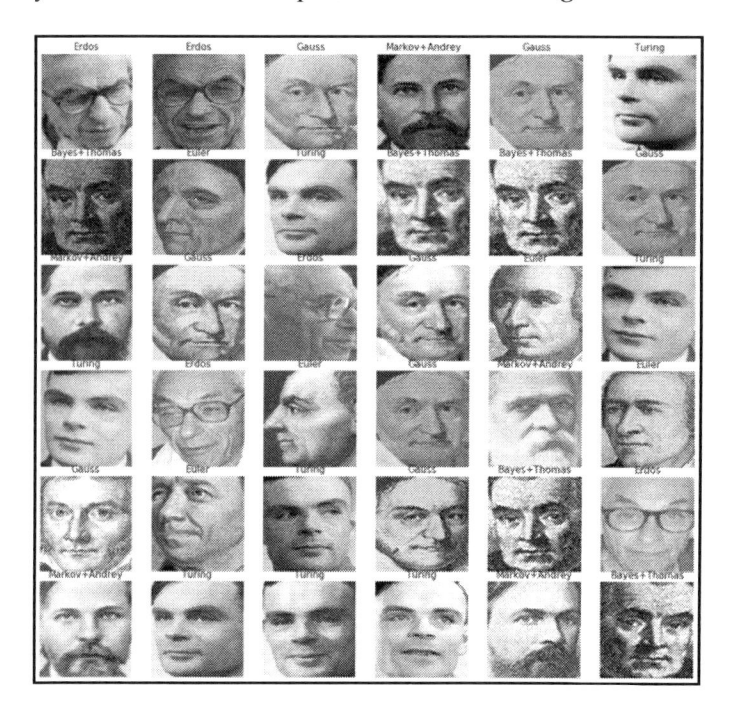

7. Define the following function to obtain the face embedding for each of the given faces. Use the pre-trained model to predict the face embedding given an input face being extracted:

   ```
   def get_embedding(model, face):
       yhat = model.predict(np.expand_dims(face, axis=0))
       return yhat[0]
   ```

8. Load the compressed data and uncompress it into the training and test datasets. Convert each face in the training and test datasets to an embedding. Save the face embeddings in a compressed format using the following code:

   ```
   data = np.load('images/6-mathematicians.npz')
   X_train, y_train, X_test, y_test = data['X_train'], \
           data['y_train'], data['X_test'], data['y_test']
   print('Loaded: ', X_train.shape, y_train.shape, X_test.shape,
   y_test.shape)
   # Loaded:  (72, 160, 160, 3) (72,) (36, 160, 160, 3) (36,)
   X_train_em = []
   for face in X_train:
   ```

[368]

```
        X_train_em.append(get_embedding(model, face))
    X_train_em = np.asarray(X_train_em)
    X_test_em = []
    for face in X_test:
        X_test_em.append(get_embedding(model, face))
    X_test_em = np.asarray(X_test_em)
    np.savez_compressed('models/6-mathematicians-embeddings.npz', \
            X_train_em, y_train, X_test_em, y_test)
```

9. Load the training and `test` image embeddings, normalize the input vectors, and label encode the targets for the training and `test` datasets using the following code (as pre-processing steps before fitting the SVM model):

```
data = np.load('models/6-mathematicians-embeddings.npz')
X_train, y_train, X_test, y_test = data['X_train'],
data['y_train'], data['X_test'], data['y_test']
print('Dataset: train=%d, test=%d' % (X_train.shape[0],
X_test.shape[0]))
# Dataset: train=72, test=36
in_encoder = Normalizer(norm='l2')
X_train, X_test = in_encoder.transform(X_train),
in_encoder.transform(X_test)
out_encoder = LabelEncoder()
out_encoder.fit(y_train)
y_train, y_test = out_encoder.transform(y_train),
out_encoder.transform(y_test)
```

10. Finally, train scikit-learn's linear SVM model in the training embedding dataset, predict the `test` embedding dataset, and compute the accuracy of prediction on the training and the `test` datasets:

```
model_svc = SVC(kernel='linear', probability=True)
model_svc.fit(X_train, y_train)
yhat_train, yhat_test = model_svc.predict(X_train),
model_svc.predict(X_test)
score_train, score_test = accuracy_score(y_train, yhat_train),
accuracy_score(y_test, yhat_test)
print('Accuracy: train=%.3f, test=%.3f' % (score_train*100,
score_test*100))
# Accuracy: train=100.000, test=94.444
```

As you can see, the accuracy obtained on the `test` dataset is more than 94%.

How it works...

If you choose a random face from the `test` dataset and predict the class (here, it is the name of the mathematician) along with the probability of prediction, you will get an output like this:

As you can see, the face of Bayes was recognized correctly with a probability of around 80% using the linear SVM classification model trained on the face embeddings.

The face identification problem can be converted into a multi-class classification problem in the embedding space by using the following steps:

1. First, extract the high-quality face-embedding features from a set of labeled training images of the mathematicians with the FaceNet pre-trained model.
2. Use these embedding features, along with the class label (the name of a mathematician), to train a linear SVM classifier model (using scikit-learn).
3. Finally, use the (just trained) classifier model to recognize new, unseen test images of these mathematicians by extracting the embedding features, first using FaceNet and then using the classifier to predict the name of the mathematician (along with the confidence) when given the encoded face-embedding of the face image.

Chapter 9

The preceding steps are shown pictorially (for just three class labels, for simplicity) in the following screenshot:

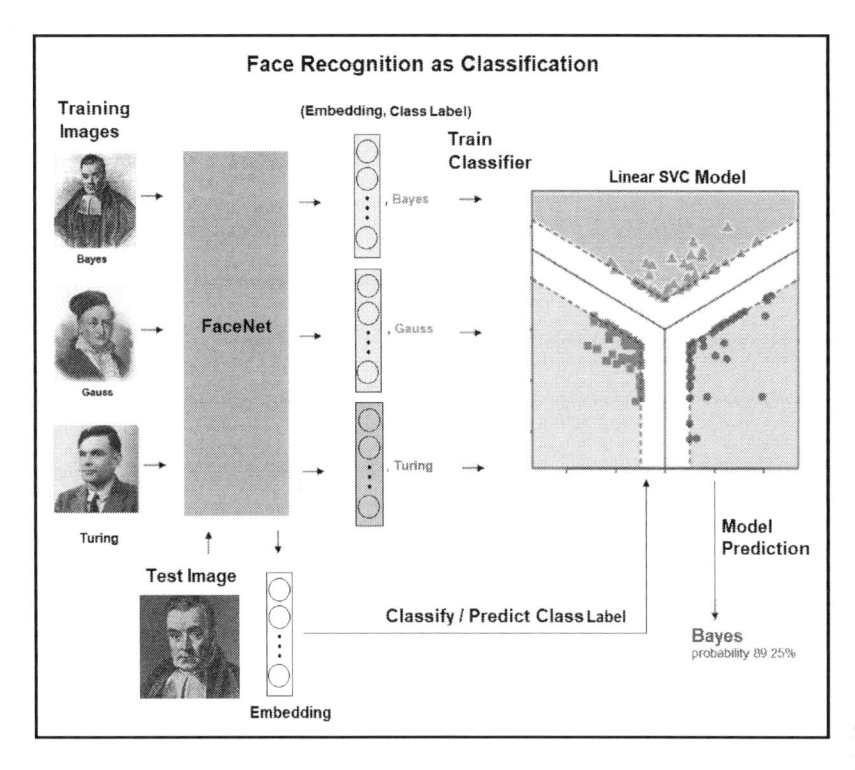

Face Recognition as Classification

The FaceNet model expects a 160×160×3 colored face image as input (any image needs to be resized to this shape) and it outputs a face embedding vector with a length of 128.

The `MTCNN()` function from the `mtcnn` library's `mtcnn` module, observed in step 2, was used to create the face detector using default weights.

In *step 10*, the `SVC` class with a linear kernel was used to train the classifier that carries out the face recognition by predicting the most probable class (that is, the mathematician's name) when given an embedding extracted (using the pre-trained FaceNet model) from a new face image of any of the mathematicians, using the trained SVM model.

> A simple **Euclidean (L2) distance** could have been used instead of the **SVM**. (Find the `class` label of the training face embedding that has the minimum L2 distance with the target face embedding. Try implementing this on your own.)

See also

For more details about this recipe, refer to the following links:

1. `https://machinelearningmastery.com/how-to-develop-a-face-recognition-system-using-facenet-in-keras-and-an-svm-classifier/`
2. `https://stackoverflow.com/questions/47068709/your-cpu-supports-instructions-that-this-tensorflow-binary-was-not-compiled-to-u`
3. `https://arxiv.org/pdf/1503.03832.pdf`
4. `https://sandipanweb.wordpress.com/2018/01/07/classifying-a-face-image-as-happy-unhappy-and-face-recognition-using-deep-learning-convolution-neural-net-with-keras-in-python/`
5. `https://www.youtube.com/watch?v=eHsErlPJWUU1ist=PLD63A284B7615313A index=14`
6. `https://www.youtube.com/watch?v=d2XB5-tuCWU`
7. `https://www.youtube.com/watch?v=EZmaYcdLfhM`
8. `https://www.thehindubusinessline.com/info-tech/google-backs-eus-proposed-facial-recognition-ban-microsoft-disagrees/article30616303.ece`
9. `https://arxiv.org/ftp/arxiv/papers/1604/1604.02878.pdf`

Age, gender, and emotion recognition using deep learning models

The age estimation of a face image can be posed as a deep classification problem using a CNN followed by an expected softmax value refinement (as can be done with a **Deep EXpectation** (**DEX**) model). In this recipe, you will first learn how to use a pre-trained deep learning model (a **WideResNet** with two classification layers added on top of it, which simultaneously estimates the age and gender using a single CNN) for age and gender recognition from a face image. We will use face images from the celebrity faces dataset for age and gender recognition. You will then implement emotion recognition using yet another pre-trained deep learning model, but this time you will need to detect the faces using a face detector (you could use transfer learning, too, and use your classifier on your own images, but this is left as an exercise for you to try).

Chapter 9

Getting ready

Download the pre-trained deep learning models from https://drive.google.com/drive/folders/0BxYys69jI14kU0I1YUQyY1ZDRUE and https://drive.google.com/file/d/0B6yZu81NrMhSV2ozYWZrenJXd1E. Extract the models to the appropriate paths in the models folder. Import the required libraries to start:

```
import cv2
import dlib
import numpy as np
from keras.models import load_model
from keras import backend as K
from keras.models import model_from_json
from glob import glob
import matplotlib.pylab as plt
```

How to do it...

Execute the following steps to implement age, gender, and emotion recognition with a pre-trained model in Keras:

1. First, load the configuration of the pre-trained model from the JSON file provided and load the model weights from the pre-trained weights file, using the following code snippet:

    ```
    json_file = open('models/model.json', 'r')
    loaded_model_json = json_file.read()
    json_file.close()
    loaded_model = model_from_json(loaded_model_json)
    loaded_model.load_weights('models/weights.29-3.76_utk.hdf5')
    ```

2. You will use dlib's frontal face detector to detect and extract faces from the input face images. Get dlib's face detector with this next line of code:

    ```
    detector = dlib.get_frontal_face_detector()
    ```

3. For each face detected in an input image with the dlib detector, predict the age and gender of the detected face with the deep-learning model by running the forward pass with the face as input and extract the predicted age and gender:

    ```
    img_size = 64
    for img_file in glob('images/musicians/*.jpg'):
        img = cv2.cvtColor(cv2.imread(img_file), cv2.COLOR_BGR2RGB)
        detected = detector(img, 0)
        if len(detected) > 0:
    ```

Face Recognition, Image Captioning, and More

```
            faces = np.empty((len(detected), img_size, img_size, 3))
            for i, d in enumerate(detected):
                x1, y1, x2, y2, w, h = d.left(),d.top(),d.right()+1,\
                                       d.bottom()+1,d.width(),d.height()
                faces[i, :, :, :] = cv2.resize(img[y1:y2+1, \
                                        x1:x2+1, :], (img_size, img_size))
            results = loaded_model.predict(faces)
            predicted_genders = results[0]
            ages = np.arange(0, 101).reshape(101, 1)
            predicted_ages = results[1].dot(ages).flatten()
```

If you run the preceding code block and draw the detected faces along with the ages and genders of the people in the images, you will get an output as in the following screenshot:

The `keras.models.model_from_json()` function was used to parse the JSON model configuration file and get a model instance.

The `keras.models.predict()` function was used to run a forward pass and generate the output age and gender predictions for the input faces.

[374]

There's more...

Similarly, use the other pre-trained model to predict the emotion in a face in a given image (use the face detector function to detect the faces first). You should get an output like this if you draw the predicted emotions of Charlie Chaplin's face:

You may want to download the five celebrities' datasets from https://www.kaggle.com/dansbecker/5-celebrity-faces-dataset and try different face images for emotion, gender, and age recognition.

See also

For more details about this recipe, use the following links:

- https://github.com/yu4u/age-gender-estimation
- https://github.com/jalajthanaki/Facial_emotion_recognition_using_Keras
- https://stackoverflow.com/questions/53859419/dlib-get-frontal-face-detector-gets-faces-in-full-image-but-does-not-get-in-c
- https://www.vision.ee.ethz.ch/en/publications/papers/articles/eth_biwi_01299.pdf

Image colorization with deep learning

In this recipe, you will learn how to use a pre-trained deep learning model to convert a grayscale image into a plausible color version. Zhang et al. propose a fully automatic image-colorization model that produces realistically colored images given a grayscale input image. The model was practiced on over a million target color images. In the testing phase, we just need to run a forward pass on the CNN to predict the output colored image when given a grayscale input. The algorithm was evaluated using a colorization Turing test, where the human participants were asked to choose between a model-generated and a ground-truth color image (which resulted in the model successfully fooling the humans in 32% of the trials). The following diagram shows the architecture of the deep CNN:

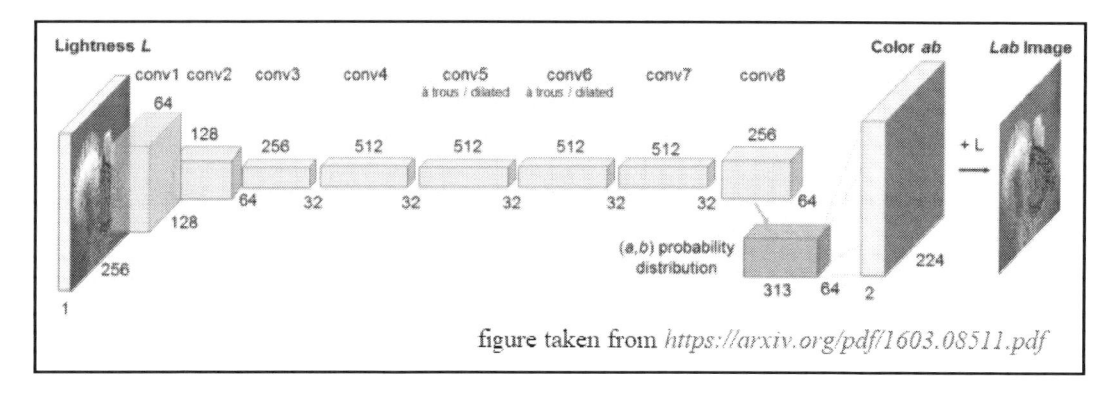

figure taken from https://arxiv.org/pdf/1603.08511.pdf

Getting ready

First, download the pre-trained Caffe model from https://github.com/richzhang/colorization/tree/master/colorization/models (for example, the colorization_deploy_v2.prototxt and .caffemodel files) and https://github.com/richzhang/colorization/blob/master/colorization/resources/pts_in_hull.npy. Import all the necessary packages using the following code block:

```
import numpy as np
import cv2
import matplotlib.pyplot as plt
import imutils
```

How to do it...

Run the following steps to implement image colorization using the pre-trained deep learning Caffe model with the `opencv-python` functions:

1. Read the model into memory from the Caffe `prototxt` and the model `weights` files:

   ```
   proto_file = "models/colorization_deploy_v2.prototxt"
   weights_file = "models/colorization_release_v2.caffemodel"
   net = cv2.dnn.readNetFromCaffe(proto_file, weights_file)
   ```

2. Load the bin centers and populate the cluster centers as 1 x 1 convolution kernels using the following code snippet:

   ```
   pts_in_hull = np.load('models/pts_in_hull.npy')
   pts_in_hull = pts_in_hull.transpose().reshape(2, 313, 1, 1)
   net.getLayer(net.getLayerId('class8_ab')).blobs = [pts_in_hull.astype(np.float32)]
   net.getLayer(net.getLayerId('conv8_313_rh')).blobs = [np.full([1, 313], 2.606, np.float32)]
   ```

3. For each of the input images, read the image from the disk, convert it to a `Lab` color space, and pull out the `L` channel using the following code snippet:

   ```
   width = height = 224
   for f in glob('images/tocolorize/*.png'):
       image = cv2.cvtColor(cv2.cvtColor(cv2.imread(f), \
               cv2.COLOR_BGR2GRAY), cv2.COLOR_GRAY2BGR)
       img_rgb = (image[:,:,[2, 1, 0]] * 1.0 / 255).astype(np.float32)
       img_lab = cv2.cvtColor(img_rgb, cv2.COLOR_RGB2Lab)
       img_l = img_lab[:,:,0]
   ```

4. Resize the lightness (`L`) channel and the image to the network input size. Run the `forward` pass to get the predicted output, as shown here:

   ```
   img_l_rs = cv2.resize(img_l, (width, height))
   img_l_rs -= 50 # subtract 50 for mean-centering
   net.setInput(cv2.dnn.blobFromImage(img_l_rs))
   ab_dec = net.forward()[0,:,:,:].transpose((1,2,0))
   ```

5. Reshape the predicted output to the input image size and convert from `Lab` to `BGR` space to get the colored output image:

```
(orig_height,orig_width) = img_rgb.shape[:2]
ab_dec_us = cv2.resize(ab_dec, (orig_width, orig_height))
img_lab_out = np.concatenate((img_l[:,:,np.newaxis], \
                              ab_dec_us),axis=2)
img_bgr_out = np.clip(cv2.cvtColor(img_lab_out, \
                       cv2.COLOR_Lab2BGR), 0, 1)
```

If you run the preceding code blocks and plot the output color images obtained from the input grayscale images, you will get an output as in the following screenshot:

The `readNetFromCaffe()` function from OpenCV-Python, downloaded in step 1, was used to load a pre-trained deep neural network model stored in the Caffe framework's format. It accepts a path to the `.prototxt` file (a text file describing the architecture of the neural net) and a path to the `.caffemodel` file (a file storing the pre-trained weights for the model).

See also

For more details about this recipe, use the following links:

- https://arxiv.org/pdf/1603.08511.pdf
- https://github.com/richzhang/colorization/blob/master/colorization/
- https://github.com/opencv/opencv/blob/master/samples/dnn/colorization.py
- http://richzhang.github.io/colorization/
- https://www.youtube.com/watch?v=M4WOPN3qjVI
- https://www.youtube.com/watch?v=vEoAGeu3NLQ

Automatic image captioning with a CNN and an LSTM

Automatic captioning of an image is a popular problem in AI that connects image processing and computer vision with NLP. In this recipe, you will learn how to use a pre-trained generative model (known as **Show and Tell**) based on a deep recurrent neural network architecture that can be used to generate captions (complete sentences in a natural language describing the contents of an image). The model was trained with the objective to maximize the likelihood of the input caption texts given the input training images. `im2txt` is a TensorFlow implementation of the Show and Tell model that can take images as input and generate human-like captions that describe the image. The model was tested on more than 300,000 images. The model is an end-to-end deep neural network consisting of a CNN (used to learn the implicit features of an input image) followed by an RNN (used to generate captions when given the CNN features). The implementation uses **BeamSearch** to iteratively select the best k captions for an input image. The following diagram shows the architecture of the Show and Tell model:

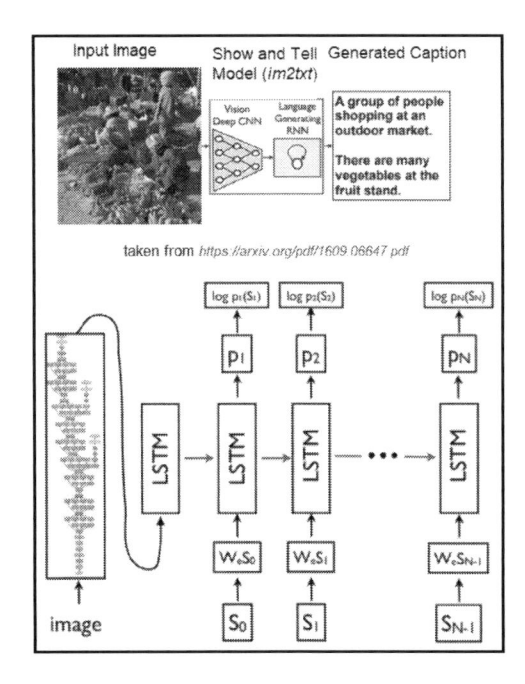

Getting ready

First, clone the repository (using `https://github.com/tensorflow/models/`) to a folder in your local machine. Then, copy the `models/tree/master/research/im2txt/im2txt` folder to the `models` folder used in this chapter. Create a sub-folder, called `cpt`, and download the pre-trained model checkpoint file (`model.ckpt-2000000`) in `cpt` from `https://drive.google.com/file/d/0Bw6m_66JSYLlRFVKQ2tGcUJaWjA/`. Create an empty `__init__.py` file in `im2txt` to mark this folder as a Python package directory. The folder structure should look like this:

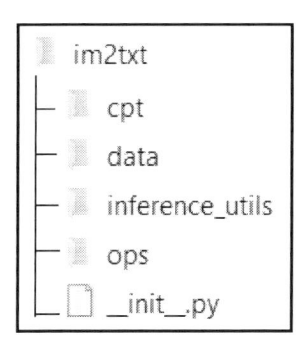

```
im2txt
├── cpt
├── data
├── inference_utils
├── ops
└── __init__.py
```

Let's import the required libraries using the following code block:

```
import os, sys
import tensorflow as tf
from glob import glob
from skimage.io import imread
import matplotlib.pylab as plt
from im2txt import configuration
from im2txt import inference_wrapper
from im2txt.inference_utils import caption_generator
from im2txt.inference_utils import vocabulary

checkpoint_dir = 'models/im2txt/cpt/'
sys.path.append(os.path.join(os.getcwd(), 'models/'))
```

How to do it...

Run the following steps to implement image captioning using a pre-trained `im2txt` model on TensorFlow:

1. The downloaded pre-trained weights checkpoint file (`model.ckpt-2000000`) contains some issues and you will most likely fail to load it. In that case, fix the issue in the checkpoint by modifying it and creating a new checkpoint file (`model2.ckpt-2000000`) inside the `models` folder using code from https://github.com/tensorflow/models/issues/466 or https://github.com/PacktPublishing/Python-Image-Processing-Cookbook/blob/master/Chapter%2009/Chapter%2009.ipynb.

2. Build the inference graph from the modified `checkpoint` file and then load the vocabulary for LSTM (a particular type of RNN that can learn long-term dependencies):

   ```
   checkpoint_path = checkpoint_dir + 'model2.ckpt-2000000'
   vocab_file = checkpoint_dir + 'word_counts.txt'

   g = tf.Graph()
   with g.as_default():
       model = inference_wrapper.InferenceWrapper()
       restore_fn = model.build_graph_from_config\
                    (configuration.ModelConfig(), checkpoint_path)
   g.finalize()

   vocab = vocabulary.Vocabulary(vocab_file)
   ```

3. Load the pre-trained model from the model `checkpoint` file using the `restore_fn()` function. Get the caption generator initialized with the pre-trained model parameters. Here, we will use the default beam search parameters (you can always explicitly specify the parameter values if you want to experiment). Ignore the beginning and end words (the start and end markers of a sentence) and output the generated captions using the following code snippet:

```
filenames = glob('images/captioning/*.png')
tf.logging.info("Running caption generation on %d files matching %s", len(filenames), filenames)
with tf.Session(graph=g) as sess:
    restore_fn(sess)
    generator = caption_generator.CaptionGenerator(model, vocab)
    for filename in filenames:
        with tf.gfile.GFile(filename, "rb") as f: image = f.read()
        captions = generator.beam_search(sess, image)
        print("Captions for image %s:" % \
              os.path.basename(filename))
        for i, caption in enumerate(captions):
            sentence = " ".join([vocab.id_to_word(w) for w in \
                                 caption.sentence[1:-1]])
            print("  %d) %s (p=%f)" % (i, sentence, \
                                       math.exp(caption.logprob)))
```

Chapter 9

If you run the preceding code block on the input images from the `images` and `captions` folders, you will generate the following captions:

[383]

As you can see, most of the captions generated are reasonably good and accurate.

How it works...

The `build_graph_from_config()` function builds the inference graph from a configuration object. It takes a model `config` object containing the configuration for building the model and a `checkpoint` path containing the `checkpoint` file. It returns a function that can be used to load the model variables from the `checkpoint` file.

The `beam_search()` function runs beam search caption generation on a single image. It accepts a TensorFlow session object and a CNN-encoded image string as input and returns a list of captions sorted by descending score.

See `caption_generator.py` for a description of the available beam search parameters.

See also

For more details about this recipe, use the following links:

- https://github.com/tensorflow/models/tree/master/research/im2txt/im2txt
- https://edouardfouche.com/Fun-with-Tensorflow-im2txt/
- https://github.com/tensorflow/models/issues/466
- https://github.com/tensorflow/tensorflow/issues/30794
- https://arxiv.org/pdf/1609.06647.pdf
- https://www.youtube.com/watch?v=yk6XDFm3J2c

Image generation with a GAN

A **generative adversarial network** (**GAN**) is a generative model that defines an adversarial net framework and is composed of a couple of models (both models are CNNs in general), namely a generator and a discriminator, with the goal of generating new realistic images when given a set of training images. These two models act as adversaries of each other: the generator learns to generate new fake images that look like real images (starting with random noise) whilethe discriminator learns to determine whether a sample image is a **real** or a **fake** image.

The generator plays the role of a counterfeiter that is trying to produce a fake image and fool the discriminator, whereas the discriminator plays the role of the police that tries to detect the fake image generated by the discriminator. We can think of this as a two-player game and competition in this game drives both teams to improve their methods until the fake images are indistinguishable from the real images (for example, the Nash equilibrium between the discriminator and generator adversaries). Once training is over, a new sample image (resembling the real image) can be generated just by running a forward propagation on the generator. Both CNN models try to optimize opposing objective (loss) functions in a **zero-sum** game. The following diagram describes the basic GAN framework and also how the GAN is trained (here, it is trained on human faces):

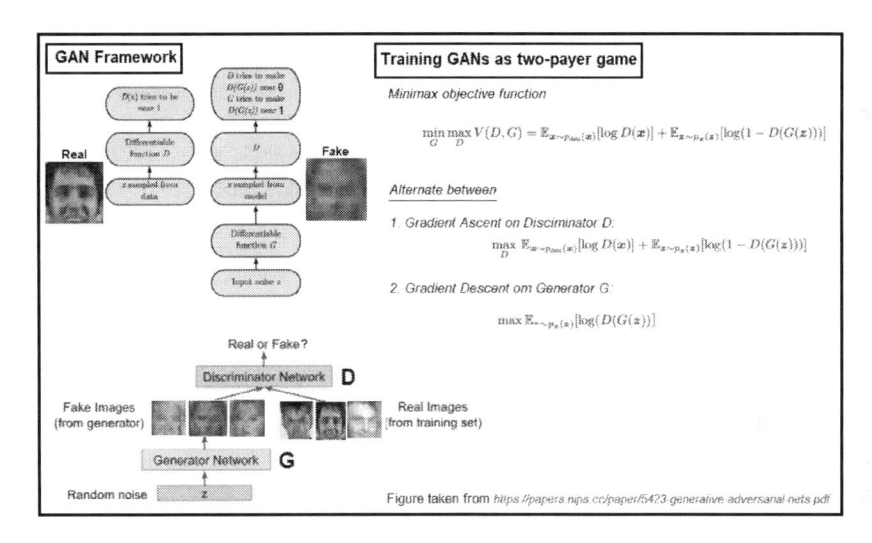

In this recipe, you will learn how to train a GAN using PyTorch to generate realistic face images, given a set of real face images. Since it is likely to take quite a long time to train the GAN, using a GPU to train a GAN is highly recommended.

Getting ready

First, download the anime face dataset from `https://www.kaggle.com/splcher/animefacedataset` (create a Kaggle account if you don't already have one) and extract the images into the `anime` sub-directory in the `images` directory (there are 63,565 images as of now). Import all the required packages using the following code block:

```
import numpy as np
from PIL import Image
```

```
import matplotlib.pylab as plt
import pickle as pkl
import torch
import torch.nn as nn
from torchvision import datasets
from torchvision import transforms
from torch.utils.data.sampler import SubsetRandomSampler
import torch.nn.functional as F
import torch.optim as optim
```

How to do it...

Run the following steps to train a GAN on the anime faces using PyTorch and to generate new realistic anime face images:

1. Define the following function to make the PyTorch data loader apply `transform` to resize the images of a given batch size from a given directory, and then return them using a Python generator:

```
def get_data_loader(batch_size, image_size, data_dir='anime/'):
    image_transforms = transforms.Compose(\
                [transforms.Resize(image_size), \
                transforms.ToTensor(), ])
    indices = np.random.choice(63565, 50000) # get 50k random
                samples
    data_loader = torch.utils.data.DataLoader( \
                datasets.ImageFolder(data_dir, \
                transform=image_transforms), \
                sampler=SubsetRandomSampler(indices),
                batch_size=batch_size)
    return data_loader

batch_size = 128
image_size = 32
anime_train_loader = get_data_loader(batch_size, image_size)

images, _ = iter(anime_train_loader).next()
```

If you plot a few sample input images from the `anime` dataset and show them using `matplotlib`, you will get an output like this:

Chapter 9

2. Define the Python class corresponding to the discriminator (D) using CNNs with the following code snippet:

```
class Discriminator(nn.Module):

    def __init__(self, conv_dim):
        super(Discriminator, self).__init__()
        self.conv_dim = conv_dim
        self.conv1 = nn.Conv2d(3, conv_dim, kernel_size=4, stride=2, \
                    padding=1, bias=False)
        self.batch_norm1 = nn.BatchNorm2d(conv_dim)
        self.conv2 = nn.Conv2d(conv_dim, conv_dim*2,kernel_size=4, \
                    stride=2, padding=1, bias=False)
        self.batch_norm2 = nn.BatchNorm2d(conv_dim*2)
        self.conv3 = nn.Conv2d(conv_dim*2, conv_dim*4, kernel_size=4, \
                    stride=2, padding=1, bias=False)
        self.batch_norm3 = nn.BatchNorm2d(conv_dim*4)
        self.conv4 = nn.Conv2d(conv_dim*4, conv_dim*8, kernel_size=4, \
                    stride=2, padding=1, bias=False)
        self.batch_norm4 = nn.BatchNorm2d(conv_dim*8)
        self.conv5 = nn.Conv2d(conv_dim*8, conv_dim*16, kernel_size=4, \
                    stride=2, padding=1, bias=False)
        self.fc = nn.Linear(conv_dim*4*4, 1)

    def forward(self, x):
        x = F.leaky_relu(self.batch_norm1(self.conv1(x)), 0.2)
        x = F.leaky_relu(self.batch_norm2(self.conv2(x)), 0.2)
        x = F.leaky_relu(self.batch_norm3(self.conv3(x)), 0.2)
        x = F.leaky_relu(self.batch_norm4(self.conv4(x)), 0.2)
```

```
x = self.conv5(x)
x = x.view(-1, self.conv_dim*4*4)
x = F.sigmoid(self.fc(x))
return x
```

3. Define the Python class corresponding to the generator (G) with CNNs using the following code snippet:

```
class Generator(nn.Module):

 def __init__(self, z_size, conv_dim):
  super(Generator, self).__init__()
  self.conv_dim = conv_dim
  self.t_conv1=nn.ConvTranspose2d(conv_dim, conv_dim*8, \
         kernel_size=4,stride=2,padding=1, bias=False)
  self.batch_norm1 = nn.BatchNorm2d(conv_dim*8)
  self.t_conv2 = nn.ConvTranspose2d(conv_dim*8,conv_dim*4, \
         kernel_size=4, stride=2,padding=1, bias=False)
  self.batch_norm2 = nn.BatchNorm2d(conv_dim*4)
  self.t_conv3 = nn.ConvTranspose2d(conv_dim*4, conv_dim*2, \
         kernel_size=4,stride=2,padding=1,bias=False)
  self.batch_norm3 = nn.BatchNorm2d(conv_dim*2)
  self.t_conv4 = nn.ConvTranspose2d(conv_dim*2, 3, kernel_size=4, \
         stride=2, padding=1, bias=False)
  self.fc = nn.Linear(z_size, conv_dim*4)

 def forward(self, x):
  batch_s = x.shape[0]
  x = self.fc(x)
  x = x.view(batch_s, self.conv_dim, 2, 2)
  x = F.relu(self.batch_norm1(self.t_conv1(x)))
  x = F.relu(self.batch_norm2(self.t_conv2(x)))
  x = F.relu(self.batch_norm3(self.t_conv3(x)))
  x = self.t_conv4(x)
  x = F.tanh(x)
  return x
```

4. Apply initial weights to the convolutional and linear layers, initialize the model weights, and build the GAN (using the given dimensions of the D and G CNNs) to obtain the discriminator and generator instances, using the following code block:

```
def init_weights_normal(m):
 classname = m.__class__.__name__
 if hasattr(m, 'weight') and (classname.find('Conv') != -1 or \
         classname.find('Linear') != -1):
  nn.init.normal_(m.weight.data, 0.0, 0.02)
```

```
    if hasattr(m.bias, 'data'):
        nn.init.constant_(m.bias.data, 0.0)

def build_GAN(d_conv_dim, g_conv_dim, z_size):
    D = Discriminator(d_conv_dim)
    G = Generator(z_size=z_size, conv_dim=g_conv_dim)
    D.apply(init_weights_normal)
    G.apply(init_weights_normal)
    return D, G

# define model hyperparams
d_conv_dim = 32
g_conv_dim = 32
z_size = 100

D, G = build_GAN(d_conv_dim, g_conv_dim, z_size)
```

5. Define the `real` and `fake` loss functions to train the discriminator and the generator networks:

```
def real_loss(D_out, smooth=False):
    batch_size = D_out.size(0)
    if smooth: # smooth, real labels = 0.9
        labels = torch.ones(batch_size)*0.9
    else: # real labels = 1
        labels = torch.ones(batch_size)
    if train_on_gpu: labels = labels.cuda()
    criterion = nn.BCELoss()
    loss = criterion(D_out.squeeze(), labels)
    return loss

def fake_loss(D_out):
    batch_size = D_out.size(0)
    labels = torch.zeros(batch_size)
    if train_on_gpu: labels = labels.cuda()
    criterion = nn.BCELoss()
    loss = criterion(D_out.squeeze(), labels)
    return loss
```

6. Initialize the optimizers to be used (`Adam`) for the discriminator and generator. Define the function to train the GAN:

```
train_on_gpu = torch.cuda.is_available()
lr = 0.0005
g_optimizer = optim.Adam(G.parameters(), lr=lr, betas=(0.3, 0.999))
d_optimizer = optim.Adam(D.parameters(), lr=lr, betas=(0.3, 0.999))

def train(D, G, n_epochs, print_every=50):
```

```
if train_on_gpu:
   D.cuda()
   G.cuda()
samples = []
losses = []
```

7. Get some fixed data (uniform random noise) for sampling. These are images that are held constant throughout training and allow us to inspect the model's performance. Train the discriminator and generator with the batch input images and iterate the training process for a given number of epochs:

```
sample_size=36
fixed_z = np.random.uniform(-1, 1, size=(sample_size, z_size))
fixed_z = torch.from_numpy(fixed_z).float()
if train_on_gpu:
  fixed_z = fixed_z.cuda()

for epoch in range(n_epochs):
  for batch_i, (real_images, _) in enumerate(anime_train_loader):
    batch_size = real_images.size(0)
    real_images = scale(real_images)
```

8. Train the discriminator on real images from the data and fake images generated by the generator, with the goal of differentiating fake images from real images:

```
if train_on_gpu: real_images = real_images.cuda()
    d_optimizer.zero_grad()
    D_real = D(real_images)
    d_real_loss = real_loss(D_real)
    z_flex = np.random.uniform(-1, 1, size=(batch_size, z_size))
    z_flex = torch.from_numpy(z_flex).float()
    if train_on_gpu: z_flex = z_flex.cuda()
    fake_images = G(z_flex)
    D_fake = D(fake_images)
    d_fake_loss = fake_loss(D_fake)
    d_loss = d_real_loss + d_fake_loss
    d_loss.backward()
    d_optimizer.step()
```

9. Train the generator with an adversarial loss to generate more realistic images to fool the discriminator:

```
g_optimizer.zero_grad()
    z_flex = np.random.uniform(-1, 1, size=(batch_size, z_size))
    z_flex = torch.from_numpy(z_flex).float()
    if train_on_gpu: z_flex = z_flex.cuda()
    fake_images = G(z_flex)
    D_fake = D(fake_images)
```

```
g_loss = real_loss(D_fake, True) # use real loss to flip labels
g_loss.backward()
g_optimizer.step()
```

10. At the end of each epoch, switch to the `eval` mode and generate new images with the generator by running a `forward` pass on the generator CNN, then again switch back to the `train` mode:

    ```
    G.eval() # switch to eval mode for generating samples
    samples_z = G(fixed_z)
    samples.append(samples_z)
    G.train() # switch back to training mode
    ```

The following screenshot shows the fake images generated by the generator after 10 epochs. Notice that they look like realistic anime face images:

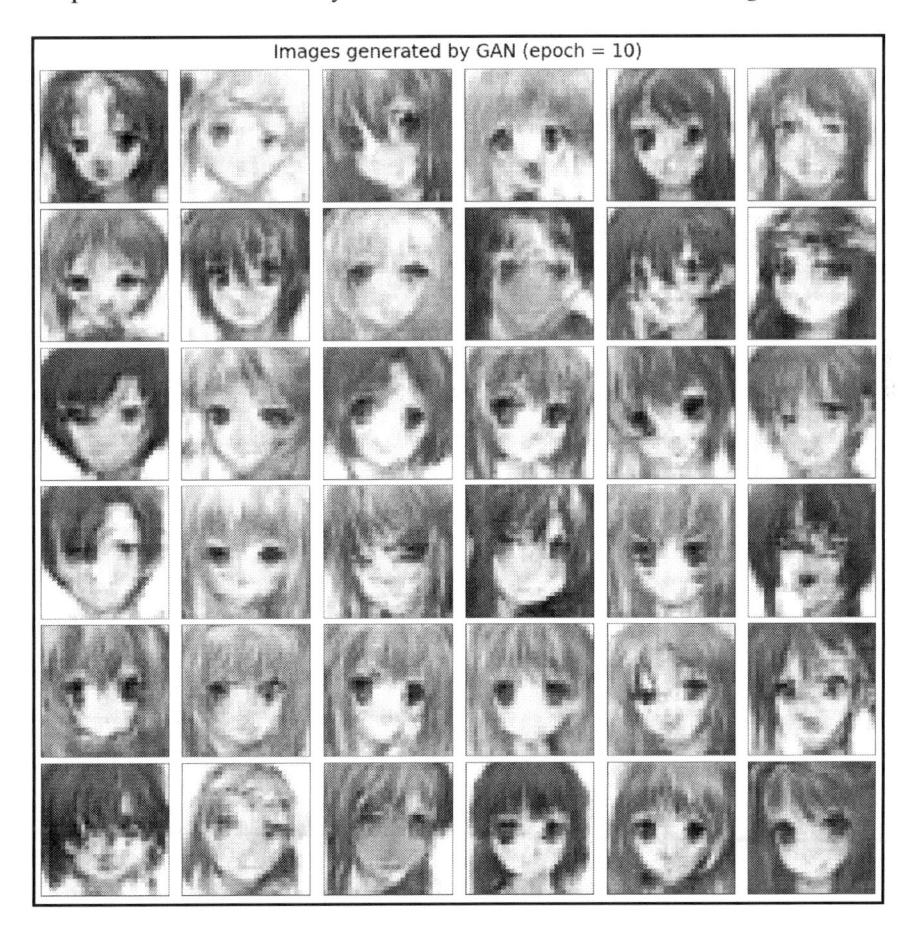

How it works...

The generator (`net`) generates new image instances, while the discriminator evaluates them for authenticity.

The adversarial training focuses on the system's weaknesses, forcing each other to improve over time (the generator gets better at generating realistic images and the discriminator gets better at differentiating the real from the fake images), until the fake images generated by the generator become indistinguishable from the real images and the discriminator can't differentiate them (at this point, the generator has learned how to generate a good image).

The discriminator is just a binary classifier that gets two batches of images as input (from real training data and from the generator) and figures out whether an image is real or fake.

The discriminator optimizes the `loss` function, composed of the sum of the real and the fake losses, implemented by the `real_loss()` and the `fake_loss()` functions, respectively.

The generator optimizes the real loss to fool the discriminator by making the generated image look more and more like the real images (starting from random noise).

The `build_GAN()` function is implemented to create and initialize the discriminator and generator networks.

There's more...

You may want to download the **CelebFaces Attributes (CelebA)** dataset from `http://mmlab.ie.cuhk.edu.hk/projects/CelebA.html`. (For example, download the aligned faces at `https://drive.google.com/drive/folders/0B7EVK8r0v71pWEZsZE9oNnFzTm8` and try to generate human face images using a GAN.)

See also

For more details about this recipe, use the following links:

- `https://arxiv.org/pdf/1406.2661.pdf`
- `https://www.youtube.com/watch?v=5WoItGTWV54`
- `https://www.youtube.com/watch?v=HGYYEUSm-0Q`

- `https://papers.nips.cc/paper/5423-generative-adversarial-nets.pdf`
- `https://www.youtube.com/watch?v=2MLJMBEQNds`

Using a variational autoencoder to reconstruct and generate images

A **variational autoencoder** (VAE) is a generative model that uses Bayesian inference and tries to model the underlying probability distribution of images so that it can sample new images from that distribution. Just like an ordinary autoencoder, it's composed of two components: an encoder (a bunch of layers that will compress the input to the bottleneck in a vanilla autoencoder) and a decoder (a bunch of layers that will reconstruct the input from its compressed representation from the bottleneck in a vanilla autoencoder). The difference between a VAE and an ordinary autoencoder is that instead of mapping an input layer to a latent variable, known as the bottleneck vector, the encoder maps the input to a distribution. The random samples are then drawn from the distribution and fed to the decoder.

Since it cannot run backpropagation and push gradients through a sampling node, a reparameterization trick is applied, where the mean and standard deviation vectors of images are learned with backpropagation by setting aside the stochastic part. The VAE's objective is a variational lower bound; it also ensures that the distribution learned is not far from the normal standard. It tries to estimate the true posterior $(p\theta(z|x))$ using variational (Bayesian) inference. The following diagram illustrates the preceding steps:

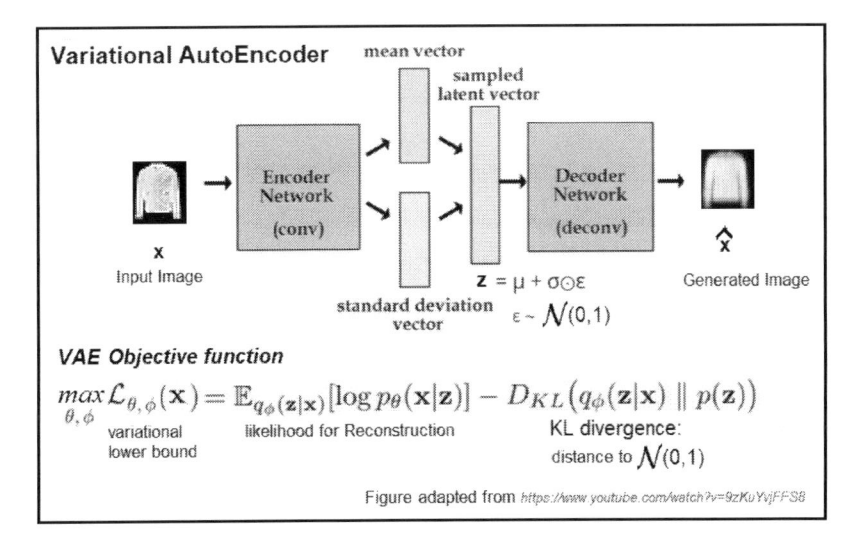

Here, $p\theta(x|z)$, z, and $q\varphi(z|x)$ represent the decoder network, the latent variable, and the encoder network, respectively. In this recipe, we will use the Fashion MNIST images dataset to train and then generate new images using a VAE, implementing it in PyTorch.

Getting ready

Let's import all the required packages using the following code snippet:

```
import gzip, os, sys
import numpy as np
from scipy.stats import multivariate_normal
from urllib.request import urlretrieve
import matplotlib.pyplot as plt
import torch
import torch.utils.data
from torch import nn, optim
from torch.autograd import Variable
from torch.nn import functional as F
from torchvision import datasets, transforms
from torchvision.utils import save_image
from torch.utils.data import DataLoader
```

How to do it...

Run the following steps to implement a VAE with PyTorch:

1. In this recipe, we will use the Fashion MNIST images as input. In order to download the training and test images and load these images, along with the ground-truth labels, to memory, the following functions need to be defined:

    ```
    def download(filename, source='http://fashion-mnist.s3-website.eu-central-1.amazonaws.com/'):
        print("Downloading %s" % filename)
        urlretrieve(source + filename, filename)

    def load_fashion_mnist_images(filename):
        if not os.path.exists(filename): download(filename)
        with gzip.open(filename, 'rb') as f:
            data = np.frombuffer(f.read(), np.uint8, offset=16)
        data = data.reshape(-1, 784)
        return data

    def load_fashion_mnist_labels(filename):
    ```

```
if not os.path.exists(filename): download(filename)
with gzip.open(filename, 'rb') as f:
    data = np.frombuffer(f.read(), np.uint8, offset=8)
return data
```

2. Load the training and test images, along with the corresponding labels, using the following code snippet and using the functions defined in the previous code snippet. Note that all the images are of a size of 28x28 (each one is flattened into a vector of 784). There are 60k training and 10k test images in the dataset:

```
train_data = load_fashion_mnist_images('train-images-idx3-
ubyte.gz')
train_labels = load_fashion_mnist_labels('train-labels-idx1-
ubyte.gz')
test_data = load_fashion_mnist_images('t10k-images-idx3-ubyte.gz')
test_labels = load_fashion_mnist_labels('t10k-labels-idx1-
ubyte.gz')
print(train_data.shape)
# (60000, 784) ## 60k 28x28 handwritten digits
print(test_data.shape)
# (10000, 784) ## 10k 2bx28 handwritten digits
```

If you plot a few *randomly chosen* images from the training dataset, you will get an output as in the following screenshot:

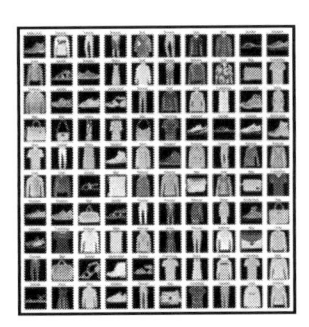

3. Define the VAE class, which has the encode(), decode(), forward(), and reparameterize() methods, by implementing a VAE, as in the following code block:

```
z_dim = 32 # latent variable dimesion

class VAE(nn.Module):

    def __init__(self):
        super(VAE, self).__init__()
```

```
            self.fc1 = nn.Linear(n*n, 512)
            self.fc21 = nn.Linear(512, z_dim) # mu
            self.fc22 = nn.Linear(512, z_dim) # sigma
            self.fc3 = nn.Linear(z_dim, 512)
            self.fc4 = nn.Linear(512, n*n)

        def encode(self, x):
         h1 = F.relu(self.fc1(x))
         return self.fc21(h1), self.fc22(h1)

        def reparameterize(self, mu, logvar):
         std = torch.exp(0.5*logvar)
         eps = torch.randn_like(std)
         return mu + eps*std

        def decode(self, z):
         h3 = F.relu(self.fc3(z))
         return torch.sigmoid(self.fc4(h3))

        def forward(self, x):
         mu, logvar = self.encode(x.view(-1, n*n))
         z = self.reparameterize(mu, logvar)
         return self.decode(z), mu, logvar
```

4. Instantiate the `VAE` class, then instantiate the `train` and `test` data loaders and initialize `optimizer` as Adam:

```
        torch.manual_seed(1)
        cuda = torch.cuda.is_available()
        batch_size, log_interval = 128, 20
        epochs, n = 50, 28
        device = torch.device("cuda" if cuda else "cpu")
        kwargs = {'num_workers': 1, 'pin_memory': True} if cuda else {}
        train_loader = DataLoader(np.reshape(X_train, (-1, 1, n, \
                    n)).astype(np.float32), batch_size=batch_size, \
                    shuffle=True)
        test_loader = DataLoader(np.reshape(X_test, (-1, 1, n, \
                    n)).astype(np.float32), batch_size=batch_size, \
                    shuffle=True)
        model = VAE().to(device)
        optimizer = optim.Adam(model.parameters(), lr=1e-3)
        #weight_decay=1e-4
```

5. Implement the `loss` function for the VAE as the **reconstruction and KL divergence losses** summed over all the elements and the batch:

```
        def loss_function(recon_x, x, mu, logvar):
         BCE = F.binary_cross_entropy(recon_x, x.view(-1, n*n), \
```

```
                    reduction='sum')
    KLD = -0.5 * torch.sum(1 + logvar - mu.pow(2) - logvar.exp())
    return BCE + KLD
```

6. Implement the `train` function:

```
def train(epoch):
  model.train()
  batch_idx = 0
  train_loss = 0
  losses = []
  for data in train_loader:
    data = data.to(device)
    optimizer.zero_grad()
    recon_batch, mu, logvar = model(data)
    loss = loss_function(recon_batch, data, mu, logvar)
    loss.backward()
    train_loss += loss.item()
    optimizer.step()
    if batch_idx % log_interval == 0:
       print('Train Epoch: {} [{}/{} ({:.0f}%)]\tLoss: {:.6f}'.format(
       epoch, batch_idx * len(data), len(train_loader.dataset),
       100. * batch_idx / len(train_loader), loss.item() / len(data)))
    batch_idx += 1
  print('====> Epoch: {} Average loss: {:.4f}'.format(epoch, \
          train_loss / len(train_loader.dataset)))
```

7. Implement the `test` function:

```
def test(epoch):
  model.eval()
  test_loss = 0
  i = 0
  with torch.no_grad():
    for data in test_loader:
      data = data.to(device)
      recon_batch, mu, logvar = model(data)
      test_loss += loss_function(recon_batch, data, mu, logvar).item()
      if i == 0: N = min(data.size(0), 8)
      comparison = torch.cat([data[:N], recon_batch.view(batch_size, \
             1, n, n)[:N]])
      i += 1
  test_loss /= len(test_loader.dataset)
  print('====> Test set loss: {:.4f}'.format(test_loss))
```

8. Train the model for `50` epochs. At the end of each epoch, evaluate the model on `test`, then use the VAE trained so far to generate images, and finally, use the mean and standard deviation vectors learned so far with some random Gaussian noise using the following code:

```
epochs = 50
for epoch in range(1, epochs + 1):
    train(epoch)
    test(epoch)
    with torch.no_grad():
        sample = torch.randn(64, 32).to(device)
        sample = model.decode(sample).cpu()
```

If you plot the images generated by the VAE at the end of all the epochs and plot the `test` images reconstructed using the model (trained in the first 20 epochs, sequentially visualized), you will get an output like this:

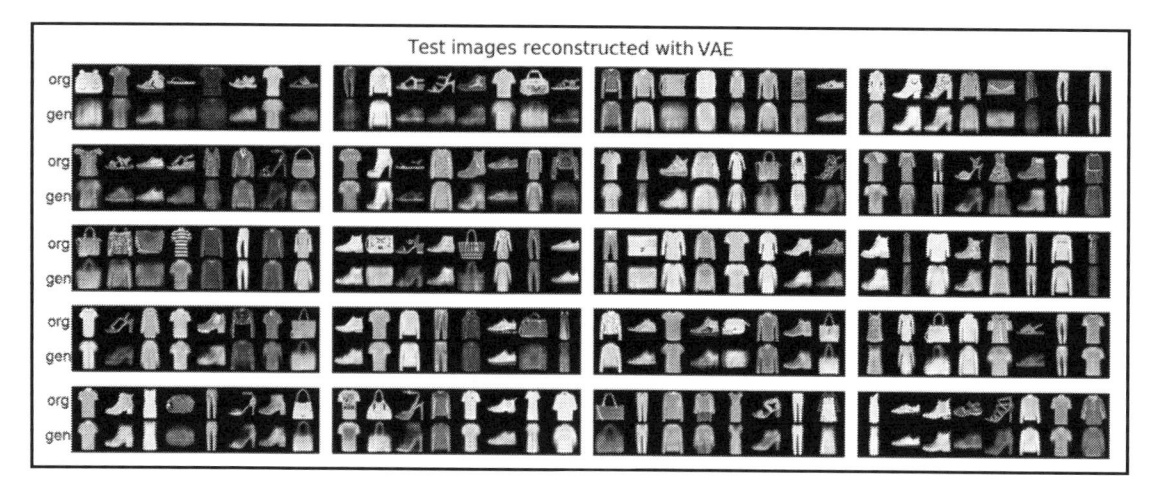

As you can see from the preceding output, the `test` image reconstruction quality becomes better as the model is trained more.

Also, if you plot the images generated by the VAE at the end of the first 20 epochs, you will get an output like this:

Notice how the quality of the generated images evolves during the training process.

Face Recognition, Image Captioning, and More

There's more...

If you have the latent variable dimension set to 2 (instead of 32), what you get is a **2D VAE**. You can use the VAE to predict the test dataset and visualize the predictions (with color codes) for the 10 Fashion MNIST products in the 2D latent space, as in the following figure:

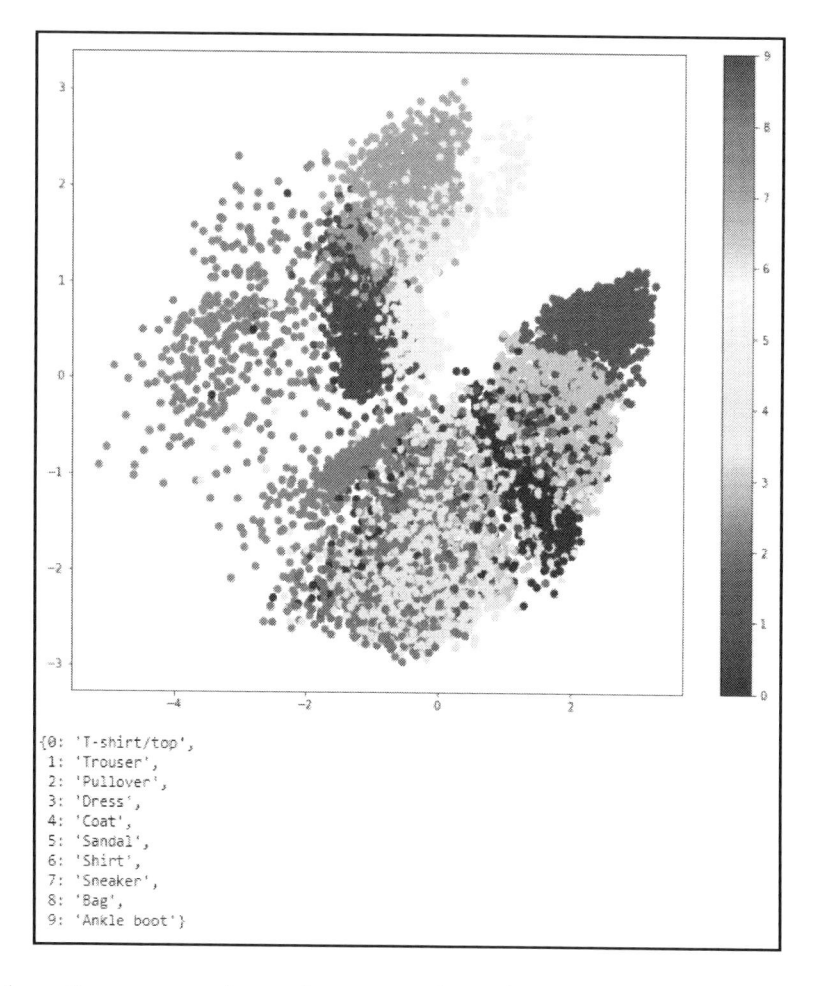

You can see how the same products cluster together. The code is left to you as an exercise.

Also, if you use the decoder to visualize the images from the latent space as you change the latent variables, you will obtain a smoothly varying space where each product transforms into another, as in the following diagram (the code is again left to you as an exercise):

Chapter 9

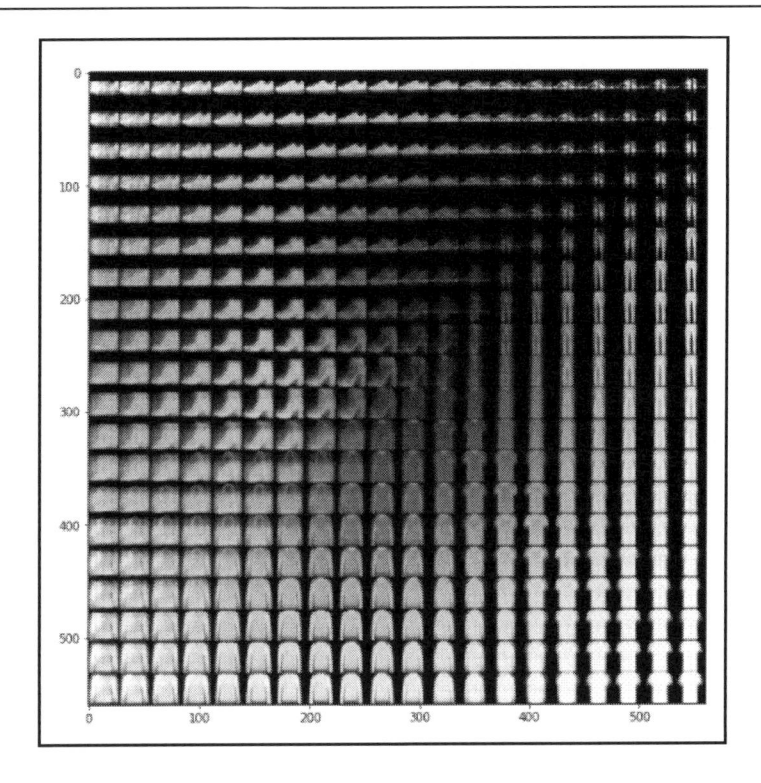

See also

For more details about this recipe, use the following links:

- https://arxiv.org/pdf/1906.02691.pdf
- https://wiseodd.github.io/techblog/2016/12/10/variational-autoencoder/
- https://www.youtube.com/watch?v=9zKuYvjFFS8
- https://www.kaggle.com/rvislaywade/visualizing-mnist-using-a-variational-autoencoder
- https://www.youtube.com/watch?v=jZcv09RA25k

Using a restricted Boltzmann machine to reconstruct Bangla MNIST images

A **restricted Boltzmann machine** (RBM) is an unsupervised model. As an undirected graphical model with two layers (observed and hidden), it is useful to learn a different representation of input data along with the hidden layer. This was the first structural building block of deep learning, particularly when the computational resources to learn about a deep neural net with backpropagation were not available (a stacked RBM was used instead). It restricts the connectivity of the network (only allowing a bipartite graph in between the hidden and observed set of nodes) to make inference easy. It is an energy-based model; the joint distribution is modeled using the **energy** function. To infer the most probable observation, we need to choose the one with the least energy. This model is generally trained on binary images. Computing the joint distribution of observed and hidden layers is intractable (as the partition function, Z, is hard to compute), although the conditional distribution is easy to compute and sample from (since the full conditional distribution factorizes). The **contrastive divergence** (CD) algorithm is used to train an RBM and minimize the average negative-log likelihood. For each training example, $x(t)$, a negative sample is generated using k steps of Gibbs sampling, starting at $x(t)$ with the **k-step contrastive divergence** (CD-k) algorithm.

Obtain the point estimates using Gibbs sampling and subsequently update the parameters W, b, and c. The basic math is depicted in the following diagram:

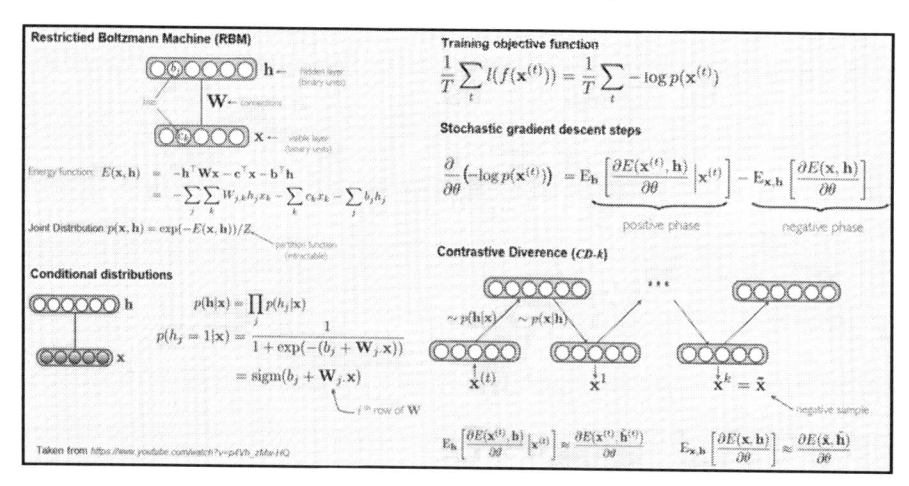

In this recipe, we will use the Numta dataset (a Bengali handwritten digits dataset) to implement the RBM and generate digits from the hidden representations using PyTorch.

Getting ready

First, download the Numta dataset from https://www.kaggle.com/BengaliAI/numta and extract the images in the `images/Numta` folder. Import the required libraries to implement the RBM with PyTorch:

```
import os
from glob import glob
import pandas as pd
import numpy as np
import torch
import torch.utils.data
import torch.nn as nn
import torch.nn.functional as F
import torch.optim as optim
from torch.autograd import Variable
from torchvision import datasets, transforms
from torchvision.utils import make_grid , save_image
from torch.utils.data import DataLoader
```

How to do it...

Run the following steps to implement the RBM with PyTorch and run inference with the Numta images dataset:

1. Read the training and test images using the following code:

```
n = 28
df = pd.read_csv('images/Numta/training-e.csv')
X_train = np.zeros((df.shape[0], n*n))
for i in range(df.shape[0]):
  img = rgb2gray(imread('images/Numta/training-e/' + \
              df.iloc[i]['filename']))
  img = resize(img, (n,n))
  X_train[i,:] = np.array([np.ravel(img)])

test_images = glob('images/Numta/testing-e/*.png')
X_test = np.zeros((len(test_images), n*n))
for i in range(len(test_images)):
  img = rgb2gray(imread(test_images[i]))
  img = resize(img, (n,n))
  X_test[i,:] = np.array([np.ravel(img)])
```

Face Recognition, Image Captioning, and More

If you display a few randomly selected images from the training dataset, you will get an output like this:

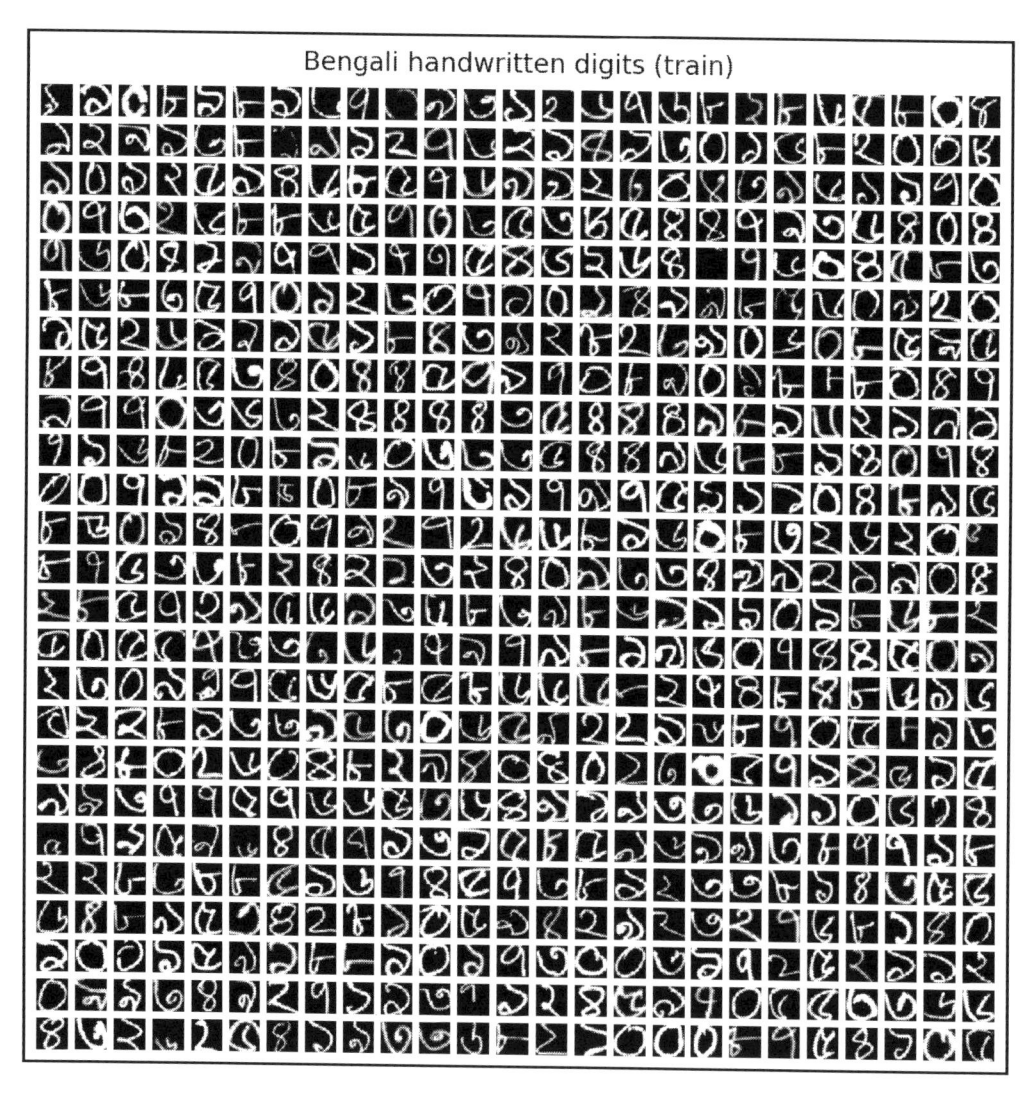

2. Implement the RBM class with the `sample_from_p()`, `v_to_h()`, `h_to_v()`, and `forward()` methods to implement a CD-k algorithm. Use the `free_method()` to compute the energy function for RBM:

```python
class RBM(nn.Module):
    def __init__(self, n_vis=784, n_hin=500, k=5):
        super(RBM, self).__init__()
        self.W = nn.Parameter(torch.randn(n_hin,n_vis)*1e-2)
        self.v_bias = nn.Parameter(torch.zeros(n_vis))
        self.h_bias = nn.Parameter(torch.zeros(n_hin))
        self.k = k

    def sample_from_p(self,p):
        return F.relu(torch.sign(p - Variable(torch.rand(p.size()))))

    def v_to_h(self,v):
        p_h = F.sigmoid(F.linear(v,self.W,self.h_bias))
        sample_h = self.sample_from_p(p_h)
        return p_h,sample_h

    def h_to_v(self,h):
        p_v = F.sigmoid(F.linear(h,self.W.t(),self.v_bias))
        sample_v = self.sample_from_p(p_v)
        return p_v,sample_v

    def forward(self,v):
        pre_h1,h1 = self.v_to_h(v)
        h_ = h1
        for _ in range(self.k):
            pre_v_,v_ = self.h_to_v(h_)
            pre_h_,h_ = self.v_to_h(v_)
        return v,v_

    def free_energy(self,v):
        vbias_term = v.mv(self.v_bias)
        wx_b = F.linear(v,self.W,self.h_bias)
        hidden_term = wx_b.exp().add(1).log().sum(1)
        return (-hidden_term - vbias_term).mean()
```

If you plot the PyTorch model, you will get an output as in the following screenshot showing the architecture of the RBM:

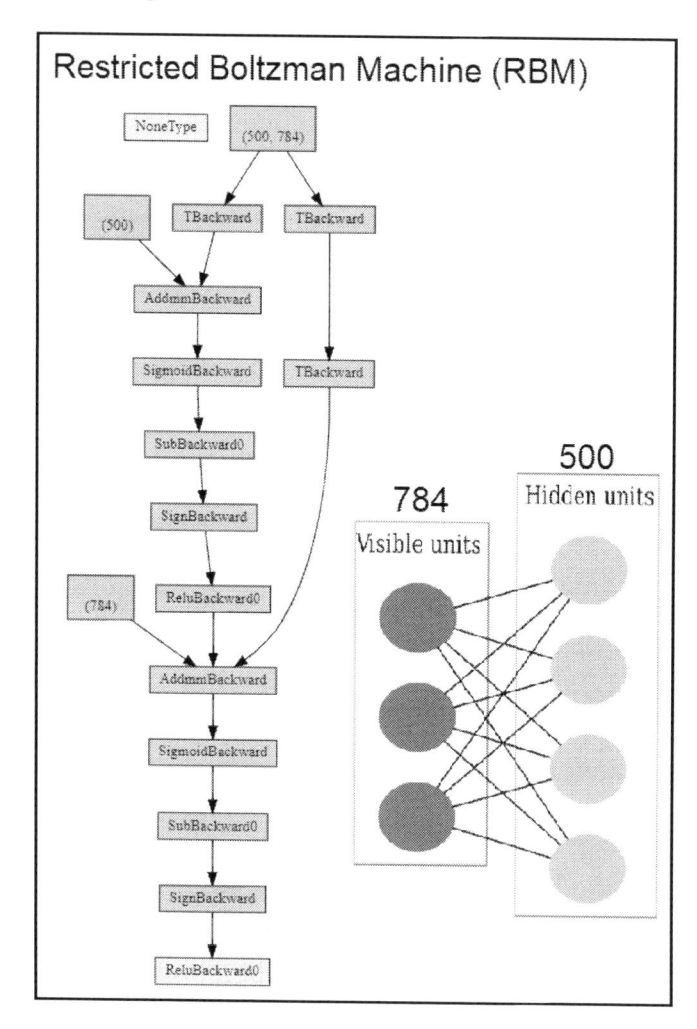

3. Train the RBM and use the learned model to reconstruct the images with the lower-dimensional representation and the hidden units using the following code block:

```
batch_size = 256 #64
train_loader = DataLoader(np.reshape(X_train, (-1, 28, \
                28)).astype(np.float32), batch_size=batch_size,
                shuffle=True)
test_loader = DataLoader(np.reshape(X_test, (-1, 28, \
```

```
                    28)).astype(np.float32), batch_size=batch_size,
                    shuffle=True)
rbm = RBM(k=1)
train_op = optim.SGD(rbm.parameters(), 0.1) #, weight_decay=1e-4)
for epoch in range(20):
  loss_ = []
  for data in train_loader:
    data = Variable(data.view(-1,784))
    sample_data = data.bernoulli()
    v,v1 = rbm(sample_data)
    loss = rbm.free_energy(v) - rbm.free_energy(v1)
    loss_.append(loss.item())
    train_op.zero_grad()
    loss.backward()
    train_op.step()
```

If you plot the original digits images and the reconstructed images with the RBM after 20 epochs, you will get the following output:

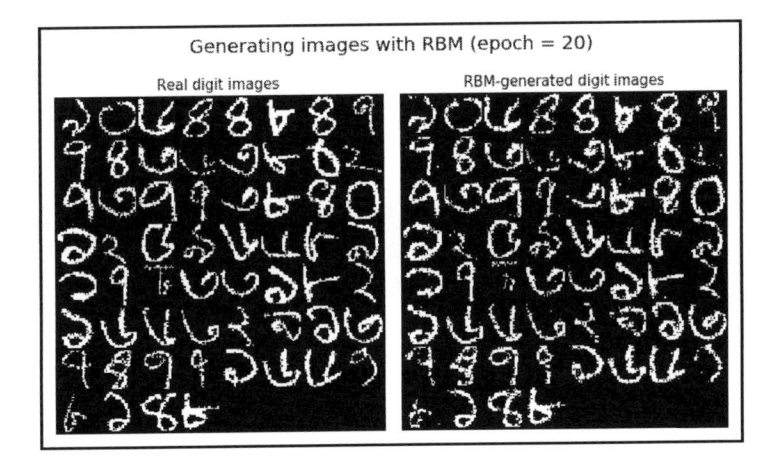

As you can see, the generated digits look more like the original digits as we train the model for more epochs.

The next screenshot shows how the features learned as weights look like in the hidden layer. If you plot the features learned at a few hidden layers, you may observe that those are quite interesting features that sort of represent the strokes of a pen while drawing a digit:

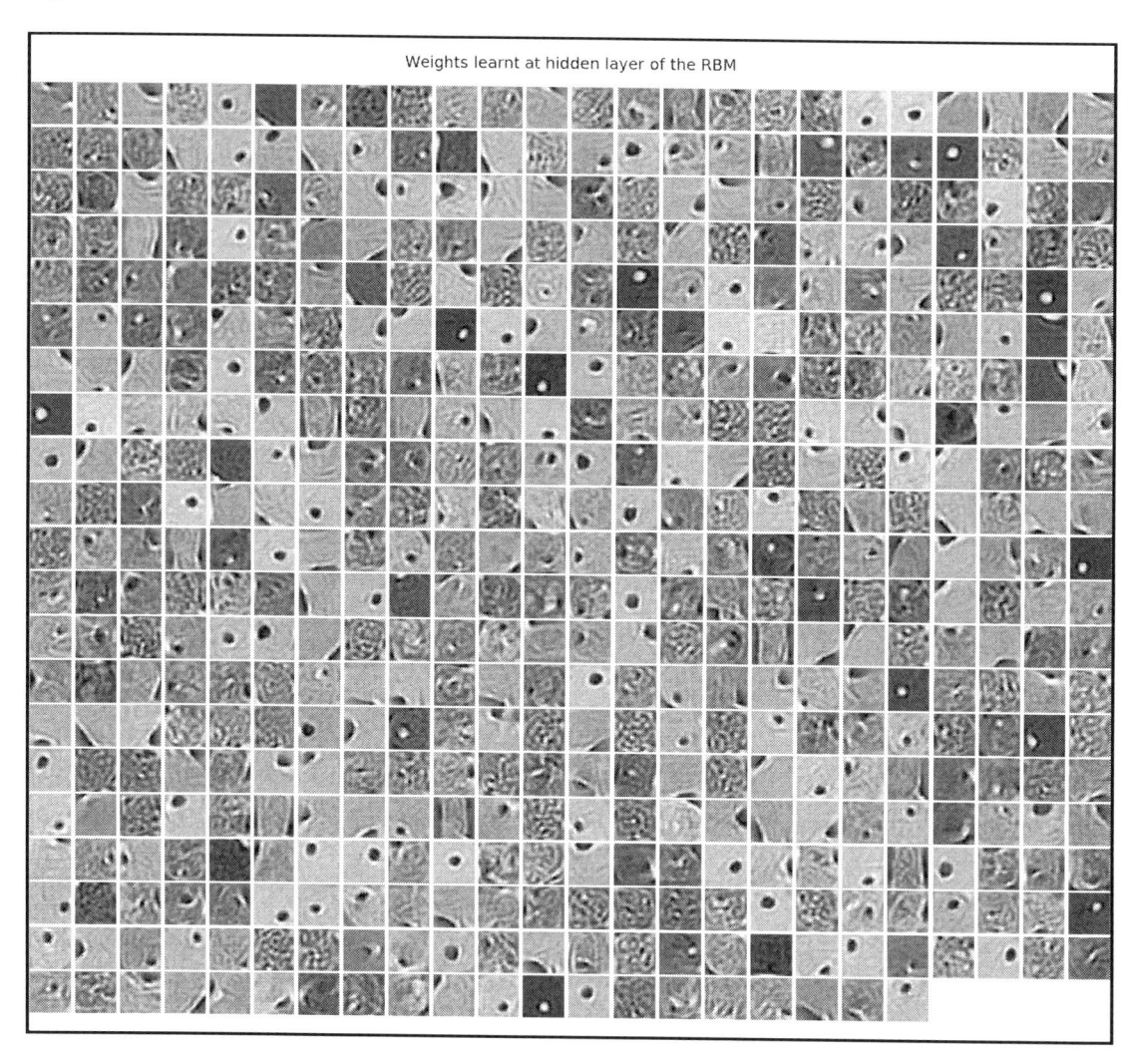

Weights learnt at hidden layer of the RBM

See also

For more details about this recipe, use the following links:

- `https://www.youtube.com/watch?v=UcAWwySuUZM`
- `https://www.youtube.com/watch?v=p4Vh_zMw-HQ`
- `https://www.cs.toronto.edu/~hinton/absps/guideTR.pdf`
- `https://www.youtube.com/watch?v=VdVYpjBWqWs`

Other Books You May Enjoy

If you enjoyed this book, you may be interested in these other books by Packt:

Hands-On Image Processing with Python
Sandipan Dey

ISBN: 978-1-78934-373-1

- Perform basic data pre-processing tasks such as image denoising and spatial filtering in Python
- Implement Fast Fourier Transform (FFT) and Frequency domain filters (e.g., Weiner) in Python
- Do morphological image processing and segment images with different algorithms
- Learn techniques to extract features from images and match images
- Write Python code to implement supervised / unsupervised machine learning algorithms for image processing
- Use deep learning models for image classification, segmentation, object detection and style transfer

Other Books You May Enjoy

PyTorch Computer Vision Cookbook
Michael Avendi

ISBN: 978-1-83864-483-3

- Develop, train and deploy deep learning algorithms using PyTorch 1.x
- Understand how to fine-tune and change hyperparameters to train deep learning algorithms
- Perform various CV tasks such as classification, detection, and segmentation
- Implement a neural style transfer network based on CNNs and pre-trained models
- Generate new images and implement adversarial attacks using GANs
- Implement video classification models based on RNN, LSTM, and 3D-CNN
- Discover best practices for training and deploying deep learning algorithms for CV applications

Leave a review - let other readers know what you think

Please share your thoughts on this book with others by leaving a review on the site that you bought it from. If you purchased the book from Amazon, please leave us an honest review on this book's Amazon page. This is vital so that other potential readers can see and use your unbiased opinion to make purchasing decisions, we can understand what our customers think about our products, and our authors can see your feedback on the title that they have worked with Packt to create. It will only take a few minutes of your time, but is valuable to other potential customers, our authors, and Packt. Thank you!

Index

A

AdaBoost ensemble classifier 359
affine transformation
  about 13
  applying 14, 15, 16
affine_transform() function 17
anisotropic diffusion
  used, with image denoising 57, 58, 59, 60
annotated image dataset
  download link 342
atlas image
  download link 251
atoms 109
autoencoder 46

B

Bangla MNIST images
  reconstructing, with restricted Boltzmann machine (RBM) 402
BeamSearch 379
binary image filters
  with SimpleITK 138, 139, 140
Binary Robust Independent Elementary Features (BRIEF)
  about 190
  reference link 193
blob detection
  with erosion 161
  with LOG scale-space 159
  with morphological watershed 156, 158, 159
blob separation
  with erosion 161
blue-yellow color component 10
bounding box closing 143
brain tumor segmentation
  with deep learning 255

with, deep learning 253

C

caffe model
  download link 317
Caltech101 images
  download link 276
Canny
  used, for edge detection 25, 74
cartoonish images
  creating 26, 27, 28, 29
CelebFaces Attributes (CelebA)
  download link 392
CIELAB (Lab) 10
classifier, for smile detection
  download link 359
CNN
  used, for automatic image captioning 379, 380, 381, 383, 384
colored image
  brightness, modifying with Lab color space 12
Constrained Least Squares (CLS) filter
  image, restoring 89, 90, 91, 93
content-based image retrieval (CBIR) 213
contrast-limited adaptive histogram equalization (CLAHE) 315
contrastive divergence (CD) algorithm 402
cover image 118
CSRT tracker 352
cumulative distribution function (cdf) 62
cv2.inpaint() function 101

D

Deep EXpectation (DEX) 372
deep instance segmentation
  with pretrained mask-RCNN model 267, 268, 269, 271, 272

deep learning model
  human pose estimation 316, 318, 320, 322
  traffic signs, classifying 305, 306, 308, 310, 312, 314, 315
  using, for age recognition 372, 373
  using, for emotion recognition 372, 373
  using, for gender recognition 372, 373
deep learning
  image completion, with inpainting 105, 106, 108
  using, for brain tumor segmentation 253, 255
  using, for image colorization 376, 377, 378
DeepLabV3 model
  using, for semantic segmentation 260, 261, 264
denoising autoencoder
  about 46
  used, for image denoising 46, 48, 50, 51, 52, 53
Depth Of Field (DOF) 17
dictionary 109
dictionary learning
  image, restoring 109, 110, 112
  used, for restoring image 109
Difference of Gaussian (DoG) 23, 81
dilation 126
dilation by reconstruction
  with skimage 141, 142, 144, 146
discrete Fourier transform (DFT)
  about 53
  used, for image denoising 53, 54
discrete wavelet transform (DWT)
  about 53
  used, for image denoising 53, 55, 56
dlib library's face detector
  using 187, 188
dlib
  using, for face alignment 182, 183, 185, 186, 187
draw_box() function 348

E

EAST text detector model
  download link 354
ECC algorithm
  used, for image alignment 177, 179, 180, 181
  using 182
edge detection

  about 73
  implementing, with LoG/zero-crossing 75, 76
  implementing, with wavelets 77, 78
  techniques 25
  with Canny 73, 74
  with CannyEdgeDetection() function 79
  with LoG/zero-crossing 73
  with wavelets 73
Efficient and Accuracy Scene Text detection (EAST) 353
EM algorithm
  reference link 244
erosion
  about 126
  using, for blob separation and detection 161
Euclidean (L2) distance 371
expectation-maximization (EM) 244, 251
Extended Difference of Gaussian (XDOG) 22, 24

F

face alignment
  about 182
  with dlib 182, 183, 185, 186, 187
face cascade classifier, parameters
  minNeighbors 362
  minSize 362
  scaleFactor 361
face detection
  with Viola-Jones/Haar-like feature 359, 360, 362
face detector function
  using 375
face morphing
  implementing 204, 205, 206, 210, 212
face recognition
  issues 364
  using, FaceNet 364, 365, 366, 367, 368, 370, 371
FaceNet
  about 364
  using, for face recognition 364, 365, 366, 367, 368, 370, 371
Faster R-CNN model
  object detection, implementing 337, 340, 342
  reference link 338
filters

applying, for image denoising 42, 43, 46
focus stacking (extended depth of fields)
  about 33
  implementing, with mahotas 33, 35
fully connected (FC) 296, 297
fully convolutional network (FCN)
  about 332
  using, for semantic segmentation 264, 266
Fully-Convolutional deep learning Network (FCN) 105

G

Gabor filter banks
  textures, classifying 282, 283, 284, 286, 288
Gaussian 22
Gaussian mixture model (GMM) 244
Generative Adversarial Network (GAN)
  about 384
  used, for image generation 384, 385, 387, 388, 389, 390, 392
German Traffic Sign Recognition Benchmark (GTSRB) 305
Gibbs sampler 88
GMM-EM algorithm
  used, for segmenting MRI image 251, 252, 253
  using, for skin-color segmentation 244, 245, 247, 249
  with skin-color segmentation 250
gradient blending
  performing 70, 72
Graph 342
green-red color component 10

H

Haar-like feature 359
handwritten digit images
  clustering, with SOM 236, 237, 238
histogram equalization
  performing, with createCLAHE() function 65
  used, for improving image contrast 61, 63, 64
histogram matching
  about 65
  application example 69
  implementing 66, 67, 68
histogram of oriented gradients (HOG)
  about 275, 324
  object detection, implementing 324, 326, 327, 330
hit-or-miss transform 147
HOG descriptors
  about 324
  usage 324
homography
  applying 17, 18, 19, 20, 21
HSV color space 35
HSV
  color, used for object detection 35, 36, 37, 38, 39
human pose estimation
  reference link 322
  with deep-learning model 316, 318, 320, 322
hysteresis thresholding
  applying 80

I

image alignment
  with ECC algorithm 177, 179, 180, 181
image captioning
  with CNN 379, 380, 381, 383, 384
  with LSTM 379, 380, 381, 383, 384
image classification
  reference link 294
  transfer learning 295, 296, 298, 299, 301, 302, 304
image colorization
  with deep learning 376, 377, 378
image completion
  with inpainting 105, 106
image contrast
  improving, with histogram equalization 61, 63
image denoising
  filters, applying 42, 43, 46
  with anisotropic diffusion 57, 58, 59, 60
  with colored images 53
  with denoising autoencoder 46, 48, 50, 51, 52
  with PCA/DFT/DWT 53, 55, 56
image inpainting
  about 99, 100, 101
  with convex optimization 103, 104
image mosaicing 194

image mosaicing (panorama)
  using 194, 195, 196, 197, 198, 199, 202
  with OpenCV-Python 201
image search engine
  implementing 213, 214
  implementing, steps 218, 219, 221, 222
image segmentation
  with self-organizing map (SOM) 231, 232, 233, 235
image stitching 194
image
  classifying, with PyTorch 289, 290, 291, 292, 294
  classifying, with scikit-learn 275, 276, 278, 279, 280, 281
  compressing, with wavelets 115, 116, 117, 118
  generating, with variational autoencoder (VAE) 393, 394, 395, 398, 399
  reconstructing, with variational autoencoder (VAE) 393, 394, 395, 398, 399
  restoring, with Constrained Least Squares (CLS) filter 89, 90, 91, 93
  restoring, with dictionary learning 109, 110, 112, 113
  restoring, with Markov Random Field (MRF) 95, 96, 97, 98
  restoring, with Wiener filter 84, 86, 87
  segmenting, with morphology 152
  similarity, finding between with SIFT 214, 215, 217
  text detection/recognition, with EAST/Tesseract 353, 354, 355, 357, 358
input images
  download link 296
isotropic diffusion 61
ISRO public images gallery
  reference link 240

K

k-step contrastive divergence (CD-k) algorithm 402
KCF tracker 352
keras-frcnn
  reference link 342

L

Lab color space
  RGB, converting into 10
  used, for modifying colored image brightness 12
  using 13
labeled faces in the wild (lfw) 46
Laplacian 102
Laplacian of Gaussian (LoG) 75
light art/long exposure
  about 30
  simulating 30, 32, 33
local binary pattern (LBP) 288
LoG and zero-crossing
  edge detection, implementing 75, 76
LOG scale-space
  using, for blob detection 159
logistic regression 275
Long Short-Term Memory (LSTM)
  about 358
  used, for automatic image captioning 379, 380, 381, 384
lowpass filter (LPF) 55
LSB data hiding 118

M

mahotas
  metrics, computing 135, 136
  morphological image filters 136, 137
  used, for implementing focus stacking 33, 35
Markov Chain Monte Carlo (MCMC) 88
Markov Random Field (MRF)
  image, restoring 95, 96, 97, 98
Mask R-CNN model
  object detection, implementing 343, 344, 346, 347, 348
  reference link 344, 348
medical image registration
  with SimpleITK 170, 171, 172, 173, 174
medical image segmentation 250, 258
mesh-warping algorithm 204
metrics
  computing, with mahotas/scikit-image 135, 136
morphological closing and opening
  objects, counting 163

morphological filters 134, 135
morphological image filters
    with mahotas 136, 137
morphological operators 126, 127, 129, 130, 131,
    132, 133
morphological pattern matching
    about 147
    implementing 148, 149, 150, 151
morphological watershed
    about 153, 154
    using, for blob detection 156, 158, 159
morphology
    image, segmenting 152
MOSSE tracker 352
MRI image
    segmenting, with GMM–EM 251, 252, 253
    segmenting, with watershed 256
MS-COCO dataset
    download link 348
MS-COCO image dataset
    reference link 336
multi-person dataset (MPI) 317
multiple object tracking
    reference link 352
    with OpenCV-Python 349, 350, 351
    with python-opencv 352

O

object detection
    implementing, with Faster R-CNN model 337,
        340, 342
    implementing, with HOG 326, 327, 328, 330
    implementing, with Mask R-CNN model 343,
        344, 346, 347, 348
    implementing, with SVM 324, 326, 327, 328,
        330
    implementing, with YOLO v3 model 331, 332,
        333, 335, 336
    reference link 330
object tracking 349
objects
    counting 160, 164
    detecting, with colors in HSV 35, 36, 37, 38, 39
online dictionary learning 113, 114
OpenCV-Python

image mosaicing (panorama) with 201
    multiple object tracking 349, 350, 351, 352
OpenPose, working
    greedy inference 316
    keypoints localization 316
    part affinity fields (PAFs) 316
Optical Character Recognition (OCR) 354
Otsu
    used, for thresholding 226, 227, 228

P

PACAL VOC image dataset 331
panorama image 194
Partial Differential Equation (PDE) 102
Peak Signal-to-Noise Ratio (PSNR) 42, 86
pencil sketches, for images
    creating 22, 23, 24, 25, 26
perspective transformation
    applying 17, 18, 19, 20, 21
pickled dataset
    download link 305
postporess() function 348
pretrained mask-RCNN model
    using, for deep instance segmentation 267, 268,
        269, 271, 272
principal component analysis (PCA)
    about 53
    used, for image denoising 53, 55, 56
probability density function (pdf) 244
proportion (percentage)
    using 223
PSNR value
    using 57
pyramid blending
    using 203
PyTorch
    image, classifying 289, 290, 291, 292, 294

R

Random Sample Consensus (RANSAC) 189
RandomWalk segmentation
    using 243
    with scikit-image 239, 240, 242, 243
RANSAC algorithm
    using, for homography 189, 190, 191, 192, 194

[419]

using, for robust match 189, 190, 191, 192, 194
Region Proposal Network (RPN) 337
registration 169
resize_crop() function
　implementing 212
ResNet 293
ResNet101 338
restricted Boltzmann machine (RBM)
　used, for reconstructing Bangla MNIST images 402, 403, 405, 406, 407
RGB image
　converting, into grayscale 11
　converting, into Lab color space 10
rgb2lab() function
　using 12, 13
Riddler–Calvard
　used, for thresholding 226, 227, 228
ROI Align module 343
ROI Pooling 343

S

Scale-Invariant Feature Transform (SIFT)
　about 195
　used, for finding similarity between image 214, 215, 217
scikit-image library functions
　using 11
scikit-image
　implementations, using 46
　metrics, computing 135, 136
　using, for RandomWalk segmentation 239, 240, 242, 243
scikit-learn
　image, classifying 275, 276, 278, 279, 280, 281
　reference link 282
seamless cloning
　with OpenCV-Python 71
search engine (SE) 213
self-organizing feature map (SOFM) 232
self-organizing map (SOM)
　used, for clustering handwritten digit images 236, 237, 238
　using, for image segmentation 231, 232, 233, 235
semantic segmentation

　about 259, 260
　with DeepLabV3 model 260, 262, 264
　with FCN 264, 266
Show and Tell model 379
siamese network 364
SimpleITK filter
　using 176
SimpleITK observers
　using 174
SimpleITK
　binary image filters 138, 139, 140
　used, for medical image registration 170, 171, 172, 173, 174
skimage
　dilation by reconstruction 141, 142, 143, 144, 146
skin-color segmentation
　download link 245
　with GMMEM algorithm 244, 245, 247, 249, 250
SOM algorithm 231
sparse coding 109
steganalysis
　using 118, 120, 122
steganography
　using 118, 120, 122
stego text 118
support vector machine (SVM)
　about 268, 324
　object detection, implementing 324, 326, 327, 330

T

target area 177
tensorflow object detection model zoo
　reference link 338
Tesseract
　installation link 354
text detection
　about 353
　in images, with EAST/Tesseract 353, 354, 355, 357, 358
　reference link 358
text recognition
　in images, with EAST/Tesseract 353, 354, 355,

[420]

357, 358
  reference link 358
texture images
  download link 283
textures
  classifying, with Gabor filter banks 282, 283,
    284, 286, 287
  reference link 288
thresholding algorithms
  for binary segmentation 229
  with Otsu 226, 227, 228
  with Riddler–Calvard 226, 227, 228
traffic signs
  classifying, with deep-learning model 305, 306,
    308, 310, 312, 314, 315
  reference link 315
transfer learning
  for image classification 295, 296, 298, 299,
    301, 302, 304
  reference link 304
triplet loss function 364

V

variational autoencoder (VAE)
  using, to generate images 393, 394, 395, 398,
    399
  using, to predict test dataset 400
  using, to reconstruct image 393, 394, 395, 398,
    399
Viola-Jones 359

W

warp() function 21
watershed
  used, for segmenting MRI image 256
wavelets
  used, for compressing image 115, 116, 117,
    118
  used, for implementing edge detection 77, 78
White Gaussian Noise (WGN) 90
WideResNet 372
Wiener filter
  image, restoring 84, 86, 87
winning neuron 231

Y

YOLO v3 model
  about 332
  download link 332
  object detection, implementing 332, 333, 335,
    336
  reference link 336
You Only Look Once (YOLO) 331

Z

zero-crossing
  computing, algorithm 80

Printed in Great Britain
by Amazon